Aging and the Family

Aging and the Family

Edited by

Stephen J. Bahr
Brigham Young University

Evan T. Peterson
Brigham Young University

Lexington Books
D.C. Heath and Company/Lexington, Massachusetts/Toronto

Library of Congress Cataloging-in-Publication Data

Aging and the family.
  Includes index.
1. Aged—United States—Family relationships.
2. Aged—United States—Social conditions. I. Bahr,
Stephen J. II. Peterson, Evan T.
HQ1064.U5A6337   1989   306.8'7   88–23040
ISBN 0–669–17702–4 (alk. paper)

Published simultaneously in Canada
Printed in the United States of America
International Standard Book Number: 0–669–17702–4
Library of Congress Catalog Card Number 88–23040

The paper used in this publication meets the minimum requirements of American National Standard for Information Sciences—Permanence of Paper for Printed Library Materials, ANSI Z39.48–1984. ∞™

89 90 91 92 8 7 6 5 4 3 2 1

Contents

Preface

One of the major demographic trends that has occurred in recent decades has been the increase in life expectancy. This increase in longevity, along with the decline in fertility, has produced what has been termed "the graying of America." The proportion of the population that is over age 65 has increased substantially and will continue to increase during the next two decades. Many people will spend more years of their lives in middle age and retirement than they did raising children.

The demographic trends have not been followed by a commensurate amount of research on aging. Although the amount of gerontological research has increased, research on family relationships during the later stages of the life span has been inadequate. Textbooks on family life typically have one chapter to cover the many years spent in launching children, middle age, retirement, and widowhood.

This book examines aging from a family perspective. Its aims are to assess the current state of knowledge, to present new data in several important areas, and to stimulate future research. The data presented are relevant to a number of social issues and will be useful to students, teachers, researchers, and policymakers who are interested in aging or the family. Certainly, those who are interested in the family will find this book informative. Social gerontologists will find it useful, even though their field is broader than the scope of this book. And it could be used as a supplemental text in sociology, family science, and social gerontology courses.

The contributors to this volume were selected because of their research interests, not because of disciplinary affiliation. Each author was instructed to review and integrate current literature, to identify areas in which research is needed, and where possible to report new research findings.

The prologue is an overview of the aging family from a developmental perspective. It provides a brief review of the research.

In Part I, major *family transitions* during the later stages of the life cycle are examined—namely, launching children, retirement, and widowhood. Chapter 1 reviews what is known about the transition to the empty nest, while in chapter 2 the effects of retirement on marital division of labor are analyzed. The data show why it is important to study retirement from a family perspective. A model for understanding how people adjust to the stresses of widowhood is presented in chapter 3. Chapter 4 reports the extent of remarriage among the elderly and the satisfaction and stability of their remarriages.

The final two chapters in Part I concern leisure and religion. Neither is viewed as a common transition in the life course, yet both are important. Chapter 5 reviews trends in recreation and education as people age, while chapter 6 is a study of how faith changes for men and women across the life span.

Part II, includes four chapters on *family relationships* among the aged. Satisfaction, conflict, and the division of labor of golden wedding couples are the focus of chapter 7. The nature of grandparenting is discussed in chapter 8, while elderly parent-child relationships are examined in chapter 9. The final chapter in Part II is a report on the extent to which genealogists may be characterized as elderly and what functions genealogy serves for people.

Health is one of the major social issues of our time, and it has become more important as the population ages. Four aspects of health among the elderly are examined in Part III. Chapter 11 reviews major physical illnesses of the elderly and how they impact on families. The mental health of the elderly and its impact on families is the focus of chapter 12. The topic of chapter 13 is burden experienced by caregivers of the dependent elderly; a propositional theory is developed that integrates research and identifies major social characteristics associated with burden. In chapter 14 estimates of the prevalence of elder abuse are reported, and common characteristics of the abused and the abuser are identified.

Part IV contains two chapters on *economics*. Are the elderly worse off or better off economically than they were in 1970? How does the economic well-being of the elderly compare with the economic well-being of the general population? These questions are answered in chapter 15, along with a report on where the elderly get their income and how they spend it. Then the problem of providing financially for the dependent elderly is addressed in chapter 16.

What is the future for the elderly and their families? What social changes can we expect? What are some areas of needed research? The epilogue concludes the book by addressing these questions.

This book provides an introduction to aging from a family perspective. It reviews existing research and presents new data on transitions, family relationships, health, and economic well-being. Many subjects traditionally covered in social gerontology texts are not discussed, such as ethnic group differences, the impact of crime, transportation and housing problems, civic and political activities, and death and grief. However, most of the research on these topics has been focused on the aging individual, not on the aging family. The authors' aim has been not to produce another social gerontology book but to present data with special relevance to the aging family.

Acknowledgments

We gratefully acknowlege the many who have contributed to this book. Norene Petersen and Kimberly Hanson provided excellent clerical services. The Family and Demographic Research Institute and the College of Family, Home, and Social Sciences at Brigham Young University provided institutional support.

Prologue: A Developmental Overview of the Aging Family

Stephen J. Bahr

amilies follow a pattern of development over time in which they expand, change, and contract. This process of transformation can be divided into stages corresponding to major transitions over the family's history. These stages are usually referred to as the stages of the family life cycle.

There are a variety of ways to delineate life-cycle stages, depending on what transition points are considered critical. The most widely used set of family life-cycle categories is Duvall and Hill's (1948) eight stages, which are as follows: (1) married couples (without children), (2) childbearing families (oldest child birth to 30 months), (3) families with preschool children (oldest child 2½ years to 6 years), (4) families with schoolchildren (oldest child 6 to 13 years), (5) families with teenagers (oldest child 13 to 20 years), (6) families launching young adults (first child's to last child's leaving home), (7) middle-aged parents (empty nest to retirement), and (8) aging family members (retirement to death of one spouse). Widowhood could be added as a ninth stage, from the death of one spouse to the death of the other. The beginning of each stage of the family life cycle is a transition that requires a change of roles and tasks.

One of the limitations of family research has been a neglect of the later stages of the life cycle. The purpose of this chapter is to identify major changes in the family life cycle during the past century and provide an overview of research on the last three stages of the life cycle.

Life-Cycle Changes

Two of the most significant changes in family life during the past century have been the increase in longevity and the decrease in fertility. Since 1900, life expectancy in the United States has increased by more than twenty-five years. In 1900, it was less than 50 years, compared with 75 years in 1985 (Bengtson 1986). In 1957, the total fertility rate was 3.7 children per woman, while in 1984 it was 1.8 children per woman (Bengtson 1986).

These changes have compressed the childbearing and child-rearing years and extended the middle and later stages of the family life cycle. In 1984, men married at age 26 and women at age 24, on the average (National Center for Health Statistics 1987a, 4). The average woman will have two children, at ages 26 and 29. The retirement age is 65, and life expectancy for men and women is 71 and 78, respectively (National Center for Health Statistics 1987b).

Using these statistics, a profile of the family life cycle of the average couple has been constructed. The average couple spends two years as a married couple without children, eighteeen years in the child-rearing stages, ten years launching their two children, nine years in middle age between launching and retirement, and six years as a retired couple. The wife spends nine years as a widow following her husband's death.

The average woman will spend almost as much time retired and widowed as she did raising children at home. She will spend twenty-five years in the last three stages of the life cycle, plus nine more years as a widow, compared with only twenty-one years in the first five stages of the family life cycle.

Overview of the Research

What follows as a brief review of research on the last three stages of the family life cycle—middle age (empty nest), retirement, and widowhood. This overview sets the stage for more detailed reviews in the later chapters.

Middle Age

Middle age is the period between the launching of the last child and retirement. A period of assessment and adjustment, it is sometimes termed the "mid-life crisis" for men and the "empty-nest syndrome" for women. There is often a shift in time perspective from "time lived" to "time left" (Ciernia 1985a; Hagestad and Burton 1986; Tamir 1982).

At this period in their lives many men realize that they are not going to reach the occupational goals they earlier set for themselves. Other men, who have met their goals, often feel dissatisfied and wonder if their sacrifices have been worth it. In either case, men at this stage often feel a need for more personal fulfillment. They may disengage from work somewhat and put more emphasis on family life or on other personal relationships (Tamir 1982).

Women also evaluate their accomplishments and desires at mid-life. Some regret not having had the opportunity for career development that most men have had. Others feel lost when their children leave and wonder what their role is. Many embark on professional careers during this period (Poloma et al. 1981). Some enter college to obtain a degree as well as to achieve independence and a sense of identity (Hildreth et al. 1983). Others move in and out of the labor force (Moen 1986).

During this stage in life, many men become more sensitive and nurturant as they place more emphasis on relationships. At the same time, women tend to become more assertive, independent, and interested in mastery of the outside world (Hagestad and Burton 1986). Rossi (1986) noted that men and women do not lose their existing traits but rather add new traits to their existing repertoire. As a result, gender roles within the family tend to become more androgynous as aging occurs (Rossi 1986; Tamir 1982).

Some have suggested that divorce, drinking, and suicide become more common during middle age because of the mid-life crisis. Although some may react to middle age in these ways, there is no evidence that this is a general tendency. Divorce and heavy drinking actually tend to go down at mid-life, while suicide rates vary little between young adulthood and middle age (Ciernia 1985b). A more extensive review of research on the transition to the empty nest is provided by Barber in chapter 1.

Marital Satisfaction, Divorce, and Remarriage in Middle Age. Marital satisfaction tends to increase somewhat after children leave home (Brubaker 1985; Treas and Bengtson 1987). Rearing children is stressful, and companionship and shared activities tend to increase after the children are launched.

The divorce rate is not high among middle-aged couples, although it has increased in recent years. Smyer and Hofland (1982) estimated that divorces among couples in middle age constitute about 17 percent of all divorces. The difficulty in adjusting to divorce increases as age increases, which makes middle-age divorce more stressful than divorce earlier in the life cycle (Berardo 1982).

Remarriage is fairly common among middle-aged divorced and widowed persons, although remarriage rates decline as age increases and are much higher among men than among women (National Center for Health Statistics 1987a). An examination of remarriage among middle-aged and elderly persons is given in chapter 4.

Grandparenting. Most people become grandparents during their middle years, although there is considerable variation in the exact age at which people become grandparents. About three-fourths of all individuals over age 65 have living grandchildren (Brubaker 1985, 70).

Most people enjoy being grandparents and feel it is an important role.

About 80 percent of grandparents are happy with their relationships with their grandchildren. A majority of grandparents say that grandparenting is easier than parenthood and enjoy it more than parenthood (Brubaker 1985). Grandfathers are somewhat less satisfied with grandparenthood than grandmothers (Thomas 1986). Middle-aged grandparents (aged 45 to 60) tend to be more willing to give advice and to take responsibility for watching and disciplining a grandchild than grandparents who are older than 60 (Thomas 1986).

About three-fourths of grandparents see a grandchild at least once a week (Troll 1983). A good grandparent is described as one who shows love, who sets a good example, who helps if asked, and who does not spoil the grandchild or interfere with parental upbringing (Brubaker 1985).

Grandparents want to be involved, but generally they do not want to be surrogate parents. When grandparenting comes too early, it is stressful and may be rejected, especially if too much responsibility is placed on the grandparent (Hagestad and Burton 1986). In chapter 8, Peterson reviews the research on grandparenting.

Caregiving. There is a strong norm that care of elderly parents is the responsibility of their children (Campbell and Brody 1985; Martin et al. 1987). The better the parent-child relationship, the greater the responsibility felt by adult children; daughters feel more responsibility than sons (Brubaker 1985; Martin et al. 1987).

Caregivers are usually middle-aged women who have many other demands placed on them. They provide substantial amounts of money, child care, and emotional support to their own children, while at the same time they offer emotional support and care to their parents (Troll 1982). Sons become caregivers only if there is no female sibling available (Horowitz 1985).

The well-being of middle-aged caregivers depends on their health, their social contacts, their affection for their parents, and their financial stress. If they have good health, they are able to withstand the burden much more easily. Having adequate social contacts with other people decreases the amount of stress associated with care of an elderly parent. Affection for the parent also tends to be associated with less burden. Finally, financial stress tends to be associated with greater burden (Stull et al. 1986). An in-depth review of research on burden among caregivers is presented by Barber in chapter 13.

Retirement

The retirement stage of the family life cycle typically begins at age 65, when the husband retires. Married women tend to retire earlier than unmarried women, primarily to synchronize their retirement with their husbands'. Because the wife tends to be younger than the husband, he tends to retire before she does.

Adjusting to Retirement. The actual effect of retirement on a marriage depends on the relationship that existed before retirement. On the one hand, retirement provides opportunities for companionship that did not exist when one or both spouses were employed. On the other hand, the additional time together may increase tension and conflict among couples who do not enjoy being together (Brubaker 1985).

Hill and Dorfman (1982) studied a sample of wives whose husbands had recently retired. The wives reported that increased companionship, increased flexibility of schedule, and increased time available for desired activities were some of the positive aspects of retirement. Some of the negative aspects of retirement were financial problems and too much togetherness. Health of husband, adequate income, husband's participation in household tasks, and joint decision making were all correlated with the satisfaction of the wife with retirement (Hill and Dorfman 1982).

The preretirement division of labor tends to continue after retirement, with women doing more of the household work than men (Brubaker 1985). If the wife's health deteriorates, the husband's involvement in household chores increases significantly. A systematic analysis of how retirement affects division of labor among couples is presented by Szinovacz in chapter 2.

There is usually a reduction in income following retirement, and expenditure patterns change considerably. Chen and Chu (1982) found that couples over age 65 tend to spend higher proportions of their income on food, utilities, and medical care than do couples under age 65. Nonretired couples spend relatively more on clothing, household furnishings, transportation, and recreation. Chapter 15 presents a review of income and expenditure patterns of elderly couples.

Health and financial problems decrease retirement satisfaction, and the unmarried are less satisfied than the married. The retirement experience appears to be similar for both men and women, although women tend to have somewhat lower satisfaction because they tend to have had lower incomes and are less likely to be married (Maxwell 1985; Seccombe and Lee 1986).

There is a popular conception that loneliness is a serious problem among the aged (Harris 1981). However, Revenson and Johnson (1984) found that loneliness decreases as age increases, and that people over age 65 have less loneliness than any other age group. Neither gender nor living alone was related to loneliness; however, they found that the loss of an intimate attachment through divorce or widowhood was related to loneliness.

Golden Wedding Couples. About 80 percent of first marriages are dissolved by divorce or death before they reach their fiftieth anniversary (Glick and Norton 1977). The 20 percent that to make it to their golden wedding anniversary tend to be very satisfied with their marriages. Retirement has enabled them to spend much time together, and they share many household and leisure activities. They report that the most satisfying periods of their lives were childbearing, the preschool years, and the period after retirement. The least satisfying years were childbearing, launching, and middle age (Brubaker 1985). In chapter 7, Condie reports on the satisfaction, conflict, and division of labor among a sample of golden wedding couples.

Divorce and Remarriage After Retirement. The divorce rate among elderly couples is small—less than 3 percent, according to Uhlenberg and Myers (1981). Remarriage rates among persons over age 65 are relatively low. About five out of every thousand divorced women over age 65 remarry each year. By comparison, about twenty-four of every thousand divorced men over age 65 remarry each year. Comparable rates among widowed persons are two for women and sixteen for men, respectively (National Center for Health Statistics 1987a, 13). A thorough examination of remarriage among the elderly is presented by Bowers and Bahr in chapter 4.

Physical Health. Satisfaction with retirement is affected by health. In illness in either spouse will have a major impact on an older couple. Caring for an ill spouse over a long period of time is physically and emotionally draining. Social support from others and the good health of the caregiver are important in adjusting to the caregiver role (Brubaker 1986). Physical health and caregiving are the topics of chapters 11 and 13, respectively.

Mental Health. Retired people are in the process of role disengagement. Their children are raised, and they are no longer employed. They may become depressed and feel that they no longer have a purpose in life. Being married has a significant influence on the mental health of retired persons. A variety of indicators of psychological adjustment and subjective well-being have been found to be higher among the elderly who are married compared with those who are not married (Ferraro and Wan 1986; Lawton et al. 1984; Leonard 1982; Revenson and Johnson 1984).

Mental health is also affected by the quality of the marriage. Older couples with substantial marital conflict tend to have higher levels of depression than do couples with lower levels of conflict (Keith and Schafer 1986).

Having friends to associate with is critical for the mental health of elderly persons; it buffers the effects of stress (Baldassare et al. 1984; Cohen et al. 1985; Ward et al. 1985). Income and physical health are other factors associated with the mental health of the aged (Ferraro and Wan 1986; Leonard 1982; Raymond et al. 1980).

A thorough review of research on the mental health of the elderly is presented in chapter 12 by Murphy. She identifies the major types of cognitive dysfunctions and how they impact on families.

Widowhood

An extensive review of the research on widowhood is presented by Pitcher and Larson in chapter 3. In the present section only a brief overview of the adjustment to widowhood is provided.

It is usually the woman who is faced with widowhood, as 70 percent of women outlive their husbands (Treas and Bengtson 1987). In only a small percentage of cases does widowhood occur suddenly, without warning. In the majority of cases there is a struggle with health before the death, and usually the surviving wife cares for her ill husband before he dies (Brubaker 1985).

The adjustment to widowhood usually has three stages (Brubaker 1985). First, there is a crisis in which there is grief, disbelief, and a sense of loss and abandonment. Mourning is accompanied by extensive involvement with family and friends. During this period bereaved individuals tend to have significantly more depression and psychopathology than nonbereaved persons (Farberow et al. 1987).

The second stage is a transitional period in which people try to establish a life without their spouse. During this period one begins to form a new identity as an unmarried person. Support from friends and family tends to decrease somewhat during this stage.

The final stage is the establishment of a new lifestyle. This is the reorganization of one's life as a single person; for some, remarriage occurs (Brubaker 1985). The adjustment process appears to be similar for both men and women in terms of emotional problems, depression, and life satisfaction (Feinson 1986; Lund et al. 1986).

The loss of a companion is difficult to adjust to and is a major reason for loneliness in late life (Clark et al. 1986; Revenson and Johnson 1984; Singh and Gill 1986). However, loneliness tends to decrease with time as involvement with friends increases (Revenson and Johnson 1984; Roberto and Scott 1986). Developing a network of friends that enables one to express feelings is particularly important in adjusting to widowhood (Dimond et al. 1987; Ferraro et al. 1984; Haas-Hawkings et al. 1985).

Forty-one percent of women over age 65 live alone, and the proportion of older men and women living with their children has declined by 50 percent during the past thirty-five years (Brubaker 1985; U.S. Bureau of the Census 1986, 46). However, living alone does not mean widowed persons are isolated. The widowed who live alone tend to have more involvement with children, siblings, relatives, and friends than do elderly married individuals (Brubaker 1985).

Summary

During the past century longevity has increased dramatically while fertility has decreased. This has compressed the childbearing and child-rearing years and extended the middle and later stages of the family life cycle.

Middle age is the period between the launching of the last child and retirement; it typically lasts about nine years. During this period family roles tend to become more androgynous, marital satisfaction increases, and couples usually become grandparents. In middle age, many face the dual demands of helping their adult children and caring for their aged parents. Female children usually do most of the caregiving. The extent of burden in caring for an aging parent depends on the health of the caregiver, having adequate social contacts, affection for the parent, and the amount of financial stress.

The retirement period typically lasts about six years for couples. Being married, having high marital satisfaction, having adequate income, enjoying good physical health, and having friends are all positively associated with satisfaction with retirement and good mental health.

About seven out of ten women outlive their husbands. The average married woman will be a widow for nine years. Friendship networks are important for adjustment to widowhood.

References

Baldassare, Mark, Sarah Rosenfield, and Karen Rook. 1984. The types of social relations predicting elderly well-being. *Research on Aging* 6:549–59.

Bengtson, Vern L. 1986. Sociological perspectives on aging, families and the future. In M. Bergener (ed.), *Dimensions in Aging: The 1986 Sandoz Lectures in Gerontology.* London: Academic Press.

Berardo, Donna Hodgkins. 1982. "Divorce and remarriage at middle age and beyond." *Annals of the American Academy of Political and Social Science* 464:132–39.

Brubaker, B. 1986. "Caring for a dependent spouse." *American Behavioral Scientist* 29:485–96.

Brubaker, Timothy H. 1985. *Later Life Families.* Beverly Hills, CA: Sage Publications.

Campbell, Ruth, and Elaine M. Brody. 1985. "Women's changing roles and help to the elderly: Attitudes of women in the United States and Japan." *The Gerontological Society of America* 25:584–92.

Chen, Yung-Ping, and Kwang-Wen Chu. 1982. "Household expenditure patterns. The effect of age of family head." *Journal of Family Issues* 3:233–50.

Ciernia, James R. 1985a. "Death concern and businessmen's mid-life crisis." *Psychological Reports* 56:83–87.

———. 1985b. "Myths about male midlife crises." *Psychological Reports* 56:1003–1007.

Clark, Phillip G., Robert W. Siviski, and Ruth Weiner. 1986. "Coping strategies of widowers in the first year." *Family Relations* 35:425–30.

Cohen, Carl I., Jeannie Teresi, and Douglas Holmes. 1985. "Social networks, stress, and physical health: A longitudinal study of an inner-city elderly population." *Journal of Gerontology* 40:478–86.

Dimond, Margaret, Dale A. Lund, and Michael S. Caserta. 1987. "The role of social support in the first two years of bereavement in an elderly sample." *The Gerontologist* 27:599–604.

Duvall Evelyn M., and Reuben L. Hill. 1948. *Report of the Committee on the Dynamics of Family Interaction*. Washington, DC: National Conference on Family Life.

Farberow, Norman L., Dolores E. Gallagher, Michael J. Gilewski, and Larry W. Thompson. 1987. "An examination of the early impact of bereavement on psychological distress in survivors of suicide." *The Gerontologist* 27:592–98.

Feinson, Marjorie Chary. 1986. "Aging widows and widowers: Are there mental health differences?" *International Journal of Aging and Human Development* 23:241–55.

Ferraro, Kenneth F., Elizabeth Mutran, and Charles M. Barresi. 1984. "Widowhood, health, and friendship support in later life." *Journal of Health and Social Behavior* 25:245–59.

Ferraro, Kenneth F., and Thomas T.H. Wan. 1986. "Marital contributions to well-being in later life." *American Behavioral Scientist* 29:423–37.

Glick, Paul C., and Arthur J. Norton. 1977. "Marrying, divorcing, and living together in the U.S. today." *Population Bulletin* 32: 1–39. Washington, DC: Population Reference Bureau.

Haas-Hawkings, Gwen, Sandra Sangster, Michael Ziegler, and David Reid. 1985. "A study of relatively immediate adjustment to widowhood in later life." *International Journal of Women's Studies* 8:158–67.

Hagestad, Gunhild O., and Linda M. Burton. 1986. "Grandparenthood, life context, and family development." *American Behavioral Scientist* 29:471–84.

Harris, L. 1981. *Aging in the Eighties: America in Transition*. Washington, DC: National Council on Aging.

Hildreth, Gladys J., Peggye Dilworth-Anderson, and Sabrina M. Rabe. 1983. "Family and school life of women over age fifty who are in college." *Educational Gerontology* 9:339–50.

Hill, Elizabeth A., and Lorraine T. Dorfman. 1982. "Reaction of housewives to the retirement of their husbands." *Family Relations* 31:195–200.

Horowitz, Amy. 1985. "Sons and daughters as caregivers to older parents: Differences in role performance and consequences." *The Gerontologist* 25:612–17.

Keith, Pat M., and Robert B. Schafer. 1986. "Housework, disagreement and depression among younger and older couples." *American Behavioral Scientist* 29:405–22.

Lawton, M. Powell, Miriam Moss, and Morton H. Kleban. 1984. "Marital status, living arrangements, and the well-being of older people." *Research on Aging* 6:323–45.

Leonard, W. M., II. 1982. "Successful aging: An elaboration of social and psychological factors." *International Journal on Aging and Human Development* 14:223–32.

Lund, D. A., Michael S. Caserta, and Margaret F. Dimond. 1986. "Gender differences through two years of bereavement among the elderly." *The Gerontologist* 26:314–20.

Martin, Mary E., C. Ko, and Vern L. Bengtson. 1987. "Filial responsibility and patterns of caregiving in three generation families." Paper presented at Pacific Sociological Association meeting, Eugene, Oregon, April 1987.

Maxwell, Nan L. 1985. "The retirement experience: Psychological and financial linkages to the labor market." *Social Science Quarterly* 65:22–33.

Moen, Phyllis. 1986. "Women's life transitions in the middle years: A longitudinal analysis." Paper prepared for presentation at the annual meetings of the American Sociological Association, New York, August 1986.

National Center for Health Statistics. 1987a. "Advance report of final marriage statistics, 1984." *Monthly Vital Statistics Report*, vol. 36, no. 2, supp.(2). DHHS Pub. No. (PHS) 87–1120. Hyattsville, Maryland: Public Health Service.

———. 1987b. "Advance report of final mortality statistics, 1985." *Monthly Vital Statistics Report*, vol. 36, no. 5, supp., DHHS Pub. No. (PHS) 86–1120. Hyattsville, Maryland: Public Health Service.

Poloma, Margaret M., Brian F. Pendleton, and T. Neal Garland. 1981. "Reconsidering the dual-career marriage." *Journal of Family Issues* 2:205–24.

Raymond, Edward F., T. J. Michals, and Robert A. Steer. 1980. "Prevalence and correlates of depression in elderly persons." *Psychological Reports* 47:1055–61.

Revenson, Tracey A., and Jeffrey L. Johnson. 1984. "Social and demographic correlates of loneliness in late life." *American Journal of Community Psychology* 12:71–85.

Roberto, Karen A., and Jean Pearson Scott. 1986. "Confronting widowhood." *American Behavioral Scientist* 29:497–511.

Rossi, A. S. 1986. "Sex and gender in an aging society." *Daedalus* 115:141–69.

Seccombe, Karen, and Gary R. Lee. 1986. "Gender differences in retirement satisfaction and its antecedents." *Research on Aging* 8:426–40.

Singh, G. M., and S. Gill. 1986. "Problems of widowhood." *The Indian Journal of Social Work* 37:67–71.

Smyer, Michael A., and Brian F. Hofland. 1982. "Divorce and family support in later life." *Journal of Family Issues* 3:61–77.

Stull, D. E., Karl D. Kosloski, and Rhonda J.V. Montgomery. 1986. "Predictors of well-being among caregivers of the elderly." Paper presented at the 57th annual meeting of the Pacific Sociological Association, Denver, Colorado, April 1986.

Tamir, L. M. 1982. "Men at middle age: Developmental transitions." *Annals of the American Academy of Political and Social Science* 464:47–56

Thomas, Jeanne L. 1986. "Age and sex differences in perceptions of grandparenting." *Journal of Gerontology* 41:417–23.

Treas, J., and Vern L. Bengtson. 1987. "The family in later years." In Marvin B. Sussman and Suzanne K. Steinmetz (eds.), *Handbook of Marriage and the Family*. New York: Plenum Press.

Troll, Lillian E. 1982. "Family life in middle and old age: The generation gap." *The Annals of the American Academy of Political and Social Science* 464:38–46.

———. 1983. "Grandparents. The family watchdogs." In Timothy H. Brubaker (ed.), *Family Relationships in Older Life*. Beverly Hills: Sage Publications.

Uhlenberg, Peter, and Mary Anne P. Myers. 1981. "Divorce and the elderly." *The Gerontologist* 21:276–82.

U.S. Bureau of the Census. 1986. *Statistical Abstract of the United States: 1987* (107th ed.). Washington, DC: U.S. Government Printing Office.

Ward, Russell A., Mark LaGory, and Susan R. Sherman. 1985. "Social networks and well-being in the older population." *Sociology and Social Research* 70:102–11.

Part I
Transitions

In Part I, the authors identify some of the major transitions that occur within the family. The chapters have been arranged, as far as possible, in terms of a developmental framework. First comes the empty-nest stage, which is discussed in chapter 1. It typically occurs around middle age and requires some adjustment as the children start to leave the home.

Other transitions soon follow, and in some cases go on simultaneously with the empty-nest phase of the family life cycle. Retirement is the next major transition, and chapter 2 examines how retirement affects the division of labor of couples.

Another major transition is widowhood, which one-fourth of all married women face by age 65. In chapter 3 there is a review of stresses associated with widowhood and ways people adjust to those stresses.

One possible adjustment to widowhood is remarriage. An increasing and significant number of the elderly are getting remarried. Chapter 4 is a study of the amount and nature of remarriage among the elderly.

The final two topics in this section are leisure and religion. Although they do not fit neatly into a developmental framework, leisure and religion change over the life span. While leisure activities are important for all families, the nature of the activities changes after retirement. For example, while adult education is open to adults of any ages, it seems to have special appeal to the elderly. A majority of them feel as if they should spend more time in adult education than in viewing television, even though they tend to spend more time viewing television. Leisure and education among the elderly are discussed in chapter 5.

Then there is the matter of religion. A high percentage of the elderly believe in the existence of Deity, and religious activity and faith are important aspects of their lives. The faith development of men and women over the life span is discussed in chapter 6.

1
Transition to the Empty Nest

Clifton E. Barber

I n this chapter, the term *empty nest* refers to the years a couple spend together between the launching of their last child and the death of one of the spouses. The transition to the empty nest begins when the first child is launched from the home and ends when the last child departs. This chapter is about how parents react to and evaluate this transition.

The Empty Nest as a Twentieth-Century Phenomenon

It is estimated that in 1900 the empty nest lasted an average of two years and often occurred in a couple's old age. Since that time, however, trends such as smaller family size, closer spacing of children, and increased longevity have resulted in a longer empty-nest period. On the average, couples today experience the launching of their last child during middle age and can expect to remain in the empty-nest period for at least thirteen years and often much longer (Glick 1977).

For example, the average couple who married in 1960 and had children during the ensuing five years would have launched their last child in 1985, at which time the husband would have been about 47, and the wife two years younger. Subsequently, they could expect to remain in the empty-nest period for thirteen to eighteen years before the advent of retirement and for over twenty years before the death of the husband at age 70.

As one of the most dramatic changes to have emerged in the family life cycle pattern in this century (Glick 1977), the empty nest has understandably become the center of attention for an increasing number of popular articles as well as empirical investigations.

The majority of this literature has focused on eight areas of inquiry: (1) demarcation of the empty-nest transition, (2) parental responses to the empty-nest transition, (3) gender differences in these reactions, (4) cohort differences in these reactions, (5) ethnic differences in these reactions, (6) changes in marital relationships, (7) the impact of the empty-nest transition on parent-child relationships during and after launching, and (8) the reversible nature of the empty-nest transition. Consequently, the research reviewed in this chapter is organized around these eight topics.

Demarcation of the Empty-Nest Transition

Most researchers have assumed that the empty-nest period is inaugurated when the youngest child turns 18 (Glenn 1975) or when a particular launching event occurs, such as marriage or graduation from high school (Deutscher 1964; Harkins 1978; Lowenthal and Chiriboga 1972; Lurie 1974). Other researchers have simply left the point of launching vague and undefined, being content to refer to it as a "letting go" of the children, or having them "leave home" (Kimmel 1974).

However, this assumption may not be valid from the perspective of parents. For example, when Barber (1979, 1980, 1981) asked parents to describe the circumstances surrounding the departure of their children, most mentioned a wide variety of "marker" events: marriage, entering military service, attending college, and getting a job. Interestingly, there was no consensus concerning which event was most likely to signal the transition to the empty nest. In fact, many parents in these studies balked at being asked to identify a particular event. They insisted instead that the departure of their children was more accurately described as a sequence of events—a launching *process*—that is experienced as a gradual "weaning" of the children, as one parent in the study called it. This "weaning" may be precipitated by a particular event, such as entering military service, or it may culminate in a single event, such as marriage, but the dominant feature of the departure of one's children is that it is a gradual process, not an abrupt change of status resulting from the occurrence of any particular event.

Further, confirmation that the transition to the empty nest is predicated on subjective criteria rather than on discrete events is found in the Transitions Study by Lowenthal and her colleagues at the Langley Porter Neuropsychiatric Institute (Lowenthal, Thurnher and Chiriboga 1975; Spence and Lonner 1971). In that study, twenty-seven men and twenty-seven women were identified as approaching the empty nest in that their youngest child was about to graduate from high school. In spite of the fact that all these parents were approaching the same event, interviews with them disclosed that some felt they had completed the transition to the empty nest, but others perceived it was yet to come. In the words of the researchers; "It appears that the transition involves more than what is encompassed by the graduation of one's child from high school" (Spence and Lonner 1971, 371). Spence and Lonner (1971) concluded that the transition to the empty nest is more accurately expressed in much broader and more subjective terms than simply the result of the occurrence of a particular event. For most parents in the Transitions Study, the critical variable in the transition to the empty nest was their own perceptions regarding the child's movement toward independence and adulthood. More important, these perceptions were often relatively independent of particular events demarcating the attainment of adulthood (for example, graduation from high school and marriage).

If particular events do not serve as reliable markers of the launching of children, what subjective criteria *do* parents employ in gauging their children's movement toward adulthood (and implicitly their own movement toward the empty nest)? Answers to this question are found in Barber's (1980) study wherein parents reported that the launching status of their children was tied more to subtle changes involving independence than to specific events. The first of these changes dealt with the parents' perception of qualitative changes in the parent-child relationship. As one mother put it,

> [t]here's a difference between having a child leave home and live somewhere else and having a child have their heart somewhere else. They can live a long way from you and still be close to you emotionally. I don't mean that they're dependent on you, but you feel like nothing has changed in your relationship with them. But when they start to depend on someone else and feel closer to them than to you, then you feel like you're losing them . . . they're gone then.

The second criterion was the extent to which parents perceived their children to be both emotionally and financially independent. For example, one father commented,

> He's [the father's son] still living here at home, but he has his own car, pays his own bills and the rent, and makes his own decisions. I don't know what my wife would say, but as far as I'm concerned, I feel he's on his own.

The emphasis on parental perceptions in determining progress through the empty-nest transition is important in two respects. First, it serves to alert researchers to the dangers inherent in conceptually and operationally defining the empty nest solely in terms of discrete events. And second, it illustrates a void in the empty-nest literature by suggesting that research needs to be conducted in which launching events (as well as the duration of the transition itself) are considered as *dependent* variables. The assumption that the transition to the empty nest is embodied in a particular event such as the graduation of the youngest child from high school seems unwarranted since the symbolic value or meaning of such an event varies considerably from parent to parent.

Parental Responses to the Empty-Nest Transition

Folklore and popular literature have often portrayed the transition to the empty nest as a time of crisis for most middle-aged parents, particularly mothers. In addition, many early studies on changes in marital quality over the life cycle have reported high levels of marital conflict and low marital satisfaction during the transition to the empty nest (Dizard 1968; Pineo 1961). For example, Rollins and Feldman (1970) reported that the lowest point with regard to present marital quality was expressed by respondents who were in the launching stage of the family life cycle.

However, more recent studies have supported neither the dire rhetoric of the "empty-nest syndrome" nor the findings of early investigations portraying the empty nest as a time of individual, marital, and family crisis (Barber 1980; Hagestad 1980; Lewis, Freneau, and Roberts 1979; Lowenthal and Chiriboga 1972; Spence and Lonner 1971). For example, Barber (1980) reported that the majority of parents in his study of couples in rural Pennsylvania evaluated the departure of their children in mostly positive terms. Positive aspects of emptying the nest were (1) relief from the relentless responsibility of day-to-day caring for children and (2) increased freedom and privacy. Collectively, these positive changes contributed to a marked improvement in marital relationships as well as to a sense of individual well-being.

According to Hagestad (1980), one of the major problems in studying the empty-nest transition is the lack of conceptual and theoretical interpretations of the *positive* effects of children leaving home. In testing her theoretical notions, Hagestad (1980) reported that the majority of middle-aged mothers in her study painted a rather positive picture of the empty-nest experience. These mothers indicated that the empty nest afforded them an opportunity to indulge in interests they had previously repressed. And perhaps more important, many of these mothers viewed their adult children as valuable "interpersonal resources" contributing to their (the mothers') sense of well-being.

All this is not to imply that the departure of one's children is devoid of family disruptions or of challenges to parents' individual well-being. Undoubtedly it is not. But the bulk of recent research in this area indicates that the empty-nest period is something that many parents look forward to, prepare for, and do not find exclusively stressful.

In most instances parents experience a mixture of both positive and negative reactions to the departure of their children (Barber 1980; Deutscher 1964). In examining points of stress in family transitions, Scherz (1971) suggested that when a change to a succeeding stage of the family life cycle (for example, the transition to the emtpy nest) is imminent, the stress experienced by family members is a product of wishing to retain the status quo and at the same time of wishing or hoping for change. These stresses she called transitional or "maturational crises." Each maturational crisis carries with it a mourning for the relationships that must be relinquished. And as in all mourning, there are temporary, mixed feelings of sorrow and happiness, often mild depression, and a desire to hold on to the old while simultaneously pressing ahead toward the new.

Although Scherz's (1971) proposal offers a partial explanation for why parents harbor mixed feelings as their children leave home, it does not explain *why* there are differences in the ways parents respond to and evaluate the empty-nest transition. Some of the most important differences in parental responses to the empty nest have been attributed to gender. Consequently, it is to this topic that we now turn.

Gender Differences and the Empty Nest

For a number of years, feelings of worry, dissatisfaction, loneliness, and depression have been portrayed in the literature as the standard reaction of women to the launching of their children. Collectively, these negative responses have been referred to as the "empty-nest syndrome."

Why has the empty-nest syndrome been used to describe women but not men? One reason is that the rhetoric of American society has proclaimed parenting as reserved primarily for women and as a major focus and key source of identity in their lives. Following this supposition to its conclusion, it has been presumed that the loss of the parental role during the empty-nest transition resulted in greater stress for women.

This reasoning has been prevalent in the literature for over thirty years. For example, in the late 1950s Phillips (1957) proposed that because the adult female gains her identity primarily from the parenting role, the loss of this intimate and frequently enacted role resulted in greater disorientation and dissatisfaction for her than for her male counterpart, whose identity was believed to stem mainly from his provider role. Twenty years later, Williams (1977) continued this line of reasoning by suggesting that those who experience the empty-nest period as particularly stressful are housewives who (1) are experiencing loss of the maternal role, (2) have been overprotective and overinvolved in the lives of their children, and (3) have believed that if they subordinated all their own needs to their children's needs, they would be content.

Empirical evidence supporting the existence of the "empty-nest syndrome" for women has been inconsistent. On the one hand, researchers have found that women evaluate the empty-nest stage as being equally satisfying or more satisfying than previous stages in the family life cycle (Axelson 1960; Campbell 1975; Lowenthal and Chiriboga 1972). Bart

(1971), Curlee (1969), and Lurie (1974), however, found evidence supporting the notion that the empty nest is a period of crisis for women. An important note with regard to these latter three studies is that they were all based on clinical samples and as such may not be representative of the way in which women generally respond to the departure of their children.

In contrast to the research and theory on women and the empty-nest transition, very little is known about how men react to the departure of children from the home. The lack of research implies that men may be relatively unaffected by the departure of their children, or at least that this period does not pose as great a threat to their individual well-being as it does to that of their wives. However, there is some evidence that the transition to the empty nest is difficult for some men. Because of men's traditional role as the primary economic provider, they may bemoan lost opportunities for relationships with their children (Rubin 1980). An example of this was found in Barber's (1980) study. Several fathers but *no* mothers mentioned that the empty-nest transition was difficult for them because they had failed to take advantage of the time when the children were still at home.

Barber (1980) found significant variability in the extent to which fathers found the empty-nest transition stressful. To better understand why the empty-nest transition might be more difficult for some men than for others, it is useful to review a study by Lewis et al. (1979) wherein both husbands and wives (in the same marital dyads) were interviewed regarding the experience of the launching of their last child. Although most fathers in this study were either neutral (35 percent) or felt some degree of happiness (42 percent) about their child's departure from the home, nearly a quarter of the men (22 percent) reported feeling either very unhappy or somewhat unhappy. Fathers who expressed unhappiness in the empty-nest transition were most likely to be those men who (1) had fewer children, (2) were older, (3) had the highest nurturing orientation, (4) felt most neglected by their wives, (5) received the least amount of understanding, empathy, and companionship from their wives, and (6) were the most lonely.

Lewis et al. (1979) posited a "principle of *most* interest" to explain their findings. Fathers with the most interest in their children had the more difficult time adjusting to the transition to the empty nest because they had the most to lose:

> [t]hey had the fewest children and, therefore, had more to lose emotionally with each child's leaving. They tended to be older fathers and, therefore, may have perceived fewer years to share with this child whom they feared would probably never again be so close. They also tended to perceive themselves as more nurturing and caring men, who may have had more to lose with the diminution of the full-time father role and loss of accompa-

nying identities as care-givers and nurturing persons. Finally, these were fathers who probably had the most to lose with their last child's leaving, because they tended also to report less satisfactory marriages (Lewis et al. 1979, 518).

Back (1971) reported that the departure of children from the home had a greater negative impact on fathers than on mothers. He hypothesized that this was due to gender differences in self-image. Mothers in Back's study expressed greater agreement between their real self and their appearance to others than did fathers. Back suggested that for women, being free of family obligations may allow them greater ease in accepting themselves for what they are; whereas for men, children leaving home makes them more dependent on their work role, in which they have difficulty presenting their real self-image.

In his study of empty-nest couples in rural Pennsylvania, Barber (1980) reported that the men were more likely than the women to express ambivalent or neutral feelings concerning the empty-nest transition. Lewis et al. (1979) also reported that over one-third (35 percent) of the fathers in their study felt "neutral" about the departure of their last child. Women, on the other hand, were less likely to be neutral and more likely to describe their responses to launching either in predominantly negative or in positive terms (Barber 1980; Deutscher 1962; Lowenthal and Chiriboga 1972).

Lowenthal and Chiriboga (1972) suggested that this gender difference may be an artifact of the predisposition of women in our society to more skillfully and freely express complex feelings and attitudes. During the transition to the empty nest, they found, men experienced self-evaluation and disequilibrium but might be unwilling and/or unable to clearly express their emotional responses to the transition in other than neutral or ambivalent terms.

In summary, research on the subjective well-being of mothers versus fathers in the empty nest is inconsistent, reflecting the complexity of the empty-nest transition. Nevertheless, one conclusion that can be drawn from these studies is that there is little support for the notion that the empty-nest syndrome is widespread or pertains solely to women. Contrary to previous assumptions, the well-being of fathers can also be affected by the transition to the empty nest.

Cohort Differences and the Empty-Nest Syndrome

In a presidential address to the Eastern Sociological Association, Matilda White Riley (1978) claimed that the ways in which individuals experience and cope with life transitions vary from generation to generation; that there is no set pattern of negotiating role transitions. A quote from her address emphasizes this point:

> The ways in which children enter kindergarten, or adolescents move into adulthood, or older people retire are not preordained. In this view, the life course is not fixed, but widely flexible. It varies with social change—not only with the changing nature of the family, the school, the workplace, the community, but also with changing ideas, values, and beliefs. As each new generation or cohort enters the stream of history, the lives of its members are marked by the imprint of social change and in turn leave their own imprint. (1).

Other than Barber (1979) and Borland (1982), researchers investigating parental responses to the empty-nest transition have largely ignored the possible influence of cohort membership. Barber (1979) noted that persons experiencing the launching of a last child at one point in history might have evaluated it quite differently from a group who experienced the empty-nest transition at another point in history. As an example, he cited the departure of a son to serve in the armed forces during wartime. He compared the experience of the son leaving home to serve in the military during World War II versus during the unpopular Vietnam war. Although parents during both historical periods were experiencing the empty nest transition, their reactions to it varied significantly due to the historical and social context in which it occurred.

In an important theoretical article, Borland (1982) hypothesized that the empty-nest syndrome as it applies to women is a cohort phenomenon. She noted that empty-nest research has failed to consider the changing roles of women over time as a control variable in assessing responses to the departure of children. This is a serious "flaw" in previous studies, she said, since each generation of women lives with a different ideology of what constitutes appropriate women's roles.

Borland subsequently argued that the degree to which women experience the empty-nest syndrome depends on the unique set of social circumstances in which they live, including family values and social norms concerning women's "proper" roles. Borland suggested that the generation of women who were born between 1920 and 1940, who went through the "active phase" of parenting between 1940 and 1960, and who experienced the empty-nest transition between 1960 and 1980 were more likely than other cohorts to experience the empty-nest syndrome. In the following quote, Borland (1982:122) describes why she thinks this is the case:

> Early life teachings and mother-role modeling socialized many of these women that to be feminine and happy was to be married and to become mothers who dedicated their lives selflessly to their family's needs. Most of

these women lived by that philosophy during their active parenthood years. When the maternal role ended . . . many found themselves without the major role which gave them an identity and feeling of being worthwhile for approximately 30 years.

Borland emphasized that her theoretical model was not deterministic. That is, she did not suggest that all women in a particular generation or birth cohort experience the same historical influences or react in the same way to the emptying of the nest. Individual differences as well as the influence of social class, community size, religion, and ethnicity play important roles in affecting parents' perceptions of the empty-nest transition. But her point was well taken, and future research should not overlook the hypothesis that unique historical and social circumstances affect parental reactions to and evaluations of the transition to the empty nest.

Ethnic Differences in the Empty-Nest Syndrome

Borland (1982) also addressed the question of whether there might be ethnic diferences in parental responses to the empty nest. She reviewed the historical and societal roles of black and Mexican-American women, with particular focus on family structure and ideology, on women's work roles, and on labor force participation.

Women in the Black Family

The family structure and work roles of black women suggest that the empty-nest syndrome may occur to a lesser degree for some black women than for middle-class white women. Queen and Habenstein (1974) described two forms of the black family that developed out of the traditional matriarchal family of the early twentieth century: (1) the adaptive urban matricentric black family, and (2) the acculturated middle majority black family. In the first family form, black women not only have economic roles outside the home and a residentially closer and larger family system, they also generally overlap the rearing of their own children with the rearing of grandchildren.

Borland then proposed three hypotheses regarding the empty-nest syndrome. First, she hypothesized that women in the adaptive urban matricentric black family would be less likely than middle-class white women to experience stress during the empty-nest transition. Second, since the second black family form—the acculturated middle majority black family—is very similar to the middle-class white family, Borland hypothesized that black women in this family form would experience the empty-nest syndrome to a greater extent than would their counterparts in the adaptive urban matri-centric black family. And third, since more black women have generally worked outside the home than have white women, and since there is no evidence that there has been a period of time when black females remained predominantly in the home and were exposed to the ideology that prevailed in the 1950s, Borland hypothesized that as a group, black women experi-ence the empty-nest syndrome to a lesser extent than do middle-class white women born between 1920 and 1940.

Women in the Mexican-American Family

Like the black family, the form of the Mexican-American family also varies as a result of acculturation (Bremer and Ragan 1977). First, there is the traditional extended family form, characterized by strong kinship ties, in which Mexican-American women find their major role and self-affirmation as wives and mothers. Although this family form still exists, particularly in regions in the southern United States, increased labor force participation rates among Mexican-American women together with other consequences of acculturation are moving the Mexican-American family more toward a nuclear family form.

Borland (1982) listed two hypotheses regarding the extent to which the empty-nest syndrome is experienced by Mexican-American women. First, she hypothesized that women in the emerging Mexican-American nuclear family form would experience the empty-nest syndrome more than would their counterparts in the traditional Mexican-American family form. Sec-ond, she hypothesized that the empty-nest syndrome would exist for Mexican-American women to the degree that nuclear families became phys-ically distant from one another and to the degree that they did not have meaningful alternative roles when children left the home.

Changes in Marital Relationships

Two factors make it difficult to determine marital quality after launching the last child. The first factor has to do with the length of the "couple alone again" stage. Often the empty-nest period lasts thirty, forty, or more years, and variation in relationship attributes increases with the passage of time (Troll et al. 1979). A profile of the marital relationship immediately upon entering the empty-nest transition may not—and most probably does not—serve as a reliable indicator of the future trajectory of that relationship. Personality development as well as changing economic and health condi-tions may combine to produce considerable variation in the quality of the marital relationship over the course of the empty-nest period (Hill et al. 1970; Lopata 1973).

A second factor is that the majority of studies have employed a cross-sectional research design. As such, it is impossible to discern whether the reported differences among groups of couples who are at different points in the empty-nest period actually reflect changes in marital quality over time, or simply denote cohort or generational differences (Rollins and Cannon 1974; Schaie 1967).

In spite of the difficulties involved, one fairly well-documented outcome of the departure of children is an improvement in the quality of the marital relationship (Barber 1980; Deutscher 1964; Rollins and Feldman 1970). Parents find themselves in the position of "husband and wife" again rather than primarily in the position of "father and mother." Although this realization may force them to admit that they no longer have enough in common to continue the relationship, the normal pattern is satisfaction with a loving relationship that is again allowed to flourish. Over half the parents in Deutscher's (1964) study evaluated their postparental life as preferable to their parental life; most of the others said that their married life remained about the same; and only 6 percent considered their post-parental relationship worse than it was before the children left.

The previously mentioned Transitions Study by Lowenthal et al. (1975) included two groups of middle-aged people representing two points in the empty-nest period. One group was defined as being on the verge of entering the empty nest since the youngest child was a senior in high school. The other group in this cross-sectional study consisted of empty-nest couples who were within three years of retirement. Most of the people in both these groups claimed that they had experienced positive changes in their marital relationship (Lurie 1974). However, couples in the older group (within three years of retirement) were twice as likely as those in the younger group to say they had experienced such a change (33 percent versus 15 percent) and were less likely to report negative changes (14 percent versus 38 percent). Lowenthal and her associates (1975) also reported that the empty-nest couples facing retirement expressed renewed interest in the personalities of their spouses. Eighty-two percent of both men and women in this group described their spouses in positive terms.

Whether improved marital relations in middle and later life are a chiefly a product of the launching of children, however, is questionable. Feldman (1964) compared the qualitative aspects of marriage between childless couples and older empty-nest couples who had been married the same number of years and concluded that the length of time a couple had been married was a more important determinant of marital quality than was the presence or absence of children. It may be that the qualitative aspects of marriage improve during the empty nest not because the nest is empty but because of more profound changes in individual development of the spouses themselves, as well as changes in the nature of the relationship itself (Troll 1975). For example, Reedy (1977) reported that long-married couples place greater stress on loyalty and emotional security than do couples who have been married for shorter periods of time. Parron's (1978) study of golden wedding couples reported a similar finding. Finally, Troll and Smith (1976) speculated that there is a fundamental inverse relationship between attraction and attachment over the period of time a couple is married. Attraction is high in the beginning, but attachment is low. With the passage of time, the valence of attraction wanes while the importance of attachment increases.

Impact on Parent-Child Relationships

Several researchers have reported a significant improvement in parent-child relationships during and after the empty-nest transition. Hagestad (1980), for example, suggested that adult children increasingly become resource persons for their mothers. When mothers in her study were asked what impact their college-aged children had on them, the majority responded by describing their children as an important "interpersonal resource" who contributed to their (the mothers') sense of well-being. The parents whom Barber (1980) interviewed claimed that their relationships with their adult children had improved since the children's departure. Why? The reason most frequently given was that after children "get out on their own," they appreciate their parents more and are not as critical as they were prior to leaving home.

Although this reason for improved parent-child relationships (increased appreciation of children for parents) was given by both mothers and fathers, it was most frequently given by mothers in relation to their daughters. This finding was also reported in early studies by Willmott and Young (1960) and Adams (1968). Adams suggested that daughters express a greater similarity of values with their mothers than do sons. This similarity is likely not only a product of early socialization but more important also a result of the "role convergence" that comes with marriage and parenthood on part of the daughter.

With regard to their research on mother–adult child relationships in the empty-nest transition, Spence and Lonner (1972) noted that there comes a point when women see their children no longer as children but as independently functioning adults. But they also argued that this change in perception from one way of viewing a child to another is complex. It is one thing to "be rid of the kids and the responsibility" and quite another to have a secure feeling that the children are on their own course and will demand little in the future. Thus, having one's children leave the home does not necessarily relieve one of the parent role; in fact, it may complicate the role by introducing long-distance parenting.

Spence and Lonner (1972) also observed that some mothers, although looking forward to the departure of their children from the home, expressed great hope but less confidence in their children's ability to handle the departure well. This lack of confidence created uncertainty in the minds of some mothers. When they spoke of goals and interests they wished to pursue when the children were gone, they did so in a tentative, vague, and even pessimistic manner.

The Empty Nest: A Reversible Transition?

As mentioned earlier in this chapter, many parents perceive the departure of their children as a gradual weaning process, a process defined less in terms of specific events than in terms of subtle subjective criteria based on the children's movement toward independence and adulthood. Nevertheless, most parents do have in mind an approximate "timetable" for the launching of their children that may include the occurrence of events such as completing an eduction and getting married. Although parents do not often acknowledge that specific events signal the departure of their children, they anticipate that their children will progress toward independence according to a schedule of parental expectations that may include the timing of certain events. Parents express concern both for children who are "late" and resist leaving and for those who leave before the parents feel they are ready (Barber 1979).

Furthermore, most parents expect that once their children have departed, the nest will remain empty. But for an increasing number of parents, these expectations regarding the timing and permanence of launching are not being met. For example, between 1968 and 1983, the percentage of families with one child eighteen to twenty-four years of age at home increased from 6.36 percent to 7.40 percent; in the same period the percentage of families with a child age twenty-five or older increased from 2.57 percent to 3.84 percent (U.S. Bureau of the Census 1983).

Why is it that many adult children are not leaving home or are returning home? Answers are found in the rising divorce rates, in the recently increasing age at first marriage, in a labor market with low entry salaries for the majority of young adults, in unemployment and underemployment, and in the continuing high cost of housing. All of these are encouraging adult children to linger awhile longer in the nest or to return to the nest after having left it.

How are parents responding to this trend? To begin with, they are surprised. In a recent study of adult children living with their parents, Clemens and Axelson (1985) reported that 80 percent of the parents (of a child twenty-two years or older) *had not* planned to have the child home at that time. Second, parents are not happy with this arrangement, resulting in what has been referred to as the "full-nest syndrome" (Eberle 1987). And the older the child, the less happy the parents feel about having them return to the nest (Clemens and Axelson 1985). Most parents view the resulting living arrangements as temporary and are generally unwilling to have the adult child remain in the nest indefinitely.

The popular press has picked up on this trend, and a number of articles have recently appeared commenting on the problematic aspects of adult children returning home to live with their parents (Block 1983; Ommerman 1983). Researchers, too, have felt that this phenomenon is worth investigating. Clemens and Axelson (1985), for example, recently explored some of the problematic issues involved in families where young adults had returned to live with their parents. The two problems they found most frequently cited by parents were "time of coming and going" (43.5 percent) and "cleaning and maintenance" (48.7 percent). "Entertaining friends" and "use of household resources" were other problems mentioned.

Additionally, Clemens and Axelson (1985) reported that parents' marriages are often adversely affected by the presence of adult children in the home. Almost half the parents in their studies complained that the presence of an adult child in the home had a negative effect on their marriage. Parents may find that the presence of an adult child in the home prevents them from evaluating their marital relationship and resolving latent relationship issues. They may be deprived of the new-found freedoms and privacy they enjoyed when the children first left home.

Clemens and Axelson (1985) further speculated that parents may find that their development as individuals, is hindered when the children return to the nest. The expectation of being able to take advantage of new freedoms and opportunities may be thwarted. And the stress of having an adult child in the home may also place parents in jeopardy as they try to reconcile their guilt, associated with wanting their children to "be off and gone," and the sense of responsibility they have for doing all they possibly can for the child.

However, the study by Clemens and Axelson (1985) was based on a small ($n = 32$) and unrepresentative sample derived primarily from participants in a workshop on "parenting the young adult." It is possible that their findings are biased in that many of those choosing to attend the workshop were parents experiencing problems with adult children living at home.

A study by Suitor and Pillemer (1987) provides a more accurate profile of how marriages are affected by the presence of adult children. Using a random sample of 677 older couples who were sharing a residence with at least one adult child, they found that the presence of adult children in the couples' households had *no* effect on the incidence of marital conflict.

Those couples experienced no greater marital conflict than did those couples whose nest was truly empty. This finding contributes to a growing body of literature suggesting that the presence of adult children in the home may not be as detrimental to the well-being of older couples as was once thought (Lee and Ellithorpe 1982).

Future Research

Three areas where future research is needed have been suggested throughout this chapter: (1) how men experience the empty-nest transition, (2) controlling for cohort, social class, and ethnic background in evaluating the impact of the empty-nest transition on the well-being of *both* women and men, and (3) the impact of refilling up the nest when young adult child returns home after having been launched.

A fourth suggestion is that future research should be more attuned to time-dependent factors in the empty-nest transition. Presumably, there is constant interplay between expectations formed prior to the departure of one's children and the realization or disconfirmation of these expectations during or subsequent to the time when the children leave (Klinger 1975; Stokols 1975). Given this perspective, the design of the majority of research on the empty-nest transition is inadequate since measures of parental well-being are taken at only one point in time. When this is the case, there is no way of knowing if and how parents' expectations concerning the empty nest are changed or modified over the course of the transition itself. For example, do parents "lower" their expectations to accommodate those aspects of the launching of their children that at first are not fulfilled? The answers to this and similar questions can only come from longitudinal designs that have the potential for revealing the changing expectations of parents as they experience the transition to the empty nest.

References

Adams, B. N. 1968. *Kinship in and Urban Setting*. Chicago: Markham Publishing.

Axelson, L. J. 1960. "Personal adjustment in the post-parental period." *Marriage and Family Living* 22:66–70.

Back, K. W. 1971. "Transition to aging and the self-image." *Aging and Human Development* 2:296–304.

Barber, C. E. 1979. "An experience in middle adulthood: The transition to the empty nest." In G. D. Hansen and G. R. Bascom (eds.), *Aging and Families*. Provo, UT: Brigham Young University, Division of Continuing Education.

———. 1980. "Gender differences in experiencing the transition to the empty nest:

Reports of middle-aged and older women and men." *Family Perspective* 14:87–95.

———. 1981. "Parental responses to the empty-nest transition." *Journal of Home Economics* 73:32–33.

Bart, P. 1971. "Depression in middle-aged women." In V. Bornick and B. K. Moran (eds.), *Women in Sexist Society*. New York: New American Library.

———. 1973. "Portnoy's mother's complaint." In H. Z. Lopata (ed.), *Marriages and families*. New York: Van Nostrand Reinhold.

Block, J. L. 1983. "Help! They've all moved back home!" *Woman's Day* (April 26):72, 74, 76.

Borland, D. C. 1982. "A cohort analysis approach to the empty-nest syndrome among three ethnic groups of women: A theoretical position." *Journal of Marriage and the Family* 44:117–29.

Bremer, T. H., and Ragan, P. K. 1977. "The effect of the empty-nest on the morale of Mexican American and White women." A paper presented at the 30th annual meeting of the Gerontological Society, San Francisco, November 1977.

Campbell, A. 1975. "The American way of mating: Marriage yes, children only maybe." *Psychology Today* 8(May):37–43.

Clemens, A. W., and Axelson, L. J. 1985. "The not-so-empty-nest: The return of the fledgling adult." *Family Relations* 34:259–64.

Curlee, J. 1969. "Alcoholism and the empty-nest." *Bulletin of the Menninger Clinic* 33:165–71.

Deutscher, I. 1962. "Socialization for postparental life." In A. Rose (ed.), *Human Behavior and Social Processes*. Boston: Houghton-Mifflin.

———. 1964. "The quality of postparental life." *Journal of Marriage and the Family* 26:52–59.

———. 1969. "From parental to postparental life." *Sociological Symposium* 3:47–60.

Dizard J. 1968. *Social Change in the Family*. Chicago: Community and Family Study Center, University of Chicago.

Eberle, N. 1987. "The full-nest syndrome." *Woman's Day* 58 (July 7):60, 62, 65.

Feldman, H. 1964. "Development of the husband wife relationship." Preliminary report, Cornell Studies of Marital Development: Study in the Transition to Parenthood. Ithaca, NY: Department of Child Development and Family Relationships. New York State College of Home Economics, Cornell University.

Glenn, N. D. 1975. "Psychological well-being in the postparental stage: Some evidence from national surveys." *Journal of Marriage and the Family* 37:104–10.

Glick, P. C. 1977. "Updating the life cycle of the family." *Journal of Marriage and the Family* 39:5–13.

Hagestad, G. O. 1980. *Role Change and Socialization in Adulthood: The Transition to the Empty Nest*. Unpublished manuscript. State College, PA: The Pennsylvania State University.

Harkins, E. B. 1978. "Effects of empty nest transition on self-report of psychological and physical well-being." *Journal of Marriage and the Family* 40:549–56.

Hill, R., Foote, N., Aldous, J., Carlson, R. and MacDonald, R. 1970. *Family Development in Three Generations*. Cambridge, MA: Schenkman.

Kimmel, D. C. 1974. *Adulthood and Aging: An Interdisciplinary, Developmental View*. New York: John Wiley and Sons.

Klinger, E. 1975. "Consequences of commitment to and disengagement from incentives." *Psychological Review* 82:26–44.

Lee, G. R., and Ellithorpe, E. 1982. "Intergenerational exchange and subjective well-being among the elderly." *Journal of Marriage and the Family* 44:217–24.

Lewis, R. A., Freneau, P. J., and Roberts, C. L. 1979. "Fathers and the postparental transition." *Family Coordinator* 28:514–20.

Lopata, H. Z. 1973. *Widowhood in an American City*. Cambridge, MA: Schenkman.

Lowenthal, M. F., and Chiriboga, D. 1972. "Transition to the empty nest: Crisis, challenge or relief?" *Archives of General Psychiatry* 26:8–14.

Lowenthal, M. F., Thurnher, M., and Chiriboga, D. 1975. *Four Stages of Life*. San Francisco: Jossey-Bass.

Lurie, E. E. 1974. "Sex and stage differences in perceptions of marital and family relationships." *Journal of Marriage and the Family* 36:260–69.

Ommerman, B. 1983. "Going back to the nest: Tips on coping with the return of adult children." *Roanoke Times and World News* C (March 10):1,4.

Phillips, B. S. 1957. "A role theory approach to adjustment in old age." *American Sociological Review* 22:212–17.

Pineo, P. C. 1961. "Disenchantment in the later years of marriage." *Marriage and Family Living* 23:3–11.

Queen, S. A., and Habenstein, R. 1974. "The contemporary Black American family." In *The Family in Various Cultures* (4th ed.). New York: Lippincott.

Reedy, M. N. 1977. *Age and Sex Differences in Personal Needs and the Nature of Love: A Study of Happily Married Young, Middle-Aged, and Older Couples*. Unpublished doctoral dissertation, University of Southern California, Los Angeles.

Riley, M. W. 1978. "Aging, social change, and the power of ideas." A presidential address delivered to the Eastern Sociological Society, Philadelphia.

Rollins, B. C., and Cannon, K. L. 1974. "Marital satisfaction over the family life cycle: A re-evaluation." *Journal of Marriage and the Family* 35:271–82.

Rollins, B. C., and Feldman, H. 1970. "Marital satisfaction over the family life cycle." *Journal of Marriage and the Family* 32:20–28.

Rose, A. M. 1955. "Factors associated with the life satisfaction of middle-class, middle-aged persons." *Journal of Marriage and the Family* 17:15–19.

Rubin, L. B. 1980. "The empty nest: Beginning or ending?" In L. A. Bond and J. C. Rosen (eds.), *Competence and Coping in Adulthood*. Hanover, NH: University Press of New England.

Saunders, L. 1969. *Social Class and the Postparental Perspective*. Unpublished doctoral dissertation, University of Minnesota.

Schaie, K. W. 1967. "Age changes and age differences." *The Gerontologist* 1 (part I):128–32.

Scherz, F. H. 1971. "Maturational crises and parent-child interaction." *Social Casework* 36:362–69.

Spence, D., and Lonner, T. 1971. "The 'empty nest': A transition within motherhood." *Family Coordinator* 20:369–75.

Stokols, D. 1975. "Toward a psychology of alienation." *Psychological Review* 82:26–44.

Suitor, J. J., and Pillemer, K. 1987. "The presence of adult children: A source of stress for elderly couples?" *Journal of Marriage and the Family* 49:717–25.

Troll, L. E. 1975. *Early and Middle Adulthood.* Monterey, CA: Brooks/Cole.

Troll, L. E., Miller, S. J., and Atchley, R. C. 1979. *Families in Later Life.* Belmont, CA: Wadsworth.

Troll, L. E., and Smith, J. 1976. "Attachment through the life span: Some questions about relations in later life." *Human Development* 3:156–71.

U.S. Bureau of the Census. 1983. "Marital Status and Living Arrangements: March 1982." *Current Population Reports,* series P-20, no. 380. Washington, DC: U.S. Government Printing Office.

Waller, W. 1937. "The rating and dating complex." *American Sociological Review* 2:727–34.

Williams, J. H. 1977. "Middle age and aging." In *Psychology of Women: Behavior in a Biosocial Context.* New York: Norton.

Willmott, P., and Young, M. 1960. *Family and Class in a London Suburb.* London: Routledge and Kegan Paul.

2
Retirement, Couples, and Household Work

Maximiliane Szinovacz

Over two decades ago Lipman (1961, 267) wrote, "Retirement of the male from the occupational system represents a major crisis in marital adjustment." Despite Lipman's early conceptualization of retirement as a couple event, the prevailing approach to retirement remains individualistic: most studies investigate the impact of retirement only on the retiree and consider few if any spouse and/or couple characteristics (except marital status per se). Consequently, little more is known about the marital contingencies and consequences of retirement than was known in the 1960s.

Yet the need to include couple, family, and household conditions in retirement research and to view retirement as an important event in the life of spouses has become increasingly clear. For instance, recent research shows that spouses time their retirement in relation to each other (Henretta and O'Rand 1983; Campione 1987; Szinovacz in press). It has also been suggested that inclusion of spouse characteristics is needed to reach a clearer picture of sex differences in the antecedents and consequences of female retirement (George et al. 1984; Gratton and Haug 1983). Furthermore, with the rise in female labor force participation, more couples experience dual retirement transitions and are required to adjust to each other's retirement.

Given the prevalent individualistic approach to retirement, it seems appropriate to begin this chapter with a brief review of the demographic and theoretical bases justifying a couple approach to the retirement transition. Later sections will focus on one central issue in couples' adaptation to retirement—namely, the division of household work.

This research was funded by a grant from the AARP Andrus Foundation. Additional funds were provided by the School of Home Economics, University of Illinois.

Retirement as a Couple Event: Demographic and Theoretical Bases

Demographic Changes and the Timing of Retirement

During the past quarter of a century, pronounced changes have occurred both in the retirement patterns of married men and in the labor force participation of married women. In 1960, over 90 percent of married men aged 45 to 64 and 37 percent of married men aged 65 or over were in the labor force; by 1986, these proportions had decreased to 82 percent and 17 percent, respectively. At the same time, labor force participation rates of middle-aged married women increased rapidly: for married women aged 35 to 44, labor force participation rose from 36 percent in 1960 to 69 percent in 1986; for the 45-to-64 age group, the comparative proportions are 34 percent and 50 percent. Only a minority of married women continued to work past age 65: 6 percent in 1960 and 7 percent in 1986 (U.S. Bureau of the Census 1987).

These trends imply, first, that employment of both spouses has become the "normative" pattern for middle-aged couples. Thus, more and more couples experience the retirement of both spouses. Furthermore, the trend toward earlier retirement among married men suggests a convergence in spouses' retirement age and consequently an increase in the number of couples who face retirement jointly or within a short time period.

Research on couples' retirement timing substantiates these trends. It has been shown that spouses' labor force participation constitutes one of the strongest predictors of older individuals' continued labor force participation (Clark et al. 1980; Anderson et al., 1980; Henretta and O'Rand 1980; Campione 1987) and that married women retire earlier than unmarried women, whereas married men tend to delay retirement, presumably to realize a joint retirement transition. This latter trend seems contingent on couples' age homogamy (Atchley 1976a; Atchley and Miller 1983; Palmore 1965; Shaw 1984).

Systems Theory

Interdependence and feedback are central concepts of systems theory (Kantor and Lehr 1975). The assumption of interdependence of system parts implies that changes in one part of the system will affect other system parts. From this perspective, the retirement of one spouse will necessitate adjustments on the part of both spouses, and the retiree's adjustment will be contingent not only on his or her own experiences but also on the effect retirement has on the spouse, as well as on the spouse's ability to adjust to changed life circumstances.

Several research findings support this view. Data on housewives' reactions to their husbands' retirement demonstrate that housewives adapt their own routines to oblige the retired husbands and that their failure to do so may negatively impact on husbands' and the couples' postretirement adjustment (Lipman 1960, 1961; Keating and Cole 1980). Other research suggests that spousal support is essential for retirees' and couples' postretirement adjustment (Heyman and Jeffers 1968; Brubaker 1985a) and that retirees' own life satisfaction is contingent on the life satisfaction of the spouse (Atchley and Miller 1983). In addition, the retirement of even one spouse affords changes in the couple's time schedules and activity patterns. Increased free time for leisure activities, less time pressure, and an increased focus on the marital relationship have been noted as positive consequences of husbands' and wives' retirement (Fengler 1975; Keating and Cole 1980; Hill and Dorfman 1982; Dorfman and Hill 1986; Szinovacz 1980).

Changes in internal or external circumstances may bring about temporary system instability. In such events, feedback processes elicit system responses that safeguard system maintenance either through adaptive change (positive feedback) or through the reestablishment of the prior equilibrium state (negative feedback) (Kantor and Lehr 1975; Buckley 1967). Evidence from the retirement literature suggests that both general marital system responses and adjustments made by the other spouse help prevent adjustment problems on the part of the retiree and on the part of the couple. For example, several studies indicate that married individuals face fewer retirement problems than nonmarried individuals, even if such variables as health or income are controlled (Mutran and Reitzes 1981; Beck 1982; Seccombe and Lee 1986). Other research shows that wives' tendency to retire together with or close to their husbands may prevent and/ or reduce adjustment problems faced by retired "house husbands" (Szinovacz in press).

Role Theory

Cooley's (1922) concept of the looking-glass self perhaps best epitomizes the notion that individuals' self-concept evolves from the roles they play and from others' perceptions of these roles and of the individual's role performance (see also Burgess 1973). Since spouses' occupational roles also constitute part of their family role repertory (provider role or helper in the provider role—Hood 1986), relinquishing these roles requires a redefinition of marital roles for and by both spouses. Indeed, research suggests that failure to redefine marital roles upon retirement can result in adjustment problems. Lipman (1961, 268, 271) found, for example, that "the retired person who views himself as a good economic provider is twice as likely to have low morale as the male who views his marital role as expressive" and that "wives (of retirees) who adhered to the traditional sentiment of the women's role (good homemaker) manifested the largest percentage of low morale." If both spouses retire and especially if they retire at different times, several shifts in role conceptions may be necessary (for instance, the shift from "husband as main provider in a dual-earner couple" to "house-husband in a wife-single-earner couple" and then to "husband in a dual-retired couple").

Other findings confirm that reduced sex-role segregation and the increased participation of retired husbands in household tasks promote post-retirement adjustment (Kerckhoff 1966; Keith and Brubaker 1979). Such redistribution of marital role responsibilities after retirement may also be necessary to prevent feelings of unfavorable inequity, especially on the part of wives (Schafer and Keith 1981), and to align role responsibilities with role- and/or age-related personality changes toward androgyny (Gutmann et al. 1980; Sinnott 1977; McGee and Wells 1982).

It has also been suggested that mutual "reality construction" (Berger and Kellner 1964) and "matching of developmental careers" (Foote 1956) are ongoing marital processes and prerequisites for marital adjustment. Consequently, the failure of one spouse to redefine his or her role in terms of role changes brought about by his or her own retirement or by the retirement of the spouse will hinder adaptation to the retirement transition. In commenting on Crawford's (1971) study of couples at the preretirement stage, Rapoport and Rapoport (1975, 291) demonstrated that some spouses dread the changes they know will be required of them:

> In conventional families where there is a sharp segregation of male and female roles, neither the men nor the women are prepared for what is to happen. Many men tend not to understand that their wives have a personal life organized around the central fact that men are not there during the work days, and many women accordingly find it difficult to incorporate a masculine presence around the house for more than the accustomed times. One wife is reported as saying, "I married him for better or worse, but not for lunch."

Several studies on housewives of retired husbands have shown that "having the husband underfoot" is a common complaint (Lipman 1960, 1961; Heyman and Jeffers 1968; Fengler 1975; Hill and Dorfman 1982). Other wives see it as their duty to stage an active and involved retirement life for their husbands, efforts that are not always appreciated (Keating and Cole 1980). These studies and the theoretical premises of role theory leave little doubt that joint decision-making on retirement roles and renegotiation of responsibilities are essential if the couple is to achieve a mutually rewarding retirement experience (Keith and Brubaker 1979; Dorfman and Hill 1986). And research on retirement timing indicates that consideration of the spouse's retirement plans and discussions about retirement with the spouse may play a significant role in anticipatory socialization for retirement (Prentis 1980; Shaw 1984; Evans et al. 1985).

Developmental Theory

Past research on retirement not only focused on individuals, it also treated retirement as an isolated life event (Stull and Hatch 1984). Yet developmental theory stresses that both the asynchronization of life events in relation to other life circumstances and the accumulation of life events increase stress and deter adjustment (Holmes and Rahe 1967; Seltzer 1976; Morgan 1977). The demographic changes described above suggest that couples will increasingly be faced with a dual-retirement process, either jointly or a few years apart. As shown in figure 2–1, the first alternative—joint retirement—implies simultaneous life changes for both spouses. In the second case, both spouses will experience sequential changes, each of which requires adjustments by both spouses. Either situation constitutes an accumulation of life events that, if the premises of developmental theory hold, may hinder adjustment at least on a short-term basis. To date, research evidence pertaining to this assumption is not available.

In addition, one or both of the transitional stages depicted in figure 2–1 may be associated with specific adaptation problems. The single-retired wife may feel pushed into a full-time housewife role that she is not willing to assume, and the single-retired husband may feel forced into an involuntary "house husband" role that he is equally unwilling to perform. Some research suggests that it is primarily the latter pattern that reduces adjustment (Szinovacz in press). Atchley and Miller (1983) found no significant differences in couples' life satisfaction scores by retirement pattern, but their data support the trend shown in this chapter's data: that couples with an employed wife and a retired husband scored lowest on life satisfaction.

Developmental theory further posits that the timing of and control over life events are crucial for adaptation (Morgan 1977; Seltzer 1976; Neugarten 1977). Research on retirement timing suggests that women, motivated by their husbands' retirement, often approach retirement off-time (early) and to some extent relinquish control over their retirement timing to the husband—that is, they give in to his pressure (Anderson et al. 1980; Henretta and O'Rand 1980, 1983; Clark et al. 1980; Atchley 1976a; Palmore 1965; Shaw 1984; Campione 1987; Szinovacz in press). And even if both spouses participate equally in the timing decision-making process, negotiating the timing of both spouses' retirement is clearly a more complex process than deciding on the husband's retirement in single-earner couples (Szinovacz in press). Dissatisfaction with the outcomes of these negotiations and the perception of retirement as off-time may result in lowered adjustment.

Finally, marital and familial circumstances other than spouses' retirement may affect one or both spouses' retirement timing transitions and adjustment to retirement. For instance, the ill health of husbands or of other family members has been shown to precipitate wives' retirement and to hinder their adjustment if these caregiving responsibilities detain the

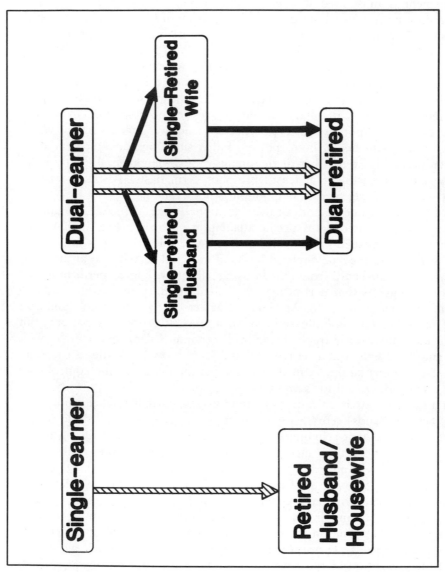

Figure 2–1. Couple Retirement Timing Patterns

retiree from involvement in her desired leisure activities (Brody et al. 1987; Crossman et al. 1981; Szinovacz, 1986–87). Other studies confirm that ill health and/or the health-related retirement of the husband is associated with lowered life satisfaction of the wife and that ill health of the wife is related to decreased life satisfaction of retired husbands (Heyman and Jeffers 1968; Hill and Dorfman 1982; Atchley and Miller 1983).

The theoretical approaches and empirical evidence discussed above substantiate the view that the retirement of either spouse constitutes a major transition for the couple and requires adjustments by both spouses. The scarce literature considering couple characteristics and responses to retirement further suggests that spouses' retirement timing in relation to each other, spouses' health, and changes in the division of household work feature among the most important contingencies of the retirement transition and adaptation process. These issues have been selected as the focus for the remainder of this chapter. Evidence from previous research and hypotheses based on these findings will be presented in the following section. This review will then be complemented with data from a recent study by the author.

Retirement and the Division of Household Tasks

Sex Difference in Household Activities after Retirement

The existing data on changes in household activity patterns following retirement are inconsistent. Some studies conducted in the 1960s, referred to in the previous section, indicated that husbands become more involved in household activities once they retire; however, their participation may be restricted to masculine tasks (Ballweg 1967; Kerckhoff 1966). A similar trend is evident in larger and more recent studies: older and/or retired men were shown to spend more time with and to carry a greater share of household work than were younger and/or employed men (Rexroat and Shehan 1987; Coverman and Sheley 1986; Altergott and Duncan 1987; George et al. 1984; Gordon et al. 1976 Dorfman and Heckert 1988; Keith et al. 1981a, 1981b). However, retirement-age women also seem to increase time spent with household activities when compared to "empty-nest" women (George et al. 1984; Rexroat and Shehan 1987; Zuzanek 1987). Other studies reported no changes or only short-lived changes in couples' division of household tasks after retirement (Brubaker and Hennon 1982; Keating and Cole 1980; Szinovacz 1980), despite expectations of increased role sharing (Dobson 1983; Brubaker and Hennon, 1982). Such nonfulfillment of role expectations may result in feelings of unfavorable inequity among older women (Schafer and Keith 1981).

In summary, the balance of findings points to an increase in household work after retirement by both men and women. This suggests the following hypothesis:

Hypothesis 1: Retirement leads to an increase in household work time on the part of both men and women.

Determinants of Change in Household Work after Retirement

Since many studies on retired spouses' division of household work contain few if any controls, little is known about the conditions under which retirees change or maintain their involvement in household work. Previous research on young couples and evidence from the retirement literature offer some insights into such conditions.

Sex Roles. Numerous studies have documented changes in sex-role attitudes toward more egalitarian norms, including the acceptance of women's employment outside the home and husbands' participation in household activities. These changes are more pronounced among selected population groups such as women, the younger age groups, higher socioeconomic status groups, and those in urban environments (Szinovacz 1984b; Scanzoni and Arnett 1987). However, normative changes pertaining to the division of household work seem to represent little more than lip-service and have not been widely implemented. For instance, Coverman and Sheley (1986) reported no significant change in husbands' housework and child care time between 1965–66 and 1975–76. Other studies showed similar findings (Nickols and Metzen 1982; Szinovacz 1984b). Nevertheless, subgroup differences in sex-role attitudes may be reflected in the extent to which men and women increase their involvement in household work after retirement.

Since current retirees belong to a sex-role traditional cohort (they married and became parents at the onset of the baby boom), high sex-role segregation among retired couples is to be expected. Yet cohort-specific norms may be counteracted by role- and age-specific changes in personality. Several researchers suggest that men's and women's personalities "mellow" or converge in the later years: men become more affiliative and women more instrumental and dominant. This convergence results in a more androgynous and complex personality profile among aged men and women (Gutmann et al. 1980; Sinnott 1977, 1982, 1984; McGee and Wells 1982). To what extent and how these personality changes are manifested in behavioral change and specifically in spouses' participation in household work is, however, not clear. It can be argued that increased androgyny in later life will be manifested in decreased sex-role segregation in household work after retirement. In other words, retirement-related increases in time spent on housework will be more pronounced for men than for women. At least for this cohort, however, such personality changes are unlikely to eliminate sex-role segregation in the division of household tasks; that is, wives of retirees and retired women will continue to bear the greater share of household work. For example, recent time-budget studies have estimated that time spent on household work by retirement-age wives exceeds their husbands' housework time by 15 to 300 percent (Altergott and Duncan 1987; Zuzanek 1987; Rexroat and Shehan 1987).

The following hypotheses can be derived from this literature:

Hypothesis 2a: Time spent on household work after retirement will be positively associated with socioeconomic status and urban residence among men and negatively associated with socioeconomic status and urban residence among women.

Hypothesis 2b: Increases in household work time after retirement will be more pronounced for men than for women.

Hypothesis 2c: Women spend significantly more time on household work than men both before and after retirement.

Ability and Need. Even though most people retire in good health, retirement for health-related reasons or to provide care for ill or disabled spouses is not uncommon (Palmore et al. 1985; Atchley and Miller 1983; Crossman et al. 1981; Brody et al. 1987). Under such circumstances, spouses' division of household tasks may become increasingly pragmatic; that is, household responsibilities are carried out by the spouse who is physically able to perform these tasks (Szinovacz 1980). Furthermore, since women bear the greater burden of household work, changes in spouses' division of household work due to disability are likely to be more pronounced if it is the wife who suffers from illness. Rexroat and Shehan (1987) found, for instance, that a wife's illness led to a significant reduction in her housework time and an increase in her husband's share in household work, whereas a husband's health was not significantly related to either spouse's household participation. Similarly, in Brubaker's (1985b) study of golden wedding couples, wives ranking low on self-reported health reported a less traditional division of household responsibilities than did healthy wives.

These findings suggest the following hypotheses:

Hypothesis 3a: Illness of the wife will be negatively related to her time involvement in household work after retirement.

Hypothesis 3b: Illness of the wife will be positively related to her husband's time involvement in household work after retirement.

Hypothesis 3c: Illness of the husband will not be significantly related to his or his wife's time involvement in household work after retirement.

Retirement Timing Patterns. Previous research on changes in household work after retirement is not only inconsistent in its findings, it has also failed to consider spouses' employment status and/or couples' retirement timing patterns. The different timing patterns shown in figure 2–1 may be associated with divergent reallocations of household duties. Research on younger couples suggests the following trends: 1) husbands and wives reduce their household work in response to their own work obligations; 2) this association is more pronounced for women; and 3) husbands' household contributions remain relatively inflexible to their employed wives' workload and overload problems (Rexroat and Shehan 1987; Fox and Nickols 1983; Nickols and Metzen 1982; Pleck 1985; Szinovacz 1984b). If these patterns hold for retirees, we can, first, expect an increase in household work time after retirement on the part of both spouses (see hypothesis 1). Second, the single-earner-retired and the dual-retired timing patterns would seem to necessitate less of a redistribution in household work than the two transitional single-retirement patterns: housewives may welcome some help from their retired husbands but reject his intrusion into their domestic realm (Lipman 1960, 1961), and dual-retired spouses may each increase their household work somewhat but strive to replace former work time with joint activities other than household work. The single-retired stage represents a drastically different situation. Here, one spouse is still subject to the time demands of gainful employment while the other is "free" to take over household chores.

Consequently, we can expect a more pronounced increase in household activities by retirees whose spouses remain employed. Given men's inflexibility toward women's workload, however, this association is likely to be more pronounced for female than for male retirees.

Hypothesis 4: Employment of the spouse will be positively related to time spent on household work after retirement; this association will be more pronounced for women than for men.

Postretirement Activities and the Meaning of Household Work. Much research has been devoted to changes in activity patterns after retirement. Some investigators suggest that retirement leads to disengagement not only from the work role but from other activities as well; others suggest that a substitution of work activities with new leisure activities occurs; and still others postulate that retirees maintain or expand their involvement in preretirement activities. Which of these patterns is followed depends on several factors, including physical ability, opportunities, and life goals. Specifically, disengagement may occur among disabled retirees and those lacking in opportunities; substitution is likely to occur if retirement is associated with a major restructuring of life goals; and continuity characterizes retirees whose life goal structure is only marginally affected by retirement (Atchley 1976b).

Housework means different things to different people—and to different researchers. Although some emphasize the oppressive and exploitative nature of housework (Hartmann 1981), others assert that at least some aspects of housework can be fulfilling and serve important familial and cultural functions (Valadez and Clignet 1984; DeVault 1987). Certainly, most housework is seen as obligatory and performed whether "liked" or not (Roadburg 1981; Moss and Lawton 1982; Lawton et al. 1986–87). Nevertheless, the flexible time schedule available to retirees may introduce an element of choice into their time expenditures on household activities. Considering the premises of both sex-role-convergence and activity-substitution/continuity theories, increases in retirees' household participation can be expected if such increases are consistent with a shift toward marriage- or family-centered life goals after retirement. Since such a shift in life goals probably constitutes a more dramatic reorientation for men than for women, and since it conforms to the enhanced affiliative needs of aging men, this association may be more pronounced for men than for women.

Based on these arguments, the following hypothesis is suggested:
Hypothesis 5: Marriage- and/or family-orientation will be positively associated with increases in time spent on household work after retirement. This association will be more pronounced for men than for women.

Sample and Methods

Data for this study are based on a stratified random sample of annuitants in Florida's State Retirement System. Stratification criteria were sex, income group (low, middle, or high, estimated from the retiree's length of service and amount of pension), and length of retirement (under one to five years). Data were collected through mailed questionnaires. The first mailing with two follow-up requests was conducted from December 1983 through early spring 1984. To correct for divergences from the stratification goals due to nonresponses, a second mailing was conducted later in the spring of 1984. The second mailing oversampled groups with high non-response rates to the first mailing. As in the case of the first mailing, two follow-up requests were mailed.

In general, stratification criteria calling for equal representation of the subgroups (by sex, income, and length of retirement) were met. Respondents in the middle-income groups were slightly underrepresented and women with high incomes were slightly overrepresented in the final sample. Of the total 2,145 mailed questionnaires, 912 were usable. One thousand one hundred twenty-seven subjects did not respond (52.5 percent), 51 questionnaires (2.4 percent) were returned for other reasons (died, moved), and 55 questionnaires (2.6 percent) were eliminated because they did not correspond with sample criteria or were only partially completed. For the following analyses, only the subsample of 611 married retirees (55 percent men) was used. (For a detailed description of data collection and sample, see Szinovacz 1984a.)

The sample is limited in two ways: it is cross-sectional, and it relies on unrelated married individuals rather than on couples. The first limitation may lead to biases resulting from respondents' inability to remember preretirement events and from the impact of current life circumstances and of social desirability on responses to attitude and adjustment scales. To correct for some of this bias, length of retirement was controlled in all analyses. Nevertheless, it must be recognized that the data on time use reflect respondents' perceptions. Retirees may have over- or underestimated time spent on household work before and after retirement, or they may have over- or underestimated the similarity in their pre- and postretirement household involvement. In the first case, a bias would result if systematic over- or underreporting occurred. Overestimates of similarity, on the other hand, would result in high associations between pre- and postretirement household work time and reduce the impact of other independent variables on postretirement household activity if preretirement household involvement is controlled. The second limitation (reliance on individuals and not on couples) was partially overcome by including questions on spouses in the questionnaires. Specifically, information was obtained on spouses' employment status and/or date of retirement and on spouses' health. Variable measurement is described in table 2–1; the distribution of the variables is shown in tables 2–3, 2–4, and 2–5.

To test the hypotheses outlined above, regressions on time spent on household work after retirement were performed for the entire sample as well as for men and women separately. In each case, two equations were run. The first equation does not control for perceptions of household work time before retirement; the second equation included this variable. Consequently, relationships in the first equation pertain to the impact of the independent variables on retirees' absolute household involvement after retirement. The second equation, controlling for preretirement household activity, provides information on predictors of household involvement after retirement, net of preretirement household activity. All other variables were forced into both equations. Mean substitution was used for missing variables. However, all missing dummy variables were coded 0.

Results

Changes in Household Activity after Retirement

The first hypothesis held that both men and women would increase time spent on household activities after retirement. This prediction is partially

Measurement of Variables

Table 2–1
Measures

Sex	Coded as dummy variable; males = 1
Age	Coded in years
Household income	Current yearly household income; respondents checked one of 26 income groups ranging from "under $2,000" to "over $50,000."
Occupational prestige	Respondents provided a job description; occupations were coded according to the NORC classification system (Davis and Smith 1983)
Size of community	Respondents checked the population size of their current residential community, ranging from 1 = "under 10,000" to 5 = "over 500,000."
Extended family	Respondents indicated whether extended family members live in the household; coded as dummy variable; 1 = yes
Length of retirement	Year of retirement was subtracted from year of survey; sample range was restricted to under one to five years.
Health	On a list of potential problems, respondents indicated that they had "somewhat" or "very serious" health problems either only after or before and after retirement.
Spouse's health	On a list of life events, respondents indicated that their spouse had a major injury or illness up to three years before or at any time after the respondent's retirement.
Motive family	On a list of retirement motives, respondents checked "my spouse retired" or "my spouse didn't want me to work" as "very" or "somewhat" important.
Motive spouse	On a list of retirement motives, respondents checked "my spouse retired" or "my spouse didn't want me to work" as "very" or "somewhat" important.
Motive self	On a list of retirement motives, respondents checked "wanted more time for myself" or "wanted to do other things" as "very" or "somewhat important"
Spouse employed Spouse housewife	On two single-item questions, respondents indicated their spouse's current employment status as well as spouse's employment status at the time of the respondent's retirement. Spouse's employment status was coded as a dummy variable, 1 = "spouse currently (and continuously) employed; for men only, a second dummy variable (1 = "housewife") was used. The omitted category consists of dual-retired couples.
Housework before Housework after	Respondents indicated on two lists of activities how much time they spent on these activities before retirement and how much time they now spend on these activities; one of the listed activities was "housework"; categories are: 1 = "never", 2 = "less than 1 hour per day", 3 = "1 hour/day," 4 = "2 hours/day," 5 = "3 hours/day," 6 = "4 hours/day," 7 = "5 or more hours/day"

confirmed by the data (see table 2–2): paired t-tests show significantly higher means for post- than for preretirement household work time for both sexes. However, these increases pertain to a minority of respondents; only 28 percent of the men and 47 percent of the women reported an increase in household work time after retirement, and 64 percent of the men compared to 39 percent of the women did not perceive retirement-related changes in household work time.

Sex Roles

Hypotheses 2a to 2c refer to the impact of gender roles on household involvement after retirement. According to hypothesis 2a, men's postretirement household involvement was expected to be positively and women's household involvement negatively related to socioeconomic status and urban residence. The data (see tables 2–4 and 2–5) show significant effects of residence on perceived postretirement household activity in the expected direction. In addition, women report significantly less household work time if their household income is high. However, none of these relationships remains significant once estimates of preretirement household work time are introduced into the equations. Thus, subgroup variations in household work time after retirement seem to stem primarily from the preretirement period.

Hypotheses 2b and 2c predict a significant effect of sex on amount of time spent on household work and a stronger increase in postretirement household activities for men compared to women. The first prediction is confirmed and the second is rejected by the data (see table 2–3). Sex (men coded 1, women 0) is negatively related to postretirement household activ-

Table 2–2
Pre- and Postretirement Housework

	Men	Women
Preretirement housework	1.99	3.80
Postretirement housework	2.31	4.25
t (paired)	−6.27**	−6.16**
Decreased	7.4 %	14.4 %
No change	64.2 %	39.0 %
Increased	28.4 %	46.6 %
Chi-square	35.74**	

**p <.01

Table 2–3
Regression on Household Activities (Total Sample) ($N=611$)

	b^a	B^b	b	B	r	Mean	SD
Household income	-0.02	-0.08	0.00	0.00	0.00	12.12	6.28
Occupation	-0.00	-0.00	0.00	0.02	0.02	47.90	14.94
Age	0.01	0.02	0.01	0.02	-0.11**	64.77	4.73
Residence	0.02	0.02	0.02	0.02	0.03	2.48	1.29
Extended family	-0.06	-0.02	-0.07	-0.02	-0.03	0.20	0.40
Years retired	0.07	0.06	0.04	0.03	0.03	3.00	1.35
Health	-0.30	-0.08*	-0.30	-0.08**	-0.11**	0.22	0.42
Spouse's health	0.29	0.06	0.34	0.08**	0.11**	0.15	0.35
Motive family	0.37	0.11**	0.19	0.05*	0.22**	0.27	0.44
Motive spouse	0.05	0.02	0.04	0.01	0.23**	0.36	0.48
Motive self	-0.01	-0.00	0.09	0.03	0.03	0.59	0.49
Spouse employed	0.36	0.09*	0.23	0.06*	0.06	0.21	0.41
Housework before	--	--	0.76	0.66**	0.76**	2.84	1.36
Housework after						3.22	1.56
Sex	-1.71	-0.54**	0.42	-0.14**	-0.57**	0.55	0.50
R^2		0.36		0.61			
Adj. R^2		0.35		0.61			
F		26.01**		68.00**			
R^2 change				0.25**			

aUnstandardized coefficients
bStandardized coefficients

*$p<.05$
**$p<.01$

Table 2–4
Regression on Household Activities (Men) ($N=336$)

	b^a	B^b	b	B	r	Mean	SD
Household income	−0.1	−0.05	0.01	0.04	0.02	11.57	6.39
Occupation	0.00	0.06	−0.00	−0.01	0.04	46.92	16.50
Age	0.01	0.05	−0.00	−0.01	0.06	65.89	4.60
Residence	0.14	0.16**	0.07	0.08	0.16**	2.45	1.28
Extended family	−0.03	−0.01	0.04	0.02	−0.02	0.21	0.41
Years retired	0.06	0.07	0.09	0.10*	0.08	3.04	1.33
Health	−0.20	−0.07	−0.20	−0.07	−0.02	0.25	0.44
Spouse's health	0.53	0.15**	0.51	0.14**	0.14**	0.12	0.33
Motive family	0.38	0.13*	0.24	0.08	0.13**	0.19	0.39
Motive spouse	−0.02	−0.01	−0.15	−0.05	0.00	0.21	0.41
Motive self	−0.01	−0.00	0.08	0.03	0.01	0.57	0.50
Spouse employed	0.36	0.12*	0.24	0.08	0.10*	0.20	0.40
Spouse housewife	−0.13	−0.05	0.03	0.01	−0.07	0.27	0.44
Housework before	--	--	0.84	0.64**	0.65**	2.01	0.90
Housework after					--	2.33	1.17
R^2	0.09			0.48			
Adj. R^2	0.05			0.46			
F	2.42**			21.03**			
R^2 change				0.39**			

^{a}Unstandardized coefficients
^{b}Standardized coefficients

$*p<.05$
$**p<.01$

Table 2-5
Regression on Household Activities (Women) (N=275)

	b^a	B^b	b	B	r	Mean	SD
Household income	−0.04	−0.16*	−0.01	−0.04	−0.16**	12.80	6.10
Occupation	−0.01	−0.09	0.00	0.04	−0.11**	49.06	12.70
Age	−0.00	−0.01	0.01	0.03	−0.02	63.38	4.57
Residence	−0.14	−0.14*	−0.06	−0.06	−0.12	2.52	1.30
Extended family	0.07	0.02	−0.13	−0.04	0.04	0.18	0.38
Years retired	0.03	0.03	−0.02	−0.02	0.05	2.95	1.37
Health	−0.54	−0.15*	−0.54	−0.15**	−0.12*	0.19	0.39
Spouse's health	0.12	0.03	0.20	0.06	0.05	0.18	0.38
Motive family	0.40	0.14*	0.19	0.07	0.16**	0.37	0.48
Motive spouse	0.09	0.03	0.13	0.05	0.05	0.56	0.50
Motive self	0.04	0.02	0.12	0.04	0.03	0.60	0.49
Spouse employed	0.40	0.13	0.26	0.08	0.01	0.23	0.42
Housework before		--	0.67	0.59**	0.58**	3.80	1.20
Housework after					--	4.24	1.36
R^2		0.10		0.39			
Adj. R^2		0.06		0.36			
F		2.40**		12.75**			
R^2 change				0.29**			

aUnstandardized coefficients
bStandardized coefficients

*$p<.05$
**$p<.01$

ity both before and after preretirement household work time is entered into the equations; that is, women report significantly more time with household activities than men after their retirement, and they are significantly more likely than men to increase household work time after the retirement transition (see also table 2–2).

Ability and Need

According to Hypotheses 3a to 3c, wives' health was expected to be negatively related to their own and positively related to the husbands' postretirement involvement in household work. In contrast, husbands' health was not expected to significantly affect their own or their spouses' household work time. The data confirm these predictions: men's reported household work time after retirement is significantly and positively related to their wives' health problems both before and after preretirement household involvement is entered into the equations; men's own health status, on the other hand, does not significantly relate to their household work time. In contrast, women report significantly less household work time if they are suffering from health problems, and this trend holds after preretirement household involvement is held constant. Women's household work time is not significantly related to illness of their husbands.

Retirement Timing Patterns

It was expected (hypothesis 4) that a spouse's continued employment would be positively associated with a respondent's postretirement household work time and that this association would be more pronounced for women. The data lend only partial support to these predictions. Both men and women reported significantly more postretirement household involvement if their spouses were still employed, but this relationship was reduced to a nonsignificant level when reported preretirement household activity was entered into the equations. Furthermore, the strength of the shown relationships is similar for men and women.

Family Orientation

It was argued (hypothesis 5) that life goals may have an important effect on postretirement changes in household activities. Specifically, it was expected that marriage- or family-oriented persons would devote more time to household activities after retirement and that this relationship would be more pronounced for men. Since the data contain no direct measure of marriage or family orientation, selected retirement motives were used as indicators of life goals. Three motives (all coded as dummy variables) were entered into the regressions: self-oriented retirement motives, spouse-oriented motives, and family-oriented motives. The data partially confirm this prediction. Men and women who retired for family-related reasons reported more time in postretirement household activity; this relationship is significant for the total sample but not for the separate regressions by sex once preretirement household involvement is entered into the equations. Furthermore, the beta coefficients are similar for men and women.

Other Effects

In addition to the predicted relations discussed above, the data reveal a strong effect of preretirement on postretirement household activity level for both sexes. As shown in table 2–2 and in the regressions, this effect is more pronounced for men than for women: preretirement activity level accounted for 39 percent of the variance in men's but only 29 percent of the variance in women's postretirement household involvement. Finally, for men but not for women, length of retirement significantly relates to postretirement household work time once preretirement involvement is controlled.

Discussion

The major purpose of the preceding analyses was to identify the extent to which and the conditions under which time spent with household activities changes after retirement. Of special interest were gender differences as well as couple characteristics (spouse's health, timing of retirement). In general, the data indicate that retirees either maintain or slightly expand their preretirement household work time, and that women are more likely than men to report increases in household work time after retirement. In addition, preretirement household involvement and sex proved to be the strongest predictors of postretirement household activities. These findings support Atchley's (1976b) contention that retirement leads to major changes in activity patterns only if it is associated with significant restructuring of life goals. However, just such a reorientation in life goals is implied in convergence theory. If, as convergence theory holds, aging individuals become more androgynous, retiring couples can be expected to move toward a less sex-role-segregated division of labor. The present data suggest that this is not the case.

Several reasons could explain this negative finding. First, retrospective data may underestimate change, especially if such change contradicts traditional sex-role norms held by the respondents; that is, men may underreport their postretirement household involvement. Apart from data limitations, predictions derived from convergence theory may not apply to this behavioral realm or to this life transition. The first possibility (aging men's enhanced affiliative needs are not fulfilled through increased involvement in household work) challenges the generalizability of convergence theory to the universe of sex-role-related behavior patterns and raises the question how and in which behavioral realms age-related personality changes manifest themselves. The second alternative pertains to the life cycle period during which the personality changes predicted by convergence theory and their manifestation in behaviors are likely to occur.

A second and related question concerned the association between respondents' life goals and their postretirement household activity. The data indicate that men and women retiring in response to family needs report more household work time than respondents who do not consider family needs as an important retirement motive. This relationship was diminished when preretirement household activity was controlled. Even though the present data do not lend themselves to definite causal interpretations, the findings suggest the following scenario: Family-oriented individuals commit more of their time to household activities before retirement than do non–family-oriented individuals; they are more inclined to retire for familial reasons; and they continue and slightly expand their relatively high household involvement after retirement. This interpretation is consistent with continuity theory. It may also imply that within-group variances and the cross-sex overlap in retirees' personality profiles are too large to expect general sex-related behavior changes such as those implied in hypothesis 2b.

One major assumption addressed in this paper was that couple characteristics play an important role in behavioral change after retirement. Two spouse characteristics were investigated: health and retirement timing. The data leave little doubt that both characteristics impact upon spouse's postretirement division of labor. Illness of the wife proved to be associated with a reorganization of household activities resulting in more involvement of the husband and less involvement of the wife. This pattern held both before and after preretirement household work time was controlled. In contrast, a husband's illness had only minor effects on men's and women's postretirement household activity. This means that the impact of health status on retirees' household involvement is contingent on the sex-segregated division of labor among retired couples. It is only if illness befalls the spouse carrying the major burden of household work (that is the wife) that a major reallocation of household duties is necessitated.

The data also confirm that spouse's continued employment is positively related to household work time on the part of the retired spouse. This relationship holds for both men and women and is slightly reduced when preretirement household involvement is controlled. Careful inspection of these results suggest a rather complex association between retirement timing and household work, especially for women. As shown in Table 3–5, the zero-order correlations between spouse's employment and postretirement household work are significant only for men. Furthermore, zero-order correlations between preretirement household work and spouse's employment are small and nonsignificant ($r = .03$ and $-.02$ for men and women, respectively). This implies, first, that some of the conditions associated with a single retired wife are related to her postretirement household activities and, second, that preretirement household involvement does not significantly differ among couples with divergent retirement timing patterns. More research is clearly needed to unveil these seemingly complex patterns. One question worth pursuing would be whether single-spouse retirement may be more acceptable among those couples in which one spouse is willing to assume greater household responsibilities after his or her retirement, thus easing overload problems for the continuing worker.

Conclusion

This chapter began with the argument that the prevailing individualistic approach to retirement is insufficient to adequately explain postretirement behaviors and attitudes, and it called for its replacement by a "couple-oriented" approach. Demographic and theoretical reasons substantiating this position were advanced, and data analyses on household work after retirement were presented, which included selected couple characteristics. The results of these analyses tend to confirm the validity of this approach: both spouse's health status and couples' retirement timing patterns proved to be important predictors of postretirement household work time. On the first issue—health status—the findings suggest a gender-specific effect: illness of the wife but not of the husband seems to bring about a redistribution of household responsibilities between spouses. This result emphasizes the need to consider the life events of both spouses (and perhaps of other family members as well) to view the couple as a system and to pay tribute to gender-role-specific variations in the predictors and consequences of postretirement activities. Findings concerning spouses' retirement timing confirmed the importance of this variable but did not lend themselves to a straightforward interpretation. More research is needed to explore the causal interactions among spouses' retirement timing patterns, the circumstances associated with these timing patterns, and their relationship to postretirement activity patterns.

Motivated at least partially by women's increased labor force participation, much research has been devoted to linkages between work and family life (see for instance Piotrowski et al. 1987). As previous research on retirement timing has shown, these linkages extend to how and when couples retire. The present chapter indicates that couple characteristics also impact on spouses' division of household work after retirement. Given these findings and given the importance of marital and familial roles for middle-aged and young-old adults, the prevalent individualistic approach in the retirement literature seems unwarranted. It presumes a separation of life spheres that hardly corresponds to retirees' own reality conceptions. Consequently, future research on retirement should address this life transition as a couple event.

Implementation of this perspective requires several adaptations in the research design of retirement studies. Sampling of couples is necessary to reach some understanding of how spouses plan the retirement transition and how these plans affect retirement adjustment. To compare the impact of divergent timing patterns over time, it will also be essential to conduct longitudinal studies that follow couples through the various phases of retirement outlined in figure 2–1. Such comparisons are especially needed to identify changes in activity patterns and adjustment resulting from the transition of dual-earner to single-retired spouse and the transition of single-retired spouse to dual-retired couple. Finally, future retirement research should acknowledge the importance of marital and familial conditions of retirement timing and adjustment through inclusion of pertinent marital and familial variables such as spouses' gender-role attitudes, marital and familial life goals, marital adjustment, marital and familial retirement motives, spouses' relative participation in the retirement decision-making process, the couple's division of labor, or the care needs of spouses and extended family.

Based on their extensive review of research on female retirement, Gratton and Haug (1983, 70) concluded: "[the] most fruitful and useful source for subsequent research on female retirement clearly lies in the analysis of the retirement decision of married couples." The demographic changes, theoretical bases, and empirical findings discussed in this chapter suggest, furthermore, that a focus on couples' retirement is necessary to gain a dynamic and fuller understanding of both men's and women's retirement.

References

Altergott, K., and Duncan, S. 1987. "Age, gender and the activities of daily life." Paper presented at the meeting of the Gerontological Society, Washington, DC.

Anderson, K., Clark, R. L., and Johnson, T. 1980. "Retirement in dual-career families." In R. L. Clark (ed.), *Retirement Policy in an Aging Society*. Durham, NC: Duke University Press.

Atchley, R. C. 1976a. "Selected social and psychological differences between men and women in later life." *Journal of Gerontology* 31:204–11.

———. 1976b. *The Sociology of Retirement*. New York: Schenkman.

———. 1982. "The process of retirement: Comparing women and men." In M. Szinovacz (ed.), *Women's Retirement: Policy Implications of Recent Research*. Beverly Hills: Sage Publications.

Atchley, R. C., and Miller, S. J. 1983. "Types of elderly couples." In T. H. Brubaker (ed.), *Family Relationships in Later Life*. Beverly Hills, CA: Sage Publications.

Ballweg, A. 1967. "Resolution of conjugal role adjustment after retirement." *Journal of Marriage and the Family* 29:277–81.

Beck, S. H. 1982. "Adjustment to and satisfaction with retirement." *Journal of Gerontology* 37:616–24.

Berger, P. L., and Kellner, H. 1964. "Marriage and the construction of reality." *Diogenes* 46:1–25.

Brody E. M. Kleban M. H. Johnsen P. T., Hoffman, C., and Schoonover C. B. 1987. "Work status and parent care: A comparison of four groups of women." *The Gerontologist* 27:201–208.

Brubaker, T. H. 1985a. *Later Life Families*. Beverly Hills, CA: Sage Publications.

———. 1985b. "Responsibilities for household tasks: A look at golden anniversary couples aged 75 years and older." In W. A. Peterson and J. Quadagno (eds.), *Social Bonds in Later Life*. Beverly Hills, CA: Sage Publications.

Brubaker, T. H., and Hennon, C. B. 1982. "Responsibility for household tasks: Comparing dual-earner and dual-retired marriages." In M. Szinovacz (ed.), *Women's Retirement: Policy Implications of Recent Research*. Beverly Hills, CA: Sage Publications.

Buckley, W. 1967. *Sociology and Modern Systems Theory*. Englewood Cliffs, NJ: Prentice-Hall.

Burgess, E. H. 1973. *On Community, Family and Delinquency. Selected Writings*. Chicago: University of Chicago Press.

Campione, W. A. 1987. "A married woman's retirement decision: A methodological comparison." *Journal of Gerontology* 42:381–86.

Clark, A. L., Johnson, T., and McDermed, A. A. 1980. "Allocation of time and resources by married couples approaching retirement." *Social Security Bulletin* 43:3–17.

Cooley, C. H. 1922. *Human Nature and the Social Order*. New York: Charles Scribner's Sons.

Coverman, B., and Sheley, J. F. 1986. "Change in men's housework and child-care time, 1965–1975." *Journal of Marriage and the Family* 48:413–22.

Crawford, M. P. 1971. "Retirement and disengagement." *Human Relations* 24:255–78.

Crossman, L., London, C., and Barry, C. 1981. "Older women caring for disabled spouses: A model for supportive services." *The Gerontologist* 21:464–70.

Davis, J. A., and Smith, P. W. 1983. *General Social Surveys, 1972–1973: Cumulative Codebook.* (Appendix F). National Opinion Research Center. Chicago: University of Chicago Press.

DeVault, M. L. 1987. "Doing housework: Feeding and family life." In N. Gerstel and H. E. Gross (eds.), *Families and Work.* Philadelphia: Temple University Press.

Dobson, C. 1983. "Sex-role and marital role expectations." In T. H. Brubaker (ed.), *Family Relationships in Later Life.* Beverly Hills, CA: Sage Publications.

Dorfman, L. T., and Heckert, D. A. 1988. "Egalitarianism in retired rural couples." *Family Relations* 37:73–78.

Dorfman, L. T., and Hill, E. A. 1986. "Rural housewives and retirement: Joint decision-making." *Family Relations* 35:507–14.

Evans, L., Ekerdt, D. J., and Bosse, R. 1985. "Proximity to retirement and anticipatory involvement: Findings from the normative aging study." *Journal of Gerontology* 40:368–74.

Fengler, A. P. 1975. "Attitudinal orientation of wives toward their husbands' retirement." *International Journal of Aging and Human Development* 6:139–52.

Foote, N. N. 1956. *Matching of Husband and Wife in Phases of Development.* Chicago: Family Study Center, University of Chicago.

Fox, K. D., and Nickols, S. Y. 1983. "The time crunch: Wife's employment and family work." *Journal of Family Issues* 4:61–82.

George, L. K., Fillenbaum, G. G., and Palmore, E. 1984. "Sex differences in antecedents and consequences of retirement." *Journal of Gerontology* 39:364–71.

Gordon, C., Gaitz, C. M., and Scott, J. 1976. "Leisure and lives: Personal expressivity across the life span." In R. H. Binstock and E. Shanas (eds.), *Handbook of Aging and the Social Sciences.* New York: Van Nostrand Reinhold.

Gratton, B., and Haug, M. R. 1983. "Decision and adaptation: Research on female retirement." *Research on Aging* 5:59–76.

Gutmann, D., Grunes, J., and Griffin, B. 1980. "The clinical psychology of later life: Developmental paradigms." In N. Datan and N. Lohmann (eds.), *Transitions of Aging.* New York: Academic Press.

Hartmann, H.I. 1981. "The family as the locus of gender, class and political struggle: The example of housework." *Signs* 6:366–94.

Henretta, J. C., and O'Rand, A. M. 1980. "Labor force participation of older married women." *Social Security Bulletin* 43:10–16.

———. 1983. "Joint retirement in the dual worker family." *Social Forces* 62:504–20.

Heyman, D. K., and Jeffers, F. C. 1968. "Wives and retirement: A pilot study." *Journal of Gerontology* 23:488–96.

Hill, E. A., and Dorfman, L. T. 1982. "Reaction of housewives to the retirement of their husbands." *Family Relations* 31:195–200.

Holmes, T. H., and Rahe, R. H. 1967. "The social readjustment rating scale." *Journal of Psychosomatic Research* 11:213–18.

Hood, J. 1986. "The provider role: Its meaning and measurement." *Journal of Marriage and the Family* 48:349–59.

Kantor, D., and Lehr, W. 1975. *Inside the Family*. San Francisco: Jossey-Bass.

Keating, N. C., and Cole, P. 1980. "What do I do with him 24 hours a day? Changes in the housewife role after retirement." *The Gerontologist* 20:84–89.

Keith P. M., and Brubaker T. H. 1979. "Male household roles in later life: A look at masculinity and marital relationships." *The Family Coordinator* 28:497–502.

Keith, P. M., Dobson, C. D., Goudy, W. J., and Powers, E. A. 1981b. "Older men: Occupation, employment status, household involvement and well-being." *Journal of Family Issues* 2:336–49.

Keith, P. M., Powers, E. A., and Goudy, W. J. 1981a. "Older men in employed and retired families." *Alternative Lifestyles* 4:228–41.

Kerckhoff, A. C. 1966. "Family patterns and morale in retirement." In I. M. Simpson and J. C. McKinney (eds.), *Social Aspects of Aging*. Durham, NC: Duke University Press.

Lawton, M. P., Moss, M., and Fulcomer, M. 1986/7. "Objective and subjective uses of time by older people." *International Journal of Aging and Human Development* 24:171–88.

Lipman, A. 1960. "Marital roles of the retired aged." *Merrill Palmer Quarterly* 6:192–95.

———. 1961. "Role conceptions and morale of couples in retirement." *Journal of Gerontology* 16:267–71.

McGee, J., and Wells, K. 1982. "Gender typing and androgyny in later life. New directions for theory and research." *Human Development* 25:116–39.

Morgan, L. A. 1977. "Toward a formal theory of life course continuity and change." Paper presented at the meeting of the Gerontological Society, San Francisco.

Moss M. S., and Lawton M. P. 1982. "Time budgets of older people: A window on four life styles." *Journal of Gerontology* 37:115–23.

Mutran, E., and Reitzes, D. C. 1981. "Retirement, identity and well-being: Realignment of role relationships." *Journal of Gerontology* 36:733–40.

Neugarten, B. L. 1977. "Personality and aging." In J. E. Birren and K. W. Schaie (eds.), *Handbook of the Psychology of Aging*. New York: Van Nostrand Reinhold.

Nickols, S. Y., and Metzen, E. J. 1982. "Impact of wife's employment upon husband's housework." *Journal of Family Issues* 3:199–216.

Palmore, E. B. 1965. "Differences in the retirement patterns of men and women." *Journal of Gerontology* 37:733–42.

Palmore, E. B., Burchett, B. M., Fillenbaum, G. G., George, L. K., and Wallman, L. M. 1985. *Retirement. Causes and Consequences*. New York: Springer.

Piotrowski, C. S., Rapoport, R. N., and Rapoport, R. 1987. "Families and work." In M. B. Sussman and S. K. Steinmetz (eds.), *Handbook of Marriage and the Family*. New York: Plenum.

Pleck, J. H. 1985. *Working Wives/Working Husbands*. Beverly Hills, CA: Sage Publications.

Prentis, R. S. 1980. "White-collar working women's perception of retirement." *The*

Gerontologist 80:90–95.

Rapoport, R., and Rapoport, R. N. 1975. *Leisure and the Family Life Cycle.* London: Routledge and Kegan Paul.

Rexroat, C., and Shehan, C. 1987. "The family life cycle and spouses' time in housework." *Journal of Marriage and the Family* 49:737–50.

Roadburg, A. 1981. "Perceptions of work and leisure among the elderly." *The Gerontologist* 21:142–45.

Scanzoni, J., and Arnett, C. 1987. "Policy implications derived from a study of rural and urban marriages." *Family Relations* 36:430–36.

Schafer, R. B., and Keith, P. M. 1981. "Equity in marital roles across the life cycle." *Journal of Marriage and the Family* 43:359–67.

Seccombe, K., and Lee, G. R. 1986. "Gender differences in retirement satisfaction and its antecedents." *Research on Aging* 8:426–40.

Seltzer, M. M. 1976. "Suggestions for the examination of time-disordered relationships." In J. F. Gubrium (ed.), *Time, Roles and Self in Old Age.* New York: Behavioral Publications.

Shaw, L. B. 1984. "Retirement plans of middle-aged married women." *The Gerontologist* 24:154–59.

Sinnott, J. D. 1977. "Sex-role constancy, biology and successful aging." *The Gerontologist* 17:459–63.

———. 1982. "Correlates of sex roles of older adults." *Journal of Gerontology* 37:587–94.

———. 1984. "Older men, older women: Are their perceived sex roles similar?" *Sex Roles* 10:847–56.

Stull, D. E., and Hatch, L. R. 1984. "Unravelling the effects of multiple life changes." *Research on Aging* 6:560–71.

Szinovacz, M. 1980. "Female retirement: Personal and marital consequences. A case study." *Journal of Family Issues* 1:423–40.

———. 1984a. *Life Events, Retirement Preparation and Adjustment to Retirement. A Comparative Study.* Final Report submitted to the AARP Andrus Foundation.

———. 1984b. "Changing family roles and interactions." *Marriage and Family Review* 7:163–201.

———. 1986–87. "Preferred retirement timing and retirement satisfaction in women." *International Journal of Aging and Human Development* 24:301–17.

———. In press. "Decision making on retirement timing." In D. Brinberg and J. Jaccard (eds.), *Dyadic Decision-making.* New York: Springer.

U.S. Bureau of the Census. 1987. *Statistical Abstract of the United States: 1988* (108th ed.) Washington, DC: U.S. Government Printing Office.

Valadez, J. J., and Clignet, R. 1984. "Household work as an ordeal: Culture of standards versus standardization of culture." *American Journal of Sociology* 89:812–35.

Zube, M. 1982. "Changing behavior and outlook of aging men and women: Implications for marriage in the middle and later years." *Family Relations* 31:147–56.

Zuzanek, J. 1987. "Till leisure us part . . ." Paper presented at the meeting of the Gerontological Society, Washington, DC, November.

3
Elderly Widowhood

Brian L. Pitcher
Don C. Larson

One particularly difficult challenge of aging is preparing for the death of a spouse, then accepting and adjusting to life without the person who has been a companion, counselor, lover, and friend throughout one's married life. From about age 45 onward, widowhood takes a rapidly increasing and very heavy toll on married couples (see table 3–1 for data on the United States). Although the increases in rates of widowhood follow the same broad pattern for both men and women, they are much more dramatic for women. Approximately one-fourth of all married women will become widows by age 65, and one-half of the remaining women will become widows by age 75. During the same age span, only one man in five will lose his wife (U.S. Bureau of the Census 1986). The mean duration of widowhood for women is fourteen years; for men it is just over six years (Soldo and Manton 1985). Although these statistics illustrate strikingly the prevalence of widowhood, they communicate nothing of the depth, variety, and complexity of the challenges faced by the widowed.

The widowed face a common problem, but there is no normative course of adjustment. Although they have in common the experiences of a prior marriage and the death of a spouse, there is considerable variation in the experiences of widowhood. The widowed are a heterogeneous group, with varied personalities, backgrounds, social lives, and support networks. Some of the widowed are financially disadvantaged; others are not. Almost all are emotionally impacted by the loss of a spouse, but some are impacted much more severely and for longer periods of time than others. Some adjust well; others do not.

It is important for future research to investigate more comprehensive theoretical models of the varied factors and conditions related to the many stresses of widowhood. Such models are useful for integrating the theoretical literature, for placing the findings of research in perspective, and for orienting future research efforts.

The purpose of this chapter is to present and overview a comprehensive theoretical framework for understanding the stresses associated with wid-

Table 3–1
Percentage Distribution of Marital Status for Older Males and Females, by Age, 1985

Marital Status	Age			
	45–54	55–64	65–74	75 +
Males	100.0	99.9	100.0	100.0
Single	6.3	6.1	5.2	5.3
Married	83.8	83.9	81.3	69.3
Widowed	1.2	3.7	9.3	22.7
Divorced	8.7	6.2	4.2	2.7
Females	100.0	100.0	100.0	100.1
Single	4.6	3.7	4.4	6.2
Married	76.3	70.0	51.1	23.8
Widowed	7.0	17.4	38.9	67.7
Divorced	12.1	8.9	5.6	2.4

Source: U.S. Bureau of the Census 1986, 39.

owhood. This theoretical framework is elaborated from recent research on models of social stress (Kahn 1973; House 1974; George 1980). It explicitly recognizes the individual's capacity to respond to stressors and is helpful in identifying the conditions under which supposed stressors have an impact. The first section of the chapter describes the theoretical framework. The second section discusses factors associated with the sources of stresses in widowhood. The third section overviews issues affecting the consequences of widowhood; and the fourth section identifies factors that mediate and condition the impact of widowhood. In each section current research is summarized and areas of needed research are identified. The concluding section discusses several major implications of this integration of the theoretical literature for understanding the stresses of widowhood and for orienting further research.

Adjustment to the Stresses of Widowhood

According to George (1980), social stress is "a social situation that poses an adaptive challenge or problem to an individual." Stressful social situations often lead to negative outcomes such as unhappiness or physical illness, unless the individual is successful in adjusting.

A fairly well-developed sociological literature deals with the effects of social, psychological, and behavioral stress factors on the etiology of physical and mental health problems. A basic model for conceptualizing the sources, mediators, and consequences of the stresses of widowhood is represented in figure 3–1. This integrated model is developed from general

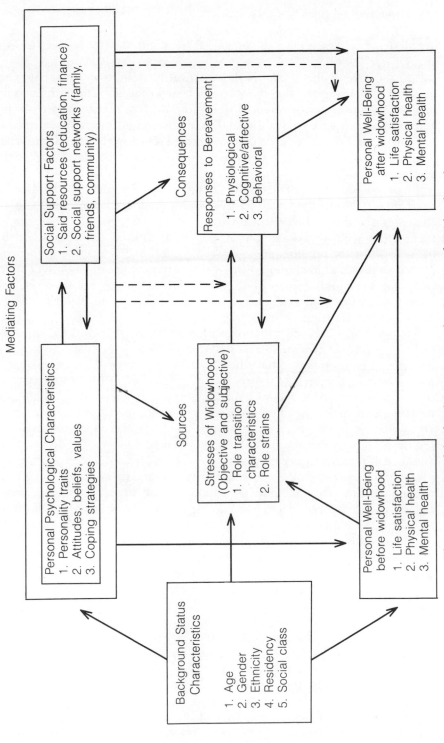

Mediating Factors

Social Support Factors
1. Said resources (education, finance)
2. Social support networks (family, friends, community)

Personal Psychological Characteristics
1. Personality traits
2. Attitudes, beliefs, values
3. Coping strategies

Consequences

Responses to Bereavement
1. Physiological
2. Cognitive/affective
3. Behavioral

Personal Well-Being after widowhood
1. Life satisfaction
2. Physical health
3. Mental health

Sources

Stresses of Widowhood
(Objective and subjective)
1. Role transition characteristics
2. Role strains

Personal Well-Being before widowhood
1. Life satisfaction
2. Physical health
3. Mental health

Background Status Characteristics
1. Age
2. Gender
3. Ethnicity
4. Residency
5. Social class

Figure 3–1. Model of Adjustment to the Stresses of Widowhood

social stress models previously suggested by Kahn (1973), House (1974), and George (1980).

At the core of this model is the question of stability versus change in personal well-being as a consequence of widowhood. Thus, the model includes two measures of personal well-being the first measuring well-being before the occurrence of widowhood, and the second measuring personal well-being after the experience of bereavement. On a general level, personal well-being has at least three dimensions—life satisfaction, physical health, and mental health.

Two major sources of stress are identified in the model: (1) characteristics of the role transition and (2) role strains associated with widowhood. Role strain in these experiences provokes changes in personal well-being—that is, it results in the adaptation, the modification, and sometimes the breakdown of the physiological or psychological organism. The immediate consequences of widowhood are the various physiological, cognitive, affective, and behavioral responses to bereavement. Over the long term, the stresses of widowhood are assumed to have significant and enduring effects on personal well-being.

In addition, this model identifies several factors that directly influence the magnitude and type of stress or condition the impact of stressors. First, the stresses of widowhood have been shown to be related to several background status characteristics such as age, gender, ethnicity, residency, and social class. Second, the model identifies types of personal psychological characteristics and social support factors that directly affect both objective and subjective levels of stress, as well as condition the impact of stress on responses to bereavement and long-term personal well-being. Factors to be considered in the category of personal psychological characteristics include personality traits; attitudes, beliefs, and values about the stresses; and the coping strategies that an individual tends to use in responding to stress. Relevant social support factors include social resources (such as education and finances) and exposure to and integration into social support networks (family, friends, and community).

Overall, figure 3–1 summarizes the sources, mediators, and consequences of the stresses of widowhood. "The stresses of widowhood" refers to the adaptive challenges associated with the transition to widowhood and the continuing experience of the widowhood role. The extent of the stresses is directly associated with the various psychological, social, and status characteristics of widowhood. In turn, the stresses of widowhood have direct impacts on bereavement responses and on long-term personal well-being. The impact of the stresses, however, are to some extent mediated and/or conditioned by the various psychological and social support characteristics.

The linkages in figure 3–1 also represent the various major areas of research on widowhood. Considerable research has already explored the consequences of widowhood, the bereavement process, and the impact of background status characteristics, personal psychological characteristics, and social support factors. To understand the stresses of widowhood, the following sections discuss basic theoretical issues and the findings of research on the sources of stress, or the consequences of stress, and on factors that alter the impact of stress.

The Sources of Stress in Widowhood

This section discusses several issues relevant to the genesis and nature of the stresses of widowhood. The work of Pearlin and associates (Pearlin and Lieberman 1979; Pearlin 1982, 1983) has been central to the development of a conceptual framework for understanding the sources of social stress. According to their framework, the stresses of widowhood are associated either with the *role transition* from the spouse role to the widowhood role or with the *role strains* created by persistent problems in widowhood.

Transition to the Widowhood Role

Role transitions are generally distinguished into two main types: normative and nonnormative. Normative role transitions are those associated with life-cycle changes (for example, entry into a marital role during young adulthood, retirement, and the "on time" death of a spouse). Although most normative role transitions are not particularly disruptive, widowhood tends to be an exception. Nonnormative role transitions, such as divorce or the "premature" death of a spouse, are unexpected and often severely disruptive.

Using George's (1980) typology of difficulties associated with role transitions, it appears that the following characteristics of the transition to widowhood may create significant difficulties in adjustment.

1. *The personal significance of the transition to widowhood.* This characteristic refers to how important the roles exited or entered are for the personal identity and life satisfaction of the individual. Most studies point out that marital satisfaction is high among older couples and that they typically report fewer problems and feelings of inadequacy than younger couples (Troll et al. 1979; George 1980). Marriage provides a basis of social integration and support conducive to maintaining personal well-being. It represents an enduring relationship based on bonds of love and solidarity (Blau 1981). Research has shown that the role of wife is central to the identity of women, particularly traditional homemakers with middle-class backgrounds.

The death of a spouse is an intense and wrenching emotional experience that evokes grief. This personal loss may be especially severe for the elderly. Because of diminished confidence, lower perceived attractiveness, and limited personal resources, some elderly view marriage relationships as irreplacable and nontransferable. For these reasons, widowhood is a major personal change for most of the current generation of elderly women and men.

2. *The normative significance of widowhood.* This characteristic refers to the importance of the roles that are being exited and entered, and the rewards and sanctions that follow. In American society the roles of husband and wife have traditionally been honorable and highly desirable. The widowed person, in contrast, occupies a marginal social role. In our society widowed persons immediately lose several privileges that they enjoyed while married. For example, because they lack a marriage partner, the widowed are often excluded from leisure activities with their married friends. Also, our culture is uncomfortable with death and grieving; thus the widowed are discouraged from openly engaging in "grief work."

It has even been suggested that the life circumstances of the elderly widowed have several similarities to those of stigmatized minorities (Karp and Yoels 1982). Stigmas associated with the role of widow and the perceived costs of widowhood interfere with the widowed's accepting the new status and learning the new role.

3. *The effect of widowhood on established patterns of behavior and relationships.* The stress of a role transition depends on how disruptive the change is on current behavior and interaction patterns. The transition to widowhood creates several changes in behavior and interaction patterns, some of which are positive and some of which are negative. The loss of a spouse requires a restructuring of personal and family time. Hypothetically, one might have greater freedom of choice, but diminished resources and limited support and companionship restrict opportunities for activity.

Widowhood also requires change in one's role set. The family is obviously not the same as it was. Relationships are lost, added, or redefined. These changes and losses are particularly important determinants of well-being in widowhood.

4. *The nature and number of socializing experiences for widowhood.* Anticipatory socialization in preparation for the expected transition helps to alleviate the stresses of change. However, an unexpected or early occurrence of a life-change—such as "early" widowhood—precludes these prior socializing experiences. People who have previous experience with life changes are generally more successful with adjustment to widowhood. Although the death of a spouse in later life or after a lingering illness might offer one more of an opportunity to prepare, the degree to which individuals seek out socialization experiences and prepare for these events varies widely. Even the most predictable transitions are problematic for many. In

addition, although anticipatory grief may alleviate the stress of change, it does not eliminate the intense pain caused by the actual loss.

The knowledge that death is approaching apparently allows for some anticipatory "grief work" and forces the surviving spouse to redefine his or her role and imagine a changed lifestyle (O'Laughlin 1983). But the available evidence indicates that the most difficult and severe bereavement reactions are those associated with unanticipated deaths.

5. *The vagueness of role expectations about widowhood.* Clearly defined norms regarding expected changes in relationships with children, siblings, and in-laws following the death of a spouse are lacking. It is not even clear how the widowed should feel about the departed spouse. This is more problematic for the younger widowed, since there are few young widowed persons from whom they can learn the appropriate feelings, attitudes, and behavior.

The Role Strains of Widowhood

Role strains are the persistent, low-key frustrations and hardships with which individuals must contend in their daily occupational and family roles. Research summarized by Pearlin (1983) suggests that role strains tend to have an even greater impact on individual psychological well-being than do role transitions. Of the six types of role strain identified by Pearlin (1983), the following four are particularly relevant to widowhood:

1. *The role tasks of widowhood.* One immediate consequence of widowhood is a multiplication of the tasks one must perform. For women, these new tasks include increased responsibilities for family finances, home and automobile maintenance, and driving. For men, the new tasks include housekeeping and cooking, and for some, maintenance of extended family contacts. The first type of role strain involves the relationship of the individual's skills, interests, and resources to the expectations and requirements of the new tasks to be performed.

It is not just the nature of the new role tasks but also the subjective evaluations of these tasks that determine the stress experienced. Strain is created both by the workload and by the feelings about assuming responsibilities formerly performed by the spouse.

2. *Interpersonal conflicts in widowhood.* Conflicts in social relationships are an important potential source of role strain. They may involve misunderstandings or disagreements over routine role expectations, and they need not be overt.

Conflicts in widowhood usually involve family and friendship relations. They often begin when friends and acquaintances attempt to dictate to the widowed how the grief experience "should" occur. Continuing conflicts between children and widowed parents often arise from differing expectations regarding the services and support each should provide. Among friends, conflicts may arise due to perceptions of inequities regarding the emotional investments in or the needs of each for the relationship.

3. *Captivity in the widowhood role.* This type of role strain occurs when a person is involuntarily bound to a role while desiring another. Role captivity is problematic for some but not all of the widowed. Men are less captive in the widowhood role than women; elderly men have remarriage rates about seven times higher than those of women (U.S. Senate Select Committee on Aging 1986). However, Lopata (1980) reported that 75 percent of her sample of older widows did not wish to remarry. They gave as reasons a fear of the loss of their independence, a fear of fortune seekers, and their reluctance to nurture another spouse facing death. On the other hand, some widows do wish to remarry and are frustrated by their inability to re-enter the married status. Various living arrangements such as living alone, living with children, or institutionalized living may also be stressful for those desiring another type of living status.

4. *Role restructuring in widowhood.* The final type of role strain involves the redistribution of resources, power, or status within social relationships over time, for example, is the restructuring of relationships between elderly parents and their adult children. During old age, parents who were providers and caregivers gradually become recipients of care. Adult children may feel obligated to take an increasing responsibility for such diverse areas as "urging the parent to go to the doctor for hearing problems, taking over holiday dinner rituals, urging parents not to be idle," and so forth (Pearlin 1983). Such broad restructuring of the behaviors, concerns, and responsibilities of parents and children may not fit one's self-image and is potentially stressful for parent-child relations.

Other changes commonly associated with widowhood, such as losses in personal resources and social support, often precipitate role restructuring. A restructuring of socioeconomic status and prestige relationships frequently accompanies widowhood, especially for women. Adjustment to role restructuring requires letting go of the old and learning new ways of relating and behaving (Pearlin 1983). This is difficult not only for the widowed but also for their children, other family members, and friends.

In summary, the death of a spouse is only a part of the story in understanding the stresses of widowhood. The nature, circumstances, and perceptions of the transition from married to single contribute to the immediate impacts. The five characteristics of the transition to widowhood are important for understanding the potential stresses of the transition. Furthermore, the four role strains associated with the way the new role becomes organized with other elements of life affect the long-term impact of the experience.

This discussion has also summarized critical role characteristics that create ongoing stresses within widowhood. Pearlin (1983) cautions that it is important to consider the subjective dispositions that individuals bring to their roles. "Whether or not a condition is experienced as innocuous or as a hardship frequently depends on how individuals' subjective values and aspirations combine with the conditions" (Pearlin 1983).

Overall, research on life change consistently indicates that the stresses of widowhood are associated with health loss and depression. Pearlin (1982) cites the following reasons:

> First, widowhood usually involves the loss of an important relationship, and second, it involves movement out of one status and into another one, movement that by itself may test the adjustment capacities of people. But it often happens that along with widowhood there are also alterations in the social and economic foundations of our lives, and we have some indication that it is the adverse changes in the more persistent conditions of life that account for much of the depression that accompanies widowhood (Pearlin 1982, 61).

The Consequences of Widowhood

The model of stresses in widowhood presented in figure 3–1 assumes that the multiple strains of widowhood provoke change—that is, that they may result in the adaptation, modification, and sometimes the breakdown of the physiological or psychological organism. Various specific health-related consequences of widowhood have been widely studied, and research studies in general, have found decreased levels of satisfaction and increased levels of illness and mortality (Balkwell 1985). Some of the specific findings of this body of research are summarized below.

Widowhood is particularly painful during the bereavement stage, which may last from twelve to eighteen months. A number of authors have suggested that the process of grief includes two to five identifiable stages, progressing from acute grief (mourning) to the reconstruction of an identity as a partnerless person (Tyhurst 1958; Bowlby 1961; Parkes 1972; Glick et al. 1974). These stages of grief can be experienced either in an abnormal or in a normal way. Abnormal grief is distinguished by a lack of personal well-being—that is, the pain is retained rather than released, and the loss is viewed as ending all familiar patterns of life. In contrast, normal grief is characterized by an ability to change and an ability to manage the stresses of this period of intense physical, mental, and social difficulty.

Early research into grief identified several characteristics of an abnormal grief response (Lindemann 1944). These include a lack of emotional reaction; personality changes; hostility to unrelated objects, organizations, or persons; and a retreat from social activity. Normal grief includes physical and psychological effects such as shock, physical symptoms (bodily distress, weakness), emotional release (tears, laughter, and anger), panic, depression, isolation, and difficulty in functioning in a normal way. The ability to regain hope and an eventual readjustment to the changes in one's life are also characteristics of the normal grief process. This readjustment involves role redefinitions for the individual.

Grief responses during bereavement are marked by several turning points in which significant changes in feelings, attitudes, and behavior are experienced. Emotional upheaval and role distress lessen as the individual works through these stages.

Oftimes people avoid those who are progressing through bereavement. One reason is their fear of the pain of grief. This fear results in a withdrawal of support at a time when the grieving individual needs it the most. Consequently, many widowed tend to respond to grief alone. The grief avoidance by family and friends has a negative impact on the widowed. Grief work is social in nature, and the widowed need support from family and friends.

This understanding of grief and "grief work" has been the basis for numerous community-based intervention programs and support-group systems. Yet in spite of the application of these process concepts, little substantive research has been done to understand what factors may modify this grief timeline.

Besides the short-term impact of bereavement, research has identified several long-term deleterious consequences of widowhood. These chronic impacts are often unrelated to the degree of success in immediate adjustment during "grief work."

Fenwick and Barresi (1981) investigated the effects of loss of spouse on perceived health and number of days spent ill in bed. They found that the subjective health conditions of older persons mediated the effects of widowhood on objective health. Ferraro (1985) observed that sex and age were the two primary characteristics involved in perceived health. Women and the old-old tended to be optimistic in their health evaluations. Hyman (1983) reported finding no differences for women, but perceptions of poorer health and less satisfaction among older widowed or divorced/separated men than among the married.

In a recent comprehensive analysis of the effects of widowhood, Helsing et al. (1981) found that widowhood was associated with increased mortality risk for men but not for women. This finding held even after controlling for age, age at first marriage, cigarette smoking, church attendance, and socioeconomic status. Earlier studies had found higher death rates during the first two years and particularly during the first six months. However, in the Helsing et al. (1981) study, the increased mortality risk persisted throughout a ten-year follow-up period. The increased risks of widowhood included infectious diseases, accidents, and suicides for men, and cirrhosis of the liver for women (Helsing et al. 1982).

With respect to life satisfaction, the most comprehensive findings were reported by Hyman (1983), based on his comparative analyses of several cross-sectional and longitudinal data sets. He noted that compared with their married counterparts, both widows and widowers reported less overall satisfaction, especially with family life. Also, this negative effect tended to be more prevalent among widowers than among widows. On the other hand, the married and formerly married showed no differences in their satisfaction with their financial situation. He concluded that the elderly tend to accept or perhaps become resigned to their relative deprivation.

It is difficult to summarize the diverse findings on the effects of widowhood for individual mental health. One important finding is that psychological states are most unstable during the early stages of acute grief. According to the process inherent in social breakdown theory (Kuypers and Bengston 1973), when the elderly lose valued roles and support systems, they are especially vulnerable to the effects of negative labeling. On the other hand, caution should be exercised about overstating this impact of widowhood. The available research suggests that identities tend to be preserved and negative self-evaluation tends to be the exception rather than the rule (George 1980). In a variety of analyses, Hyman (1983) found that misanthropy and anomia (measures of mental health) were equally prevalent among the married and unmarried elderly.

Loneliness is an almost universal long-term consequence of the death of a spouse. Several studies have identified loneliness as one of the most significant problems of widowhood (Lopata et al. 1982; Vinick 1983; Clark et al. 1986). Based on analyses from several samples of widows, the correlates of loneliness seem to be having few or no children; having physical health problems; experiencing the sudden or unexpected loss of the spouse; idealizing the spouse; age; being widowed less than six years; being withdrawn from social activities; and having a weak friendship system (Blieszner 1986).

Factors Mediating and Conditioning the Stresses of Widowhood

As indicated in Figure 4–1, the stresses of widowhood are mediated and conditioned by various background status factors, personal psychological characteristics, and social support factors. To understand the process of adjustment to widowhood, it is important to specify the interdependencies among these particular factors. This section overviews current research on these relationships.

Background Status Factors

A great deal of social science research has documented that an individual's location in the social system has a significant influence on what might be called his or her life chances—desirable outcomes and lifestyle experiences. Incorporated in models of social stress is the underlying premise that life-course roles, expectations, and demands are structured differentially depending on age, gender, ethnicity, residency, and social class. Status characteristics are assumed to be relevant for differentiating (1) levels of personal well-being, (2) social support resources and personal psychological characteristics, as well as (3) the subjective and objective stresses of widowhood. Current empirical findings regarding the impacts of these variables are reviewed below.

Age. Blau (1981) posited that adjustment to widowhood is more difficult when it places the individual in a position at variance from his or her own age and sex peers. She concluded that the detrimental effects of widowhood on friendship and social participation patterns are less for people over 70 because they have many widowed peers with whom to share this experience. For the widowed who are still in their sixties or younger, widowhood is not "normal," social supports are not as available, and the widowed are less likely to have anticipated and prepared psychologically for widowhood. On the other hand, when widowhood is postponed until the later years, the risks of ill health are greater, and fewer of one's close friends may still be available or able to render support.

Although the experiences of widowhood may differ significantly for the young-old versus the old-old, one group may not necessarily fare better overall than the other. The younger widowed typically express lower levels of life satisfaction but have higher rates of remarriage. The older widowed express higher life satisfaction but have lower rates of remarriage (George 1980). Many of the younger widowed view widowhood as a temporary state and seek actively to return to the spousal role. The older widowed are more likely to view and accept widowhood as a permanent role. As noted earlier, the older widowed may report higher levels of satisfaction because they have resigned themselves to the widowed role.

Gender. Unquestionably, the two most significant differences between widows and widowers are prevalence and duration. Atchley (1987) reported that a majority of older women are widowed by age 70, but for men a majority do not become widowers until after age 85. Older widows outnumber widowers by a factor of five. Because of gender differences in life expectancy and remarriage rates, there are striking differences in the probability of living with a spouse in the later years. These differences have important implications for the availability, size, and scope of supportive networks available to older men and women (Sauer and Coward 1985).

Several comparisons between widows and widowers have investigated whether widowhood is more difficult for widows or for widowers (Berardo 1970). So-called gender differences in the stresses and consequences of widowhood are attributable not to gender itself but to the differential social conditions and experiences of men and women.

Overall, research tends to support the conclusion that being married is more critical to the well-being and life expectancy of men than of women (Hess and Waring 1983). Widowers are more prone to illnesses, emotional disturbances, and early death than widows (Scott and Kivett 1985). Although no apparent differences exist in the extent to which widows and widowers experience loneliness, some evidence indicates that widowers are cut off from their families more than widows (Troll et al. 1979). Consistent with our cultural stereotype that men should not exhibit signs of emotional need or dependency, they tend to shun counseling and psychological support services (Clark et al. 1986). Accepting assistance with instrumental tasks, such as housekeeping and cooking, is more acceptable.

Research results portray widows as having greater difficulty than widowers in the areas of finances and maintaining their own homes. Widows also perceive themselves as more vulnerable to burglary, vandalism, and the like. Glick et al. (1974) suggested that women tend to hold deeper emotional attachments to marriage and that they need a longer grieving period than men. On the other hand, it may be that men have been socialized to deny their grief and to move more quickly toward restructuring their lives (Ward 1984).

Ethnicity. There are widespread variations among ethnic groups in the expectations and experiences of marriage and widowhood. Some evidence indicates that nonwhites and persons in close-knit ethnic communities are often characterized by more structured roles for widows, less of a couple-orientation between husband and wife, and more developed support systems for the widowed (Lopata 1973; Morgan 1984; George 1980). For example, significant racial differences have been found with respect to length of mourning. Atchley (1986) reported that because black marriages are characterized by more overt hostility, there may be less emotional trauma associated with the death of spouse. On the other hand, Wilkinson (1980) found that white males grieve for shorter periods than nonwhite males.

Ide et al. (1986) compared Anglo, Mexican-American, and American

Indian widows and noted race differences both in the probability of the widowed living alone and in perceptions of advantages and disadvantages. Anglo widows were more likely to live alone than Mexican-American widows, who often lived with other family members. Whereas some Mexican-American widows were able to assume that the family would care for them, the American Indian widows felt that they must care for the rest of the family. Ide et al. (1986) also noted that community resources were much better developed to meet the needs of the Anglo widows.

Residency. Residency status is another particularly salient variable for differentiating the impact of the stress of widowhood. Lopata (1978) suggested that modern urban communities have weaker kinship and informal social support systems. But the widowed in rural areas may be disadvantaged with respect to more formal support systems such as health care. Further research is needed to clarify the relationship between residency and social isolation.

Social class. Lifestyle differences associated with social class also tend to be important in determining the stresses of widowhood. There tends to be greater sharing of social roles, activities, and friendships in middle-class than working-class marriages. In working-class marriages, women tend to emphasize the mother role more than the wife role, while middle-class women tend to balance their roles as wife and mother. Consequently, it is expected that middle-class women will experience more trauma associated with the death of their husband than working-class women will (Ward 1984; Lopata and Brehm 1985). However, middle-class women usually have developed wider networks of personal relationships and social activities, have a better education and more self-confidence, and have greater resources available to them to help adjust and reconstruct the role of widow once the period of deep grieving is over.

Psychological Characteristics

Figure 4–1 indicates that psychological characteristics such as personality traits; attitudes, values, and beliefs; and coping strategies are significant in conditioning the stress process. This is an important area for further research. The direct, indirect, and mediating effects of psychological characteristics on the experience of widowhood are extremely difficult to conceptualize, measure, and interpret, however.

Personality Traits. Theory and research on personality and behavior suggest that several stable personality traits have important consequences for how individuals perceive and respond to social stimuli such as various changes associated with widowhood. For example, dimensions of the self-concept—self-confidence (efficacy) and self-esteem—are theoretically relevant in mediating the effects of life stress. Thoits (1983) argued that it is not the life events themselves but the perceived controllability and predictability of the events and consequences that affect outcomes such as depression. Persons with a greater sense of personal control or efficacy tend to have a more positive outlook on life and evidence better mental and physical health (cf. Seeman and Seeman 1983; Seligman 1975). These traits are effective resources in adjusting to the changes required by stress. Communication skills, interpersonal competence, and ease in interpersonal interaction also are useful resources in adjusting to stress.

Attitudes, Beliefs, and Values. Attitudes, beliefs, and values regarding marriage, family, the meaning and sanctity of life, and death are relevant for understanding an individual's affective, cognitive, and behavioral responses to the loss of a spouse. Further research needs to be conducted to identify the specific relevant attitudes and clarify the nature of these relationships.

Coping Strategies. A third psychological characteristic posited to condition the relationship between the stress of widowhood and personal well-being is coping strategies. A critical question in coping research is how and under what conditions various types of coping variables are effective in modifying the linkage between stress and outcomes. Coping strategies are defined as

> typical, habitual preferences for ways of approaching problems, for example a tendency to withdraw from rather than move toward people, to deny rather than ruminate over difficulty, to be active rather than reactive, or to blame others rather than oneself (Megahan 1983, 159).

Pearlin (1982) suggested that individual coping strategies involve either

> (1) seeking to alter the situations that give rise to the adverse forces, (2) attempting perceptually and cognitively to reshape the meaning of the forces in a way that reduces their threat, or (3) by establishing devices that enable them to live with distress without being overwhelmed by it (Pearlin 1982, 68).

On the other hand, coping efforts are

> specific actions (covert or overt) taken in specific situations that are intended to reduce a given problem or stress (e.g. appraise the problem, express or inhibit emotions, begin a new activity, ask for help, or refuse to think about it) (Megahan 1983, 159).

George (1980) noted that there is limited evidence regarding the effectiveness of specific coping strategies for adjustment to widowhood. Two commonsense approaches, "keeping busy" and "time heals all wounds," are often reported by widowed persons (Glick et al. 1974). Medications are frequently used, although the excessive or prolonged use of drugs or alcohol often signals significant maladjustment. Further research is needed to explore the effectiveness of specific coping strategies.

Transitions to and conditions of widowhood clearly affect personal well-being, but these effects are mediated by personality traits; by attitudes, beliefs, and values; and by coping strategies. Pearlin (1982) suggested that people respond to stress by three distinct but not mutually exclusive methods: (1) by selectively using their own personal coping style; (2) by utilizing personal resources such as self-efficacy and self-esteem; and (3) by establishing and using social support networks. This third method, social support, is the focus of discussion in the following section.

Social Support Factors

Two sources of social support are discussed here: social resources and social support networks. The availability of social resources is a key factor in adjustment to the stress of life change. Social resources confer status, autonomy, flexibility, security, and predictability, and they lessen constraints. Finances and education are two critical social resources. The services provided by social support networks—most notably the family, friends, and often community support groups—are also very important for maintaining personal well-being.

Social Resources. Financial resources are especially important for buffeting the negative stresses of widowhood (Atchley 1975). Income adequacy is important as a determinant of participation and access to other resources. It is well known that widows as a group have the lowest income of any segment of our population. In 1984, the median income of widows was only $6,568 (U.S. Senate Select Committee on Aging 1986), which means that one-half of all widows received less than this. The picture is even worse for minority women, whose income and education levels tend to be much lower.

Education is another important social resource because it entails knowledge and experience in planning, working within social organizations, and coping options. Lopata and Brehm (1985) noted that less educated older women tend to be socialized into passivity vis-à-vis the world outside the home and that they lack the knowledge and the confidence to adjust proactively on the changes of widowhood.

Social Support Networks. Various studies have strongly indicated that the presence of family, peers, or friends who assist with emotional management and coping during bereavement are very important in an individual's adjustment as a widowed person (Balkwell 1985; Roberto and Scott 1986; Lopata 1979). Unfortunately, the widowed frequently lose the support of family and friends who themselves are unable to cope with the bereavement or the altered role relationships (Stevens-Long 1984). Support networks involve exchanges of various types—financial, service, social, or emotional—all of which are relevant for maintaining an optimum style of life. Particularly important in widowhood, however, are emotional supports. A friendship in which one's innermost thoughts and feelings can be freely shared is a most critical asset in maintaining stable psychological well-being (Balkwell 1985; Thoits 1983). The stage of the widowed in the bereavement process, as well as the source, type, and quality of social support, are all important factors (Bankoff 1983).

The family is the most important support system for the elderly widowed. The elderly receive 80 to 90 percent of necessary services from their families (Gerontological Society 1986). Adult children are the most likely to provide aid and support, then grandchildren and siblings. The elderly who have no children tend to substitute other relatives or nonrelatives in the role of primary caregiver. Usually only one person in a family is selected as the primary caregiver, and this is most often a female (Longino and Lipman 1985). Also, there tends to be gender-role specialization in support networks. Men usually specialize in doing things, while women are more likely to provide emotional support.

Lopata (1979) reported that in her sample of urban widows, the support from extended kin and friends tended to be superficial and highly exaggerated. This was often because they lacked socialization in bereavement and were at a loss regarding how or what to do. Nevertheless, these findings reinforce the importance of adult children for widows. In their study of young-old widows (age 60 to 75), Beckman and Houser (1982) found that childless widows were more lonely and dissatisfied and were in lower states of general well-being than were widowed mothers.

This is not to suggest that friends are not important to the social networks of the widowed. But friends tend to be important more for social or companionship support than for economic or service support (Lopata 1981). Petrowsky (1976) found higher levels of interaction among widowers than among widows. In her study of changes in friendship patterns with widowhood, Lopata (1981) found that one-third of the widows kept their old friends but did not make new ones, one-third reported that they had both old and new friends, a few reported that they had no friends the year preceding their husband's fatal illness or accident, and one in six reported that they had no friends either before or after widowhood. Apparently some widows were totally socially isolated.

Hyman's (1983) research indicated that widowhood may not have negative effects on informal social relations among older women. He suggested that, if anything, it heightened the interactions. However, among men he found that widowhood neither diminished nor heightened interaction. Based on a study of attendance at religious services, he also concluded that widowhood had no effect on the spiritual involvement of men or women. Finally, it is important to note that widowers are less likely to receive assistance from support systems (Hyman 1983).

A dating relationship can be very healthy for the elderly widowed because it provides an intimate relationship where personal feelings can be expressed. The dating partner may not necessarily duplicate the former spousal role nor do things provided by other members of one's social network. But the dating partner can provide unique contributions in the areas of companionship, emotional caregiving, reinforced self-esteem, provision of a sexual partner, and opportunities for self-disclosure (c.f. Bulcroft and O'Connor 1986).

Religious groups, social agencies, and various other kinds of community support groups also are important social support networks for the widowed. Various widow-to-widow programs have been effective in assisting and supporting the newly widowed.

Conclusions

The literature reviewed in this chapter reveals the complexity of widowhood. The experience is varied, and standard stereotypes of widowhood are frequently incorrect. Relationships among causal factors tend to involve complex interdependencies and interactions. Simple cause-effect relationships are not particularly descriptive of the experience of widowhood.

The purpose of this chapter has been to develop and describe a theoretical approach that integrates various sets of factors relevant for understanding the stresses of widowhood. First, the actual and perceived stresses of widowhood vary remarkably among individuals, depending on their personal experiences in marriage and in widowhood. Status variables and personal psychological characteristics are important in understanding the perceived levels of stress associated with becoming and remaining widowed. The responses to and the impacts of these stresses are mediated and conditioned by one's psychological characteristics and social resources. In understanding the impacts of widowhood it is important to differentiate immediate consequences (bereavement experience) from long-term responses and impacts.

Using the model in figure 3–1, this chapter has attempted to review and integrate current research. We now discuss some needed directions for future research.

Although it is common to compare married and widowed persons, it is also important to investigate variations among the widowed. Just as there is great variation with respect to the experiences and satisfactions of marriage, there is also great variation among the widowed. It is surprising how little we know concerning incumbents' attitudes about widowhood or why they feel that way. Future research should systematically investigate specific stressors of widowhood, why and to what degree they are perceived as stressful, and under what conditions these stressors tend to occur. The typology developed earlier on sources of stress can be used to orient the further assessment of these issues. There is a need to develop typologies of stressful conditions and experiences in widowhood. Further research is needed on the prevalence of each type of experience and on what differentiates the impact of these experiences.

Further investigations of the effects of status variables are also relevant to this elaboration of the sources of stress. However, much more needs to be known than simply whether age, gender, ethnicity, residency, or social class makes a difference. It is important to know what it is about age, gender, and so on that makes a difference and why. The typology identifying causes of perceptions of stress could help identify specific hypotheses regarding the effects of status variables. Further research is needed to identify and compare the specific effects of these variables.

This chapter has suggested that personal well-being may be divided into three specific dimensions: life satisfaction, physical health, and mental health. In prior research innumerable outcome measures have been used, often without a careful consideration of their relevance or relationship to an overall outcome concept, such as personal well-being, and without consideration of how these various outcome variables may relate to and impact one another. It would be well for future research to give more emphasis to the comparability and relevancy of findings for different outcome measures for understanding consequences in general, and to further investigate the mutual effects of multiple consequences, such as life satisfaction, physical health, and mental health, on each other.

A particularly fruitful area for continued research is the specification of theories and the investigation of conditions assumed to mediate the effects of stress on well-being. Much emphasis in the next generation of research will be given to the testing of interaction hypotheses specifying that such-and-such will have an impact on such-and-such under the following conditions and/or in the presence of the following factors. The present interest in social psychology on the effects of social support will continue and expand. This research will need to be systematically integrated and linked with the overall stress theoretical framework depicted in figure 3–1. There is a need for an expansion of research on personal psychological characteristics. Conceptually, theoretically, and methodologically, studies of personality traits; attitudes, beliefs, and values; and coping strategies are especially challenging. In addition, at some point social scientists must begin to assess more carefully the effects of the physical as well as the psychological and social characteristics on the various dimensions of well-being.

Two basic keys for the rapid success of future research will be (1) the development of more carefully constructed theories and hypotheses specifying multivariate and interactive relationships, and (2) the design of research studies and the collection of reliable data to test complicated relationships among specific variables under specified conditions. At present, statistical analysis procedures pose less of a limitation. Since the 1960s there have been remarkable advances in the sophistication of statistical analysis methods. Wholistic conceptual frameworks, such as the model suggested in this chapter, should be developed and tested to obtain a more precise understanding of the specific sources, mediators, and consequences of stress in widowhood, and the interactive relations among the salient factors.

References

Atchley, R. C. 1975. "Dimensions of widowhood in later life." *The Gerontologist* 15:176–78.

——. 1987. *Aging: Continuity and Change* (2nd ed.). Belmont, CA: Wadsworth.

——. 1986. *The Social Forces in Later Life*. Belmont, CA: Wadsworth.

Balkwell, C. 1985. "An attitudinal correlate of the timing of a major life event: The case of morale in widowhood." *Family Relations* 34:577–81.

Bankoff, E. A. 1983. "Social support and adaptation to widowhood." *Journal of Marriage and the Family* 45:827–39.

Beckman, L. J., and Houser, B. B. 1982. "The consequences of childlessness on the social-psychological well-being of older women." *Journal of Gerontology* 37:243–50.

Berardo, F. M. 1970. "Survivorship and social isolation." *Journal of Marriage and the Family* 19:11–25.

Blau, Z. S. 1981. *Aging in a Changing Society* (2nd ed.) New York: Franklin Watts.

Blieszner, R. 1986. "Trends in family gerontology research." *Family Relations* 35:555–62.

Bowlby, J. 1961. "Processes of mourning." *International Journal of Psychoanalysis* 42:317–40.

Bulcroft, K., and O'Connor, M. 1986. "The importance of dating relationships on quality of life for older persons." *Family Relations* 35:397–01.

Clark, P. G., Siviski, R. W., and Weiner, R. 1986. "Coping strategies of widowers in the first year." *Family Relations* 35:425–30.

Fenwick, R., and Barresi, C. M. 1981. "Health consequences of marital status change among the elderly." *Journal of Health and Social Behavior* 22:106–16.

Ferraro, K. F. 1985. "The effect of widowhood on the health status of older persons." *International Journal Aging and Human Development* 21:9–25.

George, L. 1980. *Role Transitions in Later Life.* Monterey, CA: Brooks/Cole.

Gerontological Society of America. 1986. *The Common Stake: The Interdependency of Generations.* Washington, DC.

Glick, I. O., Weiss, R. D., and Parkes, C. M. 1974. *The First Year of Bereavement.* New York: John Wiley and Sons.

Helsing, K., Comstock, G., and Szklo, M. 1982. "Causes of death in a widowed population." *American Journal of Epidemiology* 116:524–32.

Helsing, K., Szlko, M., and Comstock, G. 1981. "Factors associated with mortality after widowhood." *American Journal of Public Health* 71:802–09.

Hess, B. B., and Waring, J. 1983. "Family relationships of older women: A women's issue." In E.W. Markson (ed.), *Older Women: Issues and Prospects.* Lexington, MA: Lexington Books.

House, J. S. 1974. "Occupational stress and coronary heart disease: A review and theoretical integration." *Journal of Health and Social Behavior* 15:12–27.

Hyman, H. H. 1983. *Of Time and Widowhood.* Durham, NC: Duke Press Policy Studies.

Ide, B., Tobias, C., and Kay, M. 1986. "Coping and health among older urban widows." *Newsletter of the Southwest Institute for Research on Women* 27 (October 1–2).

Kahn, R. L. 1973. "Conflict, ambiguity and overload: Three elements in job stress." *Occupational Mental Health* 3:2–9.

Karp, D. A., and Yoels, W. C. 1982. *Experiencing the Life Cycle: A Social Psychology of Aging.* Springfield, IL: Charles C. Thomas.

Kuypers, J. A., and Bengtson, V. L. 1973. "Social breakdown and competence." *Human Development* 16:181–201.

Lindemann, E. 1944. "Symptomatology and management of acute grief." *American Journal of Psychology* 101:141–48.

Longino, C. F., Jr., and Lipman, A. 1985. "The support systems of women." In W. J. Sauer and R. T. Coward (eds.), *Social Support Networks and the Care of the Elderly.* New York: Springer.

Lopata, H. Z. 1973. *Widowhood in an American City.* Cambridge, MA: Schenkman.

———. 1978. "Contributions of extended families to the support systems of metropolitan area widows: Limitations of the modified kin network." *Journal of Marriage and the Family* 40:355–64.

———. 1979. *Women as Widows: Support Systems.* New York: Elsevier North Holland.

———. 1980. "The widowed family member." In N. Datan and N. Lohman (eds.), *Transitions of Aging.* New York: Academic Press.

———. 1981. "The meaning of friendship in widowhood." In L. D. Steinberg (ed.), *The Life Cycle—Readings in Human Development.* New York: Columbia University Press.

———. 1982. "Lifestyles of American widows and widowers in urban America." *Educational Horizons* 60:185–90.

Lopata, H. Z., and Brehm, H. P. 1985. *Widows and Dependent Wives: From Social Problem to Federal Program.* New York: Praeger Publishers.

Lopata, H. Z., Heineman, G. D., and Baum, J. 1982. "Loneliness: antecedents and coping strategies in the lives of widows." In A. A. Peplau and D. Perlman (eds.), *Loneliness: A Source of Current Theory, Research and Therapy*. New York: John Wiley and Sons.

Megahan, E. G. 1983. "Individual coping efforts: Moderators of the relationship between life stress and mental health outcomes. In H. B. Kaplan (ed.), *Psychological Stress: Trends in Theory and Research*. New York: Academic Press.

Morgan, L. A. 1984. "Changes in family interaction following widowhood." *Journal of Marriage and the Family* 46:323–31.

O'Laughlin, K. 1983. "The final challenge: Facing death." In E. W. Markson (ed.), *Older Women: Issues and Prospects*. Lexington, MA: Lexington Books.

Parkes, C. M. 1972. *Bereavement: Studies of Grief in Adult Life*. New York: International Universities Press.

Pearlin, L. I. 1982. "Discontinuities in the study of aging." In T. K. Hareven and K. J. Adams (eds.), *Aging and Life Course Transitions: An Interdisciplinary Perspective*. New York: The Guilford Press.

———. 1983. "Role strains and personal stress. In H. B. Kaplan (ed.), *Psychological Stress: Trends in Theory and Research*. New York: Academic Press.

Pearlin, L. I., and Lieberman, M. A. 1979. "Social sources of emotional distress." In R. Simmons (ed.), *Research in Community and Mental Health*, vol. 1. Greenwich, CT: JAI Press.

Pearlin, L. I., and Schooler, C. 1978. "The structure of coping." *Journal of Health and Social Behavior* 19:2–21.

Petrowsky, M. 1976. "Marital status, sex and the social network of the elderly." *Journal of Marriage and the Family* 38:749–56.

Roberto, K. A., and Scott, J. P. 1986. "Confronting widowhood." *American Behavioral Scientist* 29 (4):497–511.

Sauer, W. J., and Coward, R. T. 1985. *Social Support Networks and the Care of the Elderly*. New York: Springer.

Schaie, K. W., and Willis, S. L. 1986. *Adult Development and Aging*. Boston: Little, Brown.

Scott, J. P., and Kivett, V. R. 1985. "Differences in the morale of older, rural widows and widowers." *Journal of Aging and Human Development* 21:121–36.

Seeman, M., and Seeman, T. E. 1983. "Health behavior and personal autonomy: A longitudinal study of the sense of control in illness." *Journal of Health and Social Behavior* 24:144–60.

Seligman, M. 1975. *Helplessness*. San Francisco: W.H. Freeman.

Silverman, P. R. 1986. *Widow-to-Widow*. Albert R. Roberts (series ed.). New York: Springer.

Soldo, B. J., and Manton, K. J. 1985. "The graying of America: Demographic challenges for socio-economic planning." *The Journal of Socio-Economic Planning Sciences* 19:227–47.

Stevens-Long, J. 1984. *Adult Life: Developmental Processes*. (2nd ed.). Palo Alto, CA: Mayfield.

Thoits, P. A. 1983. "Dimensions of life events that influence psychological distress: An evaluation and synthesis of the literature." In Howard B. Kaplan (ed.),

Psychological Stress: Trends in Theory and Research. New York: Academic Press.

———. 1985. "Self-labeling processes in mental illness: The role of emotional deviance." *American Journal of Sociology* 91:221–49.

Troll, L. E., Miller, S. J., and Atchley, R. C. 1979. *Families in Later Life.* Belmont, CA: Wadsworth.

Tyhurst, J. 1958. *The Role of Transition States—Including Disasters in Mental Illness.* In Symposium on Preventive and Social Psychiatry. Washington, DC: U.S. Government Printing Office.

U.S. Bureau of the Census. 1986. *Statistical Abstract of the United States: 1987* (107th ed.). Washington DC: U.S. Government Printing Office.

U.S. Congress. Senate. Select Committee on Aging. 1986. *Aging America: Trends and Projections* (1985–86 ed.). Washington, DC: U.S. Government Printing Office.

Vinick, B. H. 1983. "Loneliness among elderly widowers." Paper presented at the 36th annual meeting of the Gerontological Society of America, San Francisco.

Ward, R. A. 1984. *The Aging Experience: An Introduction to Social Gerontology.* New York: Harper and Row.

Wilkinson, A. M. 1980. "Factors associated with duration of bereavement." Paper presented at the 33rd annual scientific meeting of the Gerontological Society of America, San Diego, November 1980.

4
Remarriage among the Elderly

I-Chiao H. Bowers
Stephen J. Bahr

I n the United States more than 20 percent of all current marriages are remarriages, in which at least one spouse has been married previously (Cherlin and McCarthy 1985). Although remarriage has become relatively common as divorce rates have risen, little is known about remarriage among the elderly. Spanier and Furstenberg (1987) did an extensive review of research on remarriage but made no mention of remarriage in later life, except to say that remarriage is more common among the young than among the old. In a review of research on family life among the elderly, Treas and Bengtson (1987) made only brief mention of remarriage, noting that the rate of remarriage is much lower among elderly women than among elderly men. Norton and Moorman (1987) examined remarriage in the United States and did not even identify remarriage rates for women over age 54.

The purpose of this chapter is to provide some much-needed data about remarriage among the elderly. Five major questions are addressed: (1) How often do elderly people remarry? (2) Do remarriage rates differ between those divorced and those widowed? (3) How do remarriage rates of elderly men and women differ? (4) How stable are remarriages among the elderly? (5) Among elderly persons who have remarried, are there differences between men and women in marital happiness?

The definition of *elderly* depends on the perspective of the persons involved. Some teenagers perceive their 40-year-old parents as old. On the other hand, retired 70-year-olds may not consider themselves elderly. In this chapter *elderly* refers to those age 60 and over. However, to understand how remarriage rates change across the entire life span and to place remarriage among the elderly in perspective, it is necessary to compare them with individuals in various age categories. Thus, data are included for adults of all ages.

Literature Review

Age and Remarriage

Among both women and men, the probability of remarriage decreases as age increases (Becker et al. 1977; Glick 1984; Koo and Suchindran 1980; National Center for Health Statistics 1980; Norton and Moorman 1987; Spanier and Furstenberg 1987; Sweet 1973; Thornton 1979). One of the major reasons for this decrease is that marriage and death reduce the pool of potential partners as people get older.

Divorce, Widowhood, and Remarriage

The widowed tend to be older than the divorced and hence are less likely to remarry. In addition to age, Berardo (1982) suggested four life circumstances that also tend to make remarriage more likely for divorced persons than for widowed persons: (1) divorced persons may have young children, for whom they need to make a home; (2) divorced people are not obligated to defer remarriage out of respect for the deceased; (3) divorced persons may be more liberal; and (4) plans to remarry may have precipitated the divorce.

Gender, Age, and Remarriage

Perhaps the most striking aspect of remarriage among the elderly is the large gender difference that develops as age increases. Remarriage rates are much lower for older women than for older men (Treas and Bengtson 1987, 639).

Two major factors account for this gender difference. First, the sex ratio (the number of males per 100 females) becomes increasingly favorable toward men as aging occurs. The sex ratio is 102 among those who are 18 to 24 years old, 99 among those ages 25 to 44, 92 among those ages 45 to 64, but only 68 among those 65 years old or older (U. S. Bureau of the Census 1986, 17). The second factor is that social norms give men greater latitude in the age of their spouses. It is socially appropriate for a man to marry a much younger woman, but not for a woman to marry a younger man. These social norms further restrict the limited pool of available mates for women (Grurak and Dean 1979).

Age and Success of Remarriages

Although the likelihood of remarriage after divorce or widowhood decreases as age increases, it appears that those who remarry late in life may have more stable and satisfying marriages than those who remarry as young adults (Albrecht et al. 1983; Bumpass and Sweet 1972; Carter and Glick 1976; Norton and Glick 1979). Bernard (1971, 279) argued that "second marriages among the elderly, especially among the widowed, ended in divorce less frequently than first marriages; for the participants have the double advantage of age and experience." According to Bernard (1971, 180), remarriages among the elderly have a greater chance of success than remarriages among young adults because they are a blend of the romantic and the practical.

Studies of couples who remarry late in life have shown that these couples tend to be very satisfied with their new marriages (Brubaker 1985, 43). The major reasons for their remarriages are loneliness and the need for companionship.

Remarried men tend to be more satisfied in their marriages than remarried women (Renne 1971; White 1979; Glenn and Weaver 1977; Glenn 1981; Ishii-Kuntz 1986). To illustrate, Glenn (1981) analyzed National Opinion Research Center (NORC) data from 1972 through 1978 and found that remarried women reported less happiness than remarried men. Ishii-Kuntz (1986) replicated Glenn's study with 1980 through 1985 NORC data, and her results were similar to the findings of Glenn.

The unfavorable marriage market may be one of the reasons why women are less satisfied in remarriages than men. With few potential mates, women may have to settle for less desirable partners than do men (White 1979).

Methodology

Sample

The data used in this study were derived from two national surveys. First, the June 1985 Marital History and Fertility Survey generated by the Current Population Survey (CPS) was used to provide an overall description of remarriage. The CPS is a monthly survey conducted in approximately 57,000 randomly selected households in the United States. The present analysis includes only those men and women who have ever been married.

The second data set used in this analysis was the General Social Survey conducted by the National Opinion Research Center (NORC). Data from the 1982 through 1987 NORC surveys were pooled. The NORC data were used because they provide information on marital happiness not available in CPS data. Since there were only a small number of widowed persons in the NORC data, the analysis was conducted on a subsample of men and women who had remarried after divorce, a total of 484 men and 672 women.

Measurement of Variables

Age. For most comparisons, *age* refers to age at the time of the event, that is, age at first marriage, age at termination of first marriage, or age at second marriage. But in the NORC data, age at survey date was used to examine gender differences in marital happiness because age at marriage was unavailable.

Race. Race is a dichitomous variable in which whites were coded 0 and nonwhites were coded 1.

Previous Marital Status. There are two different categories of remarriage: remarriage after widowhood and remarriage after divorce.

Children from Previous Marriage. If a child's age was greater than the duration of the respondent's second marriage, the child was coded as from a previous marriage. Over 95 percent of women whose first marriages ended in either divorce or widowhood had at least one child.

Duration between First and Second Marriage. This is the interval between the date the first marriage was terminated and the second marriage began.

The Success of Second Marriage. If the second marriage had ended in divorce or separation by the survey date, it was coded 1, otherwise, 0. The cumulative proportion survival rate was used to estimate the probability of success of remarriage across age groups and between first and second marriages; the higher the survival rate, the higher the probability of having a successful marriage.

Marital Happiness. Marital happiness was measured on a three-point scale based on the following question: "Taking things all together, how would you describe your marriage? Would you say that your marriage is not too happy, pretty happy, or very happy?"

Global Happiness. Global happiness was measured on a three-point scale based on the following question: "Taking all together, how would you say things are these days?" Response categories were "not too happy," "pretty happy," and "very happy."

Findings

Frequency of Remarriage

The first question we address is the frequency of remarriage among the elderly. The data show that remarriage is infrequent among the elderly compared with remarriage among younger persons. Table 4–1 shows the remarriage rates for women whose first marriage ended in divorce. Among those women who divorced before age 30, 77 percent remarried, compared with 55 percent of those who divorced during their thirties and only 16 percent of those who divorced after age 60. The median age at the time of divorce for women who remarried after divorce was 26.

The remarriage rates for women whose first marriage ended in widowhood are shown in table 4–2. Of women who became widows before age 30, 73 percent remarried, compared with 50 percent of those who became widows during their thirties. Only 3 percent of those who became widows after age 60 remarried. The median age at the time of widowhood for those women who remarried after the death of their husbands was about 36. The

Table 4–1
Remarriage Rates among Women Whose First Marriages Ended in Divorce, by Age of Divorce, 1985

Age at Divorce	Total	Married Once Still Divorced	Remarried	Percent Remarried
Total	10,878	3,762	7,116	65.4
Percentage	100.0	100.0	100.0	
15–29 years	60.3	41.0	70.5	76.5
15–19	8.9	2.4	12.4	90.6
20–24	27.2	16.7	32.7	78.8
25–29	24.2	21.9	25.4	68.7
30–39 years	26.9	34.7	22.9	55.4
30–34	16.5	20.0	14.7	58.1
35–39	10.4	14.7	8.2	51.2
40–49 years	9.2	16.2	5.6	39.5
40–44	5.9	10.2	3.7	40.6
45–49	3.3	6.0	1.9	37.5
50+ years	3.5	8.1	1.1	20.2
50–54	2.1	4.7	0.7	21.2
55–59	0.8	1.8	0.3	20.9
60+	0.6	1.6	0.2	15.7
Median age	27.7	31.9	25.8	

Note: The data on this table were computed from the information obtained in the 1985 Current Population Survey.

Table 4–2
Remarriage Rates among Women Whose First Marriages Ended in
Widowhood, by Age at Widowhood, 1985

Age at Widowhood	Total	Married Once, Still Widowed	Remarried	Percent Remarried
Total	7,482	5,848	1,634	21.8
Percentage	100.0	100.0	100.0	
15–29 years	9.8	3.4	32.8	72.9
15–19	1.2	0.2	5.1	90.2
20–24	3.8	1.1	13.1	76.2
25–29	4.8	2.1	14.6	66.0
30–39 years	11.5	7.5	26.2	49.5
30–34	5.6	3.4	13.5	52.5
35–39	5.9	4.1	12.7	46.7
40–49 years	16.0	14.8	20.9	28.3
40–44	7.0	6.1	10.4	32.4
45–49	9.0	8.7	10.5	25.0
50+ years	62.5	74.4	20.0	7.0
50–54	11.4	12.2	8.6	16.5
55–59	12.5	14.2	6.1	10.7
60+	38.6	47.9	5.3	3.0
Median age	55.4	59.3	36.3	

Note: The data on this table were computed from information obtained in the 1985 Current Population Survey.

median age at the time of widowhood for those women who did not remarry after death of their husbands was 59.

Divorce, Widowhood, and Remarriage

The age distributions for divorce and widowhood are very different, as shown in tables 4–1 and 4–2. More than 60 percent of divorces occur before age 30, while more than 60 percent of widowhood occurs among those over age 50.

The remarriage rates among young widowed women are similar to those among young divorced women. Seventy-three percent of women widowed between the ages of 15 and 29 remarried, compared with 77 percent of those divorced. As age increases, the remarriage rate declines more for widowed women than for divorced women. Among women over 60, 16 percent of the divorced remarried, compared with only 3 percent of the widowed (see tables 4–1 and 4–2). Thus, widows have lower rates of remarriage than do divorced women of comparable ages. The differences are smaller among young adults and increase as age increases.

Table 4–3
Remarriage Rates, by Age, Gender, and Previous Marital Status, 1985

Age[a]	Divorced Females	Divorced Males	Widowed Females	Widowed Males
14–29 years	52.6	42.2	29.6	29.6
14–19	6.7	0.0	0.0	0.0
20–24	43.7	28.6	38.5	n/a
25–29	56.8	45.4	27.5	50.0
30–39 years	63.1	65.1	45.2	70.5
30–34	62.9	60.4	46.2	64.3
35–39	63.3	69.1	46.3	72.3
40–49 years	66.5	71.8	39.1	69.8
40–44	65.9	71.5	43.8	69.8
45–49	67.2	72.4	35.8	69.8
50+ years	71.7	76.6	20.0	44.4
50–54	67.8	72.9	31.2	50.6
55–59	68.8	72.1	28.8	56.0
60+	74.4	80.3	18.6	42.9
Total	65.4	68.9	21.8	46.6

Note: The data on this table were computed from information obtained in the 1985 Current Population Survey.

[a]*Age* refers to the age at survey date.

A comparable analysis among men was not possible because a complete marital history that showed the ages of divorce and widowhood among men was not obtained in the CPS survey. However, available data using their age at the date of the survey suggest that similar trends occur among men. Remarriage rates decrease with age, and divorced men are more likely to remarry than widowed men (see table 4–3).

Gender and Remarriage

It is well known that remarriage rates are higher for men than for women (Spanier and Furstenberg 1987, 422) and that gender differences in remarriage rates are particularly striking among the elderly (Treas and Bengtson 1987, 639). In this section, gender differences in remarriage are analyzed, using the 1985 CPS data. Because of data limitations among men, the age comparisons are based on age at survey date rather than on age at divorce or widowhood.

A comparison of remarriage rates for men and women by age and previous marital status is shown in table 4–3. Almost 69 percent of the men and 65 percent of the women remarried after their first marriages ended in divorce, while 47 percent of the men and 22 percent of the women who were widowed remarried. These figures may underestimate actual remarriage rates, since some divorced and widowed persons will remarry in the future, particularly among the younger cohorts. Nevertheless, these figures are useful for making gender comparisons.

The data in table 4–3 are consistent with previous research that has found that remarriage rates are considerably higher for men than for women. The data also confirm that remarriage is higher among divorced persons than among widowed persons. However, the age-sex comparisons in table 4–3 reveal several findings not reported in previous research. First, gender differences in remarriage after divorce are relatively modest. Among persons over age 50, the remarriage rates are 77 percent and 72 percent for men and women, respectively.

Second, among divorced persons between the ages of 14 and 29, remarriage rates are considerably *higher* for women than for men—53 percent for women, compared with 42 percent for men. Thus, divorced women do not differ greatly from divorced men in remarriage, and during their twenties divorced women are actually more likely to remarry than are divorced men.

Third, women are much less likely to remarry after widowhood than men, particularly among the elderly. Forty-three percent of widowers over age 60 remarried, compared with only 19 percent of widows over age 60. However, among persons who become widowed under age 30, women are just as likely to remarry as men. However, very few people become widows before age 30.

It should be kept in mind that the findings in table 4–3 reveal only the proportion of persons who had remarried after divorce or widowhood across age groups *at the survey date.* Caution should be used when interpreting the findings because age at survey date does not indicate the age of the persons at the time they were divorced or widowed.

The Stability of Remarriages

In this section, the stability of remarriages among elderly persons is examined, using the CPS data. The data show that remarriages among the elderly are much less likely to end in divorce than remarriages among younger persons. About 53 percent of the remarriages of women who remarried before age 50 end in divorce, compared with only 22 percent of the remarriages of women who remarried after age 50.

Cumulative marriage survival rates for the CPS women are shown in table 4–4. Among remarriages in the 10 to 15 year category, 61 percent of those remarried before 30 had survived compared with 78 percent of remarriages after age 50. Thus, about 39 percent of remarriages that occur before the age of 30 dissolve their second marriage within 15 years, compared with only 22 percent of remarriages that occur after age 50.

Table 4–4
Cumulative Marriage Survival Rates for Women,
by Age at Marriage, 1985

Age at Marriage	Duration of Marriage (years)	First Marriage[a]	Second Marriage[a]
Under 30 years			
	0–5	.90	.81
	5–10	.82	.69
	10–15	.77	.61
	15–20	.73	.56
	20–30	.68	.50
	30+	.65	.47
30–40 years			
	0–5	.92	.84
	5–10	.88	.74
	10–15	.85	.67
	15–20	.83	.64
	20–30	.81	.61
	30+	.78	.58
40–50 years			
	0–5	.94	.87
	5–10	.89	.79
	10–15	.85	.73
	15–20	.84	.71
	20–30	.83	.70
	30+	.83	---
50+			
	0–5	.93	.89
	5–10	.90	.82
	10–15	.89	.78
	15–20	.89	---
	20–30	.89	---
	30+	---	---

Note: The data on this table were computed from information obtained in the 1985 Current
Population Survey.
[a]If the cases of each category were less than 10, the cumulative proportion survived at the end
was left out.

Table 4–4 also shows that the marriage survival rate for first marriages
is greater than that for remarriages across all age groups. However, as age
at marriage increases, the difference in the marriage survival rate between
first marriages and remarriages decreases.

Regression analysis suggests that age affects the stability of remarriages,
even after race, education, number of children, and duration of marriage
are controlled (see table 4–5). The older the age at the second marriage, the
higher the probability that the second marriage will endure.

Table 4–5
Regression Analysis of Marriage Success[a] for Those Who Remarried
After the First Marriage Ended in Divorce, 1985

	Beta	P	Cumulative R^2
Age at second marriage[b]	0.13	.001	0.0179
Race	−0.07	.001	0.0227
Education	0.06	.001	0.0265
Number of children[b]	0.03	.05	0.0271
Duration	0.00	----	0.0271

Note: The data on this table were computed from information obtained in the 1985 Current Population.

[a]Marriage success was treated as a dummy variable. 0 indicates that the second marriage ended in divorce or separation; 1 indicates that the second marriage did not end in divorce by survey date.

[b]Interactive effect between age at second marriage and number of children at previous marriage was tested; the result indicates that there is no interactive effect between these two variables.

Remarriage and Happiness

In this section, the happiness of elderly persons who have remarried is examined, using the NORC data. Analysis of variance was used to compare global happiness and marital happiness across age groups for those who remarried after their first marriage ended in divorce. Those who remarried after being widowed were not included because there were insufficient cases for comparisons by age.

The mean scores on global happiness and marital happiness by age and gender are shown in table 4–6. None of the differences are statistically significant, indicating that the global and marital happiness of elderly remarried persons is just as high but not significantly higher than it is for younger remarried persons.

Analysis of variance was also used to compare men and women who had remarried on global happiness and marital happiness, as shown in table 4–7. Although men are slightly happier in their remarriages than women, the differences are not statistically significant and do not support the results of Glenn (1981) and Ishii-Kuntz (1986).

Summary and Conclusion

Seven major conclusions may be drawn from this analysis. (1) Remarriage decreases as age increases, resulting in much less remarriage among the elderly than among other age groups. (2) Divorced persons remarry more frequently than do widowed persons, even among comparable age groups, and this difference increases as age increases. (3) Although men remarry

Table 4–6
Global Happiness and Marital Happiness for Those Who Remarried After Divorce, by Age and Gender, 1982–87

Age	N	Mean	SD	F-probability
All Respondents				
Global happiness				
Under 30	99	2.15	.66	0.077
30–39	303	2.23	.64	
40–49	230	2.26	.64	
50–59	195	2.09	.67	
60+	321	2.21	.66	
Marital happiness				
Under 30	97	2.44	.68	0.408
30–39	296	2.57	.60	
40–49	222	2.56	.59	
50–59	166	2.57	.55	
60+	166	2.58	.57	
Males				
Global happiness				
Under 30	28	2.07	.66	0.362
30–39	124	2.26	.61	
40–49	120	2.23	.63	
50–59	91	2.12	.70	
60+	119	2.25	.65	
Marital happiness				
Under 30	27	2.30	.72	0.086
30–39	124	2.61	.55	
40–49	120	2.58	.54	
50–59	87	2.57	.56	
60+	100	2.64	.58	
Females				
Global happiness				
Under 30	71	2.18	.66	0.183
30–39	179	2.21	.67	
40–49	110	2.29	.65	
50–59	104	2.07	.66	
60+	202	2.19	.66	
Marital happiness				
Under 30	70	2.50	.65	0.930
30–39	172	2.53	.63	
40–49	102	2.53	.64	
50–59	79	2.57	.55	
60+	66	2.48	.56	

Note: The data on this table were computed from information obtained in the surveys conducted by the National Opinion Research Center, 1982–87.

more than women, gender differences in remarriage after divorce do not appear to be large, particularly among those under age 40. (4) After widowhood men are much more likely than women to remarry. (5) Remarriages are somewhat more likely than first marriages to end in divorce, but the older the age at remarriage, the less the chance the remarriage will end

Table 4–7
Global Happiness and Marital Happiness for Those Who Remarried After Divorce, by Age and Gender, 1982–87

Age	N	Mean	SD	F-probability
Global happiness				
Males	484	2.21	.65	0.4856
Females	672	2.19	.67	
Marital happiness				
Males	459	2.58	.52	0.1287
Females	493	2.53	.61	

Note: The data on this table were computed from information obtained in the surveys conducted by the National Opinion Research Center, 1982–87.

in divorce. (6) Elderly persons who remarry are just as happy as younger persons who remarry but are not happier. (7) There are no significant differences between the happiness of men and women who remarry.

There has been little research on remarriage among the elderly. This chapter provides some preliminary data on the frequency, stability, and happiness of remarriages among older persons. It was found that remarried elderly persons are just as happy in their marriages as remarried younger persons. Additional research is needed to document the quality of marital relationships among the remarried elderly. Brubaker (1985, 43) noted that companionship is the major reason for remarriage. He also noted that men may have more difficulty living alone than women, which may account for some of the difference in gender remarriage rates after widowhood. Since the findings here did not confirm the research of Glenn (1981) and Ishii-Kuntz (1986), additional work is needed to examine the marital satisfaction and companionship of men and women in remarriages, particularly among the elderly.

References

Albrecht, S. L., Bahr, H. M., and Goodman, K.L. 1983. *Divorce and Remarriage: Problems, Adaptations, and Adjustments.* London: Greenwood Press.

Becker, G. W., Landes, E. M., and Michael, R. T. 1977. "An economic analysis of marital instability." *Journal of Political Economy* 85:1141–87.

Berardo, D. H. 1982. "Divorce and remarriage at middle age and beyond." *The Annals of the American Academy of Political and Social Science* 464:132–39.

Bernard, J. 1971. *Remarriage: A Study of Marriage.* New York: Russell and Russell.

Brubaker, T. H. 1985. *Later Life Families.* Beverly Hills, CA: Sage Publications.

Bumpass, L. L., and Sweet, J. A. 1972. "Differentials in marital instability: 1970." *American Sociological Review* 37:251–61.

Carter, H., and Glick, P. C. 1976. *Marriage and Divorce: A Social and Economic Study.* Cambridge, MA: Harvard University Press.

Cherlin, A., and McCarthy, J. 1985. "Remarried couple households: Data from the June 1980 current population survey." *Journal of Marriage and the Family* 47:23–30.

Glenn, N. D. 1981. "The well-being of persons remarried after divorce." *Journal of Family Issues* 2 (March):61–75.

Glenn, N. D., and Weaver, C. 1977. "The marital happiness of remarried divorced persons." *Journal of Marriage and the Family* 39:331–37.

Glick, P. C. 1984. "Marriage, divorce, and living arrangements: Prospective changes." *Journal of Family Issues* 5:7–26.

Grurak, D. T., and Dean, G. 1979. "The remarriage market: factors influencing the selection of second husband." *Journal of Divorce* 3(Winter):161–71.

Ishii-Kuntz, M. 1986. "Sex and race differences in marital happiness of first married and remarried person: Update and refinement." Unpublished manuscript. Pullman, WA: Washington State University.

Koo, H., and Suchindran, C. 1980. "Effects of children on women's remarriage prospects." *Journal of Family Issues* 1(December):497–515.

National Center for Health Statistics. 1980. *Remarriage of women 15–44 years of age whose first marriage ended in divorce: United States, 1976.* Advance Data no. 58. Washington, DC: U.S. Government Printing Office.

Norton, A. J., and Glick, P. C. 1979. "Marital instability in America: Past, present, and future." In G. Levinger and O. C. Moles (eds.), *Divorce and Separation: Context, Causes, and Consequences.* New York: Basic Books.

Norton, A. J., and Moorman, J. E. 1987. "Current trends in marriage and divorce among American women." *Journal of Marriage and the Family* 49:3–14.

Renne, K. S. 1971. "Health and marital experience in an urban population." *Journal of Marriage and the Family* 33(May):338–50.

Spanier, G. B., and Furstenberg, F. F., Jr. 1987. "Remarriage and reconstituted families." In M. B. Sussman and S. K. Steinmetz (eds.), *Handbook of Marriage and the Family.* New York: Plenum Press.

Sweet, J. A. 1973. "Differentials in remarriage probabilities." Working Paper 73–29. Madison, WI: Center for Demography and Ecology.

Thornton, A. 1979. "Decomposing the remarriage process." *Population Studies* 31:383–92.

Treas, J., and Bengtson, V. L. 1987. "The family in later years." In M. B. Sussman and S. K. Steinmetz (eds.), *Handbook of Marriage and the Family.* New York: Plenum Press.

U.S. Bureau of the Census. 1986. *Statistical Abstract of the United States: 1987* (107th ed.). Washington, DC: U.S. Government Printing Office.

White, L. K. 1979. "Sex differentials in the effect of remarriage on global happiness." *Journal of Marriage and the Family* 41:869–76.

5
Leisure among the Elderly

Phileon B. Robinson, Jr.
Evan T. Peterson

In this chapter *leisure* refers to free or unobligated time. Others have given more elaborate definitions of the term (Kaplan 1975; Murphy 1975; and Nealinger 1974), but the simpler meaning is convenient and sufficient for our use (Leitner and Leitner 1985). Education and other leisure activities are discussed herein as examples of possible activities for people during their retirement. Other possible activities include a second career, volunteer work, family projects and activities, and the like.

In the past, relatively few elderly people survived the demands of their work and families, so the matter of leisure for the elderly was of no major consequence. Even today, the work ethic militates against leisure activities among many Americans. However, interest in leisure among the elderly has been growing, and leisure has become an important aspect of the lives of many elderly people. According to Huyck and Hoyer (1982, 365), "Leisure pursuits can provide a sense of individual worth, social participation, status and prestige, new experiences, opportunities to be of service, and ways to make the time pass."

There are a number of reasons for the increase in leisure time among the elderly:

1. *Increased longevity.* In the United States, both the number and the proportion of older people are increasing rapidly. In 1900, only 4 percent of the population was 65 or older. But in 1985, this age group was approximately 12 percent, and it is predicted that by the year 2020, 18 percent of the population will be 65 or over. Those 85 and older are expected to increase from 1.2 to 2.4 percent of the population. By 2005, half the U.S. population will be 50 years of age or older (Health and Human Services 1987; Thorson 1985; Davenport 1986).

2. *Earlier retirement.* When people had to work until they were physi-

cally unable to do so, leisure pursuits were rare and reserved mainly for the wealthy. But now it is becoming common for many adults to retire early, which has resulted in more opportunities for various leisure activities. Elderly people now have many different ways in which they can spend their time (American Association of Retired Persons 1987).

3. *Improved health status.* Currently, elderly people enjoy better health than they did in previous generations. This improvement opens the door to activities that would not have been possible before. A notable change during recent decades has been the shift from acute to chronic health problems (U.S. Congress 1987; Thorson 1985; Davenport 1986).

4. *Increased time available to old people for leisure activities, including educational and recreational participation.* In recent decades the work week has become shorter, while vacation and sick-leave provisions have been liberalized. In addition, some work roles become less important as aging occurs, such as professional work and activities that require great expenditures of physical energy (American Association of Retired Persons 1987). On the other hand, during this same period many of the elderly experience increased opportunities for both formal and informal learning and leisure activities with their families. It is not uncommon that these activities are influenced and encouraged by family members and take place in a family-related setting.

5. *Higher levels of formal education.* The level of formal education in our society is rising (Thorson 1985). As this happens, it seems likely that there will be more educational participation by senior citizens. The relationship between level of formal education and adult-education participation has been substantiated by numerous research studies, some of which are mentioned later in this chapter.

Elderly people constitute a major underserved adult population in American society. Various professions have begun to recognize this and to take into account the impact of the aging process on participants and prospective participants (Davenport 1986). As a result, there have been increases in programs to serve the elderly and increases in available financial resources. Unfortunately, these changes have not been followed by proportionate increases in formal educational and recreational participation by the elderly. Swaim (1983) called for a response to this situation characterized by less "programming zeal" and more "reasoned understanding." This is more likely to happen as more and better research becomes available.

This chapter reviews the research on leisure among the elderly. The first section examines types of activities that the elderly participate in and factors related to their participation. The second part section is a discussion of educational involvement and the social influences related to it. The discussion (1) identifies some of the problems for which help is needed from the research and educational community; (2) provides examples of research findings that can be useful to older people, to their families, and to professionals; and (3) gives suggestions for future research.

Leisure Activities

Types of Activities

Some research shows that older people are less likely than younger people to participate in activities such as sports and socializing but are more likely to watch television, to be involved in gardening, to sleep, or to do nothing (Harris and Associates 1975). Even so, Harris and Associates found that younger people tend to overestimate these passive activities of the elderly, as do people 65 and over when quizzed about the activities of their peers.

Riley and Foner (1968) identified some of the same leisure activities among the elderly in their earlier research: television, gardening, visiting, and reading were the major activities. Osgood (1986) found significant differences in leisure participation by age. Compared with other age groups, the older people in the study had higher levels of religious attendance, television watching, neighboring, and friendship participation.

Moss and Lawton (1982) observed the following activities among the elderly, listed in order of the greatest amount of time spent in each: watching television, rest and relaxation, reading, and family interaction. They found that most of the elderly spend much of their time in sedentary and solitary activities. McAvoy (1979) found that five activities most frequently participated in by the elderly are: visiting friends and relatives, watching television, reading, gardening, and indoor hobbies. Interestingly, McAvoy's research found that walking is the preferred activity, although television viewing is more frequently participated in by the elderly. Perhaps this is due to the physical limitations some of the elderly experience.

Extent of Participation

Typically, older people spend more time in leisure activities than do people in the middle years (Riley and Foner 1968). Some researchers have suggested that the reason the elderly do not participate in more active leisure pursuits is their lack of familiarity with many different kinds of activities; they feel incompetent or embarrassed about their participation (Atchley 1988; Miller 1965).

There is some evidence for constant declines by age in leisure participation, except for solitary activities (Gordon et al. 1976). (It should be noted that the Gordon et al. [1976] study is a cross-sectional study rather than a longtitudinal study.) There is also some evidence that males are more active than females, except in activities linked to gender roles (Gordon et al. 1976). This does not seem to hold for men and women in young and middle adulthood, however (Freysinger and Ray 1987).

Some Consequences of Leisure Activities

Edwards and Klemmack (1973) and Graney (1975) found that individuals who are active have higher levels of life satisfaction. Individuals who participate in leisure activities (taking walks, gardening, reading, playing cards, watching television, doing exercise) do not remain in hospitals as long as those who do not (Nichols et al. 1987). The work of Chambre (1987) suggested that activity is an effect of life satisfaction rather than a cause.

Those who participate in active forms of leisure report significantly greater energy, self-mastery, satisfaction, and motivational levels. Studying exercise and aesthetic types of leisure activities, Windsor et al. (1987) found that bicyclists had the lowest fatigue and highest activity scores. Within the aesthetics group, on the other hand, golfers had the greatest leisure satisfaction.

Of course, there is substantial evidence that exercise, a type of leisure activity, results in improved health (Birren 1972; Frekany and Leslie 1975; Kline 1973). Usui et al. (1986) reported that visiting with friends and the number of memberships in voluntary associations also have indirect effects of life satisfaction because of increases in self-esteem (Mann and Nelson 1986).

Social Class and Leisure Activities

The use of leisure time varies according to social class. For example, Havighurst (1961) collected data on leisure activities from a sample of elderly people in Kansas City. He found that those in the upper-middle class favored flower and landscape gardening, as well as participation in sports and voluntary associations. On the other hand, lower-middle-class and lower-class people preferred television and such things as home repairs and woodworking. Members of the lower-middle and upper-lower classes were fond of fishing. The lower-lower class ranked visiting friends and relatives along with vegetable gardening as their favorite leisure activities.

A number of other variables are also reflected in leisure activities, such as age, sex, attitudes toward aging, the availability of transportation services, the kind of recreational activity, the availability of recreational facilities, the distance from residence, and the person's interests. Finally, involvement in leisure activities reflects the state of an individuals health (Gordon et al. 1976; Schmitz-Scherzer 1976; Videbeck and Knox 1965).

Leisure and the Family

Most of the research dealing with leisure in the family looks at the family in the middle of the family life cycle rather than at the end of it. Probably the most outstanding monograph dealing with leisure in terms of the family life cycle is that by Rapoport and Rapoport (1975). According to this study, people who are motivated are preoccupied with various kinds of needs. These preoccupations may be translated into interests, and these interests may be translated into various activities. During the last years of their lives, in the period following retirement, people are concerned with a realignment of commitments that focuses on at least a couple of interests: forging a sense of integration in life and finding new meanings in life. By their mid-seventies, elderly people are preoccupied with life before death.

The relationship between leisure and the family may be similar to the the relationship between retirement and the family. Hatch (1987) suggested that although occupational circumstances are important in influencing retirement attitudes, family roles are also important. The influence of family roles on quality of life in retirement seems to differ for women and men. Research on the impact of leisure activities on the family is needed. Perhaps the key issue is not leisure per se, but the impact of complementary roles on the leisure activities of the elderly.

Dorfman and Heckert (1987) found that retired rural couples participate in a large number of joint leisure activities. Bosse et al. (1987) compared differences in stress and support among 766 workers and 741 retirees in the following areas: finances, marriage, social relations, health, and work and retirement. They found significant differences in all areas except for stress in marriage. They also found a decrease in social support among retirees.

Education

Education for the aging has expanded in recent decades. Similarly, a rapidly growing group of elderly and their families constantly looks for answers to solve the problems they face in everyday living. These people have needed, and continue to need, a source of helpful information. Specifically, they need answers from a bank of tested knowledge about the education of older people.

Many efforts have been made by researchers to provide those answers, but much remains unanswered. A continuing review needs to be made of the changes that take place over the lifetime of adults to identify areas in which research and education can be useful.

Perhaps the most significant contribution that research has made to the field of education of older adults is to provide evidence that it can be productive and beneficial. A decline in learning ability is not a necessary part of normal aging. Rather, a general slowing down occurs with increased age, and a possible impairment of the sensory processes important to many learning activities. Physical health and motivation to learn become increasingly important variables with advancing age. Continued study of these and other variables related to learning by people in this age group is needed (Botwinick 1973; Knox 1977a, 1986; Peterson 1983).

The potential of education for assisting the elderly includes the following:

1. *It can provide coping skills to meet practical challenges of daily living.* The growing complexity of our society makes educational participation by the elderly an attractive strategy for them, for their families, and for their caregivers. An example of a program designed to assist these people would be a nutrition education effort (Mitic 1985). Courses can also be made available that reflect other felt needs and developmental tasks of older adults. It has been customary in many agencies serving the elderly to conduct surveys asking them what kind of programs or services they would like. If this is done well, it can be a fruitful method for obtaining ideas that would enhance programs and make them more appealing to the target audience. The subject matter of such courses needs to reflect the ever-widening range of individual differences among adults as they grow older.

A variation on this traditional approach (Leclerc, 1985) has been suggested that would include a three-step process designed to help the elderly to (1) focus on their life situation and to discover signs of unhappiness or ill-functioning, (2) express what they would like to be, to do, or to know, and (3) identify the educational activities that correspond best to their needs. The wisdom of finding some new approach for needs assessment and reaching the target audience is evident in the fact that it is not uncommon that courses suggested by prospective students in community surveys are, in fact, currently available. Either the adults are unaware of them, or the needed motivation does not exist for them to become involved.

2. *It can enhance personal enjoyment of leisure time.* Those who make the effort to include learning activities in their lives report satisfaction and rewards from such efforts. This satisfaction brings them back again and again for more educational activity. Evidence of this can be seen in the expanding enrollments in adult-education programs during recent decades. Those associated with these programs commonly believe that a benefit is produced for the individual and for society. Lindeman (1926/1961, 5)

expressed this by saying that a major purpose of adult education was "to put meaning into the whole of life." Brockett (1987) tested to see if this type of result actually did come from educational participation. He attempted to identify ways of using education to enhance the quality of life for older people. Specifically, he looked at the use of self-directed learning projects for this purpose. He found a positive relationship between readiness for self-directed learning and life satisfaction. He also found a similar relationship between previous educational activity and life satisfaction. However, after reviewing the work of others, he noted that there is a lack of agreement on the subject and proposed further study. Although his own research gave tentative support to the long-standing assumption of professionals, empirical data are still needed.

O'Connor (1987) looked at the purposes that older people had in enrolling in a college-level educational program and found that they are more likely than middle-aged students to have expressive rather than instrumental goals as their learning orientation. This investigator suggested that this type of research be conducted in different settings to identify the orientation of the students. What would be the results if the survey were taken at a senior center? At a public school adult-education program? At a church-sponsored program? In a door-to-door survey? It would be very useful to everyone involved in the administration of adult-education programs to know what the learning orientation of a particular target audience is.

Participation Rates Over the Life Cycle

As noted above, the response of the elderly to formal educational programs has been disappointing for some who have the responsibility to develop them for this age group. The societal changes of recent decades have not resulted in proportionate increases in formal educational participation by old people. Various studies have documented that much of the potential is still to be realized.

Johnstone and Rivera (1965) reported 9 percent of those aged 55 and older participated in educational programs during the previous year. Among those aged 70 and older, the participation rate dropped to 4 percent. In the survey conducted by Harris and Associates (1975), only 2 percent of the respondents were currently enrolled in continuing education programs. Cross (1981) concluded that between 5 and 10 percent of those aged 55 and older participated. A survey by the National Center for Educational Statistics revealed that only 3.1 percent of those aged 65 and older participated in educational programs (LaBuda 1987; Kay 1982).

These and other studies show that the involvement of older people in formal educational activities remains more of a potential than a reality. However, there is ample evidence that healthy older people have the ability to learn (McClusky 1971; Peterson 1983). Thus, the central questions for those who would encourage educational participation by the elderly are what older people want to learn and under what circumstances they will do so in formal settings. What are the barriers preventing their participation? Can the response of the past be changed? To what extent do adults with various characteristics experience heightened readiness to learn before, during, and after major role changes such as retirement? What are the main developmental processes that adults use to adapt to these role changes in their families, occupations, and communities? These are underlying questions for all who are concerned with this field (Knox 1987).

The relatively low participation rates of the past do not necessarily mean that they will be repeated in the future. Forecasters project moderate to substantial growth in the number of adults, including older adults, who enroll for educational courses in the 1990s. The aging of American society alone will make an important contribution to this growth (Crimmins and Riddler 1985). However, if trends of the past continue, enrollments of older adults will not keep up with those of younger adults. Hence, administrators will continue to look for effective ways to reach the older population.

The number of older people participating in formal educational programs may be discouraging to families, educators, and others who promote this type of activity. But one should be cautious about assuming that older people are not participating in learning simply because they do not enroll in large numbers for formal courses. A more complete review of what older people do shows that many of those nonparticipants are nevertheless actively engaged in self-directed learning projects. Tough (1971) and Hiemstra (1975b) suggested that adults actually increase their involvement in learning activities as they become older. This question needs careful study. It may be that with advancing age there is a general shift from institutional programs to self-directed activities. We need more information before we can make a final decision on this matter.

Since many elderly are unable to attend educational programs, self-directed learning is very attractive to them and to those who are trying to assist them. Brockett (1987) reviewed the research on the subject and concluded that about 70 percent of all adult learning activities are planned primarily by the learners themselves. Looking at this special kind of education, Hiemstra (1975b) found that 83 percent of his respondents had completed at least one learning project during the previous year. This information is much more encouraging than that related to participation in formal courses. A greater understanding of the use of self-directed learning projects by older adults would be enlightening. To what extent can adults with various characteristics become more self-directed in their learning activities? What types of learning activities will help adults to become more creative?

Correlates of Participation

In an attempt to understand better the educational participation of older adults, researchers have given a useful list of the correlates of participation. Some of these are barriers, while others are facilitators (Kerka 1986). Some of the common correlates that have been reviewed in the professional literature are the following:

> Personal, family, and home-related influences
> Cost
> Availability of opportunity
> Perception of the value of education
> Motivation and self-confidence
> Time and place

Some of these correlates are subject to influence by family, friends, and professionals, while others are fixed for all practical purposes. However, all are important in an individual's decision to participate, and all add understanding as to why some adults with a given set of characteristics will enroll for an educational program while others will not.

The socioeconomic status of a target audience can tell us much about its prospects of participation and its potential success in educational programs. It also suggests areas of needed research. For example, *formal education* is the characteristic most highly associated with educational participation (Holden 1958; Johnstone and Rivera 1965; London et al. 1963; Anderson and Darkenwald 1979). Previous education can contribute to interest, ability, access, encouragement, and reward for continuing education. But Hooper and March (1978) have cautioned that formal education alone does not predict educational participation; not even university training, either personally or by significant others.

Older students' current learning skills, both real and perceived, also have an impact on their willingness to enroll, as well as on their performance in an educational effort. They influence the perceptions that older adults have about access. Is a course out of their reach academically? Decades of time may have elapsed since their last participation, so they may feel uncertain about their chances for success. Unfortunately, some choose to refrain from trying rather than risk possible failure. Those who want to encourage participation can emphasize the educational value of the greater experience that older people bring to their learning activities. It has also proved helpful to make specific efforts to correct deficiencies in areas such as reading, note-taking, preparing for examinations, and the like.

When feasible, action research can give teachers and administrators specific information about students and their readiness to succeed. Such information will allow teachers to tailor the learning experiences to meet, as much as possible, the special needs of their clientèle. The potential for student satisfaction and program success can thus be enhanced.

There are other characteristics of older people that relate to their adult-education participation. For example, participation varies according to occupation, income, and community involvement. Videbeck and Knox (1965) concluded that the best single predictor of extent of participation is past participation.

Real or perceived access to educational programs is an important consideration. Access can be limited or enhanced by the teaching methods used, the health of the elderly, the program location, the availability of transportation, the funds to pay the cost of fees and transportation, and the adequacy of course offerings.

Peterson (1983) proposed program adjustments to accommodate the special needs of older adults, as follows: slower pacing, provision for vision and hearing problems, adequate recognition of physical, perceptual, and attitudinal changes that older adults experience, and the teaching methods that are best suited for this age group.

The preferred learning style of older adults can be considered by teachers, administrators, and families as programs are planned. Many teaching methods are available that reflect the diversity likely to be found in such groups. Good teachers in these situations seem to find ways to adapt their teaching to conform as much as possible to the preferred learning styles of the mature students (Davenport 1986). A useful research project could look at different instructional methods to see which ones are most effective in assisting older adults with various socioeconomic characteristics.

The relationship between health and participation has been reviewed by a number of researchers. Coe and Barnhill (1965) noted a moderate positive correlation between the degree of participation by elderly subjects and their perceived condition of health. Vision and hearing problems are especially challenging in an educational setting and can limit access or reduce the effectiveness and enjoyment of programs for older adults unless they are resolved in a satisfactory manner. Punch (1983) estimated that 24 percent of all persons between age 65 and 74 have some hearing loss. For those aged 75 and older, the rate increases to 39 percent. Special tuition rates, alternative scheduling, and special courses are not be very effective unless mature students enjoy the experience they have in the classroom.

If increasing numbers of older adults return to the classroom in future decades and if educators want to serve them effectively, full consideration must be given to those with losses, especially in hearing and seeing (Patterson and Berry 1987). To do otherwise would be to limit the benefit and satisfaction of many who attend and to reduce the real and perceived access for prospective students. Teachers of older adults would do well to acquaint themselves with strategies for minimizing the impact of hearing loss. Obviously, effective use of amplification equipment will help. Good management of the classroom environment will control background noises, the volume of speakers' voices, and the distance between teacher and students. A good research and demonstration project would identify specific steps that teachers and students can take early in the term to enhance hearing, seeing, and learning. In order to keep these limitations from discouraging enrollments, information needs to be communicated to prospective students about strategies that will be used to compensate for losses.

Ill health can reduce the access of older adults to formal educational programs from their earlier patterns of participation. As adults age, they experience more health constraints; the matter becomes increasingly more important with each passing year (Havighurst 1957a; Zborowski 1962; Knox 1977a). Videbeck and Knox (1965) found that health constraints increase with age and that upper-middle-class adults in their fifties and sixties reported fewer and different health constraints than adults in the same age range at lower social class levels. Bell and Force (1956) and Webber (1954) observed that older people in good health (and those from higher socioeconomic levels) tend to maintain and even to increase participation in formal associations after age 60. Teachers and administrators of adult programs could benefit from knowledge about the typical impact of various physical deficits on learning.

It is very clear that geographical accessibility is important in an older adult's decision to participate. Programs may also be inaccessible because of other perceived or actual barriers, such as informational, situational (for example, work or family responsibilities), and institutional (for example, inconvenient schedules or locations, high fees, or complicated registration procedures) (Darkenwald 1980). Miller (1967) and Boshier (1973) noted ways in which both facilitators and barriers combine to have an important impact on participation, including developmental tasks, sense of educational efficacy, and optimism about advancement (Havighurst and Orr 1956; Aslanian and Brickell 1980; Knox 1977a; London et al. 1963).

Among the many strategies that might be considered to meet these challenges are strategies to reach the older population in nontraditional ways. For example, educational programs might reach the elderly by way of radio, television, or telephone in their homes or in their nearby schools, churches, or senior centers. Those who hope to attract large numbers of elderly to community centers that are a great distance from their homes are likely to be disappointed. These strategies recognize the need to serve the elderly in locations convenient for them.

Glass and Smith (1985) examined the medium of television as a means of educational outreach for older adults. They observed that television can be a way to serve the elderly, or it can simply encourage them to be satisfied with passive, vicarious participation. There is real need for research to help educators use this medium in the most effective way, to reach the elderly in the most familiar locations possible, starting with their own homes. For example, it would help to know more about the viewing practices of the elderly. When is the best time to schedule programs for them? What is the most appealing format for such programs? What are their educational needs that can be served by television? What behavioral objectives would best satisfy these needs? How can cable television be used with them? It should prove helpful for administrators to remember that location and transportation are important in the access that the elderly have to formal programs. Many older adults lack adequate transportation and therefore are unable to get to program locations.

Social Influences

The opinions and activities of friends and relatives help explain the variation in participation rates (Bloom 1964; Robinson 1970). Older people who have friends and relatives with favorable opinions about education and who themselves participate are more likely to be participants.

Tierce and Seelbach (1987) proposed the use of elderly people as volunteers in the public schools. Such an arrangement would alleviate some economic problems, allow older people to serve as role models for the youth, possibly erase some of the common stereotypes of aging, as well as give older people an opportunity for involvement in meaningful roles. Reports about the arrangement from both the National School Volunteer Program and the Retired Senior Volunteer Program are favorable. One of the fringe benefits of such a program could be a more optimistic view of education on the part of the senior participants. Would contact with the educational system encourage the elderly to participate?

Covey (1982) found that nearly 87 percent of older attendees in college courses indicate that "spending time with others" is an important reason for their enrollment. Learning and intellectual growth are important considerations, but so is the chance to meet others.

Providing educational opportunities for the elderly in cooperation with other organizations such as professional, community, and church groups is a strategy used by many educational institutions. How to do this most effectively needs additional research.

There appears to be a continuing opportunity for families to help overcome the common barriers to participation such as health, motivation, transportation, social support, counseling, and the like. A family's encouragement may be effective. The family provides one of the few remaining places where intergenerational recreational and educational activities can take place in our age-segregated society. Research and pilot projects are needed. These projects might seek to identify the most innovative and effective examples of home learning centers for the entire family, including for the older generation. What types of learning objectives are best for intergenerational learning activities and what procedures facilitate the process?

Conclusions

It seems appropriate to emphasize again the potential importance of effective leisure activities and especially education for the elderly in the information society of the future. The increase in the number of elderly in the United States should combine with their higher level of formal education and rising expectations to change the low participation patterns of the past. Those who are concerned with research and evaluation in this dynamic field would do well to keep in touch with its growing body of professional literature. The potential research topics range from action-related questions to theory building.

Examples of past and prospective research have been given in this chapter in order to suggest ideas for the future. As U.S. demographics continue to change, the research community has the opportunity to keep others in the field abreast of them and what some of the implications of the changes are. The elderly of today are not the same as those of yesterday, and the elderly of tomorrow will not be the same as those of today. How can institutions of higher learning adapt to meet the changing circumstances? How can they serve middle-aged and elderly people better as the number of young people who enroll on campuses decreases? What can government at different levels do? What can families do? How can leisure activities be made more effective in the lives of the elderly? What is the optimal level of activity for the elderly at different ages? Would this level vary by gender role?

Research about the target audience of an institution can be a worthwhile ongoing project for researchers. Gutknecht (1986) noted the need for a continual flow of this type of information so that those in charge may make decisions on the basis of the most accurate information possible. Such research can help educators focus their research efforts.

The preparation of the research report deserves special attention. The quality of this report may well determine the extent to which the findings are made available to practitioners and, if appropriate, to the general public. Hiemstra (1987) made the following suggestions about the preparation of research reports:

1. List the potential implications.
2. Invite readers to make contact by mail or telephone to discuss the implications of the report.

3. Suggest ways in which readers can learn to read and understand such research reports better.

4. Talk with professional colleagues about research reports and their practical implications.

5. Seek appropriate public opportunities such as professional meetings to make formal presentations about research findings.

Finally, it is hoped that those involved with research projects and with the care of the elderly would be in regular touch with each other. Research findings that will help practitioners and the elderly must be communicated to the appropriate audiences, or much of their benefit is lost. Similarly, the most pressing current problems in the care of the elderly must be communicated to the research community as a guide for decisions about future topics.

References

American Association of Retired Persons. 1987. *A Profile of Older Americans*. Washington, DC: AARP.

Anderson, R. E., and Darkenwald, G. G. 1979. *Participation and Persistence in American Adult Education*. New York: College Entrance Examination Board.

Aslanian, C. B., and Brickell, N. H. 1980. *Americans in Transition: Life Reasons for Learning*. New York: College Entrance Examination Board.

Atchley, R. C. 1988. *Social Forces and Aging: An Introduction to Social Gerontology*. Belmont, CA: Wadsworth.

Bell, W., and Force, M. 1956. "Urban neighborhood types and participation in formal association." *American Sociological Review* 21:25–34.

Bloom, B. S. 1964. *Stability and Change in Human Characteristics*. New York: John Wiley and Sons.

Birren, J. E. 1972. "Time for active sports." *Retirement Living* 8:72–74.

Boshier, R. W. 1973. "Educational participation and dropout: A theoretical model." *Adult Education* 23:225–82.

Bosse R., Aldwin, C. M., Levenson, M. R., and Ekerdt, D. J. 1987. "Differences in social support among retirees and workers." Paper given at the 40th annual meeting of the Gerontological Society of America, Washington, DC.

Botwinick, J. 1973. *Aging and Behavior*. New York: Springer.

Brockett, R. G. 1987. "Life satisfaction and learner self-direction: Enhancing quality of life during the later years." *Educational Gerontology* 13:225–37.

Chambre, S. M. 1987. "Activity and life satisfaction: Unravelling causes and effects." Paper given at the 40th annual meeting of the Gerontological Society of America, Washington, DC.

Coe, R. M., and Barnhill, E. 1965. "Social participation and health of the aged." In A. M. Rose and W. A. Peterson (eds.), *Older People and Their Social World*. Philadelphia: F. A. Davis.

Covey, H. C. 1982. "Preliminary findings on designing higher education programs for older people." *Educational Gerontology* 8:463–71.

Crimmins, E. M., and Riddler, E. W. 1985. "College enrollment trends among the population thirty-five and older: 1972–1982 and projections to 2000." *Educational Gerontology* 11:363–85.

Cross, K. P. 1981. *Adults as Learners: Increasing Participation and Facilitating Learning.* San Francisco: Jossey-Bass.

Darkenwald G. G. 1980. "Continuing Education and the Hard-to-Reach Adult." In G. G. Darkenwald and G. A. Larson (eds.), *Reaching Hard-to-Reach Adults.* San Francisco: Jossey-Bass.

Davenport, J. A. 1986. "Learning style and its relationship to gender and age among Elderhostel participants." *Educational Gerontology* 12:205–17.

Dorfman, L. T., and Heckert, D. A. 1987. "Egalitarianism in retired rural couples: Household tasks, decision-making, and leisure activities." Paper given at the 40th annual meeting of the Gerontological Society of America, Washington, DC.

Edwards, J. N., and Klemmack, D. L. 1973. "Correlates of life satisfaction: A reexamination." *Journal of Gerontology* 28:497–502.

Frekany, G. A., and Leslie, D. K. 1975. "Effects of an exercise program on selected flexibility measurements of senior citizens." *The Gerontologist* 15:182–83.

Freysinger V. J., and Ray, R. O. 1987. "Activity involvement of women and men in young and middle adulthood: A longitudinal study." Paper given at the 40th annual meeting of the Gerontological Society of America, Washington, DC.

Glass, J. C., and Smith, J. L. 1985. "Television as an educational and outreach medium for older adults." *Educational Gerontology* 11:247–60.

Gordon, C., Gaitz, C. M., and Scott, J. 1976. "Leisure and lives: Personal expressivity across the life span." In R. H. Binstock and E. Shanas (eds)., *Handbook of Aging and the Social Sciences.* New York: Van Nostrand Reinhold.

Graney, M. J. 1975. "Happiness and social participation in aging." *Journal of Gerontology* 30:701–706.

Gutknecht, B. 1986. "Developing learning experiences for older adults." Paper presented at the conference of the Association of Teacher Educators, Atlanta, Georgia.

Harris, L., and Associates. *The Myth and Reality of Aging in America.* Washington, DC: The National Council on the Aging.

Hatch, L. R. 1987. "The influence of work and family on retirement." Paper given at the 40th annual meeting of the Gerontological Society of America, Washington, DC.

Havighurst, R. J. 1957a. "The leisure activities of the middle-aged." *American Journal of Sociology* 63:152–62.

Havighurst, R. J. 1957b. "The social competence of middle-aged people." *Genetic Psychology Monographs* 56:297–375.

———. 1961. "The nature and values of meaningful free-time activities." In R. W. Kleemeier (ed.), *Aging and Leisure.* New York: Oxford University Press.

———. 1972. *Developmental Tasks and Education.* New York: David McKay.

Havighurst, R. J., and Orr, B. 1956. *Adult Education and Adult Needs.* Chicago: Center for the Study of Liberal Education of Adults.

Hiemstra, R. 1975a. *The Older Adult and Learning.* Ames, IA: Department of Adult and Extension Education, Iowa State University.

————. 1975b. "The older adult's learning projects." *Educational Gerontology* 1:331–41.

————. 1987. "Turning research on older persons into daily practice." *Perspective on Aging* 16:17–19.

Holden, J. B. 1958. "A survey of participation in adult education classes." *Adult Leadership* 6:258–60.

Hooper, J. O., and March, G. B. 1978. "A study of older students attending university classes." *Educational Gerontology* 3:321–30.

Huyck, M. H., and Hoyer, W. J. 1982. *Adult Development and Aging.* Belmont, CA: Wadsworth.

Johnstone, J. W. C., and Rivera, R. J. 1965. *Volunteers for Learning.* Chicago: Aldine.

Kaplan, M. 1975. *Leisure: Theory and Policy.* New York: John Wiley and Sons.

Kay, E. R. 1982. *Participation in Adult Education in 1981.* National Center for Education Statistics. Washington, DC: U.S. Department of Education.

Kerka, S. 1986. "Deterrents to participation in adult education." Overview. ERIC Clearinghouse on Adult, Career, and Vocational Education, no. 59.

Kline, J. 1973. "Live it up and live longer." *Prevention* 25:107–108.

Knox, A. B. 1977a. *Adult Development and Learning.* San Francisco: Jossey-Bass.

————. 1977b. *Covert Research Needs Related to Systematic Learning by Adults.* Occasional Paper No. 4. Urbana-Champaign: University of Illinois.

————. 1986. *Helping Adults Learn.* San Francisco: Jossey-Bass.

————. 1987. "Reducing barriers to participation in continuing education." *Lifelong Learning* 10:7–9.

LaBuda, D. 1987. "Potential of computer technology is on the rise." *Perspective on Aging* 16(Jan-Feb):14–16.

Leclerc, G. J. 1985. "Understanding the educational needs of older adults: A new approach." *Educational Gerontology* 11:137–44.

Leitner, M. J., and Leitner, S. F. 1985. *Leisure in Later Life.* New York: Haworth Press.

Lindeman, E. C. 1926/1961. *The Meaning of Adult Education.* Montreal: Harvest House.

London, J., Wenkert, R., and Hagstrom, W. C. 1963. *Adult Education and Social Class.* Berkeley: Survey Research Center, University of California.

Mann, A. M., and Nelson, B. A. 1986. "Leisure and vitality in adulthood." Paper presented at the 39th annual meeting of the Gerontological Society of America, Chicago, IL.

McAvoy, L. H. 1979. "The leisure preferences, problems, and needs of the elderly." *Journal of Gerontology* 11:40–47.

McClusky, H. Y. 1971. *Background Report on Education.* Washington, DC: White House Conference on Aging.

Miller, H. L. 1967. *Participation of Adults in Education: A Force Field Analysis.* Syracuse, New York: Center for the Study of Liberal Education of Adults, Syracuse University.

Miller, S. 1965. "The social dilemmas of the aging leisure participant." In A. M. Rose and W. A. Peterson (eds.), *Older People and Their Social World*. Philadelphia: F. A. Davis.

Mitic, W. 1985. "Nutrition education for older adults: Implementation of a nutritional instruction program." *Health Education* 16:7–9.

Moss, M. S., and Lawton, M. P. 1982. "Time budgets of older people: A window on four lifestyles." *Journal of Gerontology* 37:115–23.

Murphy, J. R. 1975. *Recreation and Leisure Service*. Philadelphia: Lea and Febiger.

Nealinger, J. M. 1974. *The Psychology of Leisure*. Springfield, IL: C. C. Thomas.

Nichols, L., Barnes, L., Graney, M., Cloar, T., Blow, F., Ochs, M., and Strasburg, D. 1987. "Leisure activities and hospital outcome." Paper given at the 40th annual meeting of the Gerontological Society of America, Washington, DC.

O'Connor, D. M. 1987. "Elders and higher education: Instrumental or expressive goals?" *Educational Gerontology* 13:511–19.

Osgood, N. J. 1986. "Differential patterns of leisure participation by age: A preliminary analysis of data from a longitudinal community study." Paper given at the 39th annual meeting of the Gerontological Society of America, Chicago, IL.

Patterson, K., and Berry, V. 1987. "The older hearing-impaired student: Managing obstacles to learning." *Educational Gerontology* 13:505–509.

Peterson, D. A. 1983. *Facilitating Education for Older Learners*. San Francisco: Jossey-Bass.

Punch, J. 1983. "The prevalence of hearing impairments." *ASHA*:25–27.

Rapoport, R., and Rapoport, R. 1975. *Leisure and the Family Life Cycle*. London: Routledge and Kegan Paul.

Riley, M. W., and Foner, A. 1968. *Aging and Society*. Volume One: An Inventory of Research Findings. New York: Russell Sage Foundation.

Robinson, P. B., Jr. 1970. Differentiating socio-cultural characteristics of senior citizen participants in adult education activities in Utah County, Utah. Unpublished Ph.D. dissertation. Lincoln: University of Nebraska.

Schmitz-Scherzer, R. 1976. "Longitudinal change in leisure behavior of the elderly." *Contributions to Human Development* 3:127–36.

Swaim, C. R. 1983. "Educational and cultural programs for the older person: A caveat." *Gerontology and Geriatrics Education* 3:193–99.

Thorson, J. A. 1985. "Future trends in education for older adults." In R. H. Sherran and D. B. Lumsden (eds.), *Introduction to Educational Gerontology*. Washington, DC: Hemisphere.

Tierce, J. W., and Seelbach, W. L. 1987. "Elders as school volunteers: An untapped resource." *Educational Gerontology* 13:33–41.

Tough, A. 1971. "The Adult's Learning Projects." *Research in Education*. Series no. 1. Toronto: The Toronto Institute for Studies in Education.

U.S. Department of Health and Human Services. 1987. *Personnel for Health Needs of the Elderly Through the Year 2020*. Report to Congress. Washington, DC: U.S. Government Printing Office.

Usui, W. M., Himmelfarb, S. Z., and Murrell, S. A. 1986. "Activity, self-esteem, and life satisfaction." Paper given at the 39th annual meeting of the Gerontological Society of America, Chicago, Illinois.

Videbeck, R. W., and Knox, A. B. 1965. "Alternative participatory responses to aging." In A. M. Rose and W. A. Peterson (eds.), *Older People and their Social World*. Philadelphia: F. A. Davis.

Webber, I. L. 1954. "The organized social life of the retired: Two Florida communities." *American Journal of Sociology* 59:340–46.

Windsor, L. A., Gitlin, L. N., and Lawton, M. P. 1987. "Physically active elderly: A psychological profile." Paper given at the 40th annual meeting of the Gerontological Society of America, Washington, DC.

Zborowski, M. 1962. "Aging and recreation." *Journal of Gerontology* 17:302–309.

6
Faith Development of Men and Women over the Life Span

Marie Cornwall

Almost every study that examines the religiosity of men and women reports greater religiosity for women than men (Argyle and Beit-Hallahmi 1975; Carroll and Roozen 1975; Hoge and Carroll 1978; Caplow et al. 1983; de Vaus 1982, 1984; de Vaus and McAllister 1987). The findings are so consistent, it is surprising that so little attention has been given to identifying why the difference exists. While ex post facto explanations abound in the literature, there is insufficient evidence to support most of them. An age effect has also been demonstrated (Wuthnow 1976; Johnson et al. 1974; Moberg 1965), but no research to date has examined gender differences over the life course. Elderly women are frequently overrepresented in church congregations, but it is difficult to know how much of this overrepresentation is a function of differing levels of religiosity and how much is a function of woman's different mortality rates. Furthermore, new perspectives on gender differences imply differences over the life course due to the developmental tasks of men and women, but there is also an implied convergence in later stages (Gilligan 1986).

This chapter examines the source of gender differences in religiosity and suggests a direction for further research. Three questions are explored: (1) how much difference is there in the religiosity of men and women, (2) how much of the gender difference is due to religious socialization, how much to different levels of religious group association, and how much to different locations in the social structure, and (3) how does the religiosity of men and women differ across the life span?

Gender differences in religiosity are examined by partitioning the total effect of being female on six different measures of religiosity into its direct and indirect effects. Most of the gender difference is direct, although this finding may be due as much to the lack of better data needed to fully test our hypotheses. The data do suggest, however, that some of the effect is due to the indirect effect of differential religious socialization, to different levels of religious group association, and to different locations in the social structure. Distinctive patterns of male and female religiosity are also found across the age span and for different measures of religiosity, suggesting the need for more complex explanations for the gender gap in religiosity.

Theoretical Perspective

Religious Differences in Men and Women

The amount of difference in male and female religiosity varies according to the dimension of religiosity under study, according to religious group, and according to the year in which the data were collected. Gallup's (1985) surveys reported differences between men and women in church/synagogue membership (63 percent of men and 73 percent of women are members), in frequency of prayer (19 percent of men and 23 percent of women pray three times a day or more), and in level of spiritual commitment (9 percent of men and 12 percent of women scored very high on the spiritual commitment scale).

In a study of Australians, de Vaus and McAllister (1987) reported gender differences in four dimensions of religiosity. Using ten-point-scale measurements, they found that the least amount of difference was in religious experience (women scored only .5 points higher); that the most difference was in beliefs about heaven, hell, the devil, and sin (1.4 points difference); and moderate differences in the dimensions of commitment (.9) and church attendance (.8).

In an examination of religiosity among Canadians, Bibby (1987) found consistent gender differences but noted that the difference was not very large if age and education were controlled. He noted that college-educated women are only marginally more religious than college-educated men. Furthermore, he cautioned that despite gender differences, Canadian women can hardly be called devout since only about half remain religiously committed.

The gender difference also varies across religious group, with greater variation among Protestants, less variation among Catholics, and uncertain results among Jews. Lazerwitz (1970) reported that Jewish men are more religious than Jewish women. But Mueller and Johnson (1975) found higher religious participation among Jewish females.

Gender differences have varied slightly over time. In a series of Gallup surveys conducted since 1937, respondents were asked whether they believed religion could answer all or most of today's problems. In each survey, women were more likely to agree with the statement than men by a margin of 5 to 16 percent, depending upon the year the survey was conducted (Gallup 1985). In another study, de Vaus (1984) found that gender differences in church attendance varied over a 30-year period from a low of

5 percent to a high of 14 percent. Neither study found a consistent pattern over time, except that men's attitudes seemed to vary more over time than did women's.

Sources of Religious Differences in Men and Women

Any number of explanations have been offered to account for gender differences in religiosity. The most prominent include differential religious socialization, differences in patterns of group association, and different locations in the social structure.

Religious Socialization. It has generally been assumed that much of the gender difference in religiosity can be attributed to gender-role differences (Hoge and Roozen 1979). Being religious is said to come more naturally to women because the feminine attributes emphasized in Western society are more consistent with religious roles: gentleness, nurturance, submission, and conformity to social norms. In addition, women are more anxious and more affiliative—traits also congruent with traditional religious behavior (Argyle and Beit-Hallahmi 1975).

On the other hand, gender differences may also be a function of societal expectations. That is, women may be more religious because they are supposed to be more religious. Moreover, society gives women primary responsibility within the family for the religious socialization of children and for managing the religious environment of the home. These explanations may be correct, but no empirical evidence is available to test their viability. The study of religious differences has been limited to studies of sex differences, with little attention paid to gender identification. Furthermore, studies of role allocation among husbands and wives tend to ignore the distribution of religious roles within the family.

It has generally been thought that women play a vital role in the religious socialization of children. For example, in the Middletown studies (Caplow et al. 1983), it was found that almost all *men* whose mothers had no religious preference also reported no preference themselves (80 percent), but fewer than one-fourth of the *women* whose fathers had no religious preference had no preference themselves. Such findings support Freudian interpretations of a cross-sex association. However, a closer look at the data suggests an alternative explanation. In at least three-fourths of the families in which the mother reported no preference, the father also reported no preference. This means that almost all the young men who reported that their mothers had no religious preference also reported a father with no religious preference. The cross-sex effect may in fact be explained by a nonreligious home environment. When the mother has no religious preference, it is likely that there is little or no emphasis on religion in the family. When the father has no religious preference, the family may or may not give emphasis to religion.

The impact of religious socialization may be different for men than for women. If it is true that women are generally more conforming to societal expectations, then a religious home environment may be more essential for the religious development of a young man than it is for a young women.

Not enough is known about the differential effects of religious socialization on men and women. However, since socialization processes are an important factor in the religious development of an individual, it is hypothesized that other things being equal, the differences between the religiosity of men and the religiosity of women will disappear once the effect of religious socialization is taken into account.

Religious Group Association. Some have suggested that women are more religious simply because they are more likely to affiliate with religious groups. Gallup Poll data indicate that 63 percent of men and 73 percent of women are members of a church or synagogue, and that 12 percent of men and 7 percent of women report no religious preference. In the Middletown surveys (Caplow et al. 1983), 21 percent of the men and 12 percent of the women reported no religious preference, and there was a predominance of female worshippers in almost every religious preference category. Some of the gender difference in religiosity may be due to the tendency of women to affiliate with a church.

In addition to religious group membership, the type of associations one has within the religious group itself may have a significant effect on religious belief and commitment. This effect may vary depending upon whether the religious group is churchlike or sectlike. For example, research using data collected from Mormons has demonstrated a substantial association between the number of in-group friendship ties an individual has and measures of that individual's religious belief, commitment, and behavior (Cornwall 1987). The same research also suggests that belief and commitment are higher among those whose spouses are members of the same religious group. Furthermore, the effect may differ between men and women. For example, in the Middletown data, when a husband reported no religious preference, his wife also reported no religious preference about 50 percent of the time. But when the wife reported no religious preference, the husband reported no religious preference about 75 percent of the time (Caplow et al. 1983).

The differential effect of religious group association on religiosity suggests the hypothesis that, other things being equal, the differences in the religiosity of men and women will be removed once the effects of (1) religious affiliation and (2) whether one's spouse belongs to the same religious group are taken into account.

Social Location. Sociologists are most likely to turn to structural location theories to explain gender differences (de Vaus and McAllister 1987). Rather than look to psychological dispositions or differential socialization, they tend to posit that individuals' position in society and the roles they perform affect their religiosity. The three most common explanations for gender differences in religiosity due to structural location of men and women are deprivation theory, child-rearing theory, and labor force participation theory.

Deprivation theory is based on the assumption that people who are deprived or dispossessed look to religion as a means of compensation (Dittes 1971; Glock and Stark 1965; Stark and Bainbridge 1985). As explored in the literature, being female, being older, being divorced or never married, and being poor are all indicators of deprivation. Tests of deprivation theory do not support the thesis entirely, but the data do suggest that age, marital status, and socioeconomic status have an impact on religiosity. However, the effects of these variables differ depending on the dimension of religion under study. Whether the effects are due to real deprivation or perceived deprivation has yet to be established.

Child-rearing theory hypothesizes greater religiosity for women because they have primary responsibility for the religious education of their children. However, a competing theory suggests that the time-consuming task of raising children leaves little time for religious participation. A number of studies have tested the child-rearing theory (de Vaus 1982; de Vaus and McAllister 1987; Hoge and Polk 1980; Alston and McIntosh 1979). In every study, the results did not support the proposition. Although there appears to be an increase in the religious participation of women over the course of their childbearing years the same effect is also found for men. Both men and women's religious participation is higher when there are children in the home.

The labor force participation thesis, posits that as the labor force participation of women increases, their religiosity becomes more like that of men (Lenski 1953; Luckmann 1967; Martin 1967; Nelsen and Potvin 1981; Moberg 1962). The religiosity of working females, according to this theory, comes to resemble that of males more than that of females in the home. The logic behind this theory is not always clear. The labor force participation of women may be just another indication of the modernity and the accompanying trends of industrialization and specialization that naturally lead to secularization (Luckmann 1967). On the other hand, labor force participation may provide alternative sources of identity and fulfillment for women, or the time demands may preclude religious participation.

Research in the United States provides no support for the labor force participation thesis (de Vaus, 1984). But research in Australia found a significant difference in religiosity between women in the labor force and homemakers (de Vaus and McAllister 1987). Females working full time were found to be less religious than females who were full-time home-makers. Indeed, in this research females working full time actually attended church less than did males working full time.

The problem with the labor force participation theory is that it assumes that entering the labor force means the same thing for women that it does for men and therefore would have the same effect on their religiosity. Labor force participation does not really place women in the same structural location as men. Differentials in pay scales and status clearly remain, despite the increasing numbers of women who enter the labor force. Therefore, the effects of labor force participation on women's religiosity may be highly dependent upon the reasons why they enter the labor force, the type of job they have, and the amount of income they receive.

Based on past research, it appears that gender differences may be due in part to the effects of marital status, age, education, and labor force partici-pation. Men are more likely to be currently married, they do not live as long as women, they generally receive more education, and they are more likely to be in the labor force. Therefore, it may be hypothesized that the differences between the religiosity of males and that of females will be removed once the effects of marital status, age, education, and labor force participation are taken into account.

Religiosity of Men and Women over the Life Cycle

Ample evidence indicates that religiosity is related to life-cycle factors. The research shows a pattern of declining belief and activity during a person's teens and early twenties, followed by increasing levels of activity as the person reaches the late twenties and early thirties (Caplovitz and Sherrow 1977; Wuthnow and Mellinger 1978; Argyle 1958; Moberg 1965; Dittes 1969; Roozen 1980). Some have suggested that the decline in religious belief and activity in the late teens may be due to the secularizing influence of higher education (Caplovitz and Sherrow 1977; Wuthnow and Mellinger 1978). But more recent research suggests that much of the decline is due to family background and early socialization and to developmental issues of identity and commitment that confront people during adolescence and young adulthood (Albrecht et al. 1988).

The increases in religious belief and activity during the late twenties and early thirties seem to be associated with other life-cycle changes: with attainment of the childbearing and child-rearing ages, with the shouldering of adult status and responsibilities (employment, buying a home, and the like), and with subjective concerns associated with life-cycle differences, such as identity problems and worries about illness and death (Wuthnow 1976).

The literature also shows a modest decline in church/synagogue attendance—although not necessarily in private religious devotion—in the later stages of the life cycle. Johnson et al. (1974), for example, found that increased age has a positive and persistent relationship with belief, church loyalty, and practices of personal piety but a weaker relationship with congregational activity. Moberg (1965) reported that religious beliefs increase with age but that religious behavior outside the home (such as church attendance) decreases. Stark (1968) found that older cohorts scored higher on agreement with orthodox beliefs and private devotionalism, including reading and praying; however, this was not true of their church attendance. Finney and Lee (1977) concluded that when relevant controls are used in the analysis of the effect of aging on religion, "the effect of age . . . is limited to a small, positive influence on private devotional practices." Other than this small effect, age appeared to have little influence on religious participation.

The life-cycle effect is inherent in the structural location theory postulating that women are more religious during their childbearing and child-rearing years. As already mentioned, tests of the theory suggest similar effects for men. Most recently, de Vaus and McAllister (1987) examined gender differences over the life cycle with data collected from Australians. They concluded that as men and women move through the life cycle (single; married—no children; married—children in the home; and married—children left home), gender differences in religious orientation tend to decline. The greatest gender difference was found among single people, and the least among married persons whose children had left home. The presence or absence of children in the home did not seem to be an important factor influencing gender differences across the four religiosity measures they examined.

These findings raise important questions about the religiosity of men and women over the life cycle: Are the patterns similar for men and women? Is there more change for women than for men? As men and women grow older, is there a convergence in religiosity?

A relatively new approach to the study of religious change is found in the recently burgeoning field of faith development research (Fowler 1981; Fowler 1984; Stokes 1983). Drawing upon the developmental perspectives of Piaget (1965), Kohlberg (1976, 1981), and Gilligan (1979, 1982), Fowler attempted to describe religious change as it is related to the cognitive development of the individual. Differences in the faith development of women and men have not been explored as yet. But Gilligan's work suggested meaningful distinctions: if men and women must deal with different developmental tasks (achieving intimacy and attachment for men, achieving separateness and identity for women), then the consequences for religious development are significant (Gilligan 1986). Implicit in the theory is the assumption that men and women become more similar in later stages of the life cycle as they each resolve different developmental tasks. Therefore, gender differences may disappear as men and women grow older.

Methodology

The study was based on a combined sample ($n = 3,648$) from the 1983–87 NORC General Social Surveys. The survey sampled the adult, English-speaking, noninstitutionalized American population. The measures of religiosity in the survey were not ideal but provided sufficient insight to suggest directions for further research. Six were available. Information about (1) frequency of church attendance and (2) strength of religious preference were collected for all five years. Information about (3) frequency of personal prayer, (4) feeling close to God, (5) life after death, and (6) belief in the literal interpretation of the Bible were available for four of the five years.

The frequency of church attendance and personal prayer variables were measured on an ordinal scale. However, for the purposes of this study the categories have been recoded to simulate an interval scale measuring church attendance as number of times per year and prayer as number of times per week.

Measurement on other scales was ordinal as well, but in order to compare results across the several variables, the highest category of each variable was coded as equal to 100 and all other categories were coded as 0. This coding scheme increases interpretability, since the mean on each item then becomes the percent of respondents indicating that they (1) feel extremely close to God, (2) feel strongly about their religious preference, (3) believe in life after death (4) believe in the literal interpretation of the Bible (see table 6–1).

The measures of the religious socialization, religious group association, and social location variables are presented in table 6–2, along with their scoring and means. The limitations of secondary analysis are apparent in this list, particularly for measuring religious socialization and group association.

The religious socialization measures are limited to how frequently the respondent's father and mother attended church when the respondent was aged 16. The only other indicator of religious socialization is a question about the respondent's religious preference at age 16. This information was compared with the respondent's current religious preference, and the comparison was used as an indicator of the strength of religious socialization. It was assumed that if the respondent's current religious preference was the same as the respondent's religious preference at age 16, religious socializa-

Table 6–1
Religiosity Measures, Definitions, and Gender Differences

Variable	Definition	Means		Female-Male Difference	Standardized Difference
		Men	Women		
Church attendance	# of times per year	22.37	31.59	9.22	.29
Prayer	# of times per week	5.15	7.81	2.66	.52
Feel close to God	100 = feel "extremely" close 0 = feel "somewhat" close "not very" close "not at all" close "don't believe in God"	22.15	37.91	15.77	.34
Strength of religious preference	100 = "strong" 0 = "somewhat" not very strong" no religious preference	37.15	51.57	14.32	.29
Belief in life after death	100 = yes 0 = no, undecided	76.81	84.23	7.42	.19
Belief in Bible	100 = Bible "actual word of God" 0 = Bible "inspired but contains errors" "ancient book written by men"	32.84	46.49	13.65	.29

Table 6–2
Independent Variables, Definition, and Means

Total	Variable	Definition	Means Men	Women
Gender	1 = female; 0 = male	—	—	.57
Religious Socialization				
Same religion as in youth	1 = same; 0 = different	.69	.68	.69
Father's church attendance	# of times per year	30.88	33.78	32.53
Mother's church attendance	# of times per year	39.84	42.72	41.74
Religious Group Association				
Spouse same religion	1 = same; 0 = different	.45	.39	.42
Religious preference				
Liberal Protestant		.08	.08	.08
Moderate Protestant		.23	.25	.24
Black Protestant	1 = yes; 0 = no	.06	.08	.07
Conservative Protestant		.14	.16	.15
Catholic		.28	.26	.27
Jew		.03	.02	.02
Misc. religions		.07	.07	.07
Protestants—no denomination		.03	.04	.04
No preference		.08	.04	.06
Social Location				
Age	years	43.75	45.75	44.88
Formal education	# of years completed	12.82	12.40	12.58
Marital status				
Married		.62	.55	.58
Divorced	1 = yes; 0 = no	.11	.15	.13
Single/widowed		.27	.30	.29
Employment status				
full time		.67	.40	.52
part time	1 = yes; 0 = no	.08	.13	.11
full-time homemaker		.01	.33	.19
unemployed		.04	.01	.03
retired		.16	.10	.13
student, other		.04	.03	.02

tion was relatively intense and meaningful. Approximately the same proportion of men as women (69 percent) reported the same current religion as the religion of their youth. Women reported higher levels of church attendance for both their mothers and fathers than did men. This is not an uncommon occurrence (Cornwall 1988) and suggests a tendency for women to evaluate religiosity differently. There is little reason to suspect that men come from less religious families than do women.

The impact of religious group association was measured using the same categories suggested by Roof and McKinney's (1987) recent book on mainline religion. As in other studies, twice the number of men as women reported no religious preference (8 percent as opposed to 4 percent). Interpersonal associations within the same religious group are usually measured by asking the respondents how many of their five best friends belong to the same congregation. This information was not available in the data set. However, information about spouse membership was available. Forty-five percent of men reported that their spouse had the same religious preference. In contrast, only 39 percent of women did so.

Measures of social location included age, number of years of formal education, marital status, and employment status. As might be expected, the women were slightly older (by 2 years) and slightly less educated than the men. Sixty-two percent of the men were married, compared with only 55 percent of the women. The women were more likely to be divorced. Fifty-three percent of the women were currently working, although 13 percent of these were working part time. Thirty-three percent of the women were full-time homemakers. Sixty-seven percent of men were working full time.

The data analysis relied upon ordinary least squares regression. Regression estimates were used to evaluate differences in religiosity for men and women, controlling for the effects of all other variables in the model. For each regression model, the gender gap was estimated by first estimating the effect of being female and by then entering the other independent variables in blocks. The resulting change in the value of the regression coefficient for gender shows the indirect effect of the variables being entered at the particular time (Alwin and Hauser 1975). The direct effect of gender is the effect of gender that remains after all other variables have been entered into the model.

After exploring the direct and indirect effects of gender, another series of regression models was used to estimate gender differences over the life course. A second-degree polynomial regression was used to estimate the curvilinear effect of age, an effect suggested by the life-cycle literature (Kerlinger and Pehazur 1973). These regression models assumed a curvilinear age effect, different slopes for men and women (an age × gender effect), and differences in the curvilinearity of religiosity measures (age^2 × gender). Three additional variables were entered after all other variables: age^2, age × gender, and age^2 × gender. Hypothesis testing required both a significant t-value for the unstandardized coefficient and a significant change in R^2 in order to reject the null hypothesis of no effect.

Findings

Mean differences for the six religiosity measures are presented in table 6–1. As expected, the women were more religious on all six religiosity measures. Women attended church nine times more each year than men and prayed almost three times more per week. The percentage differences on each of the other belief items were approximately the same (a 16 percent difference in feeling close to God, and a 14 percent difference in strength of religious preference and in belief in the Bible as the actual word of God), but there was only a 7 percent difference in the proportion of men and women who believe in life after death. Although the women were generally more religious than the men, they were not highly religious as a group. Although 84 percent reported a belief in life after death, only half reported a belief in the Bible as the actual word of God (46 percent) or a "strong" identification with their religious preference (51 percent). On average, the women prayed about once a day, but only 22 percent reported that they felt "extremely" close to God, and as a group they attended church three out of every five weeks.

The amount of gender difference across the six measures of religiosity can best be measured by standardizing the difference. A standard measure of difference can be obtained by dividing the mean difference by the standard deviation of the variable. The resulting value is a measure of how many standard deviations of difference there are and is equivalent to the mean difference in standard scores for men and women. The standardized difference ranges from .19 to .52, an average of approximately one-third standard deviations. The greatest amount of difference was found in the frequency of personal prayer; the least amount of difference was found in belief in life after death.

An examination of the direct effect of gender is possible with regression analysis by removing the effects of differential religious socialization, religious group association, and social location. Table 6–3 presents the total effect of gender (the same effect presented in table 6–2) on line 1. The direct effect of gender is given on line 2. This is the remaining gender gap after all the variables in the equation have been taken into account. Line 3 shows the indirect effect, or the effect that can be attributed to other variables in the model. The total effect of gender on church attendance, for example, is made up of a direct effect of 6.62 (line 2) and an indirect effect of 2.60 for the other three variable sets (line 3).

The analysis suggests that much of the gender gap remains in each of the six models. For example, with all other variables entered into the model, the women attended church almost seven times more often each year than the men and prayed two times more per week. An average gender gap of .23 standard deviations remains across the six models. The gender gap appears to be much smaller for the two belief items (.15 and .16 for belief in life after death and in the Bible, respectively), compared with the other items. The largest gender gap is found in the frequency of personal prayer model (.40 standard deviations).

Gender difference, while significant, is really not very large in compari-

Table 6–3
Decomposition of Gender Effects for Six Measures of Religiosity

	Church Attendance	Pray	Feel Close to God	Strength of Preference	Belief in Life After Death	Belief in Bible
1. Total effect (lines 2+3)	9.22	2.66	15.77	14.32	7.42	13.65
	(.29)	(.52)	(.34)	(.29)	(.19)	(.29)
2. Direct effect	6.62	2.07	12.08	11.34	5.82	7.70
	(.21)	(.40)	(.26)	(.23)	(.15)	(.16)
3. Indirect effect (lines a+b+c)	2.60	.59	3.69	2.98	1.60	5.95
	(.08)	(.11)	(.08)	(.06)	(.04)	(.12)
a. religious socialization	1.07	.11	.71	1.30	.74	.59
	(.03)	(.02)	(.02)	(.03)	(.02)	(.01)
b. religious group association	.35	.15	.88	−.90	1.52	1.83
	(.01)	(.03)	(.02)	(.02)	(.04)	(.04)
c. social location	1.18	.33	2.10	2.57	−.66	3.53
	(.04)	(.06)	(.05)	(.05)	(.02)	(.07)
X̄	27.61	6.66	31.12	45.43	81.12	40.62
Standard deviation	31.42	5.16	46.31	49.80	39.14	49.12

son with the effects of other variables in the model. For example, in the church-attendance model the direct effect of being a conservative Protestant (31.48) is five times the effect of being female, and the effect of having a spouse who has the same religious affiliation (14.39) is twice the effect of being female (see table 6–4).

The decomposition of indirect effects is shown in lines a to c of table 6–3. The indirect effect of differential religious socialization seems to be the smallest. This may be due in part to inadequate socialization measures. It may also be, however, that distal effects are always of less significance than more recent effects. The indirect effect of religious group association differs depending upon the measure of religiosity under study. This is not a surprising effect, given differences in group norms and expectations regarding the various measures available. Note that the indirect effect of religious group association is greatest for the belief items (.04) and least for attendance (.01). The indirect effect of social location is the greatest across the six measures. However, as can be seen in table 6–4, the indirect effect of social location is not due to the effects of labor force participation. Employment status is not significant in any of the models, with the exception of strength of religious preference, where there is a small effect for full-time homemakers. Rather, the social location variables that reduce the gender gap are primarily education, age, and marital status.

Results of the test for a life-cycle effect differed depending upon the measure of religiosity used. The full model produced significant t-values and change in R^2 for attendance only (see figure 6–1). All things being equal, the attendance pattern for women is curvilinear, while the attendance pattern for men remains linear. The attendance patterns of young men and women do not differ very much, but there seems to be a fairly steady increase over the life cycle for women up until age 60, when attendance begins to decline.

The regression models for frequency of personal prayer and feeling close to God produce a significant change in R^2; however, the t-value for the age^2 × gender effect is not significant. This suggests a curvilinear effect of age for both men and women and an interaction effect for age and gender. Women report greater frequency of prayer than men over the entire life course (see figure 6–2). All other things being equal, young men and women are equally likely to feel "extremely close" to God. But the percent of women feeling "extremely close" to God increases at a much steeper rate over the life course until about age 60 (see figure 6–3).

Regression models for strength of religious preference and belief in the Bible produced nonsignificant change in the R^2 and t-values. The effect of age for both these models is apparently the same for both men and women, with women always slightly more religious.

The regression model for belief in life after death is perhaps the most

Table 6–4
Unstandardized Coefficients in Six Regression Models

	Attendance (N=3648)	Pray (N=2433)	Feel Close to God (N-3291)	Strength of Preference (N=2214)	Belief in Life After Death	Belief in Bible (N-2378)
Religious Socialization						
Preference same as in youth	−7.37*	−1.24*	−4.21	−3.03	−6.83	−3.73
Father's church attendance	.11*	.01*	.13*	.21*	.09*	.16*
Mother's church attendance	.16*	.02*	.12*	.11*	.06	.07
Religious Group Association						
Spouse name preference	14.39*	1.70*	9.0.*	20.63*	3.41	5.10*
Religious preference						
Liberal Protestant	15.51*	3.08*	10.87*	41.98	31.59*	6.60
Moderate Protestant	14.30*	3.11*	10.46*	31.91	31.49*	21.80*
Conservative Protestant	31.48*	4.46*	19.28*	46.04	34.31*	40.93*
Protestant—No denomination	16.32*	3.03*	12.15*	42.40	26.74*	20.66*
Black Protestant	24.31*	5.60*	28.87*	53.95	26.16*	40.38*
Catholic	22.55*	3.64*	10.80*	41.12	27.41*	5.25
Jew	4.99	1.58*	3.83	42.64	−8.90	−1.83
Misc. religions	29.60*	4.84*	17.00*	56.14	27.58*	16.49*
Social Location						
Sex	6.63*	2.07*	−12.08	11.34*	5.82*	7.70*
Education	.55*	−.06	−1.16*	.89	.16	−4.88*
Age	.19*	−.06	.46*	.38*	−.14*	−.10
Marital status						
Married	−7.39*	−1.45*	−9.30*	−15.78*	−3.03	−4.20
Divorced	−6.08*	−.51	−1.41	−9.51*	−5.99*	−3.02
Employment status						
Full time	−1.29	−.27	−.69	.94	−1.04	−2.48
Part time	.72	−.15	−.23	4.44	−.97	−3.14
Homemaker	1.99	.54	3.36	6.50*	−1.83	5.11
Constant	−17.36	−.01	.88	−40.76	55.79	79.48
R^2	.23	.26	.14	.13	.08	.25

*p = <.05

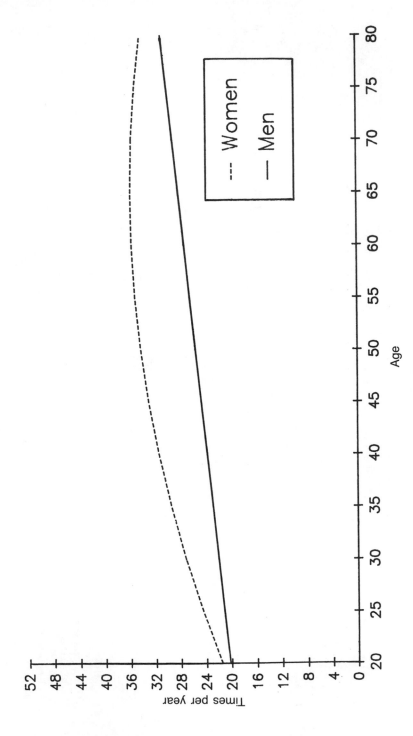

Figure 6–1. Frequency of Church Attendance

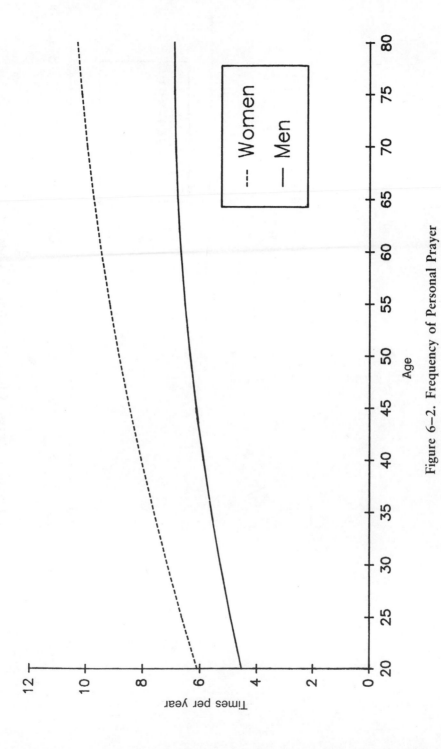

Figure 6–2. Frequency of Personal Prayer

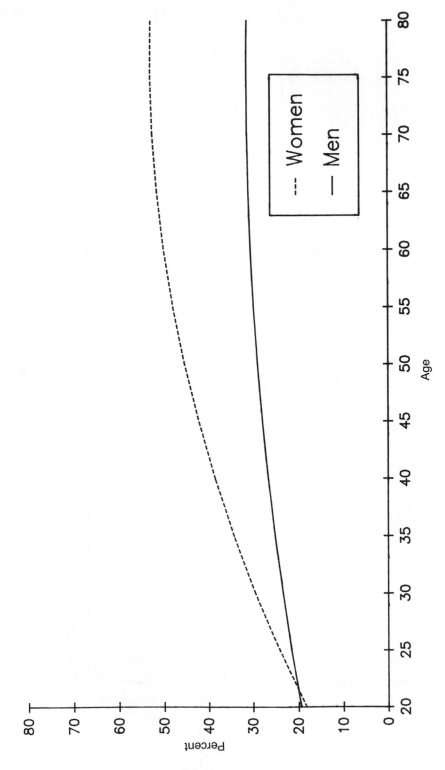

Figure 6–3. Percent Who Feel "Extremely Close" to God

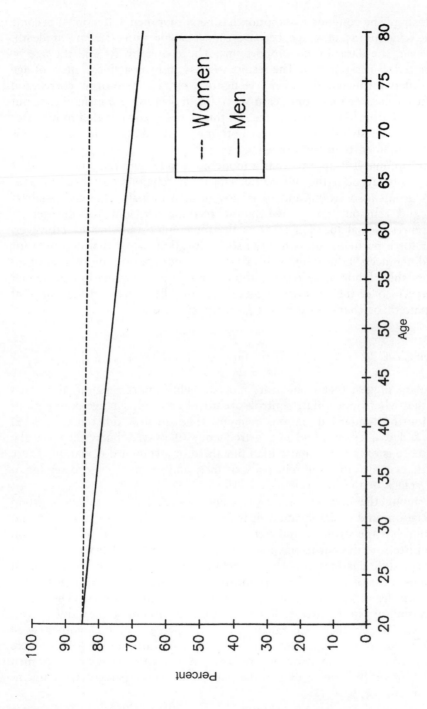

Figure 6–4. Percent Who Believe in Life after Death

surprising. The common assumption has been that men and women become more religious as they age because they become more fearful of death. However, the data do not support this. The change in R^2 and the age $\times$ gender effect is significant. The results suggest an inverse linear effect of age that differs for men and women (see figure 6–4). The zero-order correlation coefficient between age and death was -.02, indicating a nonsignificant but inverse relationship. It appears that all things being equal, belief in life after death declines slightly with age for both men and women, but the decline is greater for men than for women.

In summary, it appears that a moderate gender gap remains even after taking into account the differential effects of religious socialization, religious group association, and social location. Although religious socialization and religious group association account for some of the gender differences, social location remains the most important factor. However, labor force participation is not the social location factor that accounts for the differences. Education, marital status, and age are more important factors than labor force participation. Finally, an examination of gender differences over the life cycle suggests that the differences remain and that the pattern of change is different for men and women.

Discussion

The data suggest that women are indeed slightly more religious than men and that when appropriate controls are introduced, an average difference of one-fourth standard deviations remains. The greatest difference between men and women is found in the frequency of prayer, but even there the difference is only a little more than one-third of a standard deviation. There is little evidence that the religiosity of men and women is more similar at later stages of the life cycle.

Among the indirect effects of religious socialization, religious group association, and social location, it is apparent that for most models, social location has the strongest indirect effect. The significance of social location is consistent with conclusions made by de Vaus and McAllister (1987) but for very different reasons. They concluded that labor force participation explains most of the gender gap and that as people move through the life cycle, gender differences in religious orientation tend to decline. The inconsistent findings in the two studies may be a reflection of cultural differences. For example, in their Australian study, 23 percent of the women were working full time, 22 percent were working part time, and 4 percent were unemployed. By comparison, in the U.S. sample, 40 percent of the women were working full time, 13 percent part time, and 1 percent were unemployed.

De Vaus and McAllister (1987) gave three explanations for why labor force participation should have an effect on women's religiosity: (1) working provides a substitute for the sociopsychological benefits that individuals derive from religion and church involvement; (2) subordinate groups often adopt the values of dominant groups, and since female labor force participation does not imply equality, females will tend to modify their views toward those expressed by men in their workplace; and (3) labor force participation reduces the amount of discretionary time women have and therefore reduces time available for participation in religious activities.

The first explanation does not follow from current thinking in the sociology of religion literature, paying little attention to the function of religion in the modern world. Religion's primary function, of providing ultimate meaning and significance, cannot easily be replaced by labor force participation for either men or women (Yinger 1970; Stark and Bainbridge 1985). Futhermore, although it is true that women are subordinate in the labor force, they are also subordinate in almost all areas of life. If the second explanation were true, this generalized subordination ought to provide sufficient impetus for altering women's views consistent with the dominant culture, but it does not. Why would the impact of labor force participation be any greater? Finally, the third explanation, the lack of discretionary time for religious participation, can account only for church attendance and participation in a religious group. Yet women are still more likely then men to report a religious preference. De Vaus and McAllister (1987) need to look elsewhere for explanations about the effect of labor force participation on women's religiosity. Since working is not the norm for women in Australia, it may be that the effects of labor force participation are due to factors that influence a woman to work. For example, some religious groups emphasize the importance of women in the childbearing and child-rearing roles and discourage labor force participation. Perhaps the effects of labor force participation would be moderated if they controlled for the effects of religious preference.

Previous efforts to examine the effects of life-cycle variation on the religiosity of men and women have focused on stages in the family life cycle. The research has generally suggested that any life-cycle differences for both men and women are primarily a function of whether they have children and are concerned about socializing them properly. Since religion is the source of many cultural norms and expectations, it is thought that men and women might return to religious institutions in the process of raising their children.

This research has used age as a marker of change over the life course, which may or may not be a function of marriage and family responsibilities. It reflects a new focus on the study of adult development, particularly adult faith development, which suggests a significant association between age related developmental tasks, personality traits, and faith development (Stokes 1983; Conn 1986). The significance of this new perspective is that it recognizes that religious faith changes over the life course and that faith development is a dynamic process and therefore not necessarily linear.

Obviously, the patterns of religiosity presented in figures 6–1 through 6–3 could be due to cohort effects. The social change that has occurred in American society over the previous three or four decades could account for some of the differences. Data collected by Gallup (1985) suggest a decline in religiosity over these decades. However, it is also likely that not all of the differences are cohort differences and that patterns of men's and women's religiosity do differ over the life course.

It should be apparent by now that ex post facto explanations of gender differences in religiosity are not adequate. First, the differences may be exaggerated. Differences do exist, but once appropriate controls are introduced the already moderate differences are reduced even more. Second, studying the religiosity of men and women may require very different conceptual models. More attention needs to be given to religious socialization and religious group association. Although these factors were less able to explain the gender gap, the available measurements were insufficient to fully test the impact of religious socialization and religious group association. Third, empirical tests should take into account the differential effects of factors that are known to influence religiosity. This research has demonstrated the differential effect of age. Formal education may influence the religiosity of women very differently from the way it influences the religiosity of men. Separate conceptual models for men and women should be constructed and tested. Fourth, research on adult faith development should avoid the mistakes of other research, in which developmental models were created based on data collected from men only. The debate as to whether moral development is different for men and women still continues (Walker 1984; Lifton 1985), although generally the research has seemed to suggest that if differences exist, they are not very large. In the meantime, the study of gender differences in both religiosity and faith development can benefit from findings in the developmental literature, particularly on the importance of research designs that adequately explore differences between men and women.

The relevance of structural location to the study of gender differences appears fruitful. Other indicators of location in the social structure should be explored for their ability to explain gender differences. For example, network methodologies can be utilized as more specific measures of structural location than age, education, and marital status. As the work proceeds, however, attention must be given to the fact that being female by itself is an indicator of location in the social structure, and thus the gender difference may never be fully understood until the meaning of being female is fully explored both sociologically and psychologically.

References

Albrecht, S. L., Cornwall, M., and Cunningham, P. H. 1988. "Leaving Mormonism: Disaffection and disaffiliation." Forthcoming in D.G. Bromley (ed.), *Falling from the Faith: The Causes and Consequences of Religious Apostasy*. Beverly Hills, CA: Sage Publications.

Alston, J. P., and McIntosh, W. A. 1979. "An assessment of the determinants of religious participation." *Sociological Quarterly* 20 (Winter):49–62.

Alwin, D. F., and Hauser, R. M. 1975. "The decomposition of effects in path analysis." *American Sociological Review* 40:37–47.

Argyle, M. 1958. *Religious Behavior*. London: Routledge and Kegan Paul.

Argyle, M., and Beit-Hallahmi, B. 1975. *The Social Psychology of Religion*. London: Routledge and Kegan Paul.

Bibby, R. 1987. *Fragmented Gods: The Poverty and Potential of Religion in Canada*. Toronto: Irwin Publishing.

Caplovitz, D., and Sherrow, F. 1977. *The Religious Drop-outs: Apostasy among College Graduates*. Beverly Hills, CA: Sage Publications.

Caplow, T., Bahr, H. M., and Chadwick, B. A. 1983. *All Faithful People: Change and Continuity in Middletown's Religion*. Minneapolis: University of Minnesota Press.

Carroll, J. W., and Roozen, D. A. 1975. *Religious Participation in American Society: An Analysis of Social and Religious Trends and Their Interaction*. Hartford, CT: Hartford Seminary Foundation.

Conn, J. W. 1986. *Women's Spirituality: Resources for Christian Development*. New York: Paulist Press.

Cornwall, M. 1988. "The influence of three agents of religious socialization: Family, church, and peers." In D. L. Thomas (ed)., *The Religion and Family Connection: Social Science Perspectives*. Provo, UT: Religious Studies Center, Brigham Young University.

———. 1987. "The social base of religion: A study of factors influencing religious belief and commitment." *Review of Religious Research* 29:44–56.

DeVaus, D. A. 1982. "The impact of children on sex related differences in religiousness." *Sociological Analysis* 43:145–54.

———. 1984. "Workforce participation and sex differences in church attendance." *Review of Religious Research* 25:247–58.

DeVaus, D., and McAllister, I. 1987. "Gender differences in religion: A test of the structural location theory." *American Sociological Review* 52:472–81.

Dittes, J. E. 1969. "Psychology of Religion." In G. Lindzey and E. Aronson (ed.), *The Handbook of Social Psychology* (2nd ed., vol. 5). Reading, MA: Addison-Wesley.

———. 1971. "Conceptual deprivation and statistical rigor: Comment on 'Social deprivation and religiosity.' " *Journal for the Scientific Study of Religion* 10(Winter):393–95.

Finney, J. M., and Lee, G. R. 1977. "Age differences on five dimensions of religious involvement." *Review of Religious Research* 18:173–79.

Fowler, J. W. 1981. *Stages of Faith: The Psychology of Human Development and the Quest for Meaning*. San Francisco: Harper and Row.

————. 1984. *Becoming Adult, Becoming Christian: Adult Development and Christian Faith*. San Francisco: Harper and Row.

Gallup, G. 1985. *Religion in America: Fifty Years, 1935–1985*. Princeton, NJ: Gallup.

Gilligan, C. 1979. "Woman's place in man's life cycle." *Harvard Educational Review* 49(November):431–46.

————. 1982. *In A Different Voice: Psychological Theory and Women's Development*. Cambridge, MA: Harvard University Press.

————. 1986. "In a different voice: Visions of maturity." In J. W. Conn (ed.), *Women's Spirituality: Resources for Christian Development*. New York: Paulist Press.

Glock, C. Y., and Stark, R. 1965. *Religion and Society in Tension*. Chicago: Rand McNally.

Hoge, D. R., and Carroll, J. W. 1978. "Determinants of commitment and participation in suburban Protestant churches." *Journal for the Scientific Study of Religion* 17(June):107–27.

Hoge, D. R., and Polk, D. T. 1980. "A test of theories of Protestant Church participation and commitment." *Review of Religious Research* 21:315–29.

Hoge, D., and Roozen, D. R. 1979. "Research on factors influencing church commitment." In D. R. Hoge and D. A. Roozen (eds.), *Understanding Church Growth and Decline, 1950–1978*. New York: Pilgrim Press.

Johnson, A. L., Brekke, M. L., Strommen, M. P., and Underwager, R. C. 1974. "Age differences and dimensions of religious behavior." *Journal of Social Issues* 30:43–67.

Kerlinger, F. N., and Pehazur, E. J. 1973. *Multiple Regression in Behavioral Research*. New York: Holt, Rinehart and Winston.

Kohlberg, L. 1976. "Moral stages and moralization: The cognitive-developmental approach." In T. Lickona (ed.), *Moral Development and Behavior: Theory, Research and Social Issue*. New York: Holt, Rinehart, and Winston.

————. 1981. *The Philosophy of Moral Development*. San Francisco: Harper and Row.

Lazerwitz, B. 1970. "Contrasting the effects of generation, class, sex, and age on group identification in the Jewish and Protestant communities." *Social Forces* 49:50–58.

Lenski, G. E. 1953. "Social correlates of religious interest." *American Sociological Review* 18:533–44.

Lifton, P. D. 1985. "Individual differences in moral development: The relation of sex, gender, and personality to morality." *Journal of Personality* 53:306–34.

Luckmann, T. 1967. *The Invisible Religion*. New York: Macmillan.

Martin, D. 1967. *A Sociology of English Religion*. London: SCM Press.

Moberg, D. O. 1962. *The Church as a Social Institution*. Englewood Cliffs, NJ: Prentice-Hall.

————. 1965. "Religiosity in Old Age." *The Gerontologist* 5:78–87.

Mueller, C. W., and Johnson, W. T. 1975. "Socioeconomic status and religious participation." *American Sociological Review* 40(December):785–800.

Nelsen, H. M., and Potvin, R. H. 1981. "Gender and regional differences in the religiosity of protestant adolescents." *Review of Religious Research* 22:268–85.

Piaget, J. 1965. *The Moral Judgment of the Child*. New York: The Free Press.

Roof, W. C., and McKinney, W. 1987. *American Mainline Religion: Its Changing Shape and Future*. New Brunswick, NJ: Rutgers University Press.

Roozen, D. R. 1980. "Church dropouts: Changing patterns of disengagement and reentry." *Review of Religious Research* 21:427–50.

Stark, R. 1968. "Age and faith: A changing outlook or an old process." *Sociological Analysis* 29:1–10.

Stark, R., and Bainbridge, W. S. 1985. *The Future of Religion: Secularization, Revival, and Cult Formation*. Los Angeles: University of California Press.

Stokes, K. 1983. *Faith Development in the Adult Life Cycle*. New York: Sadlier.

Walker, L. J. 1984. "Sex differences in the development of moral reasoning: A critical review." *Child Development* 55:677–91.

Wuthnow, R. 1976. "Recent patterns of secularization: A problem of generations?" *American Sociological Review* 41:850–67.

Wuthnow, R., and Mellinger, G. 1978. "Religious loyalty, defection, and experimentation: A longitudinal analysis of university men." *Review of Religious Research* 19:234–45.

Yinger, M. 1970. *The Scientific Study of Religion*. London: Macmillan.

Part II
Family Relationships

In Part II, chapters with specific relevance to the family are presented. Although in one sense they still involve transitions, in another sense they are more directly related to the family.

First, the relationships of older married couples are discussed in chapter 7. The research dealing with stage models of individuals points out that the developmental tasks of the adult of 30 or 40 are different from those of the adult of 60 or 70; so, too, marriages that have lasted many years are different from those of a short duration. Special reference is made in this chapter to couples who have been married fifty years, the golden wedding. Their analyses of their own marriages are particularly enlightening.

There have always been grandparents, but there have not always been as many of them as there are now. Within the past several years, over forty states have passed legislation dealing with the visitation rights of grandparents with their grandchildren following the divorce of the children of the grandparents. These new laws reflect the importance and, in a sense, the redefinition of the grandparental role. In chapter 8 the available research on grandparenthood is reviewed.

Another familial relationship that has had greater impact recently is the relationship between elderly parents and their adult children, the subject of chapter 9. Once again, there have always been elderly parents whose children were adults and even middle-aged adults. But there have never been so many of them. In the past, elderly parents were cared for in the homes of their adult children more than is the case today. Now, apparently, elderly parents want to retain their independence. Their adult offspring are utilized more and more as insurance, turned to if there are no other alternatives.

A different kind of emphasis on the family is seen in the chapter 10. There, research is reported dealing with the current interest in genealogy. In most cases, those family members interested in their family's genealogy are attempting to establish linkages to a very broad extended family—certainly not to a residential family, since most of these extended family members are deceased. Except among the nobility, establishing such linkages has not been of a great deal of interest to most until recently.

7
Older Married Couples

Spencer J. Condie

As life expectancy has increased, so have the proportion of the population over age 65 and the number of elderly couples (U.S. Bureau of the Census 1987). Even with the relatively high divorce rates, it is estimated that one in every five first marriages will survive at least 50 years (Glick and Norton 1977; Brubaker 1985).

There have been scores of studies on marital relationships among young couples but relatively few studies of marital relationships in later life (Treas and Bengtson 1987). This chapter examines the marital relationships of 54 couples who have been married fifty years or more.

Four major areas are studied, after a review of the research. First, the marital satisfaction of elderly couples is explored. Second, disagreement and conflict among these couples and how they are managed is assessed. Third, how these couples divide up their household labor is discussed. Finally, the general life satisfaction of these couples and its correlates are examined.

Review of the Research

One of the major issues in the study of family life is how marital satisfaction changes over time. The results of half a century of research on this issue have been inconclusive. Tuckman and Lorge (1954), Blood and Wolfe (1960), Glass and Wright (1977), Luckey (1966), Paris and Luckey (1966) and Safilios-Rothschild (1969) reported declining marital satisfaction over time among the respondents in their respective studies. By contrast, Gass (1959), Deutscher (1964), and Glenn (1975) indicated that, if anything, marital satisfaction tends to increase throughout the family life cycle. Pineo (1961, 1969) concluded that marital satisfaction remains at rather stable levels throughout the course of married life and that most marriages are characterized by no change, regardless of whether their initial level of satisfaction was rather high or very low. Others have observed a curvilinear relationship between marital satisfaction and the various stages of the family life cycle (Terman 1938; Bossard and Boll 1955; Axelson 1960; Gurin et al. 1960; Stinett et al. 1970; Rollins and Feldman 1970; Burr 1970; Stinnett et al. 1972; Rollins and Cannon 1974; Smart and Smart 1975; Orthner 1975; Condie and Doan 1978; Schram 1979, Anderson et al. 1983; see also Spanier et al. 1975). Miller's (1976) research revealed variation on this theme with bimodal peaks of satisfaction within an overall curvilinear trend. This trend is characterized by a diminution of satisfaction during the intermediate stages and a resurgence of satisfaction during the final stages that approximated the level of satisfaction enjoyed during the initial stages.

Longitudinal data are needed to resolve these inconsistent findings. Most of the existing studies have used cross-sectional data, but cross-sectional cohorts in the later stages of the family life cycle may be merely the satisfied survivors while the dissatisfied dropouts are excluded from analysis. Nevertheless, a majority of the recent studies indicate a curviliear relationship between stage of life cycle and marital satisfaction (Treas and Bengtson 1987).

The existing research suggests that elderly couples tend to have more positive interactions and less negative sentiments than younger couples do (Treas and Bengston 1987). Perceptions of fairness are greater in couples at the later than at the earlier stages of the life cycle. Loyalty and commitment appear to be important elements in sustaining marriages over a long period (Treas and Bengtson 1987).

The overall life satisfaction of elderly couples tends to be very high (Brubaker 1985; Sporakowski and Hughston 1978; Treas and Bengtson 1987). In a study of forty couples who had reached their golden wedding anniversary, Sporakowski and Hughston (1978) asked them to retrospectively report the most and least satisfying periods of their lives. The childbearing, preschool, and aging periods were described as the most satisfying periods, while childbearing, launching, and the middle years were perceived to be the least satisfying. It is interesting that the childbearing period is listed in both categories, indicating the strains and satisfactions that accompany parenthood.

The current research shows that there is considerable sharing of household and leisure activities among elderly couples. Companionship is a key element, and conflict tends to be managed by accommodation and "give and take" (Brubaker 1985). There is also evidence that general life satisfaction is related to health as well as to marital satisfaction (Atchley and Miller 1983; Brubaker 1985).

In a study of long-term marriages, Lauer and Lauer (1987) cited commitment as one of the most important reasons for marital stability. Being one's spouse's best friend, liking one's spouse as a person, agreement on life goals, humor, playfulness, and good conflict management skills were characteristics that distinguished happily married couples from unhappily married couples.

Sample and Methods

Like Sporakowski and Hughston (1978) in their study of forty golden wedding couples, the present study began with the collecting of newspaper announcements of married couples living within one county in a western state who were celebrating their golden wedding anniversaries in the very near future. During a period of four months a list of fifty-eight couples who had been married at least 50 years was accumulated. Letters were sent to them describing the proposed study and soliciting their participation in a two-hour tape-recorded interview about their marriage experiences. Fifty-four of these couples, residing within eight different cities, agreed to be interviewed.

At the conclusion of each interview the couples were prevailed upon to respond to a 110-item questionnaire that requested a wide range of demographic information, several scale items regarding life satisfaction, items regarding marital satisfaction during each stage of the family life cycle, a detailed account of their current health status, an account of the division of labor within their home, and information on time spent in leisure pursuits, including relationships with friends and relatives.

Each of the couples had been married during the Great Depression. Without exception, all of them referred back to those early years of marriage as an extremely challenging period of time. Notwithstanding those economically trying times, 43 percent of the wives and 52 percent of the husbands had received at least some education or technical training beyond high school. Ten percent of the women and 13 percent of the men were college graduates.

Among the couples in our sample, one was childless and another was infertile but had adopted children; at the other end of the continuum was a couple who had reared ten children. The average number of children per family was 3.7.

Regarding the aggregate sources of their current income, the couples indicated that one-fourth came from individual retirement programs, fully one-half came from Social Security, one-fifth came from savings and investments, and the remaining 5 percent came from current part-time employment and other sources.

Measurement of Variables

Because questions regarding marital satisfaction during earlier life stages might be subject to selective repression or retention, three alternative techniques to measure marital satisfaction over time were used. The first measurement technique involved having the respondents indicate on a graph the level of their marital satisfaction throughout all stages of their family life cycle. The eight stages of the family life cycle were equidistantly dispersed along the abscissa (the horizontal x-axis), with increments ranging from 0 to 20 distributed along the ordinate (the vertical y-axis). Respondents were requested to mark a dot indicating their degree of marital satisfaction during each stage.

The second measurement technique involved a set of eight items mapped to each respective stage of the life cycle. Respondents were asked to indicate on a seven-point scale, ranging from "very unhappy" to "very happy," the degree of happiness they had experienced (1) before their first child was born; (2) before any children were in school; (3) when their oldest children were still in grade school, and (8) when they celebrated their golden wedding anniversary.

The third method of triangulating the concept of marital satisfaction was a replication of an approach taken previously in a cross-sectional sample of married couples (Condie and Doan 1978). Respondents were given the following instructions: "Let us assume that you could reflect your satisfaction and happiness with your marriage by different numerical values at different stages of your family life. Assume that a value of 100 indicated that you were extremely happy and a score of 0 indicated that you were extremely unhappy. Values can range anywhere between 0 and 100 with higher scores indicating greater satisfaction. What score would you assign to your marriage when . . . (1) You were newly married with no children; (2) Your oldest child was about 3 years old . . . (8) You began approaching your Golden Wedding."

Conflict was measured by asking the respondents about the degree of consensus that they had shared on the performance of activities associated with the roles of spouse and parent. The couples were asked to indicate the degree to which they had always been in agreement with regard to seven different activities within their marriage (1) when they were first married, (2) when their oldest children were in their teens, and (3) currently. These seven activities included: (1) social and recreational activities, (2) relationships with friends, (3) religious activities, (4) ways of dealing with in-laws, (5) demonstrations of affection, (6) doing household tasks, and (7) handling family finances. The couples were also asked a series of questions about division of labor, general life satisfaction, current activities, and how they managed conflict.

Findings

Marital Satisfaction

All three measures of marital satisfaction showed a curvilinear relationship with stages of the life cycle. For the sake of brevity, only the findings from the third scale are presented here, shown in figures 7–1 and 7–2.

Figure 7–1. Marital Satisfaction of Wives throughout the Family Life Cycle

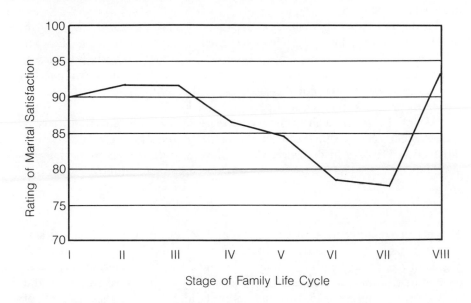

Stage of Family Life Cycle

Figure 7–2. Marital Satisfaction of Husbands throughout the Family Life Cycle

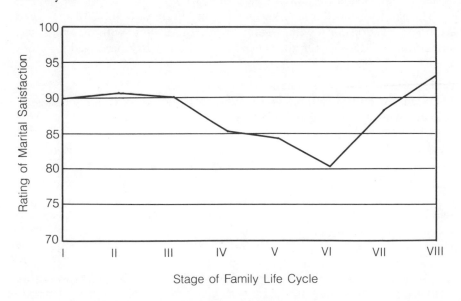

Stage of Family Life Cycle

For the wives, marital satisfaction began to wane during their childrens' transition from preschool age to entering school, and it continued to decline until the present stage, at which time they indicated an exponential increase in marital satisfaction.

Husbands also experienced a decline between the third and fourth stages of the family life cycle. However, their satisfaction began to increase as their children began to leave home. During the in-depth interviews, several of the wives identified this launching period as the most painful stage of their family life. For their husbands, this same stage was frequently a time of greater economic and personal freedom.

As noted earlier, much of the recent research also indicates that there is a curvilinear relationship between the stage of the life cycle and marital satisfaction (Treas and Bengston 1987). Several different researchers using different indicators have observed a similar curvilinear pattern.

Disagreement

The perceived agreement of husbands and wives on various activities is shown in table 7–1. The wives indicated a rather marked curvilinearity in degree of agreement, with a dramatic decline during the intermediate years on five of the seven activities in question. Only with regard to social and recreational activities and to doing household tasks did their degree of agreement increase monotonically over time. Without exception, the degree of agreement during the current stage of marriage far surpassed the degree of agreement during the initial stages of marriage.

Husbands revealed a curvilinear relationship on only three of the seven activities: relationships with friends, ways of dealing with in-laws, and doing household tasks. On the other four activities they perceived a mono-

Table 7–1
Percentage of Husbands and Wives Who "Always Agreed" on Various Activities During Three Different Stages of Marriage (in percent)

	First Married		Children in Teens		Currently	
	H	W	H	W	H	W
Social and recreational activities	17	15	26	16	43	38
Relationships with friends	38	29	21	24	44	42
Religious activities	57	58	62	54	68	70
Ways of dealing with in-laws	36	35	29	28	50	50
Demonstrations of affection	40	42	43	28	66	50
Doing household tasks	32	30	30	31	57	47
Handling family finances	40	40	51	38	70	63

tonic increase in degree of agreement with their wives from the beginning of their marriage to the present time.

Through the wide-ranging interviews, it was interesting to observe that, even in the best and longest of the marriages, universal agreement on all issues at all times was seldom a reality. Marriage was almost always a continual process of negotiation, conciliation, and construction of shared reality (see Brubaker 1985; Brubaker 1983).

Conflict Resolution

Pretest interviews indicated the wisdom of obtaining in-depth qualitative data in lieu of employing a quantitative instrument for assessing the effectiveness of various methods of conflict resolution. After half a century of matrimony, many couples had arrived at a process of mutual accommodation whereby their current relationship was almost devoid of major, enduring unresolved conflicts. The overwhelming majority of the couples insisted that both the frequency and intensity of their disagreements had decreased appreciably throughout the years. Not a single couple denied having ever experienced conflict within their marriages, but some had been more successful than others in resolving those differences. The specific methods of conflict resolution varied considerably, as indicated in the following illustrative vignettes.

Blowing Off Steam. Several couples indicated that the unfettered ventilation of emotions had been their preferred modus operandi for resolving differences early in their marriages, but most conceded that this had given way to milder conciliatory means. One of the wives confessed, however, that after trying for years to curb her sharp temper, she had concluded that "it is better for my blood pressure if I blow up and get rid of the feelings, so lately I do. I don't try to hold it in like I used to."

Alternating Anger. Half a dozen couples had achieved a measure of connubial détente through a solemn contractual agreement that "both of you not get angry at the same time." As one man described it, "If she gets mad, I'm calm enough I can hold my head and not say something I'd been sorry of, and vice versa. If I get mad, she is smart enough not to get angry too." His wife readily agreed: "It is not good for two hotheads to be together. One of you has got to stay calm."

Talking It Out. Many of the couples indicated that during the early months of marriage, the "silent treatment" was the fastest avenue to peaceful coexistence, but through years of living together they had become more adept at communicating their concerns. There were, nevertheless, a handful of couples who confessed that they are still unable to talk through their problems as easily as they would like.

One husband described a cooperative method of confronting interpersonal problems: "Well, some of the things we didn't do right. We kinda bottled them up. Then when we found out that you had to talk these things out and iron 'em out. Why, from then on you start to live a better life, that's all."

His wife agreed: "If you don't talk 'em out, you never get 'em settled. You've got to say what you think, and he's got to say what he thinks, without getting mad at each other. And that's the only way you can work any of these problems out."

Division of Labor

The 108 people in our study had been reared during an era of very well-defined demarcation between traditional female and male responsibilities within the household. One female respondent almost ecstatically expressed her joy at the current blurring of lines between stereotypical sex roles. She said, "I admire a lot of the young husbands of today in the way they do help their wives and children. It just pleases me every time I go into the grocery store and I see a young man in there doing the shopping with the baby on his back or in the cart, because you didn't see that in our day. And I think that should be a tremendous boon to families, when the husband is sharing responsibilities in rearing the children."

As men reduce their work involvement and retire, they tend to become somewhat more involved in housework (Keith and Schafer 1986). Parron and Troll (1978) observed a strong tendency among golden wedding couples to increasingly share household duties. Keith and Brubaker (1979, 50) suggested that involvement in household roles may ease the transition from work to retirement and be beneficial for self-esteem. However, preretirement patterns in division of labor tend to continue after retirement, and women continue to have the primary responsibility for household tasks (Keith and Schafer 1986). For example, Albrecht et al. (1979) observed that the degree of sharing household tasks was not significantly higher for older couples in comparison with younger married couples.

The household division of labor among the golden wedding couples is shown in table 7–2. Mowing the lawn and repairing things around the house were done almost exclusively by the husbands. Cooking, washing dishes, and cleaning were done much more by the women than by the men, although in about one-fourth of the couples the husbands and wives shared equally in getting breakfast and doing the evening dishes. Finances tended to be handled by both equally, although men were somewhat more involved than women. Grocery shopping also tended to be shared equally, although the women were somewhat more involved than the men.

Table 7–2
Current Division of Household Labor (in percent)

	Husband Always		Husband More Than Wife		Husband and Wife Equally		Wife More Than Husband		Wife Always	
	H	W	H	W	H	W	H	W	H	W
Grocery shopping	4	9	24	17	28	34	30	23	13	17
Getting breakfast	9	9	4	9	26	22	24	20	37	41
Doing the evening dishes	0	2	2	4	27	28	31	21	40	45
Straightening up living room when company comes	0	2	0	0	18	15	42	26	40	57
Mowing the lawn	95	85	5	5	0	8	0	2	0	0
Repairing things around the house	69	62	24	22	7	13	0	2	0	0
Keeping track of finances	24	15	17	26	28	23	20	15	11	21
Calling on someone to say blessing on the food	74	57	11	28	4	11	7	2	4	2

General Life Satisfaction

There has been a considerable amount of research on general life satisfaction among the elderly (Caspi and Elder 1986; Larson 1978; Spreitzer and Snyder 1974; Neugarten et al. 1961). General life satisfaction is a more inclusive category than marital satisfaction and has often been measured by the Life Satisfaction Index (LSI) developed by Neugarten et al. (1961). During the past quarter-century this scale has been modified to some degree, but it is still a widely used research instrument (Stock et al. 1986).

The LSI-A, an alternate form of the Life Satisfaction Index, contains twenty items with responses on a five-point scale, ranging from "strongly agree" to "strongly disagree." The following are examples of items on the LSI-A scale:

> These are the best years of my life.
> Most of the things I do are boring or monotonous.
> As I look back on my life, I am fairly well satisfied.

The items were factor analyzed to determine unidimensionality, and factor loadings for each respective item were then used as weightings for the responses to each item.

As shown in table 7–3, the most frequent activities among both men and women were working around the house and yard, watching television, and relaxing and taking it easy. Reading was also a common activity for these couples.

Table 7–3
Relationship Between General Life Satisfaction and Time Spent in Typical Weekly Activities

Daily or Weekly Activities	Wife Average Hours	r	Husband Average Hours	r
Watching television	13.2	.06	13.2	.13
Reading	9.7	.10	8.8	.32*
Visiting friends	4.0	.05	4.8	.15
Church-related activities	5.3	.35*	6.6	.24
Visiting children and grandchildren	8.1	.24	6.3	.22
Hobbies and recreation	7.6	.35*	7.0	.36*
Working around the house and yard	20.3	.19	12.6	.21
Relaxing and taking it easy	10.4	−.30	13.7	−.36
Working for pay	.2	**	3.6	.20
Other miscellaneous activities	1.5	**	1.5	**
Total	78.1		79.9	

*$p = .05$
**Too few cases to meaningfully compute

The general life satisfaction scores were correlated with time spent in various activities to determine if some types of activities were related to satisfaction. The results are shown in table 7–3. For women, the activities that were most strongly and positively correlated with general life satisfaction were church-related activities ($r=.35$), hobbies and recreation ($r=.35$), visiting children and grandchildren ($r=.24$), and working around the house and yard ($r=.19$). For men, those activities were hobbies and recreation ($r=.36$), reading ($r=.32$), church-related activities ($r=.24$), visiting children and grandchildren ($r=.22$), and working around the house and yard ($r=.21$).

Relaxing and taking it easy was inversely correlated with general life satisfaction for both women ($r=-.30$) and men ($r=-.36$). Although relaxing and taking it easy may appear to be deserved and rewarding, it was the *least* fulfilling activity they engaged in and tended to be related to low life satisfaction.

Correlates of General Life Satisfaction

With each couple, sources of satisfaction throughout various stages of the family life cycle were discussed. Sources of satisfaction were grouped into four categories: (1) family and friends, (2) general lifestyle, (3) leisure activities, and (4) life in general. Then correlations were computed between general life satisfaction and each of these categories to determine what areas were most important for general life satisfaction. The results are presented in table 7–4.

Among both men and women, satisfaction with standard of living and financial status had moderately strong correlations with general life satisfaction. Having satisfying hobbies and recreation was also correlated significantly with the general life satisfaction of both men and women. Satisfaction with past accomplishments was related to the general life satisfaction of the men but not the women. Similarly, satisfaction with their daily routine and spare time was correlated significantly with general life satisfaction among the men but not among the women.

When asked to reveal their greatest source of happiness, the vast majority of couples focused upon times the children had been all home together. This reaction is congruent with the observations of Sporakowski and Hughston (1978, 325), who found in their study of forty golden wedding couples that the most satisfying periods of life were the childbearing stage, the preschool stage, and the present stage. However, as shown in table 7–4, the couples' *current* relationships with their children and grandchildren elicited only a very modest correlation with life satisfaction for both wives and husbands. Geographic distances between children and grandchildren may tend to suppress large positive correlations between amount of interaction with them and life satisfaction.

Table 7–4
Correlates of General Life Satisfaction

	Wives r	Husbands r
Family and Friends		
Children	.18	.34
Grandchildren	.24	.13
Friendships	.15	.28
General Lifestyle		
Standard of living	.56*	.38*
Neighborhood	.16	.03
Financial status	.48*	.52*
Leisure Activities		
Hobbies-recreation	.42*	.46*
Daily routine	.34	.50*
Spare time	.24	.46*
Transportation	.09	.31
Life in General		
Past		
accomplishments	.27	.48*
Physical condition	.29	.27

*$p < .01$

With regard to current friendships, many couples observed that they had simply outlived most of their childhood friends or had moved too far away from them to maintain close contact. Thus, correlations between general life satisfaction and relationships with friends were only $r = .15$ for wives and $r = .28$ for husbands.

About two-thirds of the couples were "very satisfied" with their current standard of living. According to their self-reports, all the respondent owned their own homes, no matter how humble. For nearly half of them, however, home ownership was something of a mixed blessing. Only half (57 percent) of the husbands and wives (52 percent) were "completely satisfied" with the neighborhood within which they resided. For some, the demands of yardwork and home maintenance often exceeded their level of energy. For others, the increasing utility bills to be paid on a fixed income left much to be desired. Still others had a nostalgic feeling for the "old neighborhood" before these "newer families" moved in with their noisy motorcycles and teenagers with blaring radios.

Forty-two percent of the men and 30 percent of the women were very pleased with their available spare time and the way in which it was invested. General daily routine was moderately related to life satisfaction for women ($r = .34$) and quite strongly related for men ($r = .50$).

Looking back upon a lifetime spanning more than seven decades, past accomplishments were much more strongly correlated with general life satisfaction for husbands ($r = .48$) than for their wives ($r = .27$). The dramatic difference in these proportions may be indicative that many home-makers mistakenly assumed that being "just a mother" of four children was not a particularly significant accomplishment.

Health and physical well-being were increasingly important factors with the encroachment of age. Half the men and only 28 percent of the women were "very satisfied" with their current physical condition. It was apparent that health status becomes an increasingly important intervening variable with each passing year.

Summary and Conclusion

Fifty-four couples who had celebrated their golden wedding anniversary were interviewed regarding their marital satisfaction throughout the family life cycle, their methods of conflict resolution, their household division of labor, and their current sources of life satisfaction. Life respondents in several studies conducted during the past decade, these couples revealed a curvilinear trend in marital satisfaction over time. Marital satisfaction declined during the intermediate stages and then experienced a resurgence during the latter stages of the life course.

Although the frequency and intensity of conflicts had diminished over time, the methods they employed in the resolution of conflict included blowing off steam, alternating streaks of anger between spouses, the "silent treatment," and talking through differences. Their household division of labor appeared to be structured along traditional lines, with women doing much more of the cooking and cleaning while men mowed the lawn and fixed things. However, sharing domestic duties was common, and there was a relatively strong degree of interdependence.

Their participation in hobbies, recreation, and church activities was related to general life satisfaction for both husbands and wives. However, "just taking it easy" was inversely related to general life satisfaction. Satisfaction with standard of living was also correlated with general life satisfaction.

In examining the lives of fifty-four couples who had been married for half a century, it became apparent that the theoretical constructs "marital satisfaction" and "life satisfaction" are phenomenological chameleons, ever-changing amid a plethora of dynamic external realities.

Perhaps one reason family researchers are still at odds regarding the nature of marital satisfaction throughout the course of a marriage is that they persist in applying the same methodological instruments to the measurement of marital satisfaction long after the marriage has undergone its metamorphosis from the empty nest of the newlyweds to the empty nest of mature grandparents.

Perhaps researchers would be better advised to adopt a Hegelian dialectical approach to marriage, in which couples are seen as undergoing a dynamic transition from being inexperienced, isolated newlyweds, to becoming noncouples in parenthood, and then eventually arriving at a synthesis as couples once again. The antithetical stage—practicing parenthood—is so completely different from the initial thesis and the final synthesis that treating marriage as a phenomenon of eight sequential stages may cause many of the conceptual subtleties of the family life cycle to be overloaded.

Instead of concentrating their conceptual efforts upon marital and general life satisfaction, perhaps it would be better for researchers to focus upon the *social and emotional growth and psychological resilience* that couples acquire during and after the challenges of parenthood. Moreover, satisfaction scale scores begin to diminish when chronic illness and unrelenting pain take their toll. It this stage it may be indelicate and even insensitive to speak of "marital satisfaction." Perhaps it would be best to speak of "enduring love."

Additional research on marital relationships among the elderly is needed, particularly assessments of changes over time. The present research suggests that the leisure, health, and financial status of elderly are important correlates of satisfaction that need further study. One surprising finding was that relationships with friends and family are not highly correlated with life satisfaction. The role of the family in the satisfaction of elderly couples needs more intensive study.

References

Albrecht, S. L., Bahr, H. M., and Chadwick, B. C. 1979. "Changing family and sex roles: An assessment of age differences." *Journal of Marriage and the Family* 41:41–50.

Anderson, S. A., Russell, C. S., and Schumm, W. A. 1983. "Perceived marital quality and family life-cycle categories: A further analysis." *Journal of Marriage and the Family* 45:127–39.

Atchley, R. C., and Miller, S. J. 1983. "Types of elderly couples." In T. H. Brubaker (ed.), *Family Relationships in Later Life*. Beverly Hills: Sage Publications.

Axelson, L. J. 1960. "Personal adjustment in the postparental period." *Marriage and Family Living* 22:66–68.

Blood, R. O., Jr., and Wolfe, D. M. 1960. *Husbands and Wives*. New York: Macmillan.

Bossard, J. H. S., and Boll, E. S. 1955. "Marital unhappiness in the life cycle of marriage." *Marriage and Family Living* 17:10–14.

Brubaker, T. H. (ed.) 1983. *Family Relationships in Later Life*. Beverly Hills, CA: Sage Publications.

———. (ed.) 1985. *Later Life Families*. Beverly Hills, CA: Sage Publications.

Burr, W. R. 1970. "Satisfaction with various aspects of marriage over the life cycle: a random middle class sample." *Journal of Marriage and the Family* 32:29–37.

Caspi, A., and Elder, G. H., Jr. 1986. "Life satisfaction in old age: linking social psychology and history." *Journal of Psychology and Aging* 1:18–26.

Condie, S. J., and Doan, H. 1978. "Role profit and marital satisfaction throughout the family life cycle." *Journal of Comparative Family Studies* 9:257–67.

Deutscher, I. 1964. "The quality of post-parental life." *Journal of Marriage and the Family* 26:52–59.

Gass, G. Z. 1959. "Counseling implications of woman's changing role." *Personnel and Guidance Journal* 37:482–87.

Glass, S. P., and Wright, T. L. 1977. "The relationship of extramarital sex, length of marriage, and sex differences on marital satisfaction and romanticism: Athanasiou's data reanalyzed." *Journal of Marriage and the Family* 39:691–703.

Glenn, N. D. 1975. "Psychological well-being in the post-parental stage: some evidence from national surveys." *Journal of Marriage and the Family* 37:105–10.

Glick, P. C., and Norton, A. J. 1977. "Married couples and living together in the U.S. today." *Population Bulletin* 32:1–39.

Gurin, G., Verhoff, J., and Feld, S. 1960. *Americans View Their Mental Health.* New York: Basic Books.

Keith, P. M., and Brubaker, T. H. 1979. "Male household roles in life: a look at masculinity and marital relationships." *Family Coordinator* 28(4):497–02.

Keith, P. M., and Schafer, R. B. 1986. "Housework, disagreement, and depression among younger and older couples." *American Behavioral Scientist* 29:405–22.

Larson, R. 1978. "Thirty years of research on the subjective well-being of older Americans." *Journal of Gerontology* 33:109–25.

Lauer, R. H., and Lauer, J. C. 1987. "Factors in long-term marriages." *Journal of Family Issues* 7:382–90.

Luckey, E. B. 1966. "Number of years married as related to personality perception and marital satisfaction." *Journal of Marriage and the Family* 28:44–48.

Miller, B. C. 1976. "A multivariate development model of marital satisfaction." *Journal of Marriage and the Family* 38:643–657.

Neugarten, B. L., Havighurst, R. J., and Tobin, S. S. 1961. "The measurement of life satisfaction." *Journal of Gerontology* 16:134–43.

Orthner, D. K. 1975. "Leisure activity patterns and marital satisfaction over the marital career." *Journal of Marriage and the Family* 37:91–102.

Paris, B. L., and Luckey, E. B. 1966. "A longitudinal study in marital satisfaction." *Sociology and Social Research* 50:212–22.

Parron, E. M., and Troll, L. E. 1978. "Golden wedding couples: effects of retirement on intimacy in long-standing marriages." *Alternate Lifestyles* 1:447–64.

Pineo, P. C. 1961. "Disenchantment in the later years of marriage." *Marriage and Family Living* 23:3–11.

Pineo, P. C. 1969. "Development in the later years of marriage." *Family Coordinator* 18:135–40.

Rollins, B. C., and Cannon, K. 1974. "Marital satisfaction over the family life cycle: a re-evaluation." *Journal of Marriage and the Family* 36:271–82.

Rollins, B. C., and Feldman, H. 1970. "Marital satisfaction over the family life cycle: a re-evaluation." *Journal of Marriage and the Family* 32:20–28.

Safilios-Rothschild, C. 1969. "Family sociology or wives' family sociology? A cross-cultural examination of decision making." *Journal of Marriage and the Family* 31:290–301.

Schram, Rosalyn W. 1979. "Marital satisfaction over the family life cycle: A critique and proposal." *Journal of Marriage and the Family* 41:7–12.

Smart, M. S., and Smart, R. C. 1975. "Recalled, present, and predicted satisfaction in stages of the family life cycle in New Zealand." *Journal of Marriage and the Family* 37:408–15.

Spanier, G. B., Lewis, R. A., and Cole, C. L. 1975. "Marital adjustment over the family life cycle: the issue of curvilinearity." *Journal of Marriage and the Family* 37:264–75.

Sporakowski, M. J., and Hughston, G. A. 1978. "Prescriptions for happy marriage: Adjustments and satisfactions of couples married for 50 or more years." *Family Coordinator* 27:321–27.

Spreitzer, E., and Snyder, E. E. 1974. "Correlates of life satisfaction among the aged." *Journal of Gerontology* 29:454–58.

Stinnett, N., Carter, L. M., and Montgomery, J. E. 1972. "Older persons' perceptions of their marriages." *Journal of Marriage and the Family* 34:665–70.

Stinnett, N., Collins, J., and Montgomery, J. E. 1970. "Marital need satisfaction of older husbands and wives." *Journal of Marriage and the Family* 32:428–34.

Stock, W. A., Okun, M. A., and Bennin, M. 1986. "Structure of subjective well-being among the elderly." *Journal of Psychology and Aging* 1:91–102.

Terman, L. M. 1938. *Psychological Factors in Marital Happiness*. McGraw-Hill.

Treas J., and Bengtson, V. L. 1987. "The family in later years." Pp. 625–48 in M. B. Sussman and S. K. Steinmetz (eds.), *Handbook of Marriage and the Family*. New York: Plenum Press.

Tuckman, J., and Lorge, I. 1954. "Old people's appraisal of adjustment over the life span." *Journal of Personality* 22:417–22.

U.S. Bureau of the Census. 1987. *Statistical Abstract of the United States: 1988*. (108th ed.). Washington, DC: U.S. Government Printing Office.

8
Grandparenting

Evan T. Peterson

I t is difficult to describe grandparenting in our society because, contrary to several stereotypical descriptions of the role of grandparent, there are wide variations in the role (Clavan 1978). The variations in the grandparental role are reflected both in the age and in the generational diversity of grandparents in our society. Some grandparents are in their late twenties, while others are over 100 years old. Their grandchildren can be newborns or of almost any age up to around 80. The modal age for becoming a grandparent is about 50 for women and 52 for men. What this means is that grandparenting has become a middle-age experience for most Americans. People are spending more of their lives in the grandparental role than ever before.

Furthermore, an increasing number of grandparents are also great-grandparents. At the turn of the century three-generation families were common; now the four-generation family is commonplace, and five-generation families are not uncommon. According to Shanas (1978), one-half of all persons aged 65 or over with living children are members of four-generation families. The increase in the life expectancy, lower birth rates, and closer spacing between children have contributed to these changes.

In spite of the diversity and the changes that have occurred since the 1950s, there persists a fairly rigid stereotype of grandparents as gray-haired, elderly, patient, loving, kindly, and considerate (albeit forgetful) "folk" (Bischof 1976). Sometimes the grandparent stereotype becomes fused with the typically negative stereotype of elderly people in general. Occasionally, a grandfather is viewed, stereotypically, as being rather stern, rigid, and conservative and very "set in his ways." When she is differentiated from the grandfather, a grandmother is typically viewed in a more positive light. As with any other stereotype, there are gross inaccuracies with these.

It has been estimated that three-fourths of all the elderly in the nation have living grandchildren (Troll et al. 1979; Cunningham and Brookbank

1988). According to Barranti (1985), today's children can expect to spend nearly one-half of their lives as grandparents. Almost all children have at least one grandparent and, according to Harris and Cole (1980), over two-thirds have all four. However, Brody (1979) has estimated that the chance of a 10-year-old child having at least three living grandparents is 38 percent.

It seems unfortunate that such an important familial role—even if only important in terms of the duration of the role in the family life cycle, the potential interrelationships associated with the role, and the symbolic importance of the role (Bengston and Robertson 1985)—has not been researched extensively (Barranti 1985; Bengston and Robertson 1985). In this chapter, the relevant research is reviewed and suggestions made for future research.

Typologies of Grandparenting Styles

One of the earliest typologies of grandparenthood was developed by Neugarten and Weinstein (1964). They interviewed 140 grandparents and identified five types of grandparent (cf. Baranowski 1987).

The first type is the *formal* grandparent. Neugarten and Weinstein (1964) classified 31 percent of the grandmothers and 33 percent of the grandfathers as having this style. Formal grandparenting involves taking great interest in grandchildren. Grandparents of this type tend to indulge the grandchild and often provide special treats for them. They may babysit, but they typically leave the parenting to the parents.

The second type is the *fun-seeking* grandparent. Twenty-nine percent of the grandmothers and 24 percent of the grandfathers were so classified. This grandparenting type involves a very informal, playful relationship between grandchild and grandparent. The grandparent exercises little if any authority. Fun-seeking grandparent expect to have mutually satisfying emotional relationships and view grandparenting as a leisure activity.

The third type is the *parent surrogate*. Fourteen percent of the grandmothers but none of the grandfathers were typed as parent surrogates. Here the grandmother assumes the caregiving responsibilities of the parent.

The fourth type of grandparent is the *reservoir of family wisdom*. Very few of the grandparents were classified as this particular type—1 percent of the grandmothers and 6 percent of the grandfathers. In this type, the younger generations are in a subordinate position and the grandparent has the special skills and resources.

Finally, the fifth type is the *distant figure*. Nineteen percent of the grandmothers and 29 percent of the grandfathers were classified as distant figures. The grandparents were loving but remote and had infrequent contact with their grandchildren.

A second major study was done by Robertson (1977). It involved 125 grandmothers and 86 young-adult grandchildren. She identified four styles of grandmothering (cf. McGreal 1986b). Twenty-nine percent of the grandmothers were categorized as *apportioned*; that is, they were the most involved with their grandchildren. They were as concerned about doing what was right for them as they were with indulging them. Twenty-six percent of the grandmothers were categorized as *symbolic*. They were more concerned with the social meaning of their role than with the interpersonal aspects of it, and they were concerned about doing what was morally right for their grandchildren. Eleven percent were identified as *individualized* grandmothers. Here the emphasis was on the personal rewards of grandparenthood; grandchildren were used to help curb loneliness and keep them youthful. Finally, 28 percent of the grandmothers were not really involved with their grandchildren. This type was called *remote*.

Subsequently, Kivnick (1982), using qualitative data gathered from thirty grandparents and quantitative data gathered from 286 grandparents, identified five dimensions of grandparenthood. One was *centrality*, which referred to the extent to which grandparenthood is central to the life of a grandparent. The second dimension was *valued elder*, which includes two facets: the grandparent as resource person and the grandparent's concern with the regard the grandchildren have for him or her. The third dimension was *immortality through clan*, which emphasizes the continuity of the family. The fourth was *reinvolvement with personal past*, which has to do with the grandparent's sense of reliving experiences that occurred earlier in life—grandparenthood as a life review. Finally, the fifth dimension was *spoil*, the extent to which a grandparent indulges the grandchildren.

Kahana and Kahana (1971) did not devise a typology in the same sense as those discussed so far. Rather, they identified various levels of analysis in the study of grandparenthood. One level was to consider grandparenthood *as a social role*, which involves ascribed status as well as expectations of role performance. At the opposite end, grandparenthood may be viewed as an *emotional state* that is part of the individual grandparents' development. Another level was grandparenting as a *transaction* between grandchildren and grandparents, involving reciprocity and mutual influences. A fourth level was grandparenthood as part of a *group process within the family*, involving intergenerational relationships, help patterns, and family maintenance. Finally, the Kahanas considered grandparenthood as a *symbol*, which may be a reflection of aging and usefulness to society.

Kornhaber and Woodward (1981), with a sample of three hundred grandchildren under 18 years of age, identified five grandparental roles. The first was *historian*, in which the grandparent provides a sense of family history to the grandchildren. The second was *mentor*, in which the grandparent provides knowledge and wisdom to the grandchildren. *Role model* is the third role, which provides anticipatory socialization for the grandparental role to grandchildren. In the fourth role, *wizard*, the grandparent tells stories and amuses and amazes the grandchildren through imagination. Finally, the fifth role was *nurturer/great parent*, which described the most basic role a grandparent plays, in which the grandparent becomes an integral part of the grandchild's social support system.

In spite of the different methodologies employed, several conceptual similarities can be seen among these studies. Neugarten and Weinstein's "reservoir of family wisdom" resembles Kornhaber and Woodward's "mentor"; Kivnick's "valued elder", and to some extent Robertson's "symbolic" and the Kahanas' "symbol", also have similarities.

Variables Affecting Grandparenting

In this section, major variables that have been utilized in the research on grandparenting are reviewed. Most of the variables have been conceived as influences on the quality of the relationship between grandparent and grandchild. Some of the concepts used to describe the quality of that relationship are emotional closeness, emotional support, satisfaction, acceptance/rejection, and bonding.

Age of Grandchildren

There is considerable research that deals with the age of grandchildren as it impacts on the grandparent-grandchild relationship. Kahana and Kahana (1970) found that children under age 10 feel closer to their grandparents than do older grandchildren, and that grandparents like their younger grandchildren more than the older ones. Four- and 5-year-old children desired indulgence in grandparents. Those aged 8 or 9 wanted to share in some fun activities. During adolescence some grandchildren became alienated. Kahana and Kahana (1971) reported that the relationships vary with the developmental cognitive changes occurring in the grandchildren.

Clark and Anderson (1967) suggested that as children get older, the aura they might have once perceived surrounding their grandparents starts to dim. Grandparents are not viewed as being as competent as they once were. Also, grandparents tend to enjoy their grandchildren more as young children than as adolescents. Clark (1969) suggested that this may be due to younger grandchildren being more attentive than older grandchildren.

Robertson (1977) reported that grandchildren aged 18 to 24 feel a sense of responsibility toward their grandparents. They do not expect concrete rewards from them, nor do they select grandparents as companions, advisers, role models, or financial supporters. This kind of relationship is a far cry from the Kahana and Kahana (1970) report on young children's perception of grandparents. Also, some other research has suggested that many adolescents apparently turn to grandparents as special family resources (Gilford and Black 1972; Hagestad 1978).

Age of Grandparents

In Neugarten and Weinstein's (1964) study, a grandparent's age was one of the chief determinants of grandparenting type. Those grandparents over 65 more commonly used the formal style, whereas younger grandparents were fun-seeking. Perhaps people become more formal as they age, or perhaps the older cohort has a more traditional view. It is also possible that grandparents are more playful with younger grandchildren than they are with older ones. Neugarten and Weinstein (1964), as well as Boyd (1969b), said that grandparenthood is more salient in middle age than it is in old age.

Baranowski (1987), who studied a sample of 106 grandfathers, found that the older grandfathers tended to have less contact with their grandchildren than did the younger grandfathers. The gender of the grandchild was not a significant predictor of frequency or of type of interaction.

Wood and Robertson (1976) found an inverse relationship between the association of grandparents and grandchildren and the age of the grandparents. The older grandparents tended to have lowered physical mobility and fewer activities. Cherlin and Furstenberg (1985) found the same thing; the younger grandparents were more active (Johnson 1985; Thomas 1986b).

Maternal and Paternal Grandparents

Hartshorne and Manaster (1982) found that there is more interaction with maternal grandmothers than there is paternal grandmothers. Kahana and Kahana (1971) reported that maternal grandmothers and paternal grandfathers show the greatest closeness and warmth toward grandchildren (McGreal 1986a). They speculated that grandparents see grandchildren as more similar to their own children through the father-son and mother-daughter relationships. Hoffman (1979–80) found that her college-age females had more contact with and felt closer to their maternal than to their paternal grandparents. Similarly, Matthews and Sprey (1985) reported that the grandchildren in their study were most likely to describe their relationships with their maternal grandmothers as close and least likely to describe their relationships with the paternal grandparents as close.

There is also some contrary evidence. Using data from the USC Longitudinal Study of Three Generations, Miller and Bengston (1987) reported that the "matrifocal tilt" hypothesis was not supported. They found no statistically significant difference between maternal and paternal grandparental relationships with their grandchildren.

Gender of Grandparents

Atchley (1988) stated that grandmothers appear to have a somewhat better chance of developing a relationship with their granddaughters than grandfathers have with their grandsons. Hagestad's (1978) research is consistent with Atchley's position. More of the relationships are along the maternal line; grandmothers are more likely to have warm relations with their grandchildren than are grandfathers. In one review of research, Baranowski (1985) asked whether grandfathers really exist. Hagestad and Speicher (1981) described grandfathers as forgotten men. Cunningham-Burley's (1984) study of grandparent couples in Scotland looked on grandfathers as peripheral to the family system. Several other studies (Troll 1980, 1983; Russell 1986; Cherlin and Furstenberg 1985) reported that very few grandfathers spend much time with their grandchildren.

Kivett (1985) reported that elderly men view their grandfather role as somewhat unimportant. It was perceived as subordinate to other family roles, except that of sibling. This reflects a matrilateral focus in our bilateral kinship system that emphasizes the female (Yanigasako 1977).

According to Neugarten and Weinstein (1964), the "parent-surrogate" style is used consistently by grandmothers, whereas the predominant style used by grandfathers is the "reservoir of family wisdom" style.

Nye and Berardo (1973) stated that women are more likely than men to look forward to assuming the grandparent role and experience considerable anticipatory socialization (cf. McGreal 1986a). Thomas (1986a) found that grandmothers have slightly higher satisfaction with the role than do grandfathers. She suggested that the higher satisfaction scores among women may reflect a continuity of earlier and current family experiences. The research of Albrecht (1973) suggests that gender differences in grandparenting may be greater in the middle than in the lower class. Middle-class grandfathers have more interactions with their grandchildren than do lower-class grandfathers, while there are no class differences in the grandmother role.

Gender Role of Grandchildren

In Hagestad's (1982–83) study, grandfathers, sons, and grandsons talked to each other about work, education, and money more than half the time, and their views on social issues were discussed a third of the time. On the other hand, grandmothers, daughters, and granddaughters talked to each other about interpersonal relations more than half the time; the next two themes most discussed by them were health and appearance, and daily living.

There is some evidence that grandfathers feel as if they can be of greater help to their grandsons than to their granddaughters and tend to relate to them more (Cherlin and Furstenberg 1986; Hagestad 1985; Troll 1983).

In a sample of over two hundred grandparents and their grandchildren, the present author found that granddaughters are more concerned with their grandparents than are grandsons. More granddaughters worry about their grandparents, tell them they love them, talk and visit with them, think about them, pray about them, miss them, try to spend time with them, write or phone them, enjoy them, and so forth, than grandsons. Utilizing fourteen different variables measuring both behavior and attitudinal positions, the positions of the granddaughters were found to be more positive than those of the grandsons with only two exceptions (getting angry with them and criticizing them). This is probably a reflection of traditional female familial involvement (Troll 1971; Troll et al. 1979).

Contrary to these findings, Kivett (1985) reported that granddaughters are not more prominent in grandfather-grandchild relationships than grandsons. Also, O'Bryant (1987), in studying 162 widows, found that grandsons provide more types of support and more frequent support than do granddaughters. Interestingly, receipt of support was not found to be related to close feelings toward grandchildren.

Grandparental Perceptions of Their Role

Obviously, not all grandparents perceive their role in a like fashion. In Neugarten and Weinstein's (1964) study, 42 percent of the grandmothers and 23 percent of the grandfathers saw their grandparental role as a source of renewal or continuity. Twenty-seven percent of the grandmothers and 29 percent of the grandfathers saw it as having little effect on them. Nineteen percent of the grandmothers and 27 percent of the grandfathers saw it as emotional self-fulfillment.

There is some evidence (Bengtson and Kuypers 1971) that grandparents see their role as being somewhat more important, in terms of ties to their grandchildren, than do the grandchildren. This conclusion is consistent with the present author's own research. Bengston and Kuypers (1971) argued that they do so because they want to believe that they have effectively transmitted their values to their grandchildren.

On the other hand, Troll et al. (1979) pointed out that closeness is affected by the power grandparents hold, and that modern grandparents may have lost that power. Kivett (1985) concluded that among primarily working-class older men, the role of grandfather is of relatively limited instrumental value. As a matter of fact, family relationships are not very important to the morale of old men (Watson and Kivett 1976). Cath (1986) argued that grandchildren help to bring out the best in the aging generation, including feelings about the aging process itself. According to Updegraf (1968), the majority of grandparents exhibit considerable pride and pleasure from their involvement with their grandchildren. However, Lopata (1973) found that only slightly more than half of widowed grandmothers feel close to even one of their grandchildren. Wood and Robertson (1976) found that the level of involvement in grandparenting was not related to life satisfaction. They and others (Kahana and Kahana 1971; Troll 1980) have argued that the role is primarily symbolic and ritualistic and of little importance in the lives of most grandparents. Troll et al. (1979) viewed the grandparental role as peripheral for most older adults. In an exploratory study, Wentowski (1985) found that for great-grandmothers, great-grandchildren have symbolic value but they typically feel very remote from them—more so than from their grandchildren.

The Parental Generation

The role definitions of the parental generation have typically been viewed as intervening variables. The parental generation has been variously described as the middle generation, the sandwich generation, the lineage bridge, and the mediators (Hill et al. 1970; Wood and Robertson 1978; Robertson 1975, 1977). Troll (1980) saw the relationship between grandchildren and grandparents as contingent on the parental generation. Whatever it is called, this generation links grandchildren to their grandparents.

According to Allen (1976), parents are in a position to control the grandparent-grandchild relationship until the child achieves some independence. Robertson (1977) found that interaction is usually initiated by grandchildren or their parents rather than by grandparents. This was especially clear in terms of baby-sitting and home recreation. Robertson (1976) found that close to two-thirds of a sample of young adults acknowledged that their parents influenced the involvement they maintained with their grandparents. Gilford and Black (1972) found that attitudes and feelings toward grandparents are largely transmitted from parent to child and that they tend to persist. Hagestad and Speicher (1981) found that parents tend to remain as mediators of the interaction between grandparents and grandchildren even when the grandchildren are adults.

Matthews and Sprey (1985) found that when a grandchild perceives his or her parents as having a close relationship with their own parents (the child's grandparents), there is a greater likelihood that the grandchild will also have a close relationship with his or her grandparents. They concluded (1985, 624) that "close bonds between grandchildren and their paternal grandmothers are facilitated, first, by the father's being perceived as close to his mother; second, by the mother's being perceived as close to her mother-in-law; and, last, by the grandchild's having access to (i.e., living near and/or seeing often) the grandmother in childhood." However, they went on to say that close bonds with the maternal grandmother are not dependent on these factors. The significant variables are the ties between the mother and her mother (the grandmother).

Robertson (1977) found that when dissatisfactions occur between grandparents and their adult children in the middle generation, they typically center on childrearing methods. This is especially true when the grandmother plays a central role in rearing the grandchild.

Cohler and Grunebaum (1981) studied four multigenerational, working-class Italian-American families and found remarkably close relationships between the adult daughters and their mothers. The adult daughters were comfortable with their increased dependency, but the grandmothers were bothered with the demands for intimacy made by their daughters.

Divorce and Remarriage in the Parent Generation

Because of the rising divorce rate and the increasing numbers of older people, the impact of divorce on the grandparent-grandchild relationship has been considered by researchers. Wilson and DeShane (1982) pointed out that little is known about the grandparent-grandchild relationship during and after divorce. According to them, divorce has traditionally been divisive, resulting in fewer interactions between grandparents and their grandchildren. Kelly and Wallerstein (1977) suggested that some grandparents function as surrogate parents following divorce. Beal (1979) reported that adult children may deny their children access to their grandparents.

Barranti (1985) identified the following factors as determining the impact of divorce on the intergenerational relationship between grandparents and their grandchildren. One factor was the relationship that exists between them before the divorce. A second factor was the extent to which the divorce is resolved in rancor or amicably. And finally, the third factor was the extent of friction that exists between the parents and the grandparents.

In looking at fifty divorcing families over a four-year period, Johnson (1987) found that following divorce, the greatest decline in involvement was among paternal grandmothers. In another report, Johnson and Barer (1987, 334) wrote that

> It is common for the relationship between paternal grandmothers and their former daughters-in-law to continue. This relationship transcends the divorce-related pressures for dissolution, most likely because the childrearing functions performed by women continue to be coordinated in the best interests of the grandchildren and the continuity between generations.

Matthews and Sprey (1984) reported that maternal grandparents are in the best position to maintain a relationship with their grandchildren following divorce because their daughters are more likely to get custody than are their sons, and daughters are more likely to keep in close contact than sons. They also found that sons-in-law and daughters-in-law are less likely than children to remain close following divorce.

Thomas and Sanders (1985) found some evidence that marital status is associated with different views of grandparenting by their adult children. The single parents (some of whom have been divorced) in their study said that grandparents were sources of advice and support, and the married parents said that grandparents strengthened the family as well as offered life experience and knowledge of family heritage. It seems likely that grandchildren coming from an intact marriage perceive the grandparental role differently from grandchildren with single parents.

Role Socialization

Research on the socialization for grandparenthood is rather limited. While previous socialization would seem to be a significant variable impacting on grandparenting style, very few researchers have tried to establish the impact of grandchildren's experiences on their own later roles as grandparents. Kivnick (1982) found that grandparents who have positive rather than negative experiences with their own grandparents tend to view the role of grandparent as a more valued role.

Interestingly, grandchildren are apparently socialized by their relationships with their grandparents. There is evidence that grandchildren who have grandparents are less prejudiced toward elderly people (Bekker and Taylor 1966).

There is additional evidence that socialization plays a part in the grandparent role. Sussman (1965) found that grandparents who reared their children with an emphasis on the child's needs are less intrusive and authoritarian with their grandchildren.

Avoidance of Sensitive Areas

One characteristic of high-quality relationships between grandparent and grandchild is the avoidance of sensitive areas. Hagestad (1978) suggested that grandparents and their grandchildren have "demilitarized zones." They seem to form an unspoken agreement to avoid discussing certain topics. There is an agreement to disagree and avoid these topics because they are unproductive in terms of changing the other person's point of view. This is related to having some sensitivity concerning the space of the grandchild. Boyd (1969a) found that grandparents who are valued tend to be those who wait to be asked rather than impose themselves on their grandchildren.

Availability of Grandparents

Another characteristic related to satisfactory grandparent-grandchild relationships is the availability of grandparents. Matthews and Sprey (1985) found that their respondents were more likely to know a grandmother, either maternal or paternal, and least likely to know a paternal grandfather. They wrote, "Grandchildren who visited paternal grandmothers and maternal grandfathers at least three times a year were more likely than those who did not to describe their relationships as close" (Matthews and Sprey 1985, 623). Kivett (1985) reported that grandfathers generally indicated that they felt very close to the grandchild with whom they had the most contact. And perhaps grandparents have greater contact with their grandchildren than their grandchildren have with uncles, aunts, and cousins (Robins and Tomanec 1962). Harris and Associates (1975) reported that nearly half of all grandparents are in almost daily face-to-face contact with their grandchildren, and three-fourths of them see their grandchildren at least twice a month. Wood and Robertson (1978) found that feelings of closeness prevail even where interaction with grandchildren is minimal.

Suggestions for Future Research

There are numerous directions in which future research should be directed, beyond those that have been suggested. In this section, only some of the more important directions are identified.

Longitudinal research that investigates the dynamics of the relationship between grandparents and their grandchildren would seem to be especially important. Cross-sectional research of whatever quality is suspect even at its very best. The lack of confidence that comparable data are being employed tends to leave questions in the minds of those trying to investigate such a complex intergenerational dyad as grandparent-grandchild.

Very few studies address the possible differential impact of various grandchildren on a single grandparent. Most of the research deals with one grandchild of one grandparent. Obviously, most grandparents have more than one. Equally obviously, most grandparents start the role with only one grandchild. It is possible that grandparents express different types of grandparenting with different grandchildren. Perhaps there is something significant about the ordinal position with grandchildren. Is the first-born grandchild different from later-born grandchildren? Is the first-born "paternal" grandchild viewed differently by the grandparents from the way a first-born "maternal" grandchild is viewed? The different combinations and questions are almost endless. The impact of several grandchildren is also in need of examination. Does the relationship between grandparent and grandchildren vary with the number of grandchildren? What kind of relationship does an "only" grandchild have with his or her grandparents?

There is as yet very little research on the relationship between the psychosocial well-being of the grandparent and the quality of grandparenting (cf. Kivnick 1982). In addition, research is needed that examines the effects of variables such as the gender and age of the grandparent and grandchild on the psychosocial well-being of grandparent. But this is only part of the problem; there also needs to be a rigorous attempt to delineate the relevant dimensions of the grandparent-grandchild relationship. It may be necessary to view the impact of the grandparent-grandchild relationship in terms of a variety of different dependent variables. In a sense, the grandparent-grandchild dyad is analogous to (but far less complex than) the husband-wife dyad. The husband-wife relationship has been studied in terms of marital satisfaction, marital adjustment, marital happiness, marital success, marital quality, marital stability, and so forth. The concepts are related but not always well defined. What are the relevant dimensions of the grandparent-grandchild relationship? Troll (1971) has called the grandparent role an achieved rather than an ascribed role. The same could be said for the grandchild role. Clavan (1978) referred to the grandparent role as a peculiar noninstitution. The norms and sanctions of the role are poorly defined. As a result, it is difficult to measure the quality or performance aspects of the grandparent role or the grandchild role.

More extensive research on grandparent-grandchild relationships is needed. The extent of the grandparents' social support system may have an impact on their relationships with their grandchildren. There is not even adequate research on such easily quantified variables as the number of hours spent with grandchildren or frequency of contacts. Amount of exposure is another variable that needs examination. Do those grandparents who are overexposed view the role differently from those who are underexposed? Does this affect their relationships?

Of course, there is also a need for comparative data concerning ethnicity (cf. Jackson 1971) as well as socioeconomic status. Certainly more cross-cultural research is needed (cf. Olsen 1976). Although some researchers have indicated some of the demographic characteristics of their samples, others have not, leaving the reader to assume that a grandparent is simply a grandparent. Obviously, such is not the case. It is safe to conclude that much more research and more adequate theory are needed before an accurate description of the dynamics of the roles of grandparent and grandchild can be obtained.

References

Albrecht, R. 1973. "The family and aging seen cross-culturally." In R. R. Boyd and C. G. Oakes (eds.), *Foundations of Practical Gerontology*. Columbia, SC: University of South Carolina Press.

Allen, M. L. 1976. "Visitation rights of a grandparent over the objection of a parent: The best interests of the child." *Journal of Family Law* 15:51–76.

Atchley, R. C. 1988. *Social Forces and Aging*. 5th ed. Belmont, CA: Wadsworth.

Baranowski, M. D. 1985. "Men as grandfathers." In S. M. Hanson and F. W. Bozet (eds.), *Dimensions of Fatherhood*. Beverly Hills, CA: Sage Publications.

———. 1987. "The grandfather-grandchild relationship: Patterns and meaning." Paper presented at the 40th Annual meeting of the Gerontological Society of America, Washington, DC.

Barranti, C. 1985. "The grandparent/grandchild relationship: Family resource in an era of voluntary bonds." *Family Relations* 34:343–52.

Beal, E. W. 1979. "Children of divorce: A family systems perspective." *Journal of Social Issues* 35:140–54.

Bekker, L. D., and Taylor, C. 1966. "Attitudes toward the aged in a multigenerational sample." *Journal of Gerontology* 21:115–18.

Bengston, V. L., and Kuypers, J. A. 1971. "Generational differences and the developmental stake." *Aging and Human Development* 2:249–60.

Bengston, V. L., and Robertson, J. F. (eds.). 1985. *Grandparenting*. (Focus editions, vol. 74). Beverly Hills, CA: Sage Publications.

Bischof, L. J. 1976. *Adult Psychology* (2nd ed.). New York: Harper and Row.

Boyd, R. 1969a. "The valued grandparent: A changing social role. Living in a multigenerational family." Ann Arbor, Michigan. Occasional Papers in Gerontology no. 3, Institute of Gerontology, University of Michigan–Wayne State.

———. 1969b. "Emerging roles of the four-generational family." In R. Boyd and H. Oakes (eds.), *Time, Roles, and the Self in Old Age*. New York: Human Science Press.

Brody, E. 1979. "Aged parents and aging children." In P. K. Ragan (ed.), *Aging Parents*. Los Angeles: University of Southern California Press.

Cath, S. H. 1986. "Clinical vignettes: A range of grandparental experiences." *Journal of Geriatric Psychiatry* 19:57–68.

Cherlin, A., and Furstenberg, F. F., Jr. 1985. "Styles and strategies of grandparenthood. In V. L. Bengston and J. F. Robertson (eds.), *Grandparenthood*. Beverly Hills, CA: Sage Publications.

———. 1986. *The New American Grandparent*. New York: Basic Books.

Clark, M. 1969. "Cultural values and dependency in later life. In R. Kalish (ed.), *The Dependencies of Old People*. Ann Arbor, MI: Institute for Gerontology.

Clark, M., and Anderson, B. 1967. *Culture and Aging*. Springfield, IL: Charles C. Thomas.

Clavan, S. 1978. "The impact of social class and social trends on the role of grandparents." *The Family Coordinator* 27:351–57.

Cohler, B., and Grunebaum, H. 1981. *Mothers, Grandmothers, and Daughters: Personality and Child Care in Three-Generation Families*. New York: John Wiley and Sons.

Cunningham, W. R., and Brookbank, J. W. 1988. *Gerontology: The Psychology, Biology, and Sociology of Aging.* New York: Harper and Row.

Cunningham-Burley, S. 1984. " 'We don't talk about it . . . ': Issues of gender and method in the portrayal of grandfatherhood." *Sociology* 18:325–38.

Gilford, R., and Black, D. 1972. "The grandchild-grandparent dyad: Ritual or relationship." Paper presented at the annual meeting of the Gerontological Society, San Juan, PR.

Hagestad, G. O. 1978. "Patterns of communication and influence between grandparents and grandchildren in a changing society." Paper presented at the World Congress of Sociology, Sweden.

———. 1982–83. "Divorce: the family ripple effect." *Generations* 7:24–25.

———. 1985. "Continuity and connectedness." In V. L. Bengston and J. F. Robertson (eds.), *Grandparenthood.* Beverly Hills, CA: Sage Publications.

Hagestad, G. O., and Speicher, J. L. 1981. "Grandparents and family influence: Views of three generations." Paper presented at the annual meeting of the Society for Research in Child Development, Boston, MA.

Harris, D. K., and Cole, W. E. 1980. *Sociology of Aging.* Boston: Houghton Mifflin.

Harris, L., and Associates. 1975. *The Myth and Reality of Aging in America.* Washington, DC: National Council on Aging.

Hartshorne, T. A., and Manaster, G. J. 1982. "The relationship with grandparents: contact, importance, role conception." *International Journal of Aging and Human Development* 15:233–45.

Hill, R., Foote, N., Aldous, J., Carlson, R., and MacDonald, R. 1970. *Family Development in Three Generations.* Cambridge, MA: Schenkman.

Hoffman, E. 1979–80. "Young adults' relations with their grandparents: An exploratory study." *International Journal of Aging and Human Development* 10:299–309.

Jackson, J. J. 1971. "Sex and social class variations in black aged parent-adult child relationships." *Aging and Human Development* 2:96–107.

Johnson, C. 1987. "A longitudinal analysis of grandparenting after divorce." Paper presented at the 40th annual meeting of the Gerontological Society of America, Washington, DC.

———. 1985. "Grandparenting options in divorcing families: An anthropological perspective." In V. L. Bengston and J. F. Robertson (eds.), *Grandparenthood.* Beverly Hills: Sage Publications.

Johnson, C., and Barer, B. M. 1987. "Marital instability and the changing networks of grandparents." *The Gerontologist,* 27:330–35.

Kahana, E., and Kahana, B. 1970. "Grandparenthood from the perspective of the developing grandchild." *Developmental Psychology* 3:98–105.

———. 1971. "Theoretical and research perspectives on grandparenthood." *Aging and Human Development* 2:261–68.

Kelly, J. B., and Wallerstein, J. S. 1977. "Brief interventions with children in divorcing families." *American Journal of Orthopsychiatry* 47:23–29.

Kivett, V. R. 1985. "Grandfathers and grandchildren: Patterns of association, helping and psychological closeness." *Family Relations* 34:565–71.

Kivnick, H. Q. 1982. "Grandparenthood: An overview of meaning and mental health." *The Gerontologist* 22:59–66.

Kornhaber, A., and Woodward, K. L. 1981. *Grandparents/Grandchildren: The Vital Connection*. Garden City, NY: Anchor Press/Doubleday.

Lopata, H. Z. 1973. *Widowhood in an American City*. Cambridge, MA: Schenkman.

Matthews, S. H., and Sprey, J. 1984. "The impact of divorce on grandparenthood: An exploratory study." *The Gerontologist* 24:41–47.

———. 1985. "Adolescents' relationships with grandparents: An empirical contribution to conceptual clarification." *Journal of Gerontology* 40:621–26.

McGreal, C. E. 1986a. "The significance of biological renewal to grandparents: A longitudinal analysis." Paper presented at the 39th annual meeting of the Gerontological Society of America, Chicago, IL.

———. 1986b. "Grandparental role-meaning types: A critical evaluation." *Infant Mental Health Journal* 7:235–41.

Miller, R., and Bengtson, V. L. 1987. "Adult grandchildren-grandparent relationships: A test of the 'matrifocal' tilt hypothesis." Paper presented at the 40th annual meeting of the Gerontological Society of America, Washington, DC.

Neugarten, B. L., and Weinstein, K. K. 1964. "The changing American grandparent." *Journal of Marriage and the Family* 26:199–204.

Nye, F. I., and Berardo, F. M. 1973. *The Family: Its Structure and Interaction*. New York: Macmillan.

O'Bryant, S. L. 1987. "Widows' grandchildren: An examination of support and affective ties." Paper presented at the 40th annual meeting of the Gerontological Society of America, Washington, DC.

Olsen, N. A. 1976. "The role of grandmothers in Taiwanese family socialization." *Journal of Marriage and the Family* 38:363–72.

Robertson, J. F. 1975. "Interaction in three-generation families; parents as mediators: Toward a theoretical perspective." *International Journal of Aging and Human Development* 6:103–10.

———. 1976. "Significance of grandparents: Perceptions of young adult grandchildren." *The Gerontologist* 16:137–40.

———. 1977. "Grandmotherhood: A study of role conceptions." *Journal of Marriage and the Family* 39:165–74.

Robins, L. N., and Tomanec, M. 1962. "Closeness to blood relatives outside the immediate family." *Marriage and Family Living* 24:340–46.

Russell, G. 1986. "Grandfathers: Making up for lost opportunities." In R. A. Lewis and R. E. Salt (eds.), *Men in Families*. Beverly Hills, CA: Sage Publications.

Shanas, E. 1978. *A National Survey of the Aged: Final Report to the Administration on Aging*. Washington, DC: U.S. Department of Health, Education, and Welfare.

Sussman, M. B. 1965. "Relationships of adult children with their parents in the United States." In E. Shanas and G. Streib (eds.), *Social Structure and the Family: Generational Relations*. Englewood Cliffs, NJ: Prentice-Hall.

Thomas, J. L. 1986a. "Gender differences in satisfaction with grandparenting." *Psychology and Aging* 1:215–19.

———. 1986b. "Age and sex differences in perceptions of grandparenting." *Journal of Gerontology* 41:417–23.

Thomas, J. L., and Sanders, L. M. 1985. "Married and single parents' views of grandparents: A content analysis." Paper presented at the annual meeting of the Gerontological Society of American, New Orleans, LA.

Troll, L. 1971. "The family of later life: A decade review." *Journal of Marriage and the Family* 33:263–90.

———. 1980. "Grandparenting." In L. W. Poon (ed.), *Aging in the 1980's: Psychological Issues*. Washington, DC: American Psychological Association.

———. 1983. "Grandparents: The family watchdogs." In T. H. Brubaker (ed.), *Family Relationships in Later Life*. Beverly Hills, CA: Sage Publications.

Troll, L., Miller, S. J., and Atchley, R. C. 1979. *Families in Later Life*. Belmont, CA: Wadsworth.

Updegraf, S. G. 1968. "Changing role of the grandmother." *Journal of Home Economics* 60:177–80.

Watson, J. A., and Kivett, V. R. 1976. "Influences on the life satisfaction of older fathers." *Family Coordinator* 25:582–588.

Wentowski, G. J. 1985. "Older women's perceptions of great-grandmotherhood: A research note." *The Gerontologist* 25:593–96.

Wilson, K. B., and DeShane, M. R. 1982. "The legal rights of grandparents: A preliminary discussion." *The Gerontologist* 22:67–71.

Wood, V., and Robertson, J. F. 1976. "The significance of grandparenthood." In J. F. Gubrium (ed.), *Time, Roles and Self in Old Age*. New York: Human Science Press.

———. 1978. "Friendship and kinship interaction: Differential effect on the morale of the elderly." *Journal of Marriage and the Family* 40:367–75.

Yanigasako, S. 1977. "Women-centered kin networks in urban bilateral kinship system." *American Ethnologist* 4:207–26.

9
Elderly Parents and Their Offspring

Evan T. Peterson

An examination of the relationships between elderly parents and their adult offspring should begin with a description of the American family. Parsons's (1943, 1949; Parsons et al. 1955) picture of the isolated nuclear family seems essentially correct in the sense that the elderly parents of either spouse do not customarily live with their adult offspring. The neolocal residence rule operates in the early years of the family life cycle as well as in the later years. Although some interchange of aid takes place between the nuclear family and extended kin, Parsons seemed to neglect this, while Sussman and Burchinal (1962) stressed it. Sussman (1965) argued that American society has an extended-kin family system operating over several generations that is highly integrative within a network of social relations and mutual assistance. His position is different from that of Kirkpatrick (1955), who argued that the typical consequence of two-generational families intergenerational conflict is.

The pivotal point of disagreement seems to be the extent to which the two generations assist each other. However, some behavioral scientists have entered the fray, endorsing a family organizational concept other than nuclear and extended. Litwak (1960), basing his position on a sample of Buffalo, New York, housewives, suggested that there is a "modified extended family" that does not involve geographical propinquity but that consists of a series of nuclear families with strong extended family bonds. Winch (1974) preferred the term "nonisolated nuclear family." Lopata (1978a) presented evidence that indicates that the modified extended network in American metropolitan centers is in fact inactive. In the social, emotional, economic, and service support systems for the Chicago-area widows in Lopata's research, the appearance of extended kin was rather infrequent.

Hess and Waring (1978), on the other hand, argued that there is a family network but probably not a modified extended family because it is based on the amount of resources available and is typically found among the more affluent; consequently, it is strictly voluntary. They pointed out that most adult offspring provide no material support to their parents and that there is no necessary relationship between expressions of solidarity and positive affect (Arling 1976; Brown 1969; Adams 1975; Medley 1976). Clavan (1978) believed that the extended-kinship structure is not functionally central to American society, but that various forms of the extended-kinship structure exist for particular groups of urban families.

Koller (1974b) has written about the multigenerational family in which the generations, or cohorts, are linked. Families may interact with other family members of different generations.

Whatever concepts are employed, it appears that the term, *isolated nuclear family* is not an adequate description of the contemporary American family. It also appears that in American society there has not been an evolutionary development from the extended family of the colonial period to the nuclear family of today (Skolnick 1987; Greven 1970; Demos 1970; Sena 1973). According to Laslett (1978), the recent history of the family in Western Europe and North America shows that membership in most households, both past and present, was and still is composed primarily of nuclear family members.

For purposes of this chapter, it is important to distinguish between (1) the residential family and (2) the kin network to which a person belongs by blood tie or marriage (Streib 1972). The critical issues have to do with the extent of influence adult offspring have on the basic residential family of their elderly parents; what influence elderly people have on the basic residential family of their children; the interrelationships between adult offspring and their aging parents; and the composition of the basic residential family in American society.

Living Arrangements of Elderly Parents

*Elderly Parents Who Reside
with Their Adult Offspring*

How many elderly parents reside with their adult offspring? In the mid-1960s, Tibbitts (1965) observed that 21 percent of the older population were not living in their own households. He stated that about 25 percent resided with one or more of their adult offspring, either in their own households or in the households of the offspring. He suggested that the proportion of older people sharing dwellings with their adult children probably reached a peak when residential building was curtailed during World War II. Of the population aged 65 and over who have children, Stehouwer (1965) reported that 5.1 percent in Denmark, 8.1 percent in the United

States, and 13.4 percent in Great Britain lived in three-generational households. Stehouwer believed that assistance to adult offspring leads to intergenerational stress because it imposes obligations on them and their families that are difficult to meet.

Increase in the Number of Separate Households

Beresford and Rivlin (1966) observed an increasing tendency of older people to maintain separate households rather than live with either relatives or nonrelatives in the 1960s. More recent research indicates that the percentage of elderly parents who move in with their adult offspring has continued to decline. Accompanying this has been an increase in one-person households (Kobrin 1976; Siegal 1976).

Most lone households are found among the elderly; approximately three-fourths of this group are women. Not only has there been an increase in the number of one-person households, there has also been an increase in the number of one-parent households. Chevan and Korson (1972) stated that the proportion of widowed persons living alone has increased from 20 percent in 1940 to 50 percent in 1970. Koller (1974b) wrote that three-generation families have never been very popular in American society and have numbered 5 percent or less for many years (Benson 1971). This seems to be an accurate appraisal of the situation, consistent with the preferences of most people in American society. According to Troll et al. (1979, 84), "Almost all . . . surveys show that older people prefer, whenever possible, to live in their own homes but near their children."

Independent Living as a Cultural Value

Ward (1978), agreeing with Troll et al., stated that most older people prefer to live independently of their adult offspring but argued that the extended-kin network is particularly useful in assisting older people who have experienced bereavement. Older people in institutions are about 5 percent of the population over 65 (Gefland et al. 1978). Typically they entered the institution after a variety of alternatives had been tried, including living with their adult offspring (Ward 1978).

Most of the elderly prefer to live independently in their own homes. The relationship between elderly parents and their adult children and grandchildren has been described as "intimacy at a distance" (Streib 1973). One hears a note of self-reliance, independence, and dignity among the elderly (Peterson 1978; Rosenfeld 1978). These people want to maintain themselves as long as they can, and even when they cannot meet their needs, they do not want to become dependent on their own children *Dependency* is a dirty word for them (Fuchs 1972). The elderly are often quite reluctant to seek or accept help; assistance or services perceived as earned or available to all elderly are the most acceptable (Moen 1978; Schorr 1960). There is some evidence that dependency on children is alienative because of role reversal (Glasser and Glasser 1962; Kinkel 1944; Adams 1968a). Certainly, adult offspring tend to be ill prepared to make the adjustments necessitated by role reversals, as are their aging parents (Arling 1976; Gefland et al. 1978).

Consequences of Elderly Parents Living With Their Adult Offspring

Unfortunately, the consequences of living with adult offspring have not been researched adequately. Adams (1968b, 1970) stated that those families who feel they can incorporate an elderly parent into their households without trouble are willing to attempt it. However, Schorr (1960) found that strain is possible in any parent-offspring relationship when people share a household with their elderly parents. The conditions under which households are typically shared were described by Hess and Waring (1978). They pointed out that when elderly parents move in with their adult offspring, they are apt to be very frail and disoriented, and the adult offspring frequently are ambivalent about undertaking such a responsibility. Of course, another possible problem is overcrowding (Grove et al. 1979). Whatever the consequences, the general pattern in American society is for people to detach, separate, or disengage themselves from relatives or even friends who become too troublesome (Wax 1965).

Variables Associated with Intergenerational Linkages

Spatial Proximity and Frequency of Interaction

Do adult offspring disengage themselves from their elderly parents? Most research suggests that elderly people have a consistently high degree of contact with family members (Shanas 1961, 1968, 1977; Adams 1986, 1968a; Townsend 1957; Philbald and McNamara 1965; Harris and Associates 1975). Rosenfeld (1978) reported that 92 percent of the elderly have some immediate families available and that their families are the major focus of their daily lives. Estimates vary from Troll's (1971) 40 percent who are visited weekly by their adult offspring, to reports that approximately two-thirds live close to their adult offspring and see them weekly (Shanas 1961; Komarovsky 1964). On the other hand, Shanas (1980) later found that 18 percent of the elderly in the United States are living with one of their children, 34 percent live within ten minutes' distance from at least one of their children, and three-fourths of them had seen at least one of their children during the previous week. Petrowsky (1976) reported that almost three-fourths of his 173 elderly Florida residents interacted with nearby kin groups weekly. Shanas (1979) found that most elderly people live within a half hour's drive of at least one of their adult offspring. Troll et al. (1979) concluded that most young couples seem to live reasonably close to both sets of parents. These data do not indicate disengagement, although they say nothing about the quality of the interaction.

Substantial research evidence attests to the importance of adult offspring in the lives of their elderly parents (Hess and Waring 1978; Robinson and Thurnher 1979; Mancini 1979; Seelback and Hansen 1980; Archbold 1983; Frankfather et al. 1981; Troll and Bengtson 1981; Quinn 1983; Bromberg 1983). The reverse is also true; Troll (1972) found that parents are also important to their children. Even the oldest members of her sample said they still refer to their parents more frequently than they do to other people. Johnson and Bursk (1977) found that both elderly parents and adult offspring rate each other similarly, with an occasional tendency for the parents to rate their children somewhat higher than the children rate their parents.

There is also some evidence that distance has essentially no impact on the sentiment, affection, or endurance of the relationships (Climo 1986b; Litwak 1982, 1985). Some researchers have found that the quality of the relationship is unrelated either to the amount of contact or to the separations and changes in the lives of the elderly and their adult offspring (Lee and Ellithorpe 1982; Moss et al. 1985; Adams 1968b; Bowlby 1983; Troll and Smith 1976). Johnson and Bursk (1977) found that the quality of health and financial status are more important than proximity in terms of elderly parents' positive affect toward adult offspring. Interestingly, Cicirelli (1981) found that proximity is not related to common values between parent and offspring. According to Marshall and Rosenthal (1985), proximity is less important to the emotional bonds between the two than to the frequency of interactions and exchange of services.

Different parameters are involved when elderly parents need care and their adult offspring are geographically distant. The distant children feel cut off and left out of decision making. Daughters who live away tend to express guilt more frequently about not doing more for their mothers than do distant sons. Daughters also desire to spend additional time with their mothers more often than do sons (Schoonover et al. 1987).

Climo (1986a) found that when they live long distances away from each other, adult offspring and their parents have contact mostly through letters, telephone calls, and visits. He found that telephone calls may be somewhat frustrating because they exclude all forms of nonverbal communication. Litwak (1982) reported that telephone calls tend to replace visits at certain distances and that the kinds of services the offspring can provide decrease with the increase of distance. Although psychosocial supports can be maintained at a distance (Moss et al. 1985), various other services cannot be maintained (Rosow 1974; Rosenmayr and Kockeis 1963). Climo (1986b) reported that the typical adult offspring visits an average of three times in two years, while the parents typically visit slightly less frequently. As the distance between them increases, the frequency of visits decreases, the time between the visits increases, and the visits themselves tend to last for longer periods of time.

Genealogical Proximity and Frequency of Interaction

According to Aiken (1964), interaction with kin is positively related to spatial and genealogical proximity. Research shows that most interaction between kin is between parent and child (Adams 1968b; Streib 1965; Lopata 1978b).

Gender Roles and Frequency of Interaction

The interaction between aging parents and their adult offspring is primarily between females rather than males (Lopata 1978b; Aiken 1964; Johnson and Kerckhoff 1964; Straus 1969; Shanas 1968; Seelback 1978; Bromberg 1983; cf. Atchley 1988). These women are subject to greater stress than many people realize (Brody 1981). Climo (1986a, 1986b) reported that women visit their parents more often than men. He also found that as a mother ages, she tends to visit her adult offspring for longer periods of time. Atchley (1988) has written that older women who are married interact less with their children than do women who are divorced or widowed.

Age Roles and Frequency of Interaction

The interaction aging parents have with their adult offspring is closer with young-adult offspring than with older-adult offspring (Adams 1970; Aiken, 1964). Seelback (1977) reported some evidence that as older people become more dependent, they expect and receive more aid from their offspring. In terms of long-distance visiting, Climo (1986a, 1986b) found that as age increases, the frequency of visits between elderly parents and adult offspring tends to decrease.

Consequences of Intergenerational Linkages

The research findings concerning contact (as well as other aspects of the relationship) between elderly parents and their adult offspring is not completely consistent. Some of the research suggests that frequency of contact is of minimal consequence. For example, Rosow (1965) suggested that geographical distance between elderly parents and their adult offspring reduces the emotional ties and involvement between them. He (Rosow 1967) stated that the distinction between formal responsibility and intimacy has been blurred in past research. Blau (1973) argued that elderly parents are only marginally involved in their families. Treas (1977) saw the family as becoming even less central to the elderly in the future than it is now. Bell (1973) found no evidence in support of his hypotheses of a significant increase in informal social relationships toward the later stages of the family life cycle. Kinkel (1944) maintained that the obligation of children to support aged and needy parents is no longer well established in the mores of American society. Lopata (1978a) concluded that extended kin do not make much of an appearance in the economic, service, social, and emotional support systems for widows. Rosenfeld (1978) said that the elderly seem to make a pact with their adult offspring that, because of different needs, interests, and lifestyles, they will not live too far apart and will keep in touch. Rosow (1973) stated that young people have negative stereotypes about the elderly and that their attitudes do not change as a result of experience with them (Bekker and Taylor 1966).

Positive consequences of the relationship between elderly parents and their adult children and grandchildren include anticipatory socialization (Troll 1971), stable transmission of an ideology and value system (Kempler 1976), maintenance of intergenerational continuity (Sussman 1954, 1959), a mutual socializing process (Rosenfeld 1978), and reciprocity of assistance (Streib 1973; Robertson 1977).

Mutual Aid

Shanas (1973) found that adult offspring are a major source of psychosocial support for their elderly parents in several countries, including the United States. Black (1974) maintained that the family is an important source of aid and support for the majority of elderly people today. However, in terms of services, Bracey (1966) found that less than 15 percent of his elderly respondents got regular assistance with household tasks from their adult offspring. There seems to be agreement that the elderly parent will turn to his or her adult offspring first in times of crisis (Rosenfeld 1978; Lopata 1973; Goldfarb 1965; Ward 1978; cf. Kuypers and Trute 1978; Johnson and Bursk 1977).

Most of the research shows that psychosocial support is more important than economic support (Ryder 1979; Streib 1958; Treas 1977; Moriwaki 1973; Johnson 1978; Hess and Waring 1978). Sussman and Burchinal (1962) pointed out that financial assistance seems to flow more from the parents to the offspring than the reverse. There is also evidence of different perceptions of needs between elderly parents and their adult offspring (Rosenfeld 1978; Robertson 1977). And there appears to be an inverse association between elderly parents' filial responsibility expectations and their levels of life satisfaction (Seelback and Sauer 1977; Seelback 1978).

Aid is also reflected in the major role transitions that take place in the lives of aging parents. Remnet (1987) had her sample of adult offspring identify the following major role transitions in their parents' lives: divorce, grandparenthood, retirement, and widowhood. Her respondents indicated that they needed information on communication skills, normal and abnormal aging, and available community resources in order to enhance their ability to aid their parents.

Nonfamilial Social Support

Ward (1978) reported that elderly people's emotional ties to family often remain more salient than those to friends and neighbors, even when family interaction is minimal. He also noted that the extended family is not as likely to provide the elderly with relevant roles and activities on an ongoing basis as are the age peers. Messer (1968) would probably agree; he found that the elderly with older friends and neighbors tend to feel a greater sense of integration into society than do those who are primarily dependent on their adult offspring and grandchildren for their social contacts. Blau (1973) contended that with regard to morale, friends are more important than grandchildren for older persons. Adams (1971) found that friendships among elderly people are most consistently related to satisfaction. Wood and Robertson (1978) presented data that indicate the relatively greater importance of friends that grandchildren for maintaining morale in old age. Messer (1968) found that age segregation is associated with less dependency on the family as a source of morale and is not accompanied by a feeling of familial neglect. However, according to Powers and Bultena (1976), many men and women have never formed close ties outside their immediate families.

It could be that Harper et al. (1969) were correct when they stated that subcultural affiliations more precisely describe the relationship between family generational structure and intergenerational family solidarity. For example, Woehrer (1978) reported that older Scandinavian-Americans are not in close contact with the families and are relatively reluctant to reveal difficulties and request aid from their children. She said that black Americans tend to have friends who take the place of kin, whereas for Irish-Americans, the ideal was for kin to be friends. This tendency to seek nonkin was also observed among older Mormons, who do not wish to disturb their offspring with their problems and want to associate with fellow Mormons who are not necessarily kin in the later years of their lives (Peterson 1978).

Subcultural affiliations aside, it seems safe to conclude that in American society at present, the family network for older people is only one of at least two support systems. Older friends and neighbors form the second and—on a daily basis, with routine kinds of events—may even form the central support system. Adult offspring feel as if they can be called on for assistance and support, but the hope is they will never have to be.

Suggestions for Future Research

The consequences of elderly parents living with their adult offspring have not been adequately researched. While some researchers argue that it adds little if any stress, others take the opposite position and argue that, because of the advanced age of those who do move in with their adult offspring, there are serious adjustment problems.

Most of the research indicates that elderly people have a consistently high degree of contact with family members. This does not answer the question posed at the beginning of this chapter: What influences do adult offspring have on the basic residential family of their elderly parents and what influences do elderly parents have on the basic residential family of their children? Because so many adult offspring live near their parents, it appears that there is a high degree of contact. However, a clear description of the dimensions of the relationship between parents and their adult offspring is needed. They could be considered a major dependent variable that needs to be linked to some of the independent variables discussed in this chapter. Atchley (1988) identified some of the dimensions—interaction frequency and mutual aid. He also suggested that qualitative aspects, such as degree of closeness and strength of feelings, need to be considered. Are these four (interaction frequency, mutual aid, degree of closeness, and strength of feelings) the important dimensions of the relationship? Mancini and Blieszner (1986) identified the following as the core variables: affection, companionate and task interaction, exchange, and contact satisfaction. Are these the important dimensions of the relationship?

Another area for future research is the motivations on which the interrelationships are based. In a sense, the degree of affection and regard that some offspring may have about their parents as well as their sense of duty could be considered their motivations for interaction frequency and for aid. Motivations need to be researched in greater depth. In terms of the impact on the relationship, are there significant differences between adult offspring who are motivated by duty and those motivated by affection?

A strong element of independence is evident in considering the relationship between elderly parents and their adult offspring. The elderly are often reluctant to seek or accept help, possibly because dependency on children is alienative. Certainly their motivations should be critically examined, as well as the consequences of such motivations on life satisfaction or morale.

Many current researchers seem to think that the emotional ties and involvement that elderly parents have with their adult offspring have been weakened. However, some think otherwise. Most agree that family crises precipitate close relations and that psychosocial support is more important than economic support. Some longitudinal data would be helpful, as well as analyses of different cohorts. Also, what are the critical kinds of family crises that precipitate close relationships?

Researchers have documented a variety of positive consequences of the relationships between elderly parents and their adult offspring. An emerging problem that has not been adequately researched has to do with the consequences of an even broader kin network—the four-generational family (Barron and Smith 1979). The role of the grandparent is changing in that grandparenthood is becoming a middle-age event, and great-grandparenthood is emerging as the new old-age status (Wood and Robertson 1976). Grandparents can look forward to an empty-nest stage of 13 years with their spouse, compared with an average of 2 years some 80 years ago (Glick 1977). Although the empty nest transition may not be as stressful as many originally believed (Harkins 1978), the length of this stage means that families are making plans for caring for an elderly parent just as they are approaching old age themselves (Gefland et al.; Block 1978). Hill (1965) reported that when three generations of adults are living, aid tends to flow from the middle generation to the other two. These older middle-aged people tend to dominate in American society (Koller 1974a), but increasingly they must cope with the impending role changes in their own lives.

Additional research is needed on socialization into old age (Rosow 1967), as well as on the impact of socioeconomic status, the kin network, and the age of the offspring in the socialization process (Harvey and Bahr 1974; Atchley 1988; Gefland et al. 1978). It has been observed that neither elderly parents nor their adult offspring have been socialized to cope optimally with the issues generated by some of the conditions in the current intergenerational family (Shanas 1980). Few norms define intergenerational relationships, and family members are left vulnerable to various platitudes concerning duty and related concepts (Getzel 1981; Kuypers and Bengston 1983).

Additional research is also needed on the role of females in both giving and receiving increased aid. Atchley (1988) said that some researchers have found few sex differences. The consequences of changes in gender roles in American society in terms of the elderly parent–adult offspring relationship need examination.

Finally, research is needed concerning the entire kin network of the elderly. In this chapter attention was focused on the elderly parent–adult offspring relationship. What impact do elderly siblings have on each other? What impact, if any, do nieces, nephews, cousins, various children-in-law, and other relations have in the lives of elderly people in American society?

References

Adams, B.N. 1964. "Interaction theory and the social network." *Sociometry* 36:64–68.

———. 1968a. "The middle class adult and his widowed or still-married." *Social Problems* 16:50–59.

———. 1968b. *Kinship in an Urban Setting.* Chicago: Markham Publishing.

———. 1970. "Isolation, function, and beyond: American kinship in the 1960's." *Journal of Marriage and the Family,* 32:575–97.

———. 1975. *The Family: A Sociological Interpretation* (2nd ed.). Chicago: Rand McNally.

———. 1986. *The Family: A Sociological Interpretation* (4th ed.). San Diego: Harcourt Brace Jovanovich.

Adams, D. L. 1971. "Correlates of satisfaction among the elderly." *The Gerontologist* 11:64–68.

Aiken, M. T. 1964. *Kinship in an Urban Community.* Ann Arbor, Michigan: Unpublished Ph.D. dissertation. University of Michigan.

Archbold, P. G. 1983. "Impact of parent-caring on middle-aged offspring." *Journal of Gerontological Nursing* 6:78–85.

Arling, G. 1976. "The elderly widow and her family, neighbors, and friends." *Journal of Marriage and the Family* 38:757–68.

Atchley, R. C. 1988. *Social Forces and Aging* (5th ed.). Belmont, CA: Wadsworth.

Barron, G. M., and Smith, P. A. 1979. *Aging, Ageism and Society.* St. Paul, MN: West Publishing.

Bekker, L. M., and Taylor, C. 1966. "Attitudes toward the aged in a multigenerational sample." *Journal of Gerontology* 21:115–18.

Bell, B. D. 1973. "The family life cycle, primary relationships, and social participation patterns." *The Gerontologist* 13:78–81.

Benson, L. 1971. *The Family Bond, Marriage, Love and Sex in America.* New York: Random House.

Beresford, J. C., and Rivlin, A. M. 1966. "Privacy, poverty, and old age." *Demography* 3:247–58.

Black, D. 1974. "The older person and the family." In H. Davis (ed.), *Prospects and Issues.* Los Angeles: Ethel Percy Andrus Gerontology Center.

Blau, Z. S. 1973. *Old Age in a Changing Society.* New York: Franklin Watts.

Bowlby, J. 1983. "Affectional Bonds: Their Nature and Origin." In R. S. Weiss (ed.), *Loneliness: The Experience of Emotional and Social Isolation.* Cambridge, MA: The MIT Press.

Bracey, H. E. 1966. *In Retirement.* Baton Rouge, LA: Louisiana State Press.

Brody, E. M. 1981. "Social economic and environmental issues relating to aging, with some thoughts about 'women in the middle' " *The Gerontologist* 21:471–80.

Bromberg, E. M. 1983. "Mother-daughter relationships in later life: The effect of quality of relationship upon mutual aid." *Journal of Gerontological Social Work* 6:75–92.

Brown, R. 1969. "Family structure and social isolation of older persons." *Journal of Gerontology* 15:170–74.

Chevan, A., and Korson, J. 1972. "The widowed who live alone: An examination of social and demographic factors." *Social Forces* 51:45–53.

Cicirelli, V. G. 1981. *Helping Elderly Parents: The Role of Adult Children.* Boston: Auburn House.

Clavan, S. 1978. "The impact of social class and social trends on the role of grandparent." *The Family Coordinator* 27:351–57.

Climo, J. J. 1986a. "Sociodemographic correlates of the distant adult child-elderly parent relationship." Paper presented at the Third National Forum on Research on Aging, Lincoln, NE.

———. 1986b. "Visits of distant living adult children and elderly parents." Paper presented at the annual meeting of the American Anthropological Association, Philadelphia, PA.

Demos, J. 1970. *A Little Commonwealth.* New York: Oxford University Press.

Dinkel, R. M. 1943. "Parent-child conflict in Minnesota families." *American Sociological Review* 8:412–19.

Frankfather, D. L., Smith, M. J., and Caro, F. G. 1981. *Family Care of the Elderly.* Lexington, MA: Lexington Books.

Fuchs, L. H. 1972. *Family Matters.* New York: Random House.

Gefland, D. E., Olsen, J. K., and Block, M. R. 1978. "Two generations of elderly in the changing American family: Implications for family services." *The Family Coordinator* 27:395–403.

Getzel, G. S. 1981. "Social work with family caregivers to the aged." *Social Casework* 62:201–10.

Glasser, P. H., and Glasser, L. N. 1962. "Role reversal and conflict between aged parents and their children." *Marriage and Family Living* 24:46–51.

Glick, P. 1977. "Updating the life cycle of the family." *Journal of Marriage and the Family* 39:5–13.

Goldfarb, A. D. 1965. "The intimate relations of older people." In S. M. Farber (ed.), *The Family's Search for Survival.* New York: McGraw-Hill.

Greven, P. 1970. *Four Generations: Population, Land and Family in Colonial Andover, Massachusetts.* Ithaca, NY: Cornell University Press.

Grove, W. R., Hughes, M., and Galle, O. R. 1979. "Overcrowding in the home: An empirical investigation of its possible consequences." *American Sociological Review* 44:59–80.

Harkins, E. B. 1978. "Effects of empty nest transition on self-report of psychological and physical well-being." *Journal of Marriage and the Family* 40:549–56.

Harper, J. R., Wood, D., and Garza, J. M. 1969. "Ethnicity, family generational structure and intergenerational solidarity." *Sociological Symposium* 2:75–82.

Harris, L., and Associates. 1975. *The Myth and Reality of Aging in America.* Washington, DC: National Council on Aging.

Harvey, C. D., and Bahr, H. M. 1974. "Widowhood, morale, and affiliation." *Journal of Marriage and the Family* 36:97–106.

Hess, B. B., and Waring, J. M. 1978. "Changing patterns of aging and family bonds in later life." *The Family Coordinator* 27:303–14.

Hill, R. 1965. "Decision making and the family life cycle." In E. Shanas and G. F. Streib (eds.), *Social Structure and the Family: Generational Relations*. Englewood Cliffs, NJ: Prentice-Hall.

Johnson, C., and Kerckhoff, A. 1964. "Family norms, social position, and the value of change." *Social Forces* 43:149–56.

Johnson, E. S. 1978. "Good relationships between older mothers and their daughters: A causal model." *The Gerontologist* 18:301–06.

Johnson, E. S., and Bursk, B. J. 1977. "Relationships between the elderly and their adult children." *The Gerontologist* 17:90–95.

Kempler, H. L. 1976. "Extended kinship ties and some modern alternatives." *The Family Coordinator* 25:143–45.

Kinkel, R. M. 1944. "Attitudes of children toward supporting aged parents." *American Sociological Review* 9:370–79.

Kirkpatrick, C. 1955. *The Family as Process and Institution*. New York: The Ronald Press.

Kobrin, F. E. 1976. "The primary individual and the family: Changes in living arrangements in the United States since 1940." *Journal of Marriage and the Family* 38:233–39.

Koller, M. R. 1974a. "Studies of three-generational households." *Marriage and Family Living* 16:205–06.

———. 1974b. *Families: A Multigenerational Approach*. New York: McGraw-Hill.

Komarovsky, M. 1964. *Blue-Collar Marriage*. New York: Random House.

Kuypers, J. A., and Bengston, V. L. 1983. "Toward competence in the older family." In T. H. Brubaker (ed.), *Family Relationships In Later Life*. Beverly Hills, CA: Sage Publications.

Kuypers, J. A., and Trute, B. 1978. "The older family as the locus of crisis intervention." *The Family Coordinator* 27:405–11.

Laslett, B. 1978. "Family membership, past and present." *Social Problems* 25:476–90.

Lee, G. R., and Ellithrope, E. 1982. *Grandmothers, Mothers, and Daughters*. New York: Institute on Pluralism and Group Identity.

Litwak, E. 1960. "Occupational mobility and extended family cohesion." *American Sociological Review* 25:9–21.

———. 1982. *The Modified Extended Family, Social Networks, and Research Continuities in Aging*. New York: Center for Social Sciences at Columbia University.

———. 1985. *Helping the Elderly*. New York: The Guilford Press.

Levy, S. M. 1981. "The aging woman: Developmental issues and mental health needs." *Professional Psychology* 12:92–102.

Lopata, H. Z. 1973. *Widowhood in an American City*. Cambridge, MA: Schenkman.

———. 1978a. "Contributions of extended families to the support systems of metropolitan area widows: Limitations of the modified kin network." *Journal of Marriage and the Family* 40:355–64.

———. 1978b. "The absence of community resources in social systems of urban widows." *The Family Coordinator* 27:383–88.

Mancini, J. A. 1979. "Family relationships and morale among people 65 years of age and older." *American Journal of Orthopsychiatry* 49:292–300.

Mancini, J. A., and Blieszner, R. 1986. "Successful aging and close relationships with children." Paper presented at the 39th annual meeting of the Gerontological Society of America, Chicago, IL.

Marshall, V. M., and Rosenthal, C. J. 1985. "The relevance of geographical proximity in intergenerational relations." Paper presented at the annual meeting of the Gerontological Society of America, New Orleans, LA.

Medley, M. L. 1976. "Satisfaction with life among persons sixty-five and over." *Journal of Gerontology* 31:448–55.

Messer, M. 1968. "Age grouping and the family status of the elderly." *Sociology and Social Research* 53:271–79.

Moen, E. 1978. "The reluctance of the elderly to accept help." *Social Problems* 25:293–303.

Moriwaki, S. Y. 1973. "Self-disclosures, significant others and psychological well-being in old age." *Journal of Health and Social Behavior*, 14:226–32.

Moss, M., Moss, S. A., and Moles, E. 1985. "The quality of relationships between elderly parents and their out-of-town children." *The Gerontologist* 25:134–40.

Parsons, T. 1943. "The kinship system of the contemporary United States." *American Anthropologist* 45:22–38.

———. 1949. "The social structure of the family." In R. N. Anshen (ed.), *The Family: Its Function and Destiny.* New York: Harper and Brothers.

Parsons, T., and Bales, R. F., and Associates. 1955. *Family, Socialization and Interaction Process.* Glencoe, IL: The Free Press.

Peterson, E. T. 1978. "Problems of the elderly and their families." Paper presented at the Adult Education Conference, U.S.A., Portland, OR.

Petrowsky, M. 1976. "Marital status, sex, and the social networks of the elderly." *Journal of Marriage and the Family* 38:749–56.

Philbald, T. C., and McNamara, R. 1965. "Social adjustment of elderly people in three small towns." In A. Rose and W. Peterson (eds.), *Older People and Their Social World.* Philadelphia: F. A. Davis.

Powers, E. A., and Bultena, G. L. 1976. "Sex differences in intimate friendships of old age." *Journal of Marriage and the Family* 38:739–47.

Quinn, W. H. 1983. "Personal and family adjustment in later life." *Journal of Marriage and the Family* 45:57–73.

Remnet, V. L. 1987. "How adult children respond to role transitions in the lives of their aging parents." *Educational Gerontology* 13:341–55.

Robertson, J. R. 1977. "Grandmotherhood: A study of role conceptions." *Journal of Marriage and the Family* 39:165–74.

Robins, L. N., and Tomanec, M. 1962. "Closeness to blood relatives outside the immediate family." *Marriage and Family Living* 24:340–46.

Robinson, B., and Thurnher, M. 1979. "Taking care of aged parents: A family cycle transition." *The Gerontologist* 19:586–93.

Rogers, C. L., and Leichter, H. L. 1964. "Laterality and conflict in kinship ties." In W. J. Goode (ed.), *Readings on the Family and Society.* Englewood Cliffs, NJ: Prentice-Hall.

Rosenfeld, A. H. 1978. *New Views on Older Lives.* Rockville, MD: U.S. Department of Health, Education, and Welfare, National Institute of Mental Health.

Rosenmayr, L., and Kockeis, E. 1963. "Propositions for a sociological theory of aging and the family." *International Social Science Journal* 15:410–26.

Rosow, I. 1965. "Intergenerational relationships: Problems and proposals." In E. Shanas and G. F. Streib (eds.), *Social Structure and the Family: Generational Relations.* Englewood Cliffs, NJ: Prentice-Hall.

———. 1967. *Social Integration of the Aged.* New York: Free Press.

———. 1973. "And then we were old." In H. Z. Lopata (ed.), *Marriages and Families.* New York: D. Van Nostrand Company.

———. 1974. *Socialization to Old Age.* Berkeley: University of California Press.

Ryder, N. B. 1979. "The future of American fertility." *Social Problems* 26:359–70.

Schoonover, C. B., Brody, E. M., Hoffman, C., and Klegan, M. H. 1987. "Parent care and geographically distant children." Paper given at the 40th annual meeting of the Gerontological Society of America, Washington, DC.

Schorr, A. L. 1960. *Filial Responsibility in the Modern American Family.* U.S. Department of Health, Education, and Welfare, Social Security Administration.

Seelback, W. C. 1977. "Gender differences in expectations for filial responsibility." *The Gerontologist* 17:506–12.

———. 1978. "Correlates of aged parents' filial responsibility expectations and realizations." *The Family Coordinator* 27:341–50.

Seelback, W. C., and Hansen, C. J. 1980. "Satisfaction with family relations among the elderly." *Family Relations* 29:91–95.

Seelback, W. C., and Sauer, W. 1977. "Filial responsibility expectations and morale among aged parents." *The Gerontologist* 17:492–99.

Sena, J. R. 1973. *The Survival of the Mexican Extended Family in the U.S.: Evidence from a Southern California Town.* Unpublished Ph.D. dissertation. University of California, Los Angeles.

———. 1980. "Older people and their families: The new pioneers." *Journal of Marriage and the Family* 42:9–15.

Shanas, E. 1961. *Family Relationships of Older People.* Health Information Foundation.

———. 1968. *Old People in Three Industrial Societies.* New York: Atherton Press.

———. 1973. "Family-kin networks and aging in cross-cultural perspective." *Journal of Marriage and the Family* 35:505–11.

———. 1977. *National Survey of the Aged: 1975.* Chicago: University of Illinois, Chicago Circle.

———. 1979. "Social myth as hypothesis: The case of family relations of old people." *The Gerontologist* 19:3–9.

Siegal, J. S. 1976. "Demographic aspects of aging and the older population in the United States." *Current Population Reports*, series P-23, no. 59. U.S. Bureau of the Census. Washington, DC: U.S. Government Printing Office.

Skolnick, A. 1987. *The Intimate Environment: Exploring Marriage and the Family* (4th ed.). Boston: Little, Brown.

Stehouwer, J. 1965. "Relations between generations and the three-generational household in Denmark." In E. Shanas and G. F. Streib (eds.), *Social Structure and the Family: Generational Relations.* Englewood Cliffs, NJ: Prentice-Hall.

Straus, M. A. 1969. "Social class and farm-city differences in interaction with kin in relation to societal modernization." *Rural Sociology* 34:476–95.

Streib, G. F. 1958. "Family patterns in retirement." *Journal of Social Issues* 14:46–60.

———. 1965. "Intergenerational relations: Perspective of the two generations on the older parent." *Journal of Marriage and the Family* 27:469–76.

———. 1972. "Older families and their troubles: Familial and social responses." *The Family Coordinator* 21:5–19.

———. 1973. "Facts and forecasts about the family and old age." In G. F. Streib (ed.), *The Changing Family: Adaptation and Diversity.* Palo Alto, CA: Addison-Wesley.

Sussman, M. 1954. "Family continuity: Selective factors which affect relationships between families at generational levels." *Marriage and Family Living* 16:112–20.

———. 1959. "The isolated nuclear family: Fact or fiction." *Social Problems* 6:333–40.

———. 1965. "Relationships of adult children with their parents in the United States." In E. Shanas and G. F. Streib (eds.), *Social Structure and the Family: Generational Relations.* Englewood Cliffs, NJ: Prentice-Hall.

Sussman, M. B., and Burchinal, L. G. 1962. "Kin family network: Unheralded structure in current conceptualizations of family functioning." *Marriage and Family Living* 24:231–40.

Sweetser, D. A. 1966. "The effect of industrialization on intergenerational solidarity." *Rural Sociology* 31:156–70.

Tibbitts, C. 1965. "The older family member in American society." In H. L. Jacobs (ed), *The Older Person in the Family: Challenges and Conflicts.* Iowa City: The Institute of Gerontology.

Townsend, P. 1957. *The Family Life of Old People.* London: Routledge and Kegan Paul.

Treas, J. 1977. "Family support systems for the aged." *The Gerontologist* 17:486–91.

Troll, L. 1971. "The family of later life: A decade review." *Journal of Marriage and the Family* 33:263–90.

———. 1972. "The salience of members of three generation families for one another." Paper presented at the annual meeting of the American Psychological Association, Honolulu, HI.

Troll, L., and Bengtson, V. 1981. "Generations in the family." In W. Burr, R. Hill, I. Nye, and I. Reiss (eds.), *Contemporary Theories about the Family.* New York: Free Press.

Troll, L., Miller, S. J., and Atchley, R. C. 1979. *Families in Later Life.* Belmont, CA: Wadsworth.

Troll, L., and Smith, J. 1976. "Attachments through the life span: Some questions about dyadic bonds among adults." *Human Development* 19:156–70.

Ward, R. A. 1978. "Limitations of the family as a supportive institution in the lives of the aged." *The Family Coordinator* 27:365–73.

Wax, R. 1965. "A cross-cultural view of the older person in the family." In H. L. Jacobs (ed.), *The Older Person in the Family: Challenges and Conflicts.* Iowa City: The Institute of Gerontology.

Winch, R. F. 1974. "Some observations on extended families in the United States." In R. F. Winch and G. B. Spanier (eds.), *Selected Studies in Marriage and the Family* (4th ed.). New York: Holt, Rinehart and Winston.

Woehrer, C. E. 1978. "Cultural pluralism in American families: The influence of ethnicity of social aspects of aging." *The Family Coordinator* 27:329–39.

Wood, V., and Robertson, J. F. 1976. "The significance of grandparenthood." In J. F. Gubrium (ed.), *Time, Roles, and Self in Old Age*. New York: Human Science Press.

———. 1978. "Friendship and kinship interaction: Differential effect on the morale of the elderly." *Journal of Marriage and the Family* 40:367–75.

10

Extended Family Ties: Genealogical Researchers

Cardell K. Jacobson
Phillip R. Kunz
Melanie W. Conlin

Until recently, interest in ancestors, family coats-of-arms, pedigrees, and so on has largely been the domain of royalty, interested in maintaining and documenting royal lineages. There have been departures from this, such as the memorizing of ancestry among some Africans documented by Alex Haley (1976) and similar cases in South Sea cultures. But general interest in ancestral family lines has not been very great.

Even today in many areas of the United States, second and third cousins do not know that they are related, even though they live in the same locality and are even neighbors to one another. Discussions with young people show that they often do not even know what countries their ancestors came from.

But interest in genealogy has increased dramatically since the end of World War II and is now reported to be one of the three most popular hobbies in the United States (Rubincam 1978; Bidlack 1983b).

The increase that has occurred during the last fifteen years has resulted from several factors. One was the televised showing of *Roots* in 1977. Since the *Roots* phenomenon, the number of self-help books and the extent of organized travel to the "old country," where people see first-hand their ancestral lands, have increased. The Bicentennial celebration of the U.S. Constitution was another factor. But genealogical interest both preceded and postdated these events.

Another factor was the increased interest in medical histories. Diabetes, heart disease and other illnesses are sometimes transferable to succeeding generations, and knowledge of previous family medical problems is becoming increasingly important. The vast records that make up the genealogical libraries are a natural source of data about family medical histories.

The most common explanation for the current interest in genealogy, however, is a sociological one, voiced by both lay people and professionals. This explanation concerns the rapid social changes and breakdown of traditional forms of social organization that have occurred in American society.

This has resulted in an attempt to regain "roots" through the study of genealogical origins. This explanation will be examined later in the chapter.

Despite the common impression, genealogical interest is not new in the United States. There were two previous eras of high genealogical interest in the United States (Hareven 1978; Taylor 1982; Bockstruck 1983). The first began about 1870 and continued through the first decade of the twentieth century. Taylor (1982) argued that much of this early interest was a reaction to the dramatic changes accompanying the Industrial Revolution, the massive migrations of the nineteenth century, and the growth of "curiosity and appreciation of history as a consequence of the nation's Centennial observance of 1876" (1982, 24). The second era of high genealogical interest occurred in the 1920s and 1930s, possibly also in response to dramatic social changes taking place at that time.

The most recent period of genealogical interest, however, is said to differ from earlier periods. Most genealogists in earlier decades seem to have been older, usually retired people who had ample time to do the research. But present genealogical researchers are younger, are more likely to be from a minority ethnic or racial group (though the majority still tend to be White Anglo-Saxon Protestants), and are more diverse with regard to their social class and their reasons for doing genealogical research (Bidlack 1978, 1983a; Hareven 1978; Rubincam 1978; Sinko and Peters 1983). Hareven (1978, 138) stated that there has been a shift "from the search for legitimization of exclusive status to a concern with emergent identity." She also argued that this increased interest is partly the result of the ethnic revival of the 1970s.

This chapter systematically examines the social characteristics of genealogical researchers. First, the extent to which genealogists may be characterized as elderly will be determined. Second, the functions that genealogy serves for people, especially the aged, will be examined.

It may be argued that concern with genealogy is an index of the relationship of the younger generation with the older generations. Thus, how a society views its elderly people may be assessed by its interest in who they are and where they came from.

Data Sources

The data presented in this chapter are taken from three surveys conducted by the authors. The first survey was taken of members of the southeastern and the south-central chapters of the Wisconsin State Genealogical Society in the fall of 1976. All members attending the meetings were asked to complete a questionnaire concerning their interest in genealogy. Approximately 80 percent of those attending completed the questionnaire. Additional questionnaires were completed at meetings of the south-central Wisconsin chapter. These respondents are herein referred to as "the Wisconsin sample."

One way to assess whether genealogists differ from the population as a whole is to compare them with the characteristics of the residents of one area from which the sample is drawn. The 1970 census provided basic information on the population of southeastern Wisconsin. The data on the Wisconsin sample of genealogists will be compared with census data on residents of the southeastern Wisconsin counties of Washington, Milwaukee, Waukesha, Racine, Kenosha, Walworth, and Rock.

A second comparison group of respondents to this same genealogical survey is a sample of seventy-four hobbyists taking county recreational classes at one of the Milwaukee high schools, primarily in arts and crafts. Comparing the genealogists to these other hobbyists helps control for a variety of spurious variables such as social class, time available, and so on. Their similarity of backgrounds helps highlight social factors related specifically to genealogical interest. The hobbyists were asked to complete the nongenealogical portions of the questionnaire.

The second survey was obtained using questionnaires on which a family tree was drawn, with blanks provided in which respondents were to write in the names and birthplaces of their ancestors. Background information, including sex, religion, religious activity, and family reunion attendance, was also obtained. Knowledge of the names and places of birth of one's ancestors was treated as the dependent variable. Such knowledge was taken as an indirect measure of involvement with ancestors. These questionnaires were completed by students in introductory sociology classes in Utah, Canada, and Kansas. The geographical areas were selected because of convenience, although each area also represents a different social and environmental situation. This sample is referred to as "the student sample."

The third questionnaire consisted of a form similar to the one used for the student sample, but also included questions about genealogical activities. It was given to all the men and women in one Mormon ward (similar to a parish) attending services on a particular Sunday. The questionnaire was distributed in Relief Society (the organization for women) and in Priesthood Meeting (the organization for men). Those participating in other activities in the church at that time were given questionnaires to fill out during the same day. Inasmuch as a very high percentage of ward members attend meetings on any particular Sunday, the response rate was over 85 percent of the entire ward. This sample is referred to as "the Mormon ward sample."

Social Characteristics of Genealogists

The Wisconsin Sample

One hundred and forty-five of the Wisconsin sample, or 75 percent, were married. Thirteen and a half percent were single, 9.3 percent were widowed, and only 2.1 percent were divorced. These figures show that genealogists are more likely to be married than the population as a whole (61.8 percent in southeastern Wisconsin). They were divorced slightly less often (2.1 percent, compared with 3.2 percent) and widowed somewhat more often (9.3 percent, compared with 7.3 percent). Singles also appear to have relatively less interest in genealogy than others, since they constituted only 13.5 percent of the sample but 26.5 percent of the general population.

The overwhelming majority of the genealogists (88.1 percent) were female. Further, their average age was approximately 53 years, while the average age of the population as a whole was approximately 43.5 years. Thus, the Wisconsin sample of genealogists was older and more likely to be female than the population as a whole.

Sinko and Peters (1983) conducted a survey of genealogists working at the Newberry Library in Chicago. Their sample was not as skewed as the Wisconsin sample; the average age of their respondents was 47.9 years, and only 58.6 percent were female. Genealogists who use libraries may be different from those active in genealogical societies. Sinko and Peters characterized their respondents as "casual hobbyists" and "highly independent." Most were working "outside the mainstream of organized genealogy." Indeed, less than half of their sample (47.6 percent) belonged to any genealogical society.

The Mormon Sample

Since early in its history, the Church of Jesus Christ of Latter-Day Saints, or Mormons, has regarded genealogy as a significant part of its theology. This interest has not remained part of some abstract belief system but has been given an organizational structure to obtain the participation of its members.

Mormon temples were built for special religious practices in which ancestors are an integral part. For those practices to be carried out, Mormons attempt to obtain genealogical information about all Mormon family members who have died and indeed for as many people as possible who have ever lived. Thus, the Church has institutionalized the work of genealogy to "search out one's dead." Although the individual member is generally responsible for getting the work done on his or her own ancestors, the Church per se is responsible for everyone.

On two occasions, the sex distribution of people using the genealogical library facilities of the Mormons in Salt Lake City was noted. The count indicated a sex ratio of three women for each man. Registration at a recent genealogy conference indicated a sex ratio of five women for each man, according to the conference planner. The conference included Mormons as well as many people from outside the faith. A count was also taken of those in the library on two other occasions, and a similar sex ratio was found.

Analysis of the Mormon ward sample indicated that the men have the responsibility for genealogical work within the Priesthood and that specific responsibility for the work is with the high priests. The women, however, know more about ancestors and do more of the actual work in tracing ancestral roots. This may be partly because men serve as wage earners more than women do, and because women are perceived as having more time for such activity. It will be interesting to see whether this traditional gender split diminishes as more women move into the labor force.

Social Characteristics

The sex difference in genealogical interest begins much earlier than retirement years. In the student sample, the females knew more names of their ancestors than did the males. This was true for both their fathers' and their mothers' sides of the family. Thirty-two percent of the males knew four or fewer names on their fathers' side, while only 21 percent of the females knew only so few.

Numerous authors have described differences in sex roles in various aspects of the family (cf., e.g., Nye 1976; Albrecht et al. 1979). Among other tasks, the wife assumes most of the tasks related to maintaining family ties. She is more responsible for the kinship role and for dealing with the extended family, as well as for married children living away from home. Doing genealogy is a natural extension of her role. This assumption may be supported by the notion that women are more expressive and men are more instrumental. Expressiveness may tie into feelings about the family in general. Even among Mormons who have theological reasons for doing genealogical research, women are the ones who generally do the work. Also, it has been assumed that women have more time to do genealogical research since they work full time less often than do men.

In addition to being older and female, genealogists are also more likely to be retired. Fourteen percent of the Wisconsin respondents were retired, and an additional 37.7 percent were housewives. Three percent were unemployed or disabled. Seventeen percent worked part time, and 28 percent worked full time.

The Wisconsin sample appears to have come from people of professional or managerial backgrounds with higher-than-average incomes. The average 1976 family income of those employed or their spouses was

$16,646, and 17.7 percent had an income over $25,000. An examination of the occupations held by the genealogists or their spouses in the Wisconsin sample explains these relatively high income levels. Forty-three percent listed the occupation of the head of the household as professional (compared with 14.7 percent of the male population as a whole). An additional 12.9 percent listed the occupation of the head of the household as managerial (compared with 7.1 percent of the male population as a whole.) Fifteen percent listed the head of household as engaged in a clerical occupation. Only 4.3 percent listed the head of household as a laborer and 5.4 percent as a skilled laborer.

Finally, genealogists are better educated than the general population. A large majority (68.1 percent) of the Wisconsin sample had attended at least some college, and 44 percent had actually graduated from college. One-quarter (25.6 percent) had attended graduate or professional school beyond college. This compares with 55.8 percent of the population as a whole who had graduated from high school and with the 12.2 years of schooling that the average resident in the population had obtained. Again, the findings of Newberry sample obtained by Sinko and Peters (1983) are somewhere between the general population and the Wisconsin sample. Fifty-eight percent of the Newberry sample had some college training.

Clearly, however, the stereotype of the genealogist as a retired man or older woman of middle-class background is reinforced by the Wisconsin sample. Nevertheless, there is also diversity. Some working-class people are interested in genealogy. Approximately one-fourth of the respondents had incomes of less than $9,000, and over a fourth of them worked full time. And approximately one-fourth of them were under 40 years of age.

Another stereotype of genealogists is that they are obsessed. The data from the survey do not support this stereotype. One-fourth of the respondents did genealogy less than an hour a week, and three-fourths did it five hours or less a week. Only 15 percent did genealogy more than ten hours a week. Admittedly, that fifteen percent may seem to be obsessed. Sinko and Peters (1983) placed the number "who are extremely active in the field of genealogical research" at about 10 percent.

Most of the Wisconsin sample had not been involved in genealogy for a long period of time. Thirty-nine percent had been involved in genealogy for three years or less. Only 21.9 percent had been involved for over ten years.

In summary, the results of the several surveys collected on genealogists indicate that the elderly are indeed much more likely to become involved in genealogy than is the population as a whole. Most of those involved, however, are not obsessed by it, although they do spend considerable amounts of time pursuing it. Clearly, it provides a meaningful experience for them and could prove to be a useful program in retirement communities, long-term care facilities, and other places where significant numbers of middle-aged or elderly people live.

Women more than men appear to be attracted to genealogical research, probably because of sex-role socialization in earlier life. Middle- and upper-class people with high educational and occupational levels appear to be attracted to it more than working-class individuals, perhaps because of the greater time they have for such pursuits.

Social Dislocations and Genealogy

Earlier we discussed the argument that the currently high level of genealogical interest is related to social change. Several authors and lay people have proposed that those interested in genealogy are attempting to return to their roots as a result of the social dislocations they have experienced in their own lives.

Dislocations such as geographical mobility and social class mobility would seem to be related to level of genealogical interest. Other social factors, such as changes in family size, ethnicity, and religiosity, may be related to genealogical interest as well.

One type of geographical mobility is immigration. Different immigrant groups among the Wisconsin sample were compared to see if differences exist among them in level of genealogical interest. The results are presented in table 10–1. Compared with other residents of southeastern Wisconsin, the genealogists appear to derive from the older immigrant groups rather than from the more recent immigrant groups. People of German and Austrian ancestry constitute the largest proportion of (44.4 percent) the residents of southeastern Wisconsin; (U.S. Bureau of the Census 1970); they constituted 42.4 percent of the Wisconsin sample. However, this sheds little light on the relationship between length of time in the United States and genealogical interest since there have been several German migrations to the United States.

The data for the other groups listed in table 10–1 indicate that the longer the group has resided in the United States, the more interested that group is likely to be in genealogy. The English, Welsh, Irish, and Scottish constitute only 11 percent of the population in the area, but they make up 34 percent of the sample of genealogists. The 1970 census did not even list western Europeans such as the French, Belgians, and Dutch separately because of their small numbers, yet these groups constituted 6.4 percent of the genealogist sample. Scandinavians composed only 2.4 percent of the census population in the area but 10.8 percent of the respondents (U.S. Bureau of the Census 1970).

Southern and eastern European groups, on the other hand, were under-represented in the genealogist sample. Only 7 percent of the respondents listed their ancestry as Hungarian, Italian, or Polish, but 38.5 percent of all the residents of the southeastern Wisconsin are of southern and eastern

Table 10–1
Nativity of Wisconsin Sample and Southeastern Wisconsin Population

Group	Number of Respondents	Percent of Sample	Percent of Southeastern Wisconsin Population
German/Austrian	86	42.4	44.4
United Kingdom/Irish/Scottish	69	34.0	11.0
Western European	13	6.4	0.0
Scandinavian	22	10.8	2.4
Southern and Eastern European	14	6.9	38.5
Central and South American	0	0.0	3.6

Source: Combined census data for Milwaukee, Waukesha,
Racine, Kenosha, Walworth, Washington, and Rock counties (U.S.Bureau of the Census 1970).

European ancestry. There were no individuals from Mexico or other Central or Latin American countries in the genealogist sample, although 3.6 percent of the population of that part of Wisconsin are from those countries.

The genealogists of different immigrant groups also differed in the amount of genealogical work they did. Those whose ancestors came earlier showed significantly greater involvement in genealogical research than did those whose ancestors came later.

A comparison of the Wisconsin sample with the sample of other hobbyists supports the notion that genealogists generally come from older generations of immigrants. The genealogists reported that their ancestors had immigrated to the country significantly earlier than the ancestors of the hobbyists did.

The hobbyists' background characteristics were quite similar to those of the genealogists in other respects. There were no significant differences between the two samples in their subjective social class, in the social class of their parents, in their own educational level, in their marital status, or in sex composition. In addition, there were no differences between the two samples in their types of full-time occupations, their fathers' occupations, their grandparents' occupations, their present income, or the highest income levels that they had ever earned.

Significant differences between the hobbyists and the genealogists, nevertheless, emerged in three sociodemographic variables: age, present occupation, and level of father's education. The differences in present occupation and age had been expected; as already noted, older and retired individuals are more likely to be involved in genealogy. The unexpectedly low education of the genealogists' fathers may be due to the more rural origins of genealogist.

They also differed in most types of social dislocations. The genealogists tended to come from stable backgrounds rather than from turbulent ones. The frequency of changing residence, was expected to be related to genealogical interest because movers more than stayers would seem to need to establish roots. Nevertheless, the genealogists moved an average of 1.4 times in the previous five years, while the hobbyists moved an average of 2.3 times. The genealogists also moved less frequently in the previous ten years (2.3 times, compared with 3.4), and in the previous twenty years (3.2, compared with 4.2). These results are summarized in table 10–2.

A corollary notion is that those who live in cities are more interested in establishing their roots than rural people because of the disruptions and dislocations that occur in cities. This notion, however, is not supported by data from the Wisconsin sample either. The genealogists themselves tended to grow up in rural areas or smaller cities, whereas the hobbyists tended to grow up in larger cities. Moreover, the parents of the genealogists grew up in more rural areas or smaller cities than did the hobbyists' parents. The genealogists were also presently living in more rural areas. Thus, the data show that people with rural rather than urban origins, and stayers rather than movers, have higher genealogical interest.

No significant differences appeared in social class mobility. The occupational mobility of the genealogists was not significantly different from that of the hobbyists; neither was the subjective social class or the occupational mobility of the parents of the genealogists. Only the frequency of moving

Table 10–2
Frequency of Moving and City Size in Wisconsin Sample of Genealogists and Hobbyists

Variable	F-ratio	Probability	Difference
Moved in last 5 years	16.91	.01	Genealogists move less
Moved in last 10 years	10.00	.01	Genealogists move less
Moved in last 20 years	6.96	.01	Genealogists move less
Size of city while growing up	15.87	.01	Genealogists are more rural
Size of city parents lived in while growing up	7.70	.01	Genealogists' parents are more rural
Size of city where presently living	25.78	.01	Genealogists are more rural

and city size were different between the genealogists and hobbyists in the Wisconsin sample.

Data from both the student sample and the Wisconsin sample indicate that genealogists are more religious than others. Furthermore, the genealogists in the Wisconsin sample tended to describe themselves as slightly more religious than their parents, while the hobbyists described themselves as less religious than their parents.

The student sample was asked to indicate their religious activity on a scale of 1 to 10. This variable correlated positively with the number of ancestor names known. Religious denomination was also associated with number of names known, as shown in table 10–3. Mormons in the student sample knew significantly more names than did the other groups; Catholics knew somewhat more than Protestants. But all the religious groups knew more ancestor names than did those professing no religion. Reasons for the Mormon students' knowing their ancestors' names are straightforward: Mormons are encouraged to do genealogy, and the study of one's ancestry is a significant part of Mormon theology.

The relationship between family size and genealogical interest is examined in table 10–4. The genealogists and hobbyists in the Wisconsin sample did not differ in number of children or number of siblings. The grandparents of the genealogists, however, had significantly larger families than did the grandparents of the hobbyists (5.4 children, compared with 3.6). Furthermore, the decrease in the number of children from the grandparents' generation to the parents' generation was greater for the genealogists than for the hobbyists. But less change occurred for the genealogists than for the

Table 10–3
Number of Ancestor Names Known, by Religion

Religion	Names Known on Father's Side[a]				
	Four or less	Five	Six	Seven +	N
Mormon	16.8%	13.2%	35.9%	34.1%	167
Catholic	30.6	15.3	36.1	18.1	72
Protestant	39.6	22.5	23.1	14.8	169
None	34.1	26.8	26.8	12.2	41

[a]$X^2 = 44.43$

Religion	Names Known on Mother's Side[b]				
	Four or less	Five	Six	Seven +	N
Mormon	13.8%	15.6%	35.9%	34.7%	167
Catholic	22.2	18.1	36.1	23.6	72
Protestant	26.6	24.9	29.6	18.9	169
None	34.1	19.5	34.1	12.2	41

[b]$2X^2 = 26.20$

Table 10–4
Family Size Comparisons in Wisconsin Sample of Genealogists and Hobbyists

Variable	F-Ratio	Probability	Difference
Number of own children	0.64	n.s.	None
Number of siblings	0.11	n.s.	None
Number of children grandparents had more	30.24	.01	Genealogists
Change in number of children grandparents and parents had	12.28	.01	Greater change for genealogists
Change in number of children parents and respondents had	3.75	.05	Greater change for hobbyists
Birth order	0.06	n.s.	None

hobbyists in the next generation, from their parents' generation to their own. In other words, large decreases in family size appear to have occurred about a generation earlier for the genealogists than for the hobbyists. This probably reflects the older immigrant groups to which the genealogists belong. The birth rate for these older groups dropped earlier than it did for the later immigrant groups.

Finally, family reunions were examined as a predictor of genealogical interest and activity. Family reunions involve the larger extended family and often have specifically directed genealogical reports and activities. This would likely translate into greater genealogical interest and activity among respondents who are part of the reunions. The reunions would function both to commit attendees to a concern for their ancestors and to do something about that concern.

The students in the sample were asked about the attendance at family reunions. The sample was divided into those who had attended no family reunion during the previous year, those who had attended one, and those who had attended two or more. Those who had attended two or more reunions knew more family names in their own pedigree than did those who attended one or none. They also knew less about the countries from which their ancestors had come.

Summary and Discussion

The popular, intuitive characterization of the typical genealogist as an elderly, probably retired man or woman is not inaccurate. The elderly are much more interested in genealogy than younger people. The hobby appears to appeal to many. Women more than men are engaged in genealogy, at a rate that exceeds even their proportion among the elderly. Women are probably more interested because of traditional sex-role definitions; women are expected to maintain family ties and relations. Genealogists also tend to be from middle- and upper-class backgrounds rather than from working-class backgrounds. This may be because they have had more time to engage in such pursuits.

The authors know of no comparable data from other countries, although it may well exist. A comparison of this and other samples from the United States with samples from other countries should show similar age, sex, and social class distributions. We have shown that two periods of genealogical interest preceded the current one in the United States. It would be profitable to determine whether other countries experience such periodic interest. Since the history of each country differs, comparable periods to ours may not have occurred.

The popular, intuitive argument for the increase in level of genealogical interest in the United States in recent years has been that social change and dislocation produce interest in reestablishing one's roots. Certainly, phenomenal social changes have occurred in recent decades, with an attendant increase in genealogical interest. It would be risky, however, to draw any conclusions from the three periods of genealogical interest that have occurred during the last century. This proposition has not been tested here on a societal level; rather, the present study has tried to assess whether personal dislocations result in genealogical interest.

In general, support for the proposition has not been found. The association of social change and genealogical interest appears to be coincidental or the result of factors other than social change. Rather, stayers have greater interest in genealogy than movers, rural people have more interest than urban people, and the religious have more interest than the nonreligious. Furthermore, social and occupational mobility is not generally correlated with genealogical interest, although parental mobility is correlated. Descendants of older immigrants are more interested in genealogy than more recent immigrant groups. In fact, stayers and traditional people in general may be more threatened than others by "storms" of disorganization produced by rapid social change. This intriguing hypothesis could explain the apparent increase in genealogical interest during times of high social change and still be consistent with the results presented in this chapter. Unfortunately, the hypothesis cannot be tested with the present data and awaits future examination.

Thus, traditionality, not change, is related to genealogical interest. This conclusion could be verified in several other ways. Nations with varying degrees of social change and instability could be examined and compared for levels of genealogical interest. Studies of genealogists in Europe and their ethnic/immigration history would be of particular interest. Nations with varying degrees of immigration and mobility could be examined. A random sample of populations in the United States and Europe could be surveyed to determine more closely the relationship between social dislocation and level of genealogical interest. Also of interest would be the differential effect of change on traditional stayers and on more innovative, mobile elements of society. As the U.S. population continues to age and as immigrant groups reside there for longer periods of time, genealogical interest will probably continue to grow: there will be a coming of age of genealogy in American society.

References

Albrecht, S. L., Bahr, H. M., and Chadwick, B. A. 1979. "Changing Family and Sex Roles: An Assessment of Age Differences." *Journal of Marriage and the Family* 41:41–50.

Bidlack, R. E. 1978. "Genealogy as it relates to library service." In *ALA Yearbook.* Chicago: American Library Association.

———1983a. "The awakening: Genealogy as it relates to library services." *RQ* 23:171–81.

———1983b. "Genealogy today." *Library Trends* 32:7–23.

Bockstruck, L. D. 1983. "Four centuries of genealogy: A historical overview." *RQ* 23:162–70.

Haley, A. 1976. *Roots.* Garden City, N.Y.: Doubleday.

Hareven, T. K. 1978. "The search for generational memory: Tribal rites in industrial society." *Daedalus* 107:137–49.

Nye, F. I. 1976. *Role Structure and Analysis of the Family.* Beverly Hills, CA: Sage Publications.

Rubincam, M. 1978. "Genealogy for all people." *National Genealogical Society Quarterly* 66:243–51.

Sinko, P. T. and Peters, S. N. 1983. "A survey of genealogists at the Newberry library." *Library Trends,* 32:97–109.

Taylor, R. M., Jr. 1982. "Summoning the wandering tribes: Genealogy and family reunions in American history." *Journal of Social History* 16:21–37.

U.S. Bureau of the Census. 1970. *Characteristics of the Population, Wisconsin.* Washington, DC: U.S. Government Printing Office.

Part III
Health

Part III deals with the health of the elderly, both physical and mental. One of the central problems the elderly face is to adapt to changes in their mental and physical health. Depression is not uncommon among them, and their suicide rates are higher than those of any other age group. They have to learn to adapt to a weakening physical body. For the most part, such weakened health does not become particularly debilitating until toward the end of the seventies. However, they represent something to which the aging family must adapt.

In Chapter 11, Leifson identifies common physical illnesses of the elderly and discusses how they have an impact on families. Then in Chapter 12, Murphy examines cognitive functioning among the elderly and how families attempt to cope with mental impairments.

In chapter 13, Barber reviews the manner in which family care of the elderly is undertaken. The middle generation, the sandwich generation, must assume responsibility for the health care of their aging parents while, at the same time, they have responsibility for their own adolescent and young adult children. For some, the pressure from both sides is enormous.

Chapter 14 is concerned with elder abuse. In some cases, the abuser is the adult child; in other cases it is the spouse. Whatever the source, concern is growing for the welfare of the elderly who are abused—typically by members of their own families.

11
Physical Health of the Elderly: Impact on Families

June Leifson

Increased longevity has resulted in a large increase in the number of elderly people in the United States. The majority of these elderly are neither sick nor dependent on their children and do not need constant care. Less than 5 percent of persons over age 65 reside in institutions, and only 14 percent of the noninstitutionalized elderly are restricted in mobility (Siegel 1976). More than half of all persons over age 65 live with their spouse, and 30 percent live alone (U.S. Bureau of the Census 1986, 46). Compared to the elderly of the past, today's elderly enjoy better health, are better off financially, and have more leisure time. Nevertheless, it is inevitable that as they advance in years, the incidence of physical and mental impairments lead to dependency on their adult children.

The purpose of this chapter is to examine the physical health of the elderly and how it impacts on families. First, normal physiological changes that occur during the aging process and ways of adjusting to those changes are briefly reviewed. Then, common chronic illnesses of the elderly are identified. Finally, there is a discussion of the impact of the elderly's health status on families.

Normal Physiological Changes during Aging

During the aging process, hair tends to thin and whiten and vision often deteriorates (Zins 1987). Cataracts, glaucoma, and macular degeneration may affect visual images (Katzman 1983). The ability to hear decreases, particularly high pitches. Fine lines appear around the eyes and mouth; these deepen into wrinkles, and the skin loses its elasticity and smoothness. Spots of dark pigmentation sometimes appear on the skin (Zins 1987).

There is a loss of lean body mass, which results in an increase in body fat. Total body water decreases when calculated as a percent of body weight. Muscle cells are lost, which reduces strength and coordination (Gioiella and Bevil 1985). The bones absorb calcium less efficiently, which weakens them and increases the risk of fractures. The joints become stiffer, particularly the hip and knee joints. With the compression of the spinal column, the body sometimes loses one to three inches in height (Zins 1987).

Between the ages of 35 and 75, the amount of air inhaled and exhaled by the lungs decreases by 45 percent and the amount of oxygen passing into the blood decreases by about 50 percent (Zins 1987). The amount of blood pumped by the heart decreases, and muscle fibers contract more slowly. Hardening of the blood vessels creates circulatory problems, and the speed with which the nervous system can process information is reduced. The kidneys lose up to 50 percent of their capacity to filter body wastes. There is a decline in hormonal flow from the adrenal gland, which lowers the ability of the elderly to respond to stress, and for the women, menstruation ceases. The immune system becomes less efficient and lowers the body's resistance to disease.

The various cells, organs, and connective tissues do not age in the same way or at the same rate. The process may be influenced by numerous factors such as genetic background, environmental forces, exercise, lifestyle, and nutritional habits (Zins 1987). According to Fries and Crapo (1981), aging does not appear to be under the direct control of the central nervous system or the genes.

Although a great deal of research has been done on the physical aging process, there is much we do not understand. Symptoms of the normal aging process can be confused with many pathological conditions that also affect the elderly (Gioiella and Bevil 1985).

Adjusting to Aging

Adjustments in lifestyle can help people compensate for the inevitable physical changes that occur as aging progresses. Glasses usually help overcome deteriorating vision. Larger print in books and more intense lighting often make reading easier. Artificial hearing devices often compensate for hearing losses. Increasing the volume of radios and televisions helps and paying attention to nonverbal cues can assist in comprehension. Also, friends may be asked to speak louder and one at a time.

Falls cause the highest number of accidents in the elderly. This is due to decreases in vision, balance, and reaction time. The use of handrails and nonskid tape can prevent falls in bathrooms and other areas. Avoiding sudden movements can decrease the chance of falls or orthostatic hypotension.

Beginning or maintaining an exercise program can assist mobility, body image, and cardiovascular and pulmonary functioning. Proper nutrition can postpone or prevent some common chronic diseases. Persons who eat properly and abstain from alcohol and tobacco tend to be healthier. Monitoring and planning activities that allow time to rest can compensate for the decreased strength and energy.

The elderly person can compensate for changes in the immune system by taking yearly immunizations against influenza and pneumonia. Early treatment of upper-respiratory infection is important, and good diet, rest, and avoidance of undue fatigue help to decrease susceptibility to disease.

Compensating for deteriorating vision or hearing may be relatively easy, while adjusting to other physical problems may be very difficult. However, it is clear that there is wide variation in the ability of the elderly to adapt in response to the aging process (Gioiella and Bevel 1985).

Common Chronic Illnesses of the Elderly

In this section the focus is on chronic conditions, since they are the major health problems among the elderly. Five major disease categories are discussed: (1) cardiovascular, (2) cancer, (3) cerebrovascular, (4) diabetes, and (5) musculosketetal.

Three out of four deaths in the United States result from heart disease, cancer, or a stroke. The occurrence of death from cardiovascular disease and stroke has decreased within the last ten years, while deaths due to cancer have increased (Zins 1987). If heart disease were eliminated, 11.4 years would be added to those at age 65, while the elimination of cancer would add only 1.4 years at age 65. It is an interesting fact that cancer does not become increasingly common in very old people (Zins 1987).

Cardiovascular

Cardiovascular symptoms and diseases are among the most common health problems of the aged. Age-related changes affect the condition of the heart and blood vessels. The dysfunctioning of these vital organs results in a number of pathophysiological conditions. The syndrome of congestive heart failure (CHF) and the resultant circulatory congestion is a common condition. The medical prognosis for elderly people with CHF is limited. The goals for treatment include reducing the cardiac workload and reducing sodium and water retention. With pharmacological agents, activity prescription, and dietary manipulation, some relief can be obtained (Carnevali and Patrick 1986).

Coronary artery disease, with its associated chest pain, increases in the elderly in both severity and prevalence. It is present in most persons over 70 years of age. Increasing the myocardial oxygen supply and reducing the oxygen demands is the goal of treatment for this condition. The elderly can assist with the condition by avoiding undue exertion, heavy eating, and emotional stress.

Peripheral vascular disease (PVP), both the chronic and the acute form, can also affect the elderly. Treatment for PVP aims to slow the progress of the disease. Smoking is thought to play a role with the disease, and therefore the person is encouraged to discontinue smoking. Walking programs also improve muscle tone and blood flow. Pain medication and surgical interventions may be required (Carnevali and Patrick 1986).

Cancer

Cancer is complex and vast in scope and can involve numerous tissues and organs. Cancer in the elderly is viewed differently from when it occurs in a young person. "The general public, the family, and even the elderly person himself—may feel and display a 'give-up syndrome' when cancer is suspected: see nothing, expect nothing, do nothing" (Carnevali and Patrick 1986:318). Values toward cancer and the elderly make decisions concerning treatment or no treatment difficult.

Sixty-two percent of all cancer occurs among people who are aged 60 or over (Carnevali and Patrick 1986). Cancer is actually many diseases that vary in symptoms, growth rate, response to treatment, and prognosis. Cancer has a more silent and insidious course in the older person, but the proliferation rate varies. The metastatic spread from the primary site tends to be slower in the elderly than in younger persons, yet there are many exceptions to this.

The older person usually is less capable of receiving the maximum dose of chemotherapy or radiation and may have a greater chance of toxicities to the treatment. Also, the cancer is often diagnosed at a later stage of the disease than in a younger person, which can result in the treatment being one of control rather than cure. However, there are many treatment options available, and cure should be an option whenever possible. The elderly, even with uncomplicated and successful surgery for cancer, may have a prolonged low energy level. This, plus the residual fear of recurrence of cancer, can add an emotional component to the physical condition. Depression is always more probable with fatigue, as is giving up (Lewis and Collior 1987).

An additional concern with cancer in the elderly is the management of pain. There appears to be an unfounded fear that the elderly have a higher risk of drug dependency and overdose. Therefore, the older person with cancer may be at higher risk to live with severe pain. Pain management can be effective to provide a better quality of life.

Cerebrovascular

The risk of having a cerebrovascular accident (CVA) increases with the advance of age and occurs with equal frequency in both sexes. Seventy-five percent of all stroke deaths occur in people over age 70. Cerebrovascular accidents are usually the result of many factors, not one single stress. Aging is a factor; ischemia (the temporary anemia due to the obstruction of the circulation to a part) is another; while hypertension, atherosclerosis, mitral stenosis, and other types of cardiac disorders can contribute to a CVA (Carnevali and Patrick 1986).

Management consists of surgical intervention as well as drug therapy to assist in the prevention of the progression of the disease. The aggressiveness of treatment varies with signs and symptoms, with the blood vessels involved, and with the individual physician's philosophy.

The signs and symptoms of a stroke vary from very subtle cues that occur in almost any area of function to very obvious and massive ones. The signs and symptoms can be those affecting the sensory system, such as a burn that they do not recognize has happened. There may be language dysfunction, mobility difficulties, or vision and emotional problems. The person who has had a stroke and suffers residual loss often goes through a grieving process. Not only have they had a loss, but this status does not change to any great degree. Many individuals become quite dependent on their families. They do not deteriorate to any degree in their disabilities, nor get a great deal better after they have achieved the initial return of functioning. The family may want to overcare for the person rather than allow the person to struggle to function at a slow pace to do things for himself.

Diabetes

Diabetes—insulin dependent and non–insulin dependent—has increased greatly in the United States in recent years. Diabetes now affects 5 percent of the population, and the chance of becoming diabetic doubles with every decade of life. An estimated 17 percent of those aged 65 and over have diabetes (Carnevali and Patrick 1986). In 1984, 300,000 deaths in the United States were directly attributed to chronic and acute complications from this syndrome. Adiposity, which is a risk factor for diabetics, occurs normally with age as the proportion of fat to lean body mass increases. Also, because glucose intolerance is a normal concomitant of aging, the question arises as to when elevated blood glucose level is an adaptation of normal aging and when it is an indication of the onset of diabetes. Assessment of the elderly diabetic is difficult because the classic symptoms may not appear. The onset may be gradual or mild, and the first indication may be the presence of vascular or neurological changes, or infection (Gioiella and Bevil 1985).

There is debate over what constitutes good control in the elderly. Modifications of lifestyle are related to diet, medication, exercise, urine/blood testing, and hygiene. Glucose tolerance in the elderly can often be managed by diet alone. If not, oral agents or insulin may be necessary. Insulin is required for 20 percent of older persons (Gioiella and Bevil 1985). Sustained regular exercise is another important factor in the management of diabetes in older people. Even a moderate increase in exercise helps manage the diabetic condition.

Two additional control measures that are advocated are the testing and monitoring of the glucose blood level and the careful administration of hygiene practice, especially good foot care. Monitoring the glucose levels of the urine or blood can be a problem for the elderly due to normal aging and pathological change in vision. Newer glucose testing devices for the elderly are being developed. And for the diabetic, scrupulous hygiene is necessary to prevent infections that are a risk for them. Once acquired, infections are often difficult to manage because of the high blood glucose level or diminished circulation.

The main physiological problems associated with diabetes are the large vessel diseases such as arteriosclerosis, along with resultant heart diseases and hypertension. The small vessel diseases associated with the capillaries primarily are in the kidney and the eyes; and neuropathy, another problem, is usually involved in the sensory nerve of the lower extremities (Carnevali and Patrick 1986).

Because diabetes can have widespread effects on the body, many elderly people find it difficult if not impossible to accept and to implement diabetic health practices into their lifestyle. The elderly's mental status, including understanding, ability to process new information, and readiness to learn can influence their ability to assume self-management in learning and performing manual skills associated with diet, medication, and urine/blood testing.

Musculoskeletal

The effects of normal aging are associated with changes in muscles, bones or joints. The impact of these changes on the lifestyle influences strength, speed, posture, body image, independence, and safety. By the time of retirement, 80 percent of the population has some type of musculoskeletal problem (Carnevali and Patrick 1986). These high-risk conditions include falls, fractures, osteoporosis, arthritis, degenerative joint disease, and gout. All have serious implications for the elderly—mobility limitations, pain, isolation, financial expense, and psychological damage.

For rheumatoid arthritis alone, older persons can be affected by over one hundred disorders. Over 20 million people in the United States suffer symptoms severe enough to cause them to seek treatment (Carnevali and Patrick 1986). Osteoporosis, another major problem in this area, affects 15 million people. Clinical osteoporosis with its attendant fractures affects 25 percent of women over age 55, and 70 percent of all fractures in women over age 45 are incurred by women with osteoporosis (Gioiella and Bevil 1985). In individuals over age 70, the incidence of nonfatal accidents increases markedly. Falls, which usually occur in the home, constitute the greatest number of accidents in the older population. In managing musculoskeletal conditions, the focus is to help the elderly learn about and adjust to the disease, to minimize pain and stiffness, and to arrest and/or reverse functional loses. The aim is to preserve as much function as possible and to prevent crippling deformities (Gioiella and Bevel 1985).

Impact on Family Relationships

Marital Relationships

There has been little research on how chronic illness affects marital relationships. Northouse (1980) observed that following the onset of a chronic illness, communication decreased and there was a tendency to avoid sharing painful experiences and feelings with one another. Fengler and Goodrich (1979) found that wives of elderly disabled men are "hidden patients." These wives are called upon to accept responsibilities that their husbands are unable to fulfill, and the demands are constant. Employed wives work a full day and then come home to a husband who needs a great deal of care. They become the family breadwinners, carry out new domestic chores, and are required to make major decisions in areas formerly assumed by their husbands. Many of these wives need as much help and support as their husbands.

In summary, existing research indicates that chronic illness results in decreased marital communication and in stress and loneliness in the healthy spouse. There is a need for much research in this area.

Parent-Child Relationships

Research on parent-child relationships among the elderly has focused on the aged parent's perception and has neglected the viewpoint of the adult child. Only recently has awareness grown of the value of understanding the parent-child relationship from the perspective of the adult child.

Ragan (1979) found that one major crisis for adult children is the retirement of the parents. This event signifies that parents can lose their productive role and that sooner or later the parents will die. Retirement often decreases the income of parents, and adult children are concerned about being required to assume financial responsibility for their parents while they (the adult children) are still providing for their own children.

The quality of the parent-child relationship is influenced by the health status and the activity level of the aging parent. As the dependency of the parent increases and confines the adult child, irritation and relationship problems tend to increase (Shanas, 1962). For example, Robinson and Thurnher (1979) found that adult children speak positively about their parents when their parents are active and self-sufficient. However, negative appraisals occur more often when the parents are dependent and require extensive care. Feelings of irritation and exasperation are expressed because of the restraints on their lifestyle.

Relationships with Primary Caregiver

Some of the common stresses associated with caring for an elderly parent are: confinement, family adjustment, change in personal plans, competing demands on time, emotional adjustment, upsetting behavior, the parent seeming to be a different person, work adjustment, feelings of being completely overwhelmed, physical strain, financial strain, and sleep disturbance (Robinson 1983).

Family members tend to care for their impaired elderly at home even though the burden of caring is enormous. Caregivers sometimes go ten to fifteen years before resorting to a nursing home placement. Placing a parent in an institution usually occurs after a lengthy period of steady mental and physical deterioration that imposes severe stress on the adult caregivers and taxes their ability to cope (Robinson and Thurnher, 1979; Crossman et al. 1981). The adult children often suffer great pangs of guilt when institutional care becomes necessary (Tobin and Kulys 1981).

Taking care of an aging parent is not viewed simply as a burden. Many feel great satisfaction in fulfilling their responsibility to their parents. However, family bonds and the sense of responsibility do not offset the sacrifices of caregiving when the caregiver is not able to get respite from the responsibilities, and when the elderly require a high level of personal care and are not cognitively able to reciprocate in an emotional relationship (Reece et al. 1983).

The impact of caregiving affects women more than men because women are more involved in direct caregiving (Horowitz 1985; Brody 1981; Cantor 1983; Johnson 1978; Lee 1980). Three recent trends tend to make caregiving more stressful for women. First, family size has decreased, leaving fewer siblings who may share the caregiving burden. Second, there has been an increase in the number of women in the labor force (Horowitz 1985). Sixty percent of women employed in the labor force are 45 to 54 years old, the group most likely to be caregivers. Usually the combination of employment and parental care increases the number of responsibilities, resulting in more stress. Third, caregivers are increasing in age themselves, which may make it more difficult for them to care for an aging parent. Ninety percent of adult caregivers are grandparents, 46 percent are great-grandparents, and 10 percent are over age 65 (Shanas 1980). According to Peck (1983), the adult caregiver tends to be a middle-aged woman who frequently complains to her doctor about her own physical problems. Fengler and Goodrich (1979) found that all the caregivers in their study had at least one chronic condition, and two were themselves seriously disabled.

Sons tend to take on the role of caregiver only in the absence of daughters, and when they do, they tend to give less extensive support with less stress. Sons provide emotional support and financial aid but are not as helpful when it comes to instrumental, hands-on service (Horowitz 1985). Older parents with only male offspring, may not be at a disadvantage, since the combined services of sons and daughters-in-law may equal those provided by daughters alone.

Only 43 percent of the caregivers in Snyder and Keefes's (1985) study reported that they received any help, and only 28 percent indicated that family assistance was consistent and regular. Although 90 percent of the caregivers said they needed breaks from caregiving, many received only occasional help from family members. Those who had been giving care for the longest period of time were those least likely to receive support from the social-services system (Snyder and Keefes 1985).

The need and importance of providing support for family caregivers of the elderly has been well recognized (Brody 1981; Shanas 1979; Tobin 1978). Renourishing the resources of the family and/or the caregiver is vitally important. It is essential that help come, and that it come while the caregiver is still able to provide further care (Tobin 1978).

Family members are often called upon to be the primary support, whether or not they have the personal resources to cope with stressful situations. These families' stressful periods can be alleviated by assisting the caregivers to rethink how they have handled difficult crises in the past, talking with family members about the value that outside activities can have in revitalizing individual family members, maintaining quality intra-familial relationships, and providing positive reinforcements (Northouse 1980).

This discussion of caregiving as it relates to parent-child relationships has been brief; Chapter 14 of this volume provides a more extensive review of research on burden and family caregiving.

Needed Future Research

This chapter has focused on normal physical changes during aging, common chronic illnesses of the elderly, and the impact of the elderly's health status on family relationships. Research that focuses on family impacts is especially needed. There has been little research on the changes in marital relationships that accompany chronic illness. What changes occur in the marital relationship between the chronically ill person and the spouse? What changes occur in the marital relationship of the caregiver and the spouse? Additional insight and research is needed concerning the compounding variables of the elderly's condition, the family, and the environmental factors.

Research in the area of adult-child attitudes and perceptions towards a parent's aging has been limited. The effect of the length and the severity of a parent's illness on family relationships needs to be investigated. Also, acute illness needs to be examined as well as chronic illness. How does an acute illness, as opposed to a chronic illness, influence the adult child's relationship with the parent?

It is well known that when one family member changes his or her role, the new balance of roles and responsibilities shifts the family homeostasis, and the other family members feel repercussions. Future research needs to investigate the independent roles played by daughters, sons, and daughters-in-law in giving direct hands-on care. What are the unique stresses and strains of daughters-in-law in providing care under conditions of marital obligation rather than under the usual conditions of parent-child obligation? What impact do the other family members have when the caregiver is overwhelmed?

There are many questions that need to be studied. How large is the problem—how many people are engaged in caregiving, and what is the extent of their involvement? What impact does this involvement have on all their lives? What differences do various diseases, such as cancer, stroke, and heart disease, make? What are the long-term effects of a short-term health condition, compared with a long-term health condition? What are the overall costs in time, effort, and emotional? What are the rights and obligations of spouses and families in relation to the chronically elderly person?

Family policies and practices need to be developed to assist the family caregiver before burdens become unbearable, to help families to cope with the day-after-day care needed for their elderly parents or spouses. Respite care and homemaking assistance can be given, especially for the older adult caregiver whose physical capacity is limited. Transportation to health and social services can assist. Legal and financial counseling could be provided to a greater degree.

Family crisis can be prevented or modified by social and community support. Intervention is needed before and not after the family has spent all their emotional, physical, and psychological resources and energy. Our society has a value to respect and care for the elderly; thus, it is imperative to safeguard and assist the well-being of the spouse, the adult caregiver, and the family unit.

References

Archbold, P. G. 1983. "Impact of parent-caring on women." *Family Relations* 32:39–45.

Bahr, H. M. 1979. "The kinship role." In F. I. Nye (ed.), *Role Structure and Analysis of the Family*. Beverly Hills, CA: Sage Publications.

Birrin, J. E. 1964. *The Psychology of Aging*. Englewood Cliffs, NJ: Prentice-Hall.

Brody, E. M. 1981. "Women in the middle and family help to older people." *The Gerontologist* 21:471–480.

Callahan, J. J., Diamond, L. D., Giele, J. Z., and Morris, R. 1980. "Responsibility of families for their severely disabled elders." *Health Care Financing Review* 1:29–48.

Cantor, M. H. 1983. "Strain among caregivers: A study of experience in the United States." *The Gerontologist* 23:597–604.

Carnevali, D. L., and Patrick, M. 1986. *Nursing Management for the Elderly*. J. B. Philadelphia: Lippincott.

Clcirelli, V. G. 1981. *Helping Elderly Parent: The Role of Adult Children*. Boston: Cuburen House.

Crossman, L., London, C., and Barry, C. 1981. "Older women caring for disabled spouses: A model for supportive services." *The Gerontologist* 21:464–70.

Eggert, G.M., Granger, C.V., Morris, R., Pendleton, S.F. 1977. "Caring for the patient with long-term disability." *Geriatrics* 32:102–14.

Fengler, A. and Goodrich, N. 1979. "Wives of elderly disabled men: The hidden patients." *The Gerontologist* 19:175–83.

Fries, J. F. and Crapo, L. M. 1981. *Vitality and Aging*. San Francisco: W. H. Freeman.

Gioiella, E. C. and Bevil, C. W. 1985. *Nursing Care of the Aging Client: Promoting Health Adaption*. Norwalk, CT: Appleton-Century-Crofts.

Hickey, I., and Douglass, R. L. 1981. "The mistreatment of the elderly in the domestic setting: An exploratory study." *American Journal of Public Health* 71:500–507.

Horowitz, A. 1982. "The impact of caregiving of children of the frail elderly" Paper presented at the annual meeting of the American Orthopsychiatric Association, San Francisco., CA.

———. 1985. "Sons and daughters as caregivers to older parents: Differences in role performance and consequence." *The Gerontologist* 25:612–17.

Johnson, E. S. 1978. "'Good' relationships between older mothers and their daughters: A causal model." *The Gerontologist* 18:301–306.

Katzman. 1983. *The Neurology of Aging*. Philadelphia: F. A. Davis Company.

Lee, S. 1980. "Helping patient and family cope with diagnosis of a terminal illness in the hospital setting." *Canadian Journal of Psychiatric Nursing* 21:14–17.

Lewis, S. M., and Collior, I. C. 1987. *Medical-Surgical Nursing Assessment and Management of Clinical Problems* (2nd ed.). New York: McGraw-Hill.

Newman, S. 1976. *Housing Adjustment of Older People: A Report of Findings from the Second Phase.* University of Michigan, Ann Arbor: The Institute for Social Research.

Northouse, L. 1980. "Who supports the support system?" *Psychiatric Nursing* 18:11–15.

Peck, R. 1983. "Home caregivers: Toward a new partnership with doctors." *Geriatrics* 38:124–28.

Phillips, L. R. 1983. "Elder abuse—what is it? Who says so?" *Geriatric Nursing* 4:167–70.

Quinn, M. J., and Tomita, S. K. 1986. *Elder Abuse and Neglect: Causes, Diagnosis and Intervention Strategies.* New York: Springer.

Ragan, P. K. 1979. *Aging Parents.* Los Angeles: The University of Southern California Press.

Reece, D., Walz, T., and Hageboeck, H. 1983. "Intergenerational care providers of noninstitutionalized frail elderly: Characteristics and consequences." *Journal of Gerontological Social Work* 5:21–34.

Robinson, B. 1983. "Validation of a caregiver strain index." *Journal of Gerontology* 38:344–48.

Robinson, B., and Thurnher, M. 1979. "Taking care of parents: A family cycle transition." *The Gerontologist* 19:586–93.

Shanas, E. 1962. *The Health of Older People.* Cambridge, MA: Harvard University Press.

———. 1979. "The family as a social support system in old age." *The Gerontologist* 19:169–74.

———. 1980. "Older people and their families: The new pioneers." *Journal of Marriage and the Family* 43:9–15.

Siegal, J. S. 1976. "Demographic aspects of aging and the older population in the U.S." *Current Population Reports*, U.S. Bureau of the Census. Series P-23, no. 59. Washington DC: U.S. Government Printing Office.

Snyder, B., and Keefes, K. 1985. "The unmet needs of family caregivers for frail and disabled adults." *Social Work in Health Care* 10:1–14.

Steinmetz, S. K. 1978. "Battered parents." *Society* 15:15.

Stroller, E. P. 1982. "Sources of support for the elderly during illness." *Health and Social Work* 7:111–22.

Tobin, S. 1978. "The future elderly: Needs and services." *Aging* 37:279–80.

Tobin, S., and Kulys, R. 1981. "The family in the institutionalization of the elderly." *Journal of Social Issues* 37:145–57.

Treas, J. 1979. "Intergenerational families and social change." In P. Ragan (ed.), *Aging Parents.* Los Angeles: The University of Southern California Press.

Zarit, T., Reever, K. E., and Bach-Peterson, J. 1980. "Relatives of the impaired elderly: Correlates of feelings of burden." *The Gerontologist* 20:649–55.

Zins, S. 1987. *Aging in America: An Introduction to Gerontology.* Albany, NY: Delmar Publishers.

12
Cognitive Functioning of the Elderly

Millene Freeman Murphy

A critical health need of the elderly is to prevent the occurrence of cognitive impairment. Prevention can be facilitated by identifying the causes of cognitive impairment and by preventing and/or treating the problems wherever possible. If this is not done, cognitive impairment will soon become the number-one health problem of the aged (Terry and Katzman 1983). Cognitive impairment robs families and communities of productive citizens and increases the needs these individuals have for resources to assist them to maintain a satisfactory lifestyle. The impact of the increased incidence of cognitive dysfunctioning will be felt even more by the year 2000 than it is now due to the increasing percentage of older individuals in the population.

Loss of cognitive functioning is the thief of productivity and functioning in the aged. A loss subtle enough to avoid diagnosis may result in changes in lifestyle and/or social relationships. The loss may be reversible, irreversible, progressive, or improvable with treatment.

Cognitive functioning includes the organization and interpretation of sensory information and the related behavioral and/or motor output. It is dependent on the brain's ability to process information effectively. Once the loss or alteration of cognitive ability becomes obvious to other people, a diagnosis of organic mental syndrome is generally made. The Diagnostic and Statistical Manual of Mental Disorders (DSMIIIR) lists six categories of organic mental syndromes (American Psychiatric Association 1987). This chapter deals with the prevention, detection, and problems associated with cognitive impairment.

Community surveys estimate that 4 to 5 percent of the U.S. population are over age 65, do not live in institutions, and have severe cognitive dysfunction; an additional 10 percent have mild to moderate impairment. (Katzman 1976). The incidence of cognitive impairment among residents of nursing homes over age 65 is estimated at 30 to 67 percent (Clarke et al. 1986; Holzer et al. 1984; Terry and Katzman 1983). A New Haven County, Connecticut, survey showed that community residents 75 years and older have a higher incidence of cognitive impairment than do younger groups (Holzer et al. 1984). Between 5 and 10 percent of individuals aged 45 to 74, and 17 percent of individuals over 74, were affected with mild cognitive impairment. A total of 20.3 percent of individuals over age 65 showed mild to severe cognitive impairment. A study from Lestershire, England (Clarke et al. 1986), reported a somewhat lower incidence. These differences may be due to the different tools used to measure cognitive functioning and to the fact that in England a higher percentage of those with moderate to severe cognitive dysfunctioning are located in institutions. All studies found a marked increase in the percentage of individuals over 80 years old with cognitive decline. This same percentage of decrease in cognitive functioning among the aging was not found in a study of educated, upper-middle-class individuals (Thomas et al. 1985). Terry and Katzman (1983) maintained that community surveys underestimate the prevalence of cognitive impairment because the tools lack sensitivity.

The purpose of this chapter is to review research on cognitive functioning among the elderly. It is divided into five major sections. The first section identifies the major causes of cognitive impairment. In the second section is a discussion of how cognitive functioning is evaluated. The third section is an overview of the impact of cognitive impairment on survival skills. The effect of cognitive impairment on family relationships is the focus of the fourth section. Finally, the fifth section is an evaluation of health care options.

Major Causes of Cognitive Impairment

The increased longevity of the U.S. population may result in dementia becoming the number-one health problem in the United States. Delaying the onset of dementia by a decade or more would reduce the tragic impact of this group of diseases (Terry and Katzman 1983). An understanding of the etiology of cognitive impairment could pave the way for prevention strategies.

Dementia has been related to over fifty conditions (Charlton 1975; Haase 1977). Only the most common are discussed here.

Reversible Causes

Depression. Depression results in reversible decreased cognitive functioning. It has also been linked with a decrease in recent memory tasks but not with delayed recall. The individual with depression differs in these respects from the individual with dementia, whose performance is poor in both recent and delayed memory tasks. The slowing of motor response seen in normal aging increases in depression. Cole and Zarit (1984) found that in elderly males depression secondary to physical illness and hospitalization results in deficits in psychomotor speed, recognition memory, abstract abilities, and interpersonal functioning. It is possible for depression to coexist with dementia (Ebrahim et al. 1985). Treatment of depression usually results in improved mood, nutrition, and well-being even if dementia is present (Reifler and Larson 1985).

Stress. Stress has long been associated with changes in physical and cognitive functioning. Stress is brought about by a variety of physical, environmental, and psychosocial causes. It is frequently related to anxiety. The role that it plays in cognitive functioning of the healthy elderly has not been well researched.

Some clinical literature indicates that the aging process decreases the ability to cope with stress. Unpublished research data indicate that the well, active elderly feel that they handle life's problems as well or better than when they were younger. Healthy elderly with "adequate" financial resources claim that their problem-solving abilities are as good or better than they were at other times in their lives.

Individuals with mild to moderate levels of cognitive impairment are vulnerable to the effects of stress. Data from unpublished clinical case studies indicate that stress in the elderly who have cognitive impairment produces a marked decrease in cognitive functioning. The stress can come from a variety of causes, including physical illness, problems in family relationships, complex decision making, and overstimulation caused by having to deal with a variety of stimuli at once, such as large group gatherings. Stress tends to decrease effective functioning, with the result that individuals appear to have more cognitive impairment than they actually do.

Loneliness. Loneliness is another factor that makes cognitive functioning appear worse that it really might be. Loneliness frequently results in stress and/or sensory deprivation. As individuals' cognitive functioning starts to deteriorate, there is an increased tendency for them to be ignored. People may talk around them and over them but not directly to them. Conversations that ask "How is Mother doing?" directed to another sibling when Mother is sitting in a nearby room are not uncommon.

There is a tendency for people to react to cognitive impairment as an all-or-none phenomenon, yet it has different degrees. It also varies within an individual, depending on the time of day, the amount of energy present, nutritional status, stress, sensory deprivation, and a variety of other factors. Families' attempts to "protect" the aged or the impaired can result in behaviors that increase their feelings of abandonment. It is frequently difficult for family members to tolerate negative or sad feelings in people with cognitive impairment. Their lack of recognition of these feelings or treating the feelings as unimportant can create a sense of isolation in the elderly. Loneliness tends to occur, along with a lack of appropriate sensory stimulation. Impairments in vision and/or hearing make it more difficult for people to interact with the elderly. A frequent byproduct of loneliness in the aged is sensory deprivation.

Sensory Deprivation. Sensory deprivation can result in decreased cognitive functioning that may or may not be reversible. Sensory deprivation may be an acute condition, such as one in which the individual is temporarily isolated from familiar sensory input; or it may be a chronic deprivation caused by loss of sensory functioning. Longitudinal studies demonstrate the effects of hearing loss in decreasing cognitive ability better than cross-sectional studies do (Uhlman et al. 1986).

Nutrition. Nutritional factors have been linked with cognitive functioning in the aged, although both obvious malnutrition and subclinical malnutrition are also found in healthy, middle-class, educated, financially-able individuals. Cognitive functioning seems to be more affected by low intake and low serum levels of riboflavin, foliate, vitamin B_{12}, and ascorbic acid (Goodwin et al. 1983). The elderly with low nutritional risk tend to perceive themselves as healthy and having intact sensory functioning (Wolinsky et al. 1984). The role of nutrition seems to be more preventive than curative. The use of vitamin therapy to treat dementia has not met with general success (Burr et al. 1975; Kral et al. 1970; Raskind 1983; Schorah et al. 1979). Anemia may be related to a disease process, a deficit in nutritional intake, or absorption factors. Anemia has been related to decreased cognitive functioning in both infants and the elderly (Charlton 1975; Lozoff et al. 1982; Oski and Hoing 1978).

Polypharmacology. Polypharmacology is a serious problem among the aged. Prescription and over-the-counter drugs are used to manage a number of complaints, discomforts, and behavioral changes associated with aging. The interaction effects, overdosing, and build-up effects due to poor elimination of the drugs may produce toxic effects. Some older individuals have increased sensitivity to some medications, which further increases the chance of negative side effects. The medications or combination of medications may interfere with memory. Once memory starts to deteriorate, there is an increased risk that the older person may accidentally overdose on medications or take them in nontherapeutic combinations. Decreasing the number of medications and adjusting them may result in a marked improvement in cognitive functioning. Because of the physical problems that usually accompany polypharmacology, adequate medical supervision is necessary when medications are adjusted. The paradox of pharmacological treatment is that medications that decrease physical problems and improve behavioral management can also create problems in these areas. Medication management coordinated by one qualified physician or nurse practitioner can effectively reduce this problem.

Delirium, which is a short-term cause of cognitive dysfunction, has been related to the abuse of various substances, including prescription and over-the-counter medications, alcohol, and a variety of "street drugs" (DSMIIIR). The effects of long-term substance abuse have not been well documented by research. Alcohol-related dementias are the best documented, but even they remain controversial. Alcohol amnestic disorder is generally associated with years of alcohol intake and is diagnosed by ruling out all other causes of dementia. When alcohol amnestic disorder is due to a combination of years of heavy alcohol intake and thiamine deficiency, it is also known as Korsakoff's syndrome (DSMIIIR). Adequate nutritional intake and avoidance of alcohol intake are associated with improved functioning in some individuals, but the indications are that cognitive functioning is not completely restored.

Other Causes. Metabolic disorders that are rather easily diagnosed and treated may result in decreased cognitive functioning. The most common include hypothyroidism, parathyroid disease, Cushings' syndrome, and deficiencies in thiamine and/or B_{12}. Other physical disorders that interfere with cognitive functioning are infection, fever, cardiovascular disorders, heavy metal poisoning: and intoxication from alcohol, barbiturates, and psychotropic drugs (Charlton 1975). These disorders; along with poor nutrition and some medicines used to treat them, can result in altered body chemistry that may give the appearance of a psychotic episode, delirium, and/or dementia.

Structured exercise training has been linked with improved neuropsychological functioning. Aerobic exercise training seems to affect central functioning more than it affects peripheral functioning (Dustman et al. 1984).

Brain tumors can cause altered cognitive functioning. The type, size, and location of the tumor determines the amount of brain tissue destroyed by the tumor or the surgery to remove it. This in turn determines if the destruction is reversible or of a more enduring nature.

Irreversible Neurological Changes

Head Injury. Head injury is a major cause of loss of cognitive functioning in young adults. The rate of survival of individuals with moderate to severe head injuries decreases as age increases. In turn, modern technology and advances in medical and nursing sciences have increased the survival rate for those with head injuries. This increased survival rate is also linked with an increase in individuals with cognitive dysfunctioning. The highest percentage of head injuries occurs in the early twenties. Those who survive with cognitive impairment, regardless of age at the time of the head injury, eventually become aged. A follow-up study of eight-nine individuals who survived two years after a head injury showed that cognitive functioning was related to length of coma rather than age at the time of injury (Brooks et al. 1980). Physical and cognitive functioning are related to the individual's being able to survive in an independent living situation (Talmage and Collins 1983).

Compromised Circulation. Another problem associated with aging is the decreased efficiency of the circulatory system. This may result in problems which have an effect on cognition. One problem is that the heart, for a variety of reasons, may stop beating. Resuscitation of the heartbeat after the brain has gone without oxygen for three to five minutes usually results in cognitive dysfunctioning. A second problem is that the arteries may become clogged with plaques and lose their elasticity. This may result in high blood pressure and/or decreased cerebral circulation. This condition can lead to multi-infract dementia or a cerebrovascular accident (CVA). An evaluation of 189 elderly patients six months after they suffered a CVA showed that twenty-two of them had dementia. Four of these twenty-two were also depressed (Ebrahim et al. 1985). The greater the age and the more severe the stroke, the greater the cognitive impairment. Dementias from CVA or other focal neurological damage are more likely to result in immobility than are other types of dementia (MacLennan et al. 1987).

Another problem relates to the medications taken to correct hypertension. These medications can, by accidental overdose or build-up effect, lower the blood pressure to the point where the brain receives only a portion of the blood it needs. This is most likely to occur when cerebral circulation is already compromised. The end result is hypoxia of the neurons, which can result in cognitive impairment. The dementias related to circulation problems are usually not progressive unless the circulation problem continues or reoccurs.

Progressive Dementia. Dementia of the Alzheimer's type (DAT) is currently receiving a lot of attention from the media, health care professionals, and research funding. Between 50 and 60 percent of all cases of dementia are a result of DAT (Terry and Katzman 1983). Unlike the other dementias that have been discussed in this chapter, this dementia has a progressive, predictable course (Reisberg 1986). Several scales have been developed to classify the stages of DAT (Reisberg 1986). These scales are general and work well after the disease has progressed to the moderate stages, but they are less effective in early diagnostic differentiation. There are changes related to EEG patterns, and CT scans have been used to assist in the diagnostic process. Positive diagnosis can be made only with an autopsy. Newer technology such as PET scans and spectroanalysis provide additional data for research and hold the possibility that they may provide some diagnostic answers (Duara et al. 1986; Duffy et al. 1984).

In addition to DAT, other disorders selectively affect specific brain regions. The better known of these include Huntington's Chorea, Parkinson's disease, and Pick's disease. Other diseases related to dementia include chronic psychiatric illnesses, syphilis, and chronic renal, hepatic, pulmonary, or endocrine disease.

Evaluating Cognitive Function

It is important to diagnose cognitive functioning accurately since the differences in treatment implications are great. Evaluating cognitive function in the elderly is difficult because of the lack of established norms associated with healthy, educated, financially-able elderly people. Because of this lack of norms, it is difficult to tell which changes are due to the normal aging process and which are early indicators of dementia. The difficulty is compounded by the need of the elderly to appear capable and knowledgeable. If they feel that they would not be able to perform tasks or answer questions on a test at an acceptable level, they may refuse to be tested or attempt to "fake good."

There is also a lot of denial surrounding the loss of cognitive functioning. This denial can be a protective mechanism, but it can also result in maladaptive behaviors. College education is associated with an ability to cover the early signs and symptoms of loss of cognitive functioning.

The variety of measurement techniques and tools used by researchers and clinicians makes it difficult to compare the data (Albert 1984). Most of the tools provide diagnostic data for individuals with moderate to severe impairment. They lack the sensitivity needed to diagnose individuals with only slight impairment, especially if their education level is high and/or their social skills are well developed. The neuropsychological batteries that result in more definitive diagnoses are difficult to administer with moderate to severe impairment. This increases the problems in comparing longitudinal data related to progressive dementia.

Distinquishing between Types of Dysfunction

Delirium, as defined by the DSMIIIR, is generally caused by a situation that is correctable. The essential features of delirium are an inability to maintain and shift attention, easy distraction, disorganized thinking, and disorientation (Albert 1984). The sleep-wake cycle and psychomotor activity may also be disturbed.

Dementia, by contrast, is a nonspecific diagnosis of behavioral incompetence generally referred to as "brain disease." The diagnosis of dementia, like that of mental retardation, carries with it significant implications about the patient's social, economic, and legal competence (Benton and Sivan 1984). The DSMIIIR lists the essential features of dementia as impairments in memory, judgment, and abstract thinking and/or personality changes. The disturbance must be severe enough to interfere with work, social activities, or relationships with others. Dementia may also involve a variety of disturbances of higher cortical function. These disturbances vary according to the type of dementia but include disturbances in language function, "constructional ability" and motor functions (American Psychiatric Association, 1987). Other dysfunctions include agnosia (failure to recognize or identify objects) and apraxia (inability to carry out motor functions of which one is physically capable). Anxiety, depression, and/or delirium may accompany dementia.

An early change related to dementia that tends to show up in tests of cognitive functioning is a difficulty in naming familiar objects. This is also sometimes seen in normal aging, to a lesser degree. The person with dementia may combine two real words to make a new one—for example, *sand-clock* in place of *hourglass*. This combining is not generally seen in the normal aging (Albert 1984). There is a tendency for responses to proverbs and to judgment questions to be logical but more concrete (Albert 1984). Drawings with repetitious patterns tend to bring out the perseveration tendencies seen in very mild stages of dementia. Difficulty with visuospatial tasks, including inaccurate drawings and concrete responses, increases with the severity of the cognitive dysfunction.

Cognitive impairment that may not meet the diagnostic criteria of the DSMIIIR can still be disruptive to one's lifestyle. Signs that are frequently missed or ignored include subtle changes in the ability to cope with high-stress events and some difficulty in precise, high-level decision making. If one's lifestyle or job performance does not require these abilities, the symptoms are even more likely to be ignored or associated with loss of motivation or interest. Data from unpublished case studies indicate that there is also a subtle loss in the ability to be sensitive to other's needs, emotional states, and nonverbal communication. There is also a decrease in concern for personal appearance and hygiene. Obsessive-compulsive behaviors may become more pronounced. These are qualitative changes that are difficult to identify and quantify.

Diagnostic Dilemmas

Cognitive changes occurring in the normal aging must be differentiated from changes due to disease processes. There are great individual differences in the cognitive performance of the elderly; some persons are of minimal ability throughout adulthood (mental retardation), while others maintain and even improve their cognitive abilities beyond age 80. Some individuals with previously high levels of cognitive functioning suffer large decrements, which may be related to various types of dementia, to head trauma, or to a variety of reversible causes (Holzer et al. 1984).

Assessing individuals who have a short attention span coupled with a need to avoid any situation that would demonstrate their potential impairment creates dilemmas. There is a tendency in assessment to use global scales that give a general overall measure but do not pinpoint specific areas of functioning. Comprehensive neuropsychological examinations are not routinely used except in a few isolated places. Neuropsychologists disagree on the best way to assess children, resulting in a large body of literature related to child assessment. But disagreements on assessment of the elderly have not resulted in a corresponding body of literature on the elderly. Comprehensive neuropsychological assessments are best utilized in the early stages of impairment, as the tasks are too difficult for individuals with severe impairment.

Assessment Procedures

The following is a proposed model for the assessment of cognitive functioning in the elderly:

I. Evaluate the information related to the highest level of past functioning
II. Evaluate the medical history (Eisdorfer and Cohen 1980)
III. Take a complete physical examination, including serum tests to rule out metabolic and related diseases and to establish a base of nutritional adequacy
IV. Determine survival skills
   A. Activities of daily living (ADL)
      1. Dressing
      2. Feeding
      3. Bathing
      4. Toileting
      5. Grooming
   B. Social role activities
      1. Telephoning

    2. Walking upstairs

    3. Grocery shopping

    4. Preparing meals

    5. Repairing and cleaning

    6. Doing laundry

    7. Managing money

V. Evaluate sensory functions

    A. Objective evaluations

    B. Self-perception of function

VI. Evaluate nutritional status

    A. Serum levels

    B. Self-report on dietary intake

    C. Physical parameters

VII. Evaluate cognitive functioning with appropriate neuropsychological testing

    A. Attention

    B. Memory (recent and remote)

    C. Language

    D. Visuospatial ability

    E. Conceptualization

    F. Sensory discrimination and perceptual organization

    G. Intellectual functioning

    H. Judgment

    I. Problem-solving ability

VIII. Evaluate mental health with appropriate testing

    A. Lawton (1975) revision of the Philadelphia Geriatric Center Moral Scale, adapted

    B. Short Zung Scale (Tucker et al. 1987)

IX. Assess self-image

X. Assess interpersonal and social relationships

    A. Current status

    B. Comparison of current with past

A model for the treatment of Alzheimer's disease along with its assessment has also been developed. This model includes a psychiatric assessment, a physical examination, a social and environmental assessment, and psychological testing (Reifler and Larson 1985). A model developed to make quick assessments on a large scale utilizes global measures of perceived health, mental orientation, activity of daily living, perceived sensory functions, nutritional risk, and mental health (Wolinsky et al. 1984).

Several rating scales have been developed to do quick assessments of cognitive functioning. The most commonly used of these scales are the Short Portable Mental Status Questionnaire (Pfeiffer 1975), the Cognitive Capacity Screening Examination (Foreman 1987), and the Mini-Mental Status Examination (Folstein et al. 1975). After comparing the results of the above rating scales on sixty-six hospitalized elderly patients, Foreman (1987) concluded that the Cognitive Capacity Screening Examination is the most sensitive. In spite of their favorable reviews, some rating scales do not contain the information necessary to help the clinician or the researcher obtain objective data, such as the Crichton Geriatric Behavioral Rating Scale (for a favorable review, see Vardon and Blessed 1986). The Reisberg scale is a global measure of functional ability (Reisberg et al. 1982). The limitations of these scales are the gross measurements they obtain, their focus on a few specific functions rather than on the integrative functions of information processing, and the lack of items on them to test for the neuromotor dysfunctioning that accompanies most dementias.

For moderate to advanced stages of dementia, these scales are sufficient and may be all that the patient can tolerate in terms of attention, stress, and performance requirements. The early stages of dementia need more sophisticated tools. Examples of these are the Reitan Halstead Neuropsychology Battery (Reitan and Davison 1974), the Luria Neuropsychological Investigation (Blackburn and Tyrer 1985), and the Luria-Nebraska Neuropsychology Battery (Golden et al. 1985).

Neuropsychological testing is needed to accompany the complete medical evaluation. A diagnosis of dementia is made by ruling out all the other possibilities. This should be done with great care. The Philadelphia Geriatric Center Multilevel Assessment Instrument attempts to assess behavioral competence in several domains—health, activities of daily living, cognition, time use, and social interaction. The domains have sectors to measure psychological well-being and perceived environmental quality (Lawton et al. 1982).

The Impact of Cognitive Impairment on Survival Skills

Survival skills are those skills one needs to care for himself or herself or to survive within the context of the environment. These skills include the ability to perform activities of daily living (ADL) typically listed on checklists, as well as the ability to get where one wants to go, to manage one's financial matters, to make environmental adjustments, and to maintain social and occupational roles.

The impact of cognitive impairment on survival skills is best documented for dementia of the Alzheimer's type, which follows a predictive course. The impact of dementia related to other processes on survival skills is similar, but there may be more crossover between the stages. Multi-infarct dementia tends to be more associated with physical disability early in the disease. This would affect mobility and thus the ability of individuals to care for their own basic needs.

Early cognitive impairment may go unnoticed if no related physical disabilities and no changes in the overlearned, routine tasks of living, including managing finances and social schedules, appear. A difficulty with complex psychomotor skills (such as the ability to travel to new locations) may be the first to be noticed. Individuals may self-correct for mild impairment by stopping their participation in demanding occupational and social settings. The signs and symptoms related to the changes may be alarming to both patient and family. Recognition of a loss of ability makes one prone to anxiety and depression.

A mild dysfunction with no physical impairment will not prevent an individual from living independently in the community. Poor judgment and lack of impulse control may lead to financial and other difficulties. Stress can markedly compromise one's functional ability. Denial of a loss of ability provides some protection from anxiety, but it decreases the acceptance of assistance.

Moderate dysfunction results in the need for supervised living arrangements. The individual needs help with managing finances, shopping, choosing proper clothing, and caring for personal hygiene needs. Difficulties with driving arise, due to poor judgment and memory loss. Individuals frequently have difficulty understanding why the family or caregivers will not let them drive, handle motor-driven equipment, or live alone. There may be a decrease in ability to do and/or enjoy leisure activities. Interacting with the outside world becomes difficult. Stress may result in a lower functional status. Wandering may become a serious problem as the individual loses the judgment necessary to protect himself or herself from environmental hazards, especially those associated with urban living. A loss of spatial relationship abilities may also occur, which results in an inability to get from one place to another. Wandering is not limited to daytime, especially if sleep difficulties are present. Getting lost is a frequent problem.

Severe cognitive impairment results in the need for constant care and considerable help with the basic functions of dressing, bathing, and toilet use. Frustration for both patient and caregiver is increased if aphasia accompanies this stage. Marked physical disabilities associated with this stage of cognitive impairment increase the demands placed on the caregiver. This is frequently more true for dementia associated with cerebral circulation disorders than for DAT. In the final stages of DAT there is complete loss of speech, locomotion, and consciousness.

Family Relationships and Cognitive Impairment

The effect of cognitive dysfunctioning on family relationships is an area that needs more research. The growing body of research on caregiver burden does not deal directly with its overall effect on family relationships. Some clinical and case study data suggest that the effect on family relationships is tied to several variables, including the quality of the relationship, the importance of the relationship to the individuals involved, the ability of the individuals to tolerate and adapt to changes in personality and role, the ability to tolerate and cope with stress, the ability to problem-solve, self-image, the ability to deal with control and power issues, the types of personality changes involved, the behavioral problems encountered, the perceived societal roles and support, and the previous level of cognitive functioning.

The patient faces a loss of once-prized abilities and valued relationships. The family faces the loss of a person they once knew, loved, and depended on for certain functions and roles. This loss adds to the drama associated with grief resolution. Denial of the problems by both patient and family is usually the first reaction. Following denial come periods of anger, alternating with attempts to adjust to the situation. Frustrations surface as both the patient and the family are forced to learn new communication patterns and to deal with new roles. Families become so caught up in the frustration of attempting to master the new roles required of them that they are often unable to cope with the anguish and despair of the impaired individual. How families have coped with stress and loss in the past, their current relationships, and their resources of time, money, and energy set the stage for coping with the current situation. (Pridgeon 1985; Safford 1986). The grief of children and adolescent members of the family may not be recognized and dealt with due to the lack of energy and the emotional drain on adult family members.

The loss of high-level decision-making abilities, interpersonal sensitivity, and/or financial ability tends to irritate family members. In mild stages of impairment or in early stages of progressive dementia, family members often associate the impairment with the individual's aging process or with stress at work or home. The loss of sensitivity and judgment in social and financial situations both embarrasses and creates numerous difficulties for family members. Some of the behaviors have to do with overspending, using poor judgment in financial matters, being vulnerable to salespeople, and inappropriate social behavior. Alzheimer's is sometimes associated with hypersexual behavior, more frequently in males. This can result in behavior that at best concerns and irritates family and neighbors and at worst causes the affected individual to end up in court. These early changes, when the family does not know or understand what is happening, can create a great deal of stress in the relationship. By the time a diagnosis is reached, the relationship may be so strained and filled with anger that spouses and/or children have lost the ability to be supportive and may not want to have any further contact with the individual. Anger is more apparent in relationships that have previously been filled with resentment. Past issues may need to be resolved before the individual can deal with the current problems.

Reifler and Larson (1985) cited a case history in which a social worker assisted a daughter in dealing with past resentments as well as current feelings. The result was an improved relationship with her impaired parent. Professionals need to be sensitive to the fact that not all family members have the energy and resources to deal with past issues during a crisis (Safford 1986).

Assuming new roles requires education, experience, and a model to follow. These requirements often are lacking for the person suddenly thrust into a role of responsibility for someone with cognitive impairment. He or she is caught trying to meet not only the new demands created by the impaired person but also all the ongoing demands of their own personal and professional life. The lack of adequate guides and supports further drains resources. Family members do not always agree on methods to handle the problems. Old methods of problem solving may be disrupted, especially if the formerly key person is no longer able to function in that role (Pridgeon 1985; Safford 1986).

Financial burdens placed on families increase the strain. If the impaired individual or the caregiver can no longer work, a loss of income occurs. Insurance companies, including Medicare, do not cover custodial care. The loss of a pension due to the necessity of leaving a jobs before an adequate diagnosis is made and disability established (Pridgeon 1985) is another financial drain.

Families become irritated when ability loss results in annoying behaviors. The loss of cognitive mapping skills results in a decreased ability to manage financial matters and an increased risk of getting lost in familiar surroundings. The loss of recent memory is perceived as asking the same question sixty times a day; forgetting to turn off water faucets, resulting in flooding; and forgetting to turn off the stove, resulting in burned pans and potential fire danger. Wandering behavior, coupled with the inability to find one's home due to a loss of visuospatial ability, can be dangerous to the impaired and result in lost time trying to find the family member. A loss of behavioral inhibition can result in socially unacceptable behaviors, creating embarrassment for the family. The exaggeration of usual coping mechanisms can result in a denial of the problem, which can create additional burdens. A loss of memory can result in continually retelling the same stories of the past, which annoys family members (Hamner 1984).

The issue for families is how to provide the necessary supervision and/or care required today. The day-to-day problems associated with caring for an individual with cognitive impairment can be overwhelming. The frustration involved may lead to anger directed either at the impaired person who created the problem or at other family members who can't solve the problem. Problems associated with learning to accept one's limited capacity to help someone in need also arise. An important feature of mature interdependency is the ability to respond to another, yet to recognize that this response will not completely solve the other's problems. A limited ability to meet another's needs may generate feelings of anger at the one who exposes these limitations (Hirschfeld 1985).

Difficulties are encountered when one person's vulnerability may potentially become the excuse for another's mastery and dominance. Impaired persons have a need to maintain control and a sense of personal power over life's vicissitudes. They are frequently not aware of the extent of their dysfunction, or they deny it. Their struggle to maintain control and power may result in behaviors labeled "obnoxious," "stubborn," "uncooperative," "unappreciative," or worse.

When these labels are applied to an impaired person, the person is treated accordingly. This creates a struggle for power between the individual and the family. The more the family struggles for control and dominance, the more the individual fight backs with disruptive, annoying behaviors in order to maintain a sense of personal power. The behaviors used to try to control vary. Some impaired people become assaultive, aggressive, or stubborn, while others withdraw and become increasingly depressed due to humiliation; they may be demanding or passive and refuse to do what self-care they are capable of. The ability to have some control over one's life has been associated with higher levels of functioning among residents of a home for the aged (Pohl and Fuller 1980). Quality care demands that the caregivers be able to deliver care in a relationship in which dependency is not embarrassing. Technology can assist with some aspects of care, but it cannot make the difficult decisions or handle the emotional impact (Hirschfeld 1985).

Families are often in the uncomfortable position of making decisions for the impaired member (proxy decisions), either alone or in conjunction with health care professionals. Adult children may not agree on the decision-making process, let alone on the decisions made. This can negatively affect the relationships between the nonaffected parent, the children and the impaired parent. Proxy assessments demand that those making the decision have accurate knowledge of what the impaired individuals would have decided for themselves, given the ability to do so (Hirschfeld 1985).

Decision making is stressful for those with cognitive impairment. The tendency is to avoid letting them make decisions at all. However, the information necessary to make wise proxy decisions can be obtained in a less stressful manner by engaging the individual in a relaxed conversation to get their opinion. This requires a high level of communication skill, trust among family members, and their ability to agree upon goals and direction. Decisions related to the quality of life and human values can be very uncomfortable for everyone involved. Individuals can determine their own quality of life only by weighing their own unique set of priorities. The value of human life is constant, regardless of ability.

People with cognitive impairment can still retain a quality of life satisfactory to them. This is even more possible with adequate family support and with their ability to allow the impaired individual as much control as he or she is capable of. The author has interviewed several people with impaired cognitive functioning who said life was good for them and enjoyable. These people had families and caregivers who treated them with respect. They also had maintained a sense of humor and optimism about life. Relationships and interactions with children and grandchildren have the potential to be either enjoyable to both parties or extremely frustrating. In order to maintain satisfactory relationships, it is necessary for the family to be able to adjust patterns of communication and role expectations (Safford 1986).

The indications are that family relationships may be preserved by the type of health care received. Factors that help maintain relationships are early diagnosis followed by appropriate teaching related to etiology, the expected course, available treatment, and management. The availability of professionals to help family members deal with their feelings, problem solve difficult decisions, and cope with their changing roles is useful for maintaining the relationships.

Health Care Options

An estimated 1.3 million people in the United States have severe dementia, and an additional 2.8 million have mild to moderate impairment (Terry and Katzman 1983). If each of these individuals has three people who are affected by their dementia, the lives of over 12 million people in the United States are affected by dementia. DAT affects the lives of roughly 8 million people in the United States, based on an estimated 2 million people with DAT and an estimated three people whose lives are intimately affected by the DAT of each victim (Reifler and Larson 1985). The result is millions of concerned families looking for diagnostic evaluations, respite care, alternate living arrangements, and solutions to problems of how to deal with adults with limited ability either to function in their expected roles or even to properly care for themselves.

The patient with dementia does not seek community resources or health care. It is the family that seeks help for the individual and for the most part are reliable in getting the right person to the evaluation center (Reifler and Larson 1985). The indications are that neither patients nor families use community resources to help cope with the problems (Wolinsky et al. 1984). There is a particular lack of use of mental health and psychiatric care facilities. This has been attributed to physicians' being the gatekeepers for access to health care. Physicians tend not to refer patients for psychiatric or mental health evaluations or treatment (Glosser et al. 1985). Physicians are educated in the treatment of acute medical problems rather than in the day-to-day management of long-term chronic illnesses. They do not tend to refer families to nurses who are more likely to have the education and experience needed to assist families with the management of problems related to chronic illnesses. The effectiveness of nursing management of basic health care requirements has been demonstrated by Martinson's block care program (Jamison and Martinson 1983) and Burnside's (1971) intervention with those in institutions.

Other than a few centers located in large cities, comprehensive evaluations for the type and cause of cognitive impairment are lacking. The ideal would be a comprehensive evaluation by a multidisciplinary staff consisting of a psychiatrist, a gerontologist, a psychiatric nurse clinical specialist, and a neuropsychologist. Other people who should be available for consultation purposes are physicians and nurses with clinical specialties in neurology, cardiology, and related areas, as well as social workers.

The typical situation for the individual with dementia is that he or she is diagnosed by a family physician, with varying degrees of expertise, and then followed for medical treatment (Waxman and Carner 1984). Family satisfaction with this type of treatment tends to be low (Guila et al. 1985). This implies that it may not be in the best interest of patients or families for physicians to be the gatekeepers to health care services.

A comparison of physicians' ratings of their own difficulties treating individuals with DAT and families' ratings of perceived help from physicians showed that both the physicians and the families felt best about the typical medical aspects of diagnosis and the treatment of physical problems (Glosser et al 1985). Physicians had the greatest difficulty with daily management aspects of care, helping with the social and living problems caused by the dementia, nursing home placement, and referral to other health care professionals. The families were the least satisfied with these activities. There was a curvilinear relationship between family satisfaction and duration of dementia. Satisfaction was highest during the diagnostic stage and after total disability. Satisfaction was lowest in the middle stages, when patients are hardest to manage at home (Glosser et al. 1985). Treatment of dementias is primarily biopsychosocial, as no medical treatment can reverse or even effectively relieve symptoms in the nonreversible dementias. The medical model is geared toward diagnosis and the symptom relief of acute problems with medication. Other disciplines are more adapt at the psychosocial management. This does not discount the value of proper medical management for physical problems and necessary medications. It does point out the benefits of multidisciplinary management.

The current health care system and social policy reflect this bias toward the treatment of acute medical problems rather than the management of chronic illness. They also favor the physician as the key entry point into the system. This health care delivery system does not meet the needs of the millions of people with dementia or of their families. Limiting the ability of other health care providers to receive third-party payments limits health care access, effectiveness, and value to the family. That families can benefit from services from a variety of health care providers was demonstrated with a multidisciplinary approach (Reifler and Larson 1985). More research needs to be done to determine why people are not utilizing existing health services (Wolinsky et al. 1984). Other models for health care that are cost effective and responsive to the needs of both the individual and the family need to be developed.

The goals of treatment should include maintaining physical health, providing symptomatic relief where possible, and providing an optimal social and physical environment for the impaired individual that will maximize ability to function and minimize troublesome behaviors (Glosser et al. 1985). Clinical and research data indicate that maintaining cognitive functioning or gaining some improvement (not cure) is possible with a planned intervention strategy (Grusendorf 1987). The intervention that seems most successful is to reduce stress, provide adequate nutrition, treat medical problems, provide support including a positive review of past accomplishments, and provide a controlled environment that will protect the safety of individuals while letting them feel they still have control and power over their lives.

References

Albert, M. 1984. "Assessment of cognitive function in the elderly." *Psychosomatics* 25:310–17.

American Psychiatric Association. 1987. *Diagnostic and Statistical Manual of Mental Disorders* revised (3rd ed)., Washington, DC: Author.

Benton, A. L., Sivan, A. B. 1984. "Problems and Conceptual Issues in Neuropsychological Research in Aging and Dementia." *Journal of Clinical Neuropsychology* 6:57–63.

Blackburn, L. M., and Tyrer, G.M.B. 1985. "The value of Luria's Neurophychological Investigation for the assessment of cognitive dysfunction in Alzheimer-type dementia." *British Journal of Clinical Psychology* 24:171–79.

Bray, J. H., Williamson, D. S., and Malone, P. E. 1984. "Personal authority in the family system: Development of a questionnaire to measure personal authority in intergenerational family processes." *Journal of Marital and Family Therapy* 19:167–78.

Brooks, D. N., Aughton, M. R., Jones, P., and Rizvi, S. 1980. "Cognitive sequelae in relationship to early indices of severity of brain damage after severe blunt head injury." *Journal of Neurology, Neurosurgery, and Psychiatry* 43:529–34.

Burnside, I. M. 1969. "Sensory stimulation: An adjunct to group work with the aged." *Mental Hygiene* 53:281–82.

———. 1971. "Long-term group work with the hospitalized aged." *The Gerontologist* 11:213–18.

Burr, M. L., Hurley, R. J., and Sweetnam, P. M. 1975. "Vitamin C supplementation of old people with low blood levels." *Gerontology Clinics* 17:236–43.

Charlton, M. H. 1975. "Presenile Dementia." *New York State Journal of Medicine* 75:1493–95.

Clarke, M., Lowry, R., and Clarke, S. 1986. "Cognitive impairment in the elderly: A community survey." *Age and Aging* 15:278–84.

Cole, K. D., and Zarit, S. H. 1984. "Psychological deficits in depressed medical patients." *The Journal of Nervous and Mental Disease* 172:150–55.

Duara, R., Grady, C., Haxby, J., and Associates. 1986. "Positron emission tomography in Alzheimer's disease." *Neurology* 36:879–87.

Duffy, F. H., Albert, M. S., and McAnulty, G. 1984. "Brain electrical activity in patients with presenile and senile Dementia of the Alzheimer's type." *Annals of Neurology* 16:439–48.

Dustman, R. E., Ruhling, R. O., Russell, E. M., and Associates. 1984. "Aeorbic exercise training and improved neuropsychological function of older individuals." *Neurobiology of Aging* 5:35–42.

Ebrahim, S., Nouri, R., and Barer, D. 1985. "Cognitive impairment after stroke." *Age and Aging* 14:345–50.

Eisdorfer, C., and Cohen, D. 1980. "Diagnostic criteria for primary neuronal degeneration of the Alzheimer's type." *Journal of Family Practice* 11:553–57.

Fillenbaum, G. G., and Smyer, M. A. 1981. "The development, validity, and reliability of the OARS Multidimensional Functional Assessment Questionnaire." *Journal of Gerontology* 36:428–34.

Folstein, M. F., Folstein, S. E., and McHugh, P. R. 1975. "Mini-mental state: A practical method for grading the cognitive state of patients for the clinician." *Journal of Psychiatric Research* 12:189–98.

Foreman, M. D. 1987. "Reliability and validity of mental status questionnaires in elderly hospitalized patients." *Nursing Research* 36:216–20.

Glosser, G., Wexler, D., and Balmelli, M. 1985. "Physicans' and families' perspectives on the medical management of dementia." *Journal of the American Geriatric Society* 33:383–91.

Golden, C. J., Purisch, A. D., and Hammeke, T. A. 1985. *Luria-Nebraska Neuropsychological Battery: Forms I and II Manual.* Los Angeles: Western Psychological Services.

Goodwin, J. S., Goodwin, J. M., and Garry, P. J. 1983. "Association between nutritional status and cognitive functioning in a healthy elderly population." *Journal of the American Medical Association* 249:2917–21.

Grusendorf, P. E. 1987. *EEG's in Cognitive Stages of Alzheimer's Type Dementia.* Unpublished master's thesis. Provo, UT:Brigham Young University.

Guila, G., Wexler, D., and Balmelli, M. 1985. "Physicians' and families' perspectives on the medical management of dementia." *Journal of the American Geriatric Society* 33:383–91.

Haase, G. R. 1977. "Diseases presenting as dementia." In C. E. Wells (ed.), *Dementia* (2nd ed.). Philadelphia: F. W. Davis.

Hamner, M. L. 1984. "Insight, reminiscence, denial, projection: Coping mechanisms of the aged." *Journal of Gerontological Nursing* 10:66–68, 81.

Hirschfeld, M. J. 1985. "Ethics and care for the elderly." *International Journal of Nursing Studies* 22:319–28.

Holzer, C. E., III, Tischler, G. L., Leaf, P. J., and Myers, J. K. 1984. "An epidemiologic assessment of cognitive impairment in a community population." *Research in Community and Mental Health* 4:3–32.

Jacobs, J. W., Bernhard, B. A., Delgado, A., and Strain, J. J. 1977. "Screening for organic mental syndromes in the medically ill." *Annals of Internal Medicine* 86:40–46.

Jamison, M., and Martinson, I. 1983. "Block nursing: Neighbors caring for neighbors." *Nursing Outlook* 31:270–73.

Katzman, R. 1976. "The prevalence and malignancy of Alzheimer disease." *Archives of Neurology* 33:217–18.

Kral, V. A., Solyom, L., Enesco, H., et al. 1970. "Relationship of Vitamin B_{12} and folic acid to memory function." *Biological Psychiatry* 2:19–26.

Lawson, J. S., Rodenburg, M., and Dykes, J. A. 1977. "A dementia rating scale for use with psychogeriatric patients." *Journal of Gerontology* 32:153–59.

Lawton, M. P. 1975. "The Philadelphia Geriatric Center Morale Scale: A revision." *Journal of Gerontology* 30:85–89.

Lawton, M. P., Moss, M., Fulcomer, M., and Kleban, M. H. 1982. "A research and service oriented multilevel assessment instrument." *Journal of Gerontology* 37:91–99.

Loring, D. W., Keller, W. J., and Largen, J. W. 1984. "Period analysis of the EEG in early putative Alzheimer's disease." *International Journal of Neuroscience* 24:63–68.

Lozoff, B., Brittenham, G. M., et al. 1982. "The effects of short-term oral iron therapy on developmental deficits in iron-deficient anemic infants." *Journal of Pediatrics* 100:352–57.

MacLennan, W. J., Ballinger, B. R., McHarg, A., and Ogston, S. A. 1987. "Dementia and immobility." *Age and Aging* 16:1–9.

McLachlan, D. R., Dalton, A. J., Galin, H., Schlotterer, G., and Daicar, E. 1984. "Alzheimer's disease: Clinical course and cognitive disturbances." *Acta Neurologica Scandinavia* 99:83–89.

Oski, F. A., and Hoing, A. S. 1978. "The effects of therapy on the developmental scores of iron-deficient infants." *Journal of Pediatrics* 92:21–25.

Penttila, M., Partanen, J. V., Soininen, H., and Reikkinen, P. J. 1985. "Quantitative analysis of occipital EEG in different stages of Alzheimer's disease." *Electroencephalography and Clinical Neurophysiology* 60:1–6.

Pfeiffer, E. 1975. "A short portable mental status questionnaire for the the assessment of organic brain deficiency in elderly patients." *Journal of the American Geriatric Society* 23:433–41.

Pohl, J. M., and Fuller, S. S. 1980. "Perceived choice, social interaction, and dimensions of morale of residents in a home for the aged." *Research in Nursing and Health* 3:147–57.

Pridgeon, H. 1985. "Impact of Alzheimer's disease and the role of the patient's family." In V.L. Melnick and N.N. Dubler (eds.), *Alzheimer's Dementia: Dilemmas in Clinical Research*. Clifton, NJ: Humana Press.

Raskind, M. 1983. "Nutrition and cognitive function in the elderly." *Journal of the American Medical Association* 249:2939–40.

Reifler, B. V., and Larson, E. B. 1985. "Alzheimer's disease and long-term care: The assessment of the patient." *Journal of Geriatric Psychiatry* 28:9–34.

Reifler, B. V., Larson, E., Cox, G., and Featherstone, H. 1981. "Treatment results at a multispeciality clinic for the impaired elderly and their families." *Journal of the American Geriatric Society* 29:579–82.

Reisberg, B. 1985. "Alzheimer's disease update." *Psychiatric Annals* 15:319–22.

———. 1986. "Dementia: A systematic approach to identifying reversible causes." *Geriatrics* 41:30–46.

Reisberg, B., Ferris, S. H., deLeon, M. J., and Crook, T. 1982. The Global Deterioration Scale for assessment of primary degenerative dementia. *American Journal of Psychiatry* 139:1136–39.

Reitan, R. M., and Davison, L. A. 1974. *Clinical Neuropsychology: Current Status and Applications.* New York: John Wiley and Sons.

Safford, F. 1986. *Caring for the Mentally Impaired Elderly.* New York: Henry Holt and Company.

Schorah, C. J., Newill, A., Scott, D. L., et al. 1979. "Clinical effects of Vitamin C in elderly inpatients with low blood Vitamin C levels." *Lancet* 1:403–406.

Soininen, H., Partanen, J. V., Helkala, E. L., and Reikkinen, P. J. 1982. "EEG findings in senile dementia and normal aging." *Acta Neurological Scandinavia* 65:59–70.

Talmage, E. W., and Collins, G. A. 1983. "Physical abilities after head injury." *Physical Therapy* 63:2010–16.

Terry, R. D., and Katzman, R. 1983. "Senile dementia of the Alzheimer type." *Annals of Neurology* 14:497–506.

Thomas, P. D., Garry, P. J., Goodwin, J. M., and Goodwin, J. S. 1985. "Social bonds in a healthy elderly sample: Characteristics and associated variables." *Social Sciences and Medicine* 20:365–69.

Thompson, E. H., and Doll, W. 1982. "The burden of families coping with the mentally ill: An invisible crisis." *Family Relations* 31:379–88.

Tucker, M. A., Ogle, S. J., Davison, J. G., and Eilenberg, M.D. 1987. "Validation of a brief screening test for depression in the elderly." *Age and Aging* 16:139–44.

Uhlman, R. F., Larson, E. B., and Koepsell, T. D. 1986. "Hearing impairment and cognitive decline in senile dementia of the Alzheimer's Type." *Journal of the American Geriatrics Society* 34:207–10.

Vardon, V. M., and Blessed, G. 1986. "Confusion ratings and abbreviated mental test performance: A comparison." *Age and Aging* 15:139–44.

Waxman, H. M., and Carner, E. A. 1984. "Physicians' recognition, diagnosis, and treatment of mental disorders in elderly medical patients." *The Gerontologist* 24:593–97.

Wilson, H.S., and Knisel, C. 1985. *Psychiatric Nursing* (2nd ed.). Menlo Park, CA: Addison-Wesley.

Wolinsky, F. D., Coe, R. M., Miller, D. K., and Prendergast, J. M. 1984. "Measurement of the global and functional dimensions of health status in the elderly." *Journal of Gerontology* 39:88–92.

13
Burden and Family Care of the Elderly

Clifton E. Barber

C ontrary to popular myth, research indicates that families *do not* abrogate their responsibility of caring for their chronically ill and dependent elderly members (Cantor 1980, 1983; McCauley and Arling 1984; Monk 1983; Shanas 1980, 1979a, 1979b; Sussman and Peter 1981). In fact, the decision to institutionalize a spouse or parent appears to be the last rather than the first resort in providing care for the elderly (Brody 1978, 1969).

The circumstance precipitating the decision to institutionalize an elderly family member is usually that the negative consequences of providing long-term care have become too difficult for the family or the individual care-giver to bear. These negative consequences may include financial hardship, decline in physical health, strain on family relationship, and a long litany of mental symptoms of emotional strain such as depression, anxiety, frustra-tion, helplessness, sleeplessness, loneliness, and lowered morale (Barber 1986; Brody 1985; Chenoweth and Spencer 1986; Cicirelli 1981; Danis 1978; Horowitz and Dobrof 1982; Robinson and Thurnher 1979).

The term *burden* is frequently used by researchers as a central measure of the costs of caregiving and subsequently of caregiver well-being (Zarit et al. 1980; Zarit 1982). The broad appeal and frequent use of *burden* in the caregiving literature seems to justify using it as the primary measure of caregiver well-being in this chapter.

The objectives of this chapter are to (1) define the concept of caregiver burden, and (2) review the literature research on caregiving. This is done in an effort to construct a preliminary theory of caregiving wherein burden is treated as the primary dependent variable. The term *theory* as used in this chapter, refers to a set of logically related propositional statements that identify how variables are related to each other (Burr et al. 1979). The chapter concludes with a discussion of implications that this theory has for future research.

Caregiver Burden

Conceptual and Operational Definitions

In the majority of studies on caring for a dependent family member, *burden* has been conceptually defined as any cost or set of costs (the terms *consequences* and *impacts* are also used) that result from shouldering the caregiving role. Most of the operational definitions of *burden* acknowledge that caregiving has multiple consequences. For example, one frequently used measure of burden, the Burden Interview developed by Zarit et al. (1980), assesses the impact of caregiving on the caregiver in five areas: health, psychological well-being, finances, social life, and relationship with the patient. Another instrument, the Caregiver Strain Index developed by Robinson (1983), likewise takes into account multiple "costs" resulting from caregiving.

Three Problems in Measuring Caregiver Burden

Almost all attempts to operationally define *burden* share three characteristics in common. First, they all contain an explicit and exclusive focus on caregiving. Second, they require the caregiver to evaluate the impact of caregiving on a number of dimensions of *burden*. And third, they yield total scores indicating overall levels of burden felt by individual caregivers. These characteristics are worth noting because they reveal three corresponding problems that have important implications for future research and theory building in this area.

Because of the first characteristic, the specific and exclusive focus on caregiving, many burden instruments cannot be administered to noncaregivers. Consequently, there is no way to discern the relative burden (that is, burden of caregivers compared with burden of noncaregivers) that caregiving imposes. One notable exception is a study by George and Gwyther (1986) in which a general measure of well-being was employed. These researchers found that the only dimensions of burden that differentiated caregivers from noncaregivers are mental health and social participation, with caregivers showing significantly lower levels of well-being (that is, higher burden) in both instances.

Because of the second characteristic, that most measures of burden explicitly require respondents to relate certain aspects of caregiving to their impact, an unwelcome kind of confounding occurs. A presumed stressor (such as involvement in caregiving tasks) and its outcome (burden) become so intertwined that one cannot independently relate caregiving to its consequence on the well-being of the caregiver.

And because of the third characteristic, that most burden instruments generate a summary score indicative of the overall level of burden experienced by the caregiver, it is impossible to investigate the impact of caregiving on different dimensions of burden. Moreover, focusing on an overall burden score masks the distinction between objective and subjective burden. This distinction is an important one and deserves to be discussed in greater detail.

Objective versus Subjective Burden

Twenty years ago, Hoenig and Hamilton (1966) discussed the importance of differentiating between objective and subjective burden. Objective burden, they said, consists of events, happenings, and activities associated with caregiving. Subjective burden, on the other hand, is embodied in the caregiver's feelings, attitudes, and emotions. The value of this dichotomous conceptualization has been illustrated by several researchers who have found a difference not only in the incidence of subjective versus objective burden but also in the correlates of the two types of burden (Herz et al. 1976; Platt and Hirsch 1981; Thompson and Doll, 1982).

In a study by Montgomery et al. (1985), *burden* was conceptually defined as the extent of disruptions or changes in various aspects of the caregiver's life and household. *Subjective burden*, on the other hand, was defined as the caregiver's attitude toward or emotional response to the caregiving experience. Although the two types of burden are correlated, subjective and objective burden share only 12 percent of common variance, a finding congruent with Thompson and Doll's (1982) research, wherein they discovered that the factors contributing to subjective burden are different from those contributing to objective burden.

Review of the Literature

Severity of Patient Impairment and Caregiver Burden

Among the variables initially believed to exert an influence on caregiver burden was the degree of severity to which the patient (any older person cared for by another person) is impaired. Severity of impairment may be measured in terms of the duration of the patient's illness, the degree of cognitive incapacity, or the number of behavior problems manifested by the patient (Deimling and Bass 1986; Zarit and Zarit 1982a). The degree of severity of impairment on any of these measures varies from patient to patient and over time for the same patient.

The relationship between the severity of a patient's impairment and the amount of burden experienced by the individual or family caring for the patient was assumed to be positive. Hence, this theoretical proposition can be stated as follows:

Proposition 1: The more severe the patient's impairment, the greater the burden experienced by the caregiver.

Although it is intuitively appealing, Proposition 1 has not been clearly supported by research, at least not without some qualification. George and Gwyther (1986) reported that although severity of patient impairment is related to caregiver well-being, it is related only in selected instances. For example, the duration of the patient's illness does not appear to affect the caregiver on a number of measures of well-being, whereas the severity of certain symptoms (such as the incidence of disruptive behavior) does negatively influence the caregiver's self-rated health, as well as the amount of time the caregiver spends relaxing (George and Gwyther 1986).

Further, Zarit (1982) claimed that although the patient's impairment creates a situation in which burden is experienced by the caregiver, how much burden varies a great deal from caregiver to caregiver *even when the severity of patient impairment is controlled.*

This is not to say that the patient's impairment does not in any way influence the caregiver's sense of burden; undoubtedly it does. But as far as future research and practice implications are concerned, it is important to note that the patient's impairment or functional status is not the sole determinant of caregiver burden. What other factors affect the amount of burden experienced by caregivers?

A review of the literature on this question reveals that at least three additional variables influence caregiver burden: (1) the extent of the caregiver's involvement, (2) the caregiver's characteristics, and (3) the amount of social support the caregiver receives. The conceptual and operational definitions of each of these variables, together with theoretical propositions that describe their relationship to caregiver burden, are discussed in the sections that follow.

Extent of the Caregiver's Involvement and Caregiver Burden

Conceptual and Operational Definitions. The conceptual and operational definitions of *caregiving involvement* have largely been limited to quantitative measures such as the number of caregiving tasks performed and/or the amount of time the caregiver spends performing them. With two notable exceptions (Archbold 1980; Montgomery et al. 1985), very little attention has been given to qualitative measures of caregiving involvement (that is, the type of caregiving task or the perceived difficulty of performing different caregiving tasks).

Extent of Caregiving Involvement as a Determinant of Burden. What is the relationship between extent of involvement in caregiving and burden? One proposition is that the extent of caregiving involvement is positively and directly related to burden, stated as follows:

Proposition 2: The more involved the caregiver is in rendering care, the greater the burden he or she experiences.

There is only limited empirical support for this proposition. Montgomery et al. (1985) reported that extent of caregiving involvement (measured in terms of the number of caregiving tasks performed weekly) is positively related to objective—but not subjective—measures of burden. On the other hand, George and Gwyther (1986) found no relationship between the amount of time the caregiver spends in the caregiving role and feelings of burden.

These findings point to the possibility that extent of caregiving involvement is not as directly related to caregiver burden as has been supposed. Rather, extent of caregiving involvement may exercise an indirect influence on burden. At least three indirect influences are worth noting.

First, when combined with level of patient impairment, extent of caregiving involvement may indirectly influence caregiver burden. Support for Proposition 1—a positive relationship between level of patient impairment and caregiver burden—is limited, a high degree of impairment does not always result in a correspondingly high level of burden because of the extent to which the caregiver is involved in caregiving. When the caregiver's extent of involvement in caregiving is relatively low, the degree of a patient's impairment may have little or no influence on burden. But when the caregiver's extent of involvement is moderate or high and the level of patient impairment is severe, this may influence burden.

Proposition 3: The more severe the patient's impairment, the greater the burden experienced by the caregiver, but only under conditions wherein the caregiver is moderately or highly involved in caregiving.

A second indirect influence that extent of caregiving involvement may have on burden is the length of time the caregiver has actively functioned in the caregiving role. A longitudinal study by Zarit et al. (1986) found that caregivers' feelings of burden actually decreased the longer they are involved in the caregiving role. The interesting explanation offered by these researchers for this finding merits special discussion.

The longer caregivers are involved in the caregiver role, Zarit et al. (1986) argued, the more likely they are to develop effective coping and caregiving skills. The successful application of these skills subsequently engenders a sense of confidence in dealing with caregiving responsibilities and increases the caregiver's tolerance for the patient's memory and behavior problems. And increased levels of confidence and tolerance subsequently lead to decreased levels of burden. This time-dependent sequence of variables is expressed in the following three propositions:

Proposition 4a: The longer the caregiver spends in the caregiver role, the more likely he or she is to acquire a repertoire of effective strategies and skills for coping with the patient's memory and behavior problems.

Proposition 4b: The greater the caregiver's repertoire of effective coping skills, the greater his or her confidence and tolerance in dealing with the patient's memory and behavior problems.

Proposition 4c: As the caregiver's level of confidence in dealing with the patient increases and as the caregiver's tolerance for the patient's memory and behavior problems increases, his or her level of burden decreases.

A third indirect influence of caregiving involvement on burden is the caregiver's perception of the extent to which his or her freedom is restricted by caregiving. Montgomery et al. (1985) measured extent of caregiving involvement both in terms of the type and in terms of number of tasks performed. Neither of these measures of extent of caregiving involvement correlated with subjective burden, but both of them were positively correlated with objective burden, particularly with six types of caregiving tasks: nursing care, bathing, dressing, walking, transportation, and errands. A narrow interpretation of these findings leads to the conclusion that caregiving involvement is positively associated with objective burden only in these six instances; but a broader and more theoretically relevant explanation is that freedom or lack of freedom may be the central concept in explaining the link between caregiving involvement and burden.

Proposition 5: Extent of caregiving involvement is positively related to burden—particularly to objective burden—in those instances wherein the caregiver perceives that fulfilling caregiving tasks limits his or her freedom.

The Caregiver's Characteristics and Caregiver Burden

Although objective burden is best predicted by extent of caregiving involvement, subjective burden appears to be more strongly influenced by the characteristics of the caregiver, particularly the caregiver's kinship relation to the patient and the caregiver's gender (Montgomery et al. 1985).

Kinship Relation of Caregiver to Patient. How do spouses and adult children compare in terms of caregiver burden? Studies addressing this question have not yielded a clear answer. Neither Robinson (1983) nor Zarit et al. (1980) found demonstrable differences in burden between spouses and adult children. However, Reever and Bach-Peterson (1979) found that spouses reported significantly more doctors' visits and poorer self-rated health than did adult children, and that spousal caregivers exhibited lower levels of well-being on several mental health measures than did adult child caregivers. These differences persisted even when age differences among spouse and adult child caregivers were statistically controlled. In sum, the consequences for caregiving of the caregiver's kinship relation to the patient are not clear and probably vary based on the dimensions of burden being measured as well as on a variety of intervening variables.

Nevertheless, it may be profitable in this theory-building attempt to postulate that spousal caregivers, because they are comparatively more involved in caregiving, experience greater burden than do adult child caregivers:

Proposition 6: Due to their comparatively greater involvement in caregiving, spousal caregivers experience greater caregiver burden than do adult child caregivers.

This proposition may be refined by identifying and briefly discussing three explanations of why spousal caregivers may be more involved in caregiving and may experience greater burden than adult children or other family members.

First, the relatively greater burden experienced by spousal caregivers might be a product of their greater extent of involvement in caregiving due to norms governing behavior and interaction in caregiving roles. For example, Shanas (1979b) noted that family care for the elderly is seldom a shared family function. Rather, care and support are more often extended by one member of the family at a time, in a pattern referred to as the "principle of substitution." That is, care is rendered in serial order. The spouse functions as the primary caregiver; in the absence of the spouse, an adult child—usually a daughter—assumes the caregiving role; in the absence of offspring, another member of the family is responsible (for example, a sibling). Furthermore, marriage is the key relationship in the event of illness in old age. In fact, reliance on a husband or wife and his or her willingness to provide assistance is almost unquestioned. Caring for a spouse is rarely ever a matter for options; it is a given, accepted without reservation. Marriage is a complementary relationship into which interdependence and reciprocity are built as prominent features governing interaction (Johnson 1979).

Second, the relatively greater burden experienced by spousal caregivers may simply be due to the fact that their proximity to the patient results in greater caregiving involvement, which in turn produces relatively higher levels of burden for them.

Third, spousal caregivers may experience greater burden because they employ different mechanisms or strategies from those adult child caregivers employ in adapting to the caregiving role. For example, in research comparing spouse caregivers with adult child caregivers, Johnson and Catalano (1983) identified two broad categories of adaptive mechanisms among caregivers that affect the caregiver's use of supports and the level of burden: (1) distancing techniques (including the establishment of both greater physical distance and greater psychological distance), and (2) enmeshing techniques (for example, social regression and role entrenchment). Johnson and Catalano (1983) found that distancing techniques are used by the adult child more often and are associated with lower levels of burden. Enmeshing techniques, are used primarily by spouses and are associated with higher levels of burden.

These three explanations are summarized in the following proposition:

Proposition 7: Compared with adult child caregivers, the relatively greater caregiving involvement (and greater burden) experienced by spousal caregivers is a product of one or more of the following factors: (1) norms governing caregiver-patient interaction, (2) the proximity of the caregiver to the patient, and (3) the mechanisms the caregiver employs in adapting to the role of caregiving.

Gender, Caregiving Involvement, and Burden. In reviewing the literature, one is disappointed and somewhat surprised to find that most of the research on the consequences of caregiving has failed to explore the effect of the caregiver's gender on burden. However, the few studies investigating gender differences report that female caregivers experience greater burden than do male caregivers (Brody, 1981; Horowitz, 1985; Johnson and Catalano 1983). One reason for this gender difference is that women are more involved in caregiving than are men, leading to the proposition:

Proposition 8: Due to their comparatively greater involvement in caregiving, female caregivers experience greater caregiver burden than do male caregivers.

This proposition is based in part on the argument that caregiving is usually defined as an expansion of the traditional responsibilities of a wife and mother, an argument that has received substantial empirical support in the literature (Brody 1981; Fitting et al. 1986; Horowitz 1981; Cantor 1983; Johnson 1983).

In spite of findings that female caregivers experience greater burden than do their male counterparts, there are several reasons why males may be expected to experience greater burden in caregiving than females. First, more women than men are diagnosed as having Alzheimer's disease; since a greater percentage of middle-aged women entered the work force between 1950 and 1970 than men, it is likely that more men, especially husbands, will be assuming the caregiver role in the future (Brody 1985). Second, the finding that women form more intimate relationships with others in their social environment and have stronger social support systems than do men suggests that male caregivers would be more socially isolated (Lowenthal et al. 1975). Finally, Gilligan's (1982) studies on women and moral development suggest that women place greater emphasis than men on personal relationships. Consequently, if women have a stronger "ethic of care" than men have, as Gilligan suggests, and if women also have stronger supports than men have, as suggested by Lowenthal et al. (1975), then male caregivers may be expected to feel greater burden and have more difficulty adjusting to the caregiver role than female caregivers would. Future research needs to explore more fully the effect of gender differences on extent of caregiving involvement and burden.

The extent of involvement in caregiving is not the only variable explaining the relationship between caregiver's gender and burden, particulary when burden is measured in subjective terms. One study (Horowitz 1985) comparing sons and daughters as caregivers, investigated the possibility that the relatively lower feelings of burden that sons felt is a reflection of their comparatively lower levels of involvement in caregiving. When the extent of caregiving involvement was controlled, however, sex differences in feelings of burden remained. The researchers concluded that the experience of caring for an aged parent is more burdensome for daughters than sons *even when both provide similar levels of care*, leading to the question: What variables other than caregiving involvement might account for the relatively greater burden experienced by female caregivers?

Role Conflict and Perceived Lack of Freedom. One answer to this question may be that female caregivers, particularly middle-aged adult daughters, experience greater role conflict as a result of competing demands on their time. They tend to have primary responsibility for the emotional support of other family members, for household management, and for child-rearing. In many cases they are also full-time workers. The same multiple demands are seldom placed on men; this may explain why, when caring for an older parent is added to these responsibilities, the experience is more burdensome for women. Further, increased role conflict may produce feelings of being confined, of lacking freedom, which in turn produces—either directly or indirectly—high levels of burden. This explanation is expressed in the following proposition:

Proposition 9: The relatively greater burden experienced by female caregivers (compared with male caregivers) is due to one or both of the following factors: (1) female caregivers experience greater role conflict in the caregiver role than do male caregivers, and (2) female caregivers perceive a greater lack of freedom in the caregiver role than do male caregivers.

Thwarting of Expectations. Several qualitative studies have reported that assuming the caregiving role often runs counter to the expectations that many women have of taking more control of their lives and of not being locked into traditional roles. This may be particularly the case for middle-aged adult daughters who are emerging from their child-rearing responsibilities with expectations of more personal fulfillment, only to have them thwarted by a parent's disability. Brody (1981, 1985) has termed this phenomenon "the woman in the middle." Hence, another related proposition is:

Proposition 10: The relatively greater burden experienced by female caregivers (compared with male caregivers) is due to the fact that they are more likely than male caregivers to experience a thwarting of expectations when they assume the caregiving role.

Stated somewhat differently, greater caregiving burden among women may reflect the different life trajectories of men and women (Neugarten and Gutmann 1968; Lowenthal et al. 1975). In many caregiving samples women have been the traditional caregivers for children and have defined their family roles early in adulthood as those of mother, homemaker, and nurturer. However, many of these women experience a role change in their early middle years in which they find themselves no longer responsible for small children. For these women, the return to caring for a parent or a spouse represents a resumption of the caregiving role, contrary to their expectations for freedom from the responsibility of caring for others. Male caregivers, on the other hand, are often already retired and are already changing their focus from work to home. In the case of a husband caring for a wife, one can speculate that whereas he had previously defined his life in terms of the "provider" role associated with his occupation, he now is engaged in a "nurturing" role, helping his wife with the activities of daily living. According to findings published by Zarit et al. (1986), many men seem to enjoy the nurturing focus of their new caregiving role.

Different Caregiving Models. Yet another explanation for gender differences in burden might be found in the way the caregiving role is perceived by women and men. Brody (1985) suggested that daughters who are caregivers for parents have an internalized model of caregiving based on a parent-infant model, wherein they assume almost total responsibility for the care of the patient. Men, on the other hand, perceive the caregiving role based on a different model, one derived from the work setting in which the delegation of responsibility and recognition of limitations necessary to do a job are emphasized. Greater feelings of burden are associated with the parent-infant model embraced more often by female caregivers. This explanation, expressed as a theoretical proposition, would be:

Proposition 11: Female caregivers experience greater burden than do male caregivers because female caregivers adopt a caregiving model (the parent-infant model) in which they assume almost total responsibility for the care of the patient.

Amount of Social Support and Caregiver Burden

The majority of studies on caregiving acknowledge that social support is an important determinant of caregiver well-being in their choice of variables (e.g. Pratt et al. 1985; Zarit 1982). It is important to note that the majority of these studies limit conceptual and operational definitions of *social support* to quantitative measures, such as the number of visits from family and friends, the frequency of contact with community services (for example, how often there is paid help in the home), and the number of different sources of support used or available to the caregiver.

Social Support as a Determinant of Burden. The general hypothesis in this area has been that as support increases, burden decreases.

Proposition 12: There is an inverse relationship between the level of social support received or the caregiver and the caregiver's level of burden.

Support for this proposition has been limited. Zarit et al. (1980) reported that the frequency of visits from family members is the best predictor of burden for caregivers of dementia patients; the greater the number of visits, the less the burden. Horowitz (1981) tallied visits from family, friends, and various social services into an overall social-support score and found that social support is inversely related to caregiver strain.

However, not all studies have found that social support mediates feelings of burden. Pratt et al. (1985) reported that the presence of a confidant or membership in a support group did not decrease burden among caregivers of Alzheimer's patients. And Zarit and Zarit (1982a) found that the frequency of neither informal nor formal supports correlated with subjective measures of burden.

Zarit and Zarit (1982a) suggested that these equivocal findings imply that quantitative measures of social support do not always exercise a direct influence on caregiver well-being. They claim that other variables, perhaps of a more subjective nature, need to be explored. For example, in using summary scores of the frequency of contact from different sources of support, many studies have assumed that all sources of support are equal in value to the caregiver. However, visits from family members may have one kind of value to the caregiver, while paid help in the home may have another. There may also be variation in the kinds of social support needed by different caregivers. In any case, the question to be asked is: What additional variables are involved in explaining the relationship between social support and burden?

Value Congruence Between Support System and Caregiver. Cobb (1976) defined *support* as information leading a person to believe he or she is cared for, loved, and esteemed as a member of a network of mutual obligations. To this can be added Dohrenwend's (1961) observation that social support may be either positive or negative, depending on the extent to which the person's salient inner goals and values are congruent with those of the support system. Thus, a high number of contacts with a support system would alleviate burden only in instances in which the values of the support system were similar to those of the caregiver.

High levels of contact with a source of support that does not make the caregiver feel loved or esteemed, or that increases value conflict between the caregiver and the support system, may even result in increased feelings of burden. In fact, at least one caregiving study (Zarit and Zarit 1982b) reported that high levels of support (that is, high frequency of contact) are positively related to feelings of burden; the more frequent the contact, the greater the burden.

This discussion leads to the following proposition:

Proposition 13: The social support received by the caregiver reduces the caregiver's burden only when the values undergirding the source of support are congruent with those of the caregiver. When these values are not congruent, increased levels of support produce greater burden.

Gender and the Meaning of Social Support. In a similar vein, it is frequently assumed in the caregiving literature that varying levels of social support have the same effects for all caregivers. The problem with this assumption is illustrated in a study by Zarit (1982) in which she investigated the relationship between the caregiver's gender, social support, and burden. Her findings indicate that husbands as caregivers have significantly more paid help in the home than do wives, relieving them of day-to-day caregiving responsibilities that might otherwise be burdensome. But more important, husbands also seem to benefit from paid help outside and inside the home because these sources of support help them feel that someone understands what they are going through. Frequency of visits from family and friends also correlate with husbands' overall rating of the adequacy of the support they receive, which in turn is the best explanation of their relatively lower burden. Among caregiver husbands there seems to be a fairly straightforward relationship between quantitative measures of social support and feelings of burden (see Proposition 12). High levels of support result in decreased feelings of burden because husbands view these support sources as offering respite and understanding.

However, the same is not true for wives in the caregiving role. Zarit (1982) reported that several measures of social support, such as the use of a confidant and paid help inside the home, are positively correlated with feelings of burden in wives caring for husbands. That is, wives who report the highest levels of support also report the greatest burden. Several explanations can be given for this finding; the one perhaps most useful here is that rather than viewing paid help as a relief and a confirmation of her worth, the caregiver wife may experience guilt for not being able to provide the care herself. In other words, it is the *meaninq* that wives attach to hiring someone to come in and help care for their husbands that is the important factor influencing the relationship between support and burden.

Zarit (1982) also observed that whereas a husband can hire a housekeeper to come in and take over his wife's instrumental chores around the house, a wife is more likely to continue to perform those duties herself. When she does hire someone to come into the home to help, that person is likely to serve as a "sitter" which does not decrease her workload but may allow her to go out to perform other chores. The theoretical importance of this finding is expressed in the following propositions:

Proposition 14a: The relationship between the social support received by the caregiver and level of burden experienced by the caregiver is contingent on the meaning or perceived value of the support from the perspective the caregiver.

Proposition 14b: Male caregivers are more likely than female caregivers to view (attach meaning to) social support in a way that alleviates feelings of burden.

The positive correlation between social support and burden for some women may also simply reflect the fact that those who experience high levels of burden are most likely to seek and obtain support. In this latter instance, burden is viewed as a determinant of support, in which frequent use of support reflects a coping response to high levels of burden.

Summary

This chapter has reviewed the research on factors influencing the amount of burden experienced by individuals caring for elderly family members. The integration of these findings was in the form of a propositional inventory or theory in which caregiving burden was viewed as the primary dependent variable. Figure 13–1 represents a summary of this theory.

Implications for Future Research

Future measures of caregiver burden need to be constructed in such a manner that they (1) permit comparisons with noncaregivers, (2) allow the investigation of the independent effect of caregiving involvement on burden,

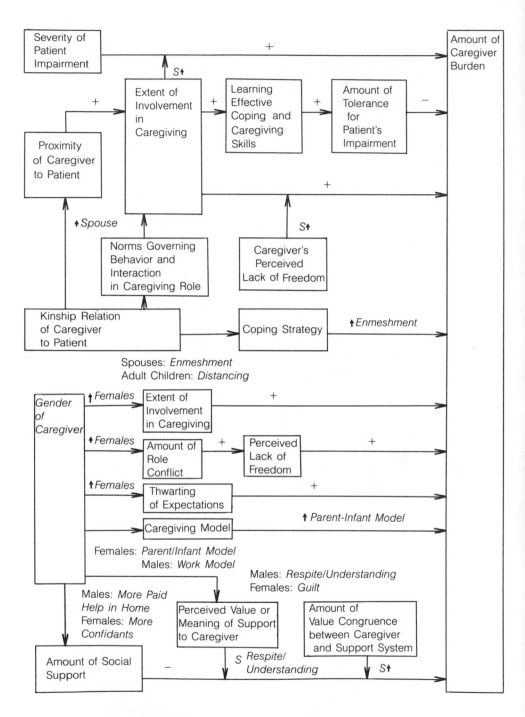

Figure 13–1. A Theory of Burden as a Dependent Variable in Family Care of the Elderly

(3) differentiate between objective and subjective burden, and (4) avoid total reliance on summary scores reflecting overall levels of burden.

Additionally, future research should investigate time-dependent aspects of caregiving. Of all the studies reviewed in this chapter, only Zarit et al. (1986) used a longitudinal research design. We know very little about how the demands of caregiving change over time or about those factors in the process of caregiving that alter feelings of burden.

The majority of caregiving research has focused on the direct influence of a given independent variable (such as caregiver's gender) on burden. Very few studies have recognized the complexity of the relationships among variables affecting amount of caregiver burden. Consequently, there is a particular need to test hypotheses involving contingent variables. For example, the positive relationship between social support and burden is contingent on the perceived value or meaning of the support to the caregiver and on the amount of value congruence between the caregiver and the support system.

References

Archbold, P. 1980. "The impact of caring for all ill elderly parent on the middle-aged offspring." *Journal of Geontological Nursing* 6:78–85.

Barber, C. E. 1986. "Correlates of subjective burden among adult sons and daughters caring for aged parents. Paper presented at the annual meeting of the American Society on Aging, San Francisco, CA.

Brody, E. M. 1969. "Follow-up study of applicants and non-applicants to a voluntary home." *The Gerontologist* 9:187–96.

———. 1978. "The aging of the family." *The Annals of the American Academy of Political and Social Science* 438:13–27.

———. 1981. " 'Women in the middle' and family help to people." Gerontologist 21:471–80.

———. 1985. "Parent care as a normative family stress." *The Gerontologist* 25:19–29.

Burr, W. R., Hill, R., Nye, F. I. and Reiss, I. L. (eds.). 1979. Contemporary Theories About the Family, vol. 1. New York: The Free Press.

Cantor, M. 1980. "Caring for the frail elderly: Impact on family, friends and neighbors." Paper presented at the 33rd annual scientific meeting of the Gerontological Society of America, San Diego, CA.

———. 1983. "Strain among caregivers: A study of experience in the United States." *The Gerontologist* 23:597–604.

Chenoweth, B., and Spencer, B. 1986. "Dementia: The experience of family caregivers." *The Gerontologist* 26:267–72.

Cicirelli, V.G. 1981. *Helping Elderly Parents: The Role of Adult Children*. Boston: Auburn House.

Cobb, S. 1976. "Social support as a moderator of life stress." *Psychosomatic Medicine* 38:300–14.

Danis, B. G. 1978. "Stress in individuals caring for ill elderly relatives." Paper presented at 31st annual meeting of the Gerontological Society of America, Dallas, TX.

Deimlng, G. T., and Bass, D. M. 1986. "Symptoms of mental impairment among elderly adults and their effects on family caregiving." *The Gerontologist* 41:778–84.

Dohrenwend, B. P. 1961. "The social psychological nature of stress: A framework for causal inquiry." *Journal of Abnormal and Social Psychology* 62:294–302.

Fitting, M., Rabins, P., Lucas, M.J., and Eastham, J. 1986. "Caregivers for dementia patients: A comparison of husbands and wives." *The Gerontologist* 26:248–52.

George, L. K., and Gwyther, L. P. 1986. "Caregiver well-being: A multidimensional examination of family caregivers of demented adults." *The Gerontologist* 26:253–59.

Gilligan, C. 1982. *In a Different Voice*. Cambridge, MA: Harvard University Press.

Gottlieb, B. H. 1983. "Social support as a focus for integrative research in psychology." *American Psychologist* 38:278–87.

Herz, M. J., Endicott, J., and Spitzer, R. E. 1976. "Brief versus standard hospitalizations: The family." *American Journal of Psychiatry* 133:795–801.

Hoenig, J., and Hamilton, M. 1966. "The schizophrenic patient in the community and his effect on the household." *International Journal of Social Psychiatry* 12:165–76.

Horowitz, A. 1981. "Sons and daughters as caregivers to older parents: Differences in role performance and consequences." Paper presented at the 34th annual meeting of the Gerontological Society, Toronto.

———. 1985. "Sons and daughters as caregivers to older parents: Differences in role performance and consequences." *The Gerontologist* 25:612–17.

Horowitz, A., and Dobrof, R. 1982. *The Role of Families in Providing Long-Term Care to the Frail and Chronically Ill-Elderly Living in the Community*. New York: Hunter College, Brookdale Center on Aging.

Johnson, C. L., 1983. "Dyadic family relations and social support." *The Gerontologist* 23:37–383.

Johnson, C. L., and Catalano, D. J. 1981. "Childless elderly and their family supports." *The Gerontologist* 21:610–18.

———. 1983. "A longitudinal study of family supports to impaired elderly." *The Gerontologist* 23:612–18.

Lowenthal, M. F., Thurnher, M., Chiriboga, D., and Associates. 1975. *Four Stages of Life: A Comparative Study of Women and Men Facing Transitions*. San Francisco, CA: Jossey-Bass

McAuley, W. J., and Arling, G. 1984. "Use of in-home care by very old people." *Journal of Health and Social Behavior* 25:54–64.

Monk, A. 1983. "Family supports in old age." *Home Health Care Services Quarterly* 3:101–11.

Montgomery, R. J. V., Gonyea, J. G., and Hooyman, N. R. 1985. "Caregiving and the experience of subjective and objective burden." *Family Relations* 34:19–25.

Neugarten, B. L., and Gutmann, D. L. 1968. "Age-sex roles and personality in middle-age: A thematic apperception study." In B. L. Neugarten (ed.), *Middle Age and Aging*. Chicago, IL: University of Chicago Press.

Platt, S., and Hirsch, S. 1981. "The effects of brief hospitalization upon the psychiatric patient's household." *Acta Psychiatrica* 64:199–216.

Pratt, C. C., Schmall, V. L., Wright, S., and Cleland, M. 1985. "Burden and coping strategies of caregivers to Alzheimer's patients." *Family Relations* 34:27–33.

Reever, K. E., and Bach-Peterson, J. 1979. *The Older Person with Senile Dementia in the Community and Their Primary Caregiver*. Unpublished master's thesis. University of Southern California.

Robinson, B. 1983. "Validation of a caregiver strain index." *Journal of Gerontology* 38:344–48.

Robinson, B., and Thurnher, M. 1979. "Taking care of parents: A family-cycle transition." *The Gerontologist* 19:586–93.

Shanas, E. 1979a. "Social myth as hypothesis: The case of the family relations of old people." *The Gerontologist* 19:3–9.

———. "The family as a social support system in old age." *The Gerontologist* 19:169–74.

Shanas, E. 1980. "Older people and their families: The new pioneers." *Journal of Marriage and the Family* 43:9–15.

Sussman, M. D., and Peter, K. 1981. *Support Networks for Families Involved in Caring for Elderly Relatives: Some Policy Initiatives*. Newark, DE: College of Human Resources, University of Delaware.

Thompson, E. H., and Doll, W. 1982. "The burden of families coping with the mentally ill: An invisible crisis." *Family Relations* 31:379–88.

Zarit, J. M. 1982. "Family role, social supports, and their relation to caregiver's burden." Paper presented at the meeting of the Western Gerontological Society, Sacramento, CA.

Zarit, J. M., Gatz, M., and Zarit, S. H. 1981. "Family relationships and burden in long-term care." Paper presented at the Annual Meeting of The Gerontological Society of America, Toronto.

Zarit, J. M., and Zarit, S. H. 1982a. "Measuring burden and support in families with Alzheimer's disease elders." A paper presented at the 35th annual scientific meeting of the Gerontological Society of America, Boston, MA.

Zarit, S. H., and Zarit, J. M. 1982b. "Families under stress: Interventions for caregivers of senile dementia patients." Psychotherapy: Theory, Research and Practice 19:461–71.

Zarit, S. H., Reever, K. E., and Bach-Peterson, J. 1980. "Relatives of the impaired elderly: Correlates of feelings of burden." *The Gerontologist* 20:649–55.

Zarit, S. H., Todd, P. A., and Zarit, J. M. 1986. "Subjective burden of husbands and wives as caregivers: A longitudinal study." *The Gerontologist* 26:260–66.

14
Elder Abuse

Melvin White

Abuse of the elderly is often regarded as a relatively recent phenomenon. However, the image of yesterday's family as a harmonious multigenerational unit appears to be largely a myth (Flandrin 1979; Stearns 1986; Reinharz 1986; Shanas 1979; Rosenmayr 1984). For generations, the elderly have suffered various types of abuse at the hands of their children (Reinharz 1986). What is recent is the increased public awareness and concern about elder abuse.

There is confusion regarding what elder abuse is and what it is not. The terms *abuse* and *neglect* are often confused; some scholars use a broad definition, while others use a narrow, restrictive definition (Douglas and Hickey 1983). This makes it difficult to compare various studies and draw reliable conclusions (Galbraith 1986).

In an attempt to provide uniformity to the area, the American Medical Association (1985) has provided the following definition of *elder abuse:*

> Abuse shall mean an act or omission which results in harm or threatened harm to the health or welfare of an elderly person. Abuse includes intentional infliction of physical or mental injury; sexual abuse, or withholding of necessary food, clothing, and medical care to meet the physical and mental health needs of an elderly person by one having the care, custody, or responsibility of an elderly person (American Medical Association 1985:967).

This chapter is divided into seven sections. The first section is a brief review of data on the incidence and prevalence of elder abuse. In the second section, major forms of elder abuse are identified. Characteristics of abused and abuser are discussed in the third and fourth sections. The fifth section reviews major risk factors that have been found to be associated with elder abuse. In section six is a discussion of prevention and treatment. The seventh section explores questions that need to be researched.

Incidence and Prevalence

There are several reasons why it is difficult to obtain valid estimates of the incidence of elder abuse: (1) Both the victim and the perpetrator tend to deny abuse or downplay its seriousness. (2) Health practitioners are unable to identify many forms of elder abuse. (3) There is a lack of uniformity in state reporting laws and record keeping. (4) Various definitions of elder abuse make it difficult to determine amounts of elder abuse.

Using a random sample, Pillemer and Sinkelhor (1988) found that about 3 percent of the elderly suffer abuse. Other estimates range from 1 percent to 10 percent. About 4 percent of abuse victims suffer moderate to severe abuse. It is estimated that the total number of elderly that are abused each year ranges from 500,000 to 2.5 million (U.S. Congress 1985).

Major Forms of Elder Abuse

Physical Abuse

Physical abuse includes the infliction of bruises, lacerations, fractures, or burns. It also includes giving the elderly excessive doses of drugs. Another form is constraining the elderly physically, such as tying them to their bed.

Psychological Abuse

Some common instances of psychological abuse are threats, insults, harrassment, and withholding affection. Refusal to allow travel, visits by friends, or attendance at church are other methods of inflicting psychological abuse.

Financial Exploitation

Another common form of abuse is the exploitation of the resources of the elderly. This usually involves the misuse of their income or other financial resources.

Neglect

In this chapter neglect is considered a type of abuse. Neglect is the failure to provide necessities. For example, the caregiver may fail to provide food, medicine, or bathroom assistance.

It is unclear which type of elder abuse is most common. Pillemer and Sinkelhor (1988) reported that physical abuse is the most common, followed by psychological abuse and neglect. Powell and Berg (1987), on the other hand, found that financial abuse is the most common, followed by psychological abuse, physical abuse, and neglect. Others have suggested that neglect is the most common type of elder abuse (Douglas and Hickey 1983; Block and Synnott 1979). The studies are consistent in showing that psychological abuse is more frequent than physical abuse.

Many elder abuse cases involve multiple forms of abuse. Powell and Berg (1987) found that physical, financial, and psychological abuse frequently occur together.

The type of elder abuse, like the incidence of elder abuse, needs better documentation. Accurate measurement of psychological abuse is extremely difficult because usually there is no physical evidence of abuse and there is no clear definition of what constitutes psychological abuse.

Characteristics of the Abused

Abused elderly persons tend to be Protestant females who are frail and mentally and/or physically impaired. They are usually between 75 and 85 years old and are dependent on the abuser to meet their needs of daily living. Abused persons often live with the abuser and are unaware of alternative living arrangements. They are often isolated and are not allowed to attend church, visit friends, or make phone calls. Many are in the working class, although significant numbers are in the middle and upper classes. Pillemer and Sinkelhor (1988) found that persons living with a spouse and one other person seem to be particularly vulnerable to maltreatment. Those living alone have a much lower rate of maltreatment than those living with others.

More women than men are abused because there are more elderly women than elderly men. However, Pillemer and Sinkelhor (1988) found that the rates of abuse are higher for men than for women. They provided two explanations for this finding. First, men are more likely than women to be living with someone rather than living alone. Second, elderly men are usually older than their wives and therefore may be more frail and vulnerable to abuse.

Characteristics of Abusers

Those who abuse elderly persons are most often family members—spouses, sons, daughters, sons-in-law, and daughters-in-law. The most frequent abuser appears to be either the spouse or the daughter of the abused. More abuse is committed by spouses than by children because more elderly live with their spouse than with their children (Pillemer and Sinkelhor 1988). However, rates of abuse are slightly higher by children than by spouses. Among elders who live with their spouses, the rate of abuse is 41 per 1,000. Among those who live with their children, the rate is 44 per 1,000.

Abusers tend to suffer from some source of stress and may be frequent users of alcohol or drugs. They tend to be white, middle-aged, and lower-middle or upper-lower class. A fear of losing control of the distribution of power and resources is frequently evident. The abuser has often cared for the abused over an extended period of time.

Risk Factors in Elder Abuse

The causes of elderly abuse are multiple, and no single theory adequately explains why older people are abused. Theories of causation frequently are grouped into three categories: (1) the psychological model, (2) the learning model, and (3) the situational model.

Psychological Model

The psychological model states that the cause of elder abuse is the mental or emotional illness of the abuser. Included in this model are abusers who abuse alcohol and drugs as well as those who have character disorders.

Learning Model

According to the learning model, abusive behavior is learned from other people. A child who grows up in a home in which the father and mother abuse their children will learn abusive behavior. They also develop feelings of resentment and anger from being abused and seek revenge for the suffering they endured as a child. The damaging attitudes of society toward the elderly reinforce attitudes developed in childhood.

Situational Model

The situational model states that abusers are neither mentally nor emotionally ill, are not abusing drugs or alcohol, and have not learned the abusive behavior from family and friends. Rather, they are normal individuals who are trying to do their best but who become overwhelmed by the stresses and demands of providing care to a helpless, dependent, and sometimes demanding individual. Stresses on the caregiver include the lack of adequate financial resources, lack of community support, and, in institutional settings, low pay and inadequately trained staff. And abused persons may actually provoke the attack of the abuser by their behavior.

These theoretical models are useful for identifying and organizing the factors that may cause elder abuse. However, no single theory adequately explains elder abuse, and many elder abuse incidents result from a combination of psychological, learning, and situational factors.

Prevention and Treatment

Prevention and treatment may focus on the abuser, on the abused, or on the relationship between the abuser and the abused. As greater understanding of the abuser is gained through research, intervention strategies can be designed to prevent or minimize those forces affecting the abuser. Knowledge of the abused may provide insights into characteristics and behaviors of the abused that may provoke an attack. Information about the interaction process between the abuser and the abused may enable society to develop better prevention and treatment strategies.

Intervention strategies may include (1) legal action to stop the abuse and punish the abuser, (2) services to provide treatment for the abuser, (3) services to relieve the family of stresses generated by caregiving responsibilities, (4) education and training to caregivers and the public in general. Of these four intervention strategies, those efforts directed toward the family may be the most productive. The family continues to be the main health care provider to elderly family members. The family also provides most of the emotional and intimate social needs of the elderly (O'Rourke 1982).

Research indicates that most adult children are concerned about their aging parents and do their best to assure that their parents receive necessary care. In most cases, children do not intentionally abuse their parents but react to a stressful situation. Therefore, programs and policies that provide family support to minimize stress are likely to be the most effective. There are two general approaches that could be used. First, the caregiver could be removed from the source of stress for a period of time. Second, support could be provided so that the caregiver does not have to shoulder the full responsibility of caring for a chronically ill parent or loved one.

Specific services may be used to support and strengthen a family under stress.

In-home support services can be designed to maximize quality of care for the patient and minimize stress for the caregiver. These services include visiting nurses and social workers, Meals on Wheels, telephone answering, home chores and repairs, and housekeeping.

Respite care may be used on a regular basis or as needed. A temporary caregiver is provided who allows the caregiver to "get away" for an hour, day, or longer. Arrangements may be made for the incapacitated elderly to stay in a nursing home, hospital, residential care, or adult day care setting for a period of time to allow the caregiver to be relieved of caretaking responsibilities.

Another useful service for caregivers is *supportive counseling*. Counseling may include helping the caregiver understand aging and the illness that the elderly person is experiencing and how best to handle stressful situations. Counseling often helps caregivers gain insight into their own fears and concerns as well as learn about community resources available to assist the elderly.

The subcommittee on health and long-term care of the House of Representatives Select Committee on Aging (U.S. Congress 1985) recommended a number of policy changes, including tax credits, respite care as reimbursable under the Medicare program, funds for shelters for abused elderly, mandatory reporting of cases of elder abuse, and free counseling to caregivers.

Government Programs to Protect the Abused Elderly

Federal and local governments have established several programs designed to protect and assist elderly individuals who are subject to abuse and neglect. Two major governmental programs in this area are the protection and advocacy program, and the long-term care ombudsman program.

The Protection and Advocacy Program. This program was first established in 1975 under Public Law 94-103. It was designed to protect elderly persons who have developmental disabilities. There are programs in every state, and the federal government assumes 100 percent of the cost of the program. Services provided under the protection and advocacy program cover a wide range of activities, including abuse and neglect, obtaining needed employment, education or medical services, financial problems, living conditions, removal of architectural barriers, and obtaining guardianship.

The methods most frequently used by protection and advocacy staff to resolve clients' problems include referral to appropriate community agencies for assistance, counseling, negotiation, and legal representation. Only about 2 percent of all client problems brought to the attention of the protection and advocacy staff are resolved through litigation. The protection and advocacy staff also play an active role in training and educational activities focused on clients, families, and guardians.

The Long-Term Care Ombudsman Program. An ombudsman is an advocate for a particular person or group to assure that their rights are protected. The long-term care ombudsman program was established in 1975 and initiated through grants to state agencies on aging to enable them to operate programs to respond to complaints made by or on behalf of residents of long-term care facilities. Drury (1985) outlined the primary functions of the long-term care ombusdman program:

1. Investigate and resolve complaints made by or for older persons in long-term care facilities. Also, investigate administrative actions that may adversely affect their health, safety, welfare or rights.

2. Monitor the development and implementation of federal, state, and local laws, regulations, and policies that relate to long-term care facilities in the state.

3. Provide information to public agencies about the problems of older persons in long-term care facilities.

4. Train volunteers to assist in the development of citizen organizations to participate in the ombudsman program.

In addition to the federally mandated functions, many states have passed laws that complement the federal requirements. The primary program objective is to provide a focal point whereby complaints regarding nursing home care can be received, investigated, and resolved as expeditiously as possible. There are insufficient data available to determine the effectiveness of the long-term care ombudsman program in preventing elder abuse or intervening in an abuse problem to minimize the impact. All states and U.S. territories are to collect information on complaints received by or on behalf of residents of long-term care facilities, and action is being taken in response to the complaints. On the basis of available information, it appears that the program is effective as a focal point for complaints and as an advocacy agency to protect the rights of long-term care residents. Certainly the program has increased the public and institutional staff awareness of potential problems and of the need to protect the rights of long-term care residents.

It should be noted that the federal government and its programs do not constitute the only approach to protecting the vulnerable elderly. Family members, neighborhood groups, churches, service organizations, and other individuals and organizations have long served as advocates for people of many different ages. In fact, the family is frequently the best and most effective advocate and ombudsman that the vulnerable elderly can have. One of the existing needs is to provide training to family members and other concerned individuals on knowledge and skills required to be an effective advocate and ombudsman.

To be effective, protective and advocacy programs require the support of adult protection and elder abuse laws. However, evidence to date indicates that much can and is being accomplished through nonlitigation procedures.

Needed Research

Research on elder abuse has consisted primarily of exploratory and descriptive studies. Attempts have been made to determine the extent and nature of elder abuse (Hudson 1986). However, because of differences in sampling and definitions of abuse, it is difficult to compare the various studies.

One obvious need for future research in elder abuse is the development of acceptable standards of definition and methodology. Such standardization would provide more definitive data upon which medical, social, and public programs can be based. Other pertinent research questions include the following: (1) What is the relationship, if any, between past incidence of family violence and present incidence of elder abuse? (2) What is the relationship between individual space requirements and elder abuse? (3) Are some forms of emotional and mental illness more closely associated with elder abuse than others? (4) What is the relationship between alcohol and drug abuse and elder abuse? (5) What is the relationship between family economic deprivation and elder abuse? (6) Are there relationships between social and psychological variables such as the age of the caregiver, the sex of the caregiver, and the health of the caregiver and elder abuse? (7) What forms of help and support do elder caregiving families need and want? (8) How do physicians and other health care providers respond to elder abuse? (9) How can those elderly individuals who are being abused be identified? (10) What intervention strategies are most effective in stopping present elder abuse and preventing future abuse? (11) What should be the role of the federal, state, and local governments in preventing, controlling, and ameliorating elder abuse? (12) Should the approach to the problem of elder abuse be punitive or rehabilitative? (13) What role should law enforcement play in dealing with elder abuse? (14) Should money be put into treatment, prevention, or both? (15) What are the ethnic and cultural variations in elder abuse? (16) What variables account for ethnic and cultural variations in elder abuse?

Many other research questions can be raised pertaining to the abuser, the abused, the family, the social policy, and the interaction of all concerned parties. Research that focuses upon the causes of abuse and neglect rather than on symptoms alone will probably prove much more useful in developing effective programs to prevent and minimize the elder abuse problem.

References

American Medical Association. 1985. "Model elderly abuse reporting act." *Journal of the American Medical Association* 257:967.

———. 1987. "Council report from the Council on Scientific Affairs." *Journal of the American Medical Association* 257:966–71

Block, M. R., and Synnott, J. D. (eds.) 1979. *The Battered Elder Syndrome: Exploratory Study*. College Park, MD: Center on Aging, University of Maryland.

Caro, F. G. 1986. "Reliving informal caregiver burden through organized services." In K. A. Pillemer and R. S. Wolf (eds.), *Elder Abuse: Conflict in the Family*. Dover, MA: Auburn House.

Douglas, R., and Hickey, T. 1983. "Domestic neglect and abuse of the elder: Research findings and a system perspective for service delivery planning." In M. W. Gailbraith (ed.), *Elder Abuse Perspectives on an Emerging Crisis*, vol. 3. Mid-America Congress on Aging.

Drury, M. 1985. "Long-term care ombudsman annual report." Salt Lake City, Utah: Division of Aging and Adult Services, Department of Social Services, State of Utah.

Fischer, D. H. 1977. *Growing Old in America*. New York: Oxford University Press.

Flandrin, J. L. 1979. *Families in Former Times: Kinship, Household and Sexuality*. (Translated R. Southern). Cambridge, MA: Cambridge University Press.

Friedmann, K. 1982. "The role of the ombudsman in the protection of citizens." In M. A. David (ed.), *An Ombudsman Perspective*. Topeka, KS: Kansas Department on Aging.

Gailbraith, M. W. (ed.) 1986. *Elder Abuse: Perspectives on an Emerging Crisis*. vol. 3. Kansas City, KS: Mid-America Congress on Aging.

Hickey, T., and Douglas, R. 1981. "Neglect and abuse of older family members: Professionals' perspective and case experience." *The Gerontologist* 21:171–76.

Hudson, M. F. 1986. "Elder mistreatment: Current research." In K. A. Pillemer and R. S. Wolf (eds.), *Elder Abuse: Conflict in the Family*. Dover, MA: Auburn House.

Mildenberger, C., and Wessman, H. C. 1986. "Abuse and neglect of elderly persons by family members." *Physical Therapy* 66:537–539.

Milt, H. 1982. *Family Neglect and Abuse of the Aged; A Growing Concern*. Public Affairs Pamphlet No. 603.

O'Rourke, M. 1982. "Legal research and services for the elderly." In Public Affairs Pamphlet No. 603:25–63.

Pillemer, K., and Sinkelhor, D. 1988. "The prevalence of elder abuse: A random sample survey." *The Gerontologist* 28:51–57.

Pillemer, K. A., and Wolfe, R. S. (eds.). 1986. *Elder Abuse: Conflict in the Family*. Dover, MA: Auburn House.

Powell, S., and Berg, R. E. 1987. "When the elderly are abused: Characteristics and interventions." *Educational Gerontology* 13:76.

Reinharz, S. 1986. "Loving and hating one's elders." In K. A. Pillemer and R. S. Wolf (eds.), *Elder Abuse: Conflict in the Family*. Dover, MA: Auburn House.

Rosenmayr, L. 1984. "Socio-cultural change in the relationship of the family to its older members, toward an integration of historical, sociological and psychiatric perspectives." Tenth International Conference of Social Gerontology 2:49–63.

Sengstock, M. L. J. "Identifying and characterizing elder abuse." Final Report submitted to the NRTA-AARP. Andrus Foundation, Institute of Gerontology, Wayne State University, Detroit, MI.

Shanas, E. 1979. "Social myth as hypothesis: Case of the family relations of old people." *The Gerontologist* 19:3–9.

Stearns, P. J. 1986. "Old age family conflict: The perspectives of the past." In K. A. Pillemer and R. S. Wolf (eds.), *Elder Abuse: Conflict in the Family*. Dover, MA: Auburn House.

Tomita, S. 1982. "Detection and treatment of elderly abuse and neglect: A protocol for health professionals." *Physical and Occupational Therapy in Geriatrics* 2:37–51.

Traxler, A. 1986. "Elder abuse laws: A survey of state statutes." In Gailbraith, M. W. (ed.), *Elder Abuse: Perspectives on an Emerging Crisis,* vol. 3. Kansas City, KS: Mid-America Congress on Aging.

U.S. Congress. 1985. House. Select Committee on Aging. Subcommittee on Health and Long-Term Care. *Elder Abuse: A National Disgrace.* Committee Publication no. 99–502.

Washington State Medical Association. 1985. *Elder Abuse: Guidelines for Intervention by Physicians and Other Service Providers.* Seattle, WA: State Medical Association.

Part IV
Economics

As noted earlier, most of the problems of the elderly seem to stem from their health or wealth. Wealth is examined in Part IV. The stereotype of the poverty-stricken elderly family is an exaggeration, but some of the elderly have serious economic problems with which to contend. Part IV deals with two aspects of the matter. First, chapter 15 reports on research dealing with the economic well-being of the aging family. Both objective and subjective measures show that the economic well-being of the elderly has improved substantially. Chapter 16 assesses the financial condition of Social Security and concludes that pessimism is unwarranted.

15

The Economic Well-Being of Aging Families

Stephen J. Bahr

T he economic status of the elderly has become an important social issue as the elderly population has expanded (U.S. Bureau of the Census 1986, 16). There is evidence that life satisfaction among the elderly is positively related to their income level (Leonard 1982; Maxwell 1985; Seccombe and Lee 1986; Singh and Gill 1986). Many adult children are concerned about having to assume financial responsibility for their elderly parents (Ragan 1979). There is debate over the value of Social Security and the tax burden required to keep it financed (Chen 1983, 1987).

The purpose of this chapter is to examine the economic well-being of elderly persons. First, trends in the economic status of the elderly are reviewed. Then the current well-being of the elderly is examined, using several different economic indicators. Third, the various sources of income among the elderly are identified. Finally, there is a brief discussion of how the elderly spend their money. Throughout this chapter the terms *elderly* and *aged* are used synonymously; both refer to people who are over age 65.

Trends in Economic Status of the Elderly

The economic status of the elderly has improved markedly over the two decades from the late 1960s to the late 1980s. One of the most frequently used indicators of economic well-being is the poverty level established by the Social Security Administration (U.S. Bureau of the Census 1986, 415). The poverty level is an estimate of the minimum income required to meet the basic necessities of life based on family size and composition. The proportion of the elderly below the poverty level decreased substantially between 1959 and 1985. In 1959, more than one-third of all persons over age 65 lived in poverty (Treas and Bengtson 1987, 630). This decreased to 25 percent in 1970 and to only 13 percent in 1985, as shown in Table 15–1. Among elderly in families, the comparable rates are 15 percent in 1970

Table 15–1
Percentage of Elderly and Nonelderly Persons Below Poverty Level, by
Race, 1970–85

	1970	1979	1985
Persons Aged 65 and Over			
All persons	24.6	15.2	12.6
White	22.6	13.3	11.0
Black	47.4	36.3	31.5
Hispanic	--	26.8	23.9
Persons in families	14.8	8.4	6.4
Persons of All Ages			
All persons	12.6	11.7	14.0
White	9.9	9.0	11.4
Black	33.5	31.0	31.3
Hispanic	--	21.8	29.0
Persons in families	10.4	10.2	12.6

Source: U.S. Bureau of the Census 1986, 442–44.

and only 6 percent in 1985. The decrease in poverty among the aged occurred among all racial groups.

In contrast, the poverty rate of nonelderly persons increased slightly from 1970 to 1985. In 1970, the poverty rate was much higher among the elderly than it was among the nonelderly, but by 1985, the poverty rate was lower among the elderly than the nonelderly (see table 15–1).

An examination of income levels shows a similar trend. Between 1970 and 1981 there was a significant increase in the median income of elderly persons (Chen 1985). From 1980 to 1984, after-tax household income increased by 13.7 percent among persons over age 65, compared with only 3.9 percent among persons under age 65 (U.S. Bureau of the Census 1986, 434). Analyses of assets and standard budgets show similar trends. The percentages of the elderly who own homes, savings accounts, checking accounts, and certificates of deposit have increased (Chen 1985).

The elderly's subjective perception of their own economic status is consistent with these objective indicators. Almost three-fourths of the elderly report that they are highly satisfied with their standard of living, which is the highest level of satisfaction of any age group (Preston 1984, 437). Overall, the data show that the economic well-being of the elderly has improved substantially during the past twenty-five years.

One important question is whether elderly women have had the same economic improvement as elderly men. Table 15–2 shows the trend in poverty level among the elderly by sex and family status. From 1970 to 1985, the poverty rate of women in families decreased from 20.1 percent to 12.1 percent. Among women not in families, the comparable percentages

Table 15–2
Percentage of Elderly Persons Below Poverty Level, by Sex and Family
Status, 1970–85

	1970	1979	1985
In Families			
Women	20.1	13.0	12.1
Men	15.9	8.4	6.0
Unrelated Individuals			
Women	49.8	30.5	27.0
Men	38.9	25.3	20.5

Source: U.S. Bureau of the Census 1986, 444

were 49.8 percent and 27.0 percent. Those decreases are comparable to the decreases observed among elderly men, although married men had a somewhat greater decrease in poverty than married women. And the poverty rates of elderly men continue to be substantially less than those among elderly women.

Current Economic Well-Being of the Elderly

The economic well-being of the elderly has improved over the past twenty-five years. This section examines in more detail the current economic status of the elderly.

The data in table 15–1 indicate that the difference between the poverty level of elderly and the poverty level of nonelderly persons is not large. In 1985, 12.6 percent of the elderly were below the poverty level, compared to 14 percent of all persons.

Family life is particularly important for the economic well-being of the elderly. Only 6.4 percent of the elderly living in a family situation are in poverty, compared with 25.6 percent of the elderly not living in a family situation (U.S. Bureau of the Census 1986, 444). Among the entire population, 12.6 percent of those living in families are in poverty, compared with 21.5 percent of persons not living in a family (U.S. Bureau of the Census 1986, 443).

One limitation of the poverty index is that it is based solely on money income; it does not reflect the fact that many low-income persons receive noncash benefits such as food stamps, Medicaid, and public housing. To overcome this limitation, the U.S. Bureau of the Census (1986) has computed poverty levels after taking into account noncash benefits. Including the market value of the noncash benefits reduces the poverty rate of the elderly from 12.6 percent to 2.9 percent. Among the general population the comparable reduction is from 14.0 percent to 9.1 percent (U.S. Bureau of the Census 1986, 446). Clearly, noncash benefits are more important to the elderly than they are to the nonelderly.

There are some important differences in economic well-being by ethnic group. As in the general population, elderly whites have less poverty than do elderly Hispanics, who in turn have less poverty than do elderly blacks, as shown in Table 15–1. Chen (1985) analyzed the poverty status of elderly families by ethnicity and gender of head. He reported that the lowest rate of poverty is among families with white male heads, while the highest rate is among aging families with black female heads. Among unrelated elderly individuals, the lowest poverty rate is among white single men and the highest rate is among black single women.

The median income of men over age 65 is $14,440, compared with $9,584 for women over age 65 (U.S. Bureau of the Census 1986, 441). A comparison of the poverty status of elderly men and elderly women by family status was presented in Table 15–2. Regardless of family status, elderly women are much more likely than elderly men to be in poverty. Being in a family benefits both men and women but is economically more beneficial for men than for women. Among elderly persons in a family situation, only 6 percent of the men are in poverty compared with 12.1 percent of the women.

The General Social Survey conducted by the National Opinion Research Center (NORC) provides a more complete financial picture of the elderly. Data from the 1983 through 1987 NORC surveys were pooled to provide adequate numbers of elderly people for analysis.

Table 15–3 shows the percent of the respondents with a total annual family income of less than $5,000, by age, sex, and marital status. The data

Table 15–3
Percentage with Total Family Income of Less Than $5,000, by Age, Sex, and Marital Status

	Age					
	Under 30	30–39	40–49	50–59	60–69	70+
Sex						
Women	14	7	8	9	13	28
Men	10	3	3	5	5	13
Marital Status						
Married	5	2	2	1	4	6
Widowed	--	22	13	24	19	33
Separated/divorced	17	13	13	15	26	35
Never married	18	10	11	29	7	21

Source: Pooled NORC surveys, 1983–87.

show that total family income is lower at the beginning and at the end of the life cycle. Women are much more likely than men to live in a family with a low income. Twenty-eight percent of the women over age 70 had a total family income of less than $5,000, compared with only 13 percent of the men.

The data also indicate that married persons are much less likely than nonmarried persons to have a low family income. The difference between married and nonmarried persons is greater among the elderly than it is among younger persons (see table 15–3). For example, among persons over age 70, 6 percent of the marrieds had family incomes of less than $5,000, compared with 33 percent of the widowed and 35 percent of the separated or divorced.

The respondents were asked how satisfied they were with their financial situation. The percent who were dissatisfied is shown in table 15–4. Among both the men and the women, the percent who were dissatisfied decreased with age. Among persons over age 70, only 15 percent of the women and 11 percent of the men were dissatisfied with their financial situation. By comparison, about one-third of the men and women aged 30 to 39 and more than one-fourth of the men and women aged 50 to 59 were dissatisfied with their financial situation. Gender differences were slight until after age 60, and then the women become somewhat more dissatisfied than the men.

Nonmarried persons tend to have much more financial dissatisfaction than do married persons. Among persons over age 70, only 8 percent of the marrieds were not satisfied with their financial situation, compared with 15 percent of the widowed and 29 percent of the separated or divorced.

Table 15–4
Percentage Who Are Dissatisfied With Their Financial Situation, by Age, Sex, and Marital Status

| | Age | | | | | |
	Under 30	30– 39	40– 49	50– 59	60– 69	70+
Sex						
Women	32	33	28	26	18	15
Men	31	34	27	27	16	11
Marital status						
Married	31	27	22	20	14	8
Widowed	--	44	27	40	22	15
Separated/Divorced	48	49	45	41	28	29
Never married	29	39	26	31	14	18

Source: Pooled NORC surveys, 1983–87.

The respondents were asked whether they perceived that their family income was far below average, below average, average, above average, or far above average. Table 15–5 shows the percentages who said their family income was far below average by age, sex, and marital status. The overall trends are similar to those shown in table 15–4. Sex differences are small until after age 70, and then more women than men report having incomes far below average. The proportion of persons who said they had very low incomes was considerably smaller among the marrieds than among the unmarrieds. Among men and among married persons, the proportion with low incomes varies little by age, although it decreases slightly after age 60. Among women and widowed persons, there is a curvilinear trend during the last three age categories. The percent who reported incomes far below average was lower among persons in their sixties than among persons in their fifties, but higher among persons beyond age 70 than among persons in their sixties.

In summary, NORC and census data show that persons over age 65 have poverty rates lower than the general population. Actual income tends to decrease after age 60, but dissatisfaction with their financial situation is lower among the elderly than among other age groups. Among the elderly, objective and perceived economic well-being is better for men than women, and for married than for unmarried persons.

Sources of Income among the Elderly

Information on how the elderly receive their income was obtained from an analysis of Current Population Survey data conducted by Upp (1983). She

Table 15–5
Percentage Who Perceive Their Family Income Is Far Below Average, by Age, Sex, and Marital Status

	Age					
	Under 30	30–39	40–49	50–59	60–69	70+
Sex						
Women	5	6	6	7	5	7
Men	6	5	6	7	4	4
Marital status						
Married	4	3	4	4	4	3
Widowed	--	22	8	10	5	7
Separated/divorced	11	10	11	15	7	11
Never married	6	7	10	7	4	11

Source: Pooled NORC surveys, 1983–87.

estimated that there are about 19 million units in the United States in which at least one member is age 65 or older. The survey included nonmarried individuals as well as couples, and the nonmarried persons were never married, separated, divorced, or widowed.

The elderly receive income from six major sources: social security, assets, earnings, government-employee pensions, private pensions, and public assistance. Table 15–6 shows the proportion of elderly persons who receive some income from these six sources. Ninety percent of the elderly receive money from Social Security. Two-thirds receive some income from assets, although this occurs more frequently among the married than among the nonmarried persons. Almost one-fourth have earnings, and 22 percent receive money from a private pension. Ten percent of the elderly receive public assistance.

Table 15–6 shows only the percentage of elderly persons who receive *any* income from the six sources and does not indicate how much income they receive from each source. Table 15–7 shows the proportion of income received from each of those six major sources. Social Security is the major income source; it accounts for 40 percent of income among people over age 65. The second most important income source is assets, which produce 22 percent of elderly people's income. Nineteen percent of elderly people's income comes from earnings. Government-employee and private pensions together make up 14 percent of elderly income, while only 1 percent is received from public assistance. Married couples receive more income from earnings and less from Social Security and public assistance than nonmarried persons do.

To determine how sources of income vary according to total level of income, Upp (1983) divided the sample into four income categories (see table 15–8). She found that low-income persons receive 79 percent of their income from Social Security and 10 percent from public assistance. They

Table 15–6
Percentage of Elderly Persons[a] with Some Income from Various Sources, by Marital Status

	All	Married Couples	Nonmarried Persons
Social Security	90	92	90
Assets	66	69	52
Earnings	23	36	13
Government-employee pensions	12	15	9
Private pensions	22	32	14
Public assistance	10	5	14

Source: Upp 1983, 5
[a]Persons aged 65 or older.

Table 15–7
Percentage of Elderly Persons'ᵃ Income Received From Various Sources, by Marital Status

	All	Married Couples	Nonmarried Persons
Social Security	40	35	48
Asset income	22	22	23
Earnings	19	24	11
Government-employee pension	7	8	7
Private pension	7	8	5
Public assistance	1	1	3

Source: Upp 1983, 5
*Persons age 65 or older.

receive only 4 percent from assets and almost none from earnings or pensions. As total income increases, earnings and assets become more important and Social Security becomes less important. Among elderly persons who receive $20,000 or more in income each year, one-third of their money is received from earnings and one-third from assets. Sixteen percent is received from Social Security and 15 percent from other pensions.

Expenditures of Money by the Elderly

Information on how the elderly spend their money is taken from the 1984 Consumer Expenditure Interview Survey, which was conducted by the U.S. Bureau of the Census (1986, 428). A sample of five thousand consumer

Table 15–8
Percentage of Elderly Persons'ᵃ From Various Sources, by Income and Marital Status

	Total Money Income			
	Less than $5,000	$5,000– $9,999	$10,000– $19,999	$20,000 or more
Social Security	79	63	39	16
Assets	4	14	21	34
Earnings	2	8	17	33
Government-employee pension	1	4	9	9
Private pension	1	6	10	6
Public assistance	10	1	0	0

Source: Upp, 1983:5
*Persons age 65 or older.

Table 15–9
Percentage of Total Income Spent on Major Budget Categories, by Age

	Age						
	Under 25	*25–34*	*35–44*	*45–54*	*55–64*	*65–74*	*75+*
Food	13	13	14	13	14	17	16
Alcohol	2	1	1	1	1	1	1
Housing	25	29	28	24	25	29	33
Clothing	5	5	5	5	5	4	3
Transportation	22	19	17	19	17	18	12
Health care	2	3	3	3	4	8	12
Other[a]	12	10	13	13	12	13	14
Life insurance	0	1	1	2	2	1	1
Pensions, social security	5	7	8	8	8	3	1
Personal taxes	13	12	10	11	12	6	8
Total income	$12,579	$24,652	$32,058	$32,285	$26,989	$16,815	$12,442

Source: U.S. Bureau of the Census 1986, 428. Based on Consumer Expenditure Interview Survey.

[a]Entertainment, personal care, reading, education, tobacco and smoking supplies, cash contributions, and miscellaneous expenditures.

units representative of the U.S. urban population were interviewed every three months over a year.

Table 15–9 shows the proportion of income spent on ten major budget categories, by age. People over age 65 spend a higher proportion of their income on housing and health care than do younger persons. For example, persons over age 70 spend one-third of their income on housing, compared with only 25 percent for those between the ages of 55 and 64. Health care takes 12 percent of the income of people over age 75, compared with only 4 percent for those between the ages of 55 and 64. And the elderly spend a somewhat higher percent of their income on food than persons under age 65 do.

By contrast, the elderly spend a considerably smaller proportion of their income on transportation, pensions, and taxes than do younger persons. They also spend somewhat less on clothing.

Some of the differences in expenditure patterns may be due to differences in income. For example, actual expenditures for food and housing may not change when people retire, but the proportion of their incomes spent on food and housing may increase because their incomes decrease. Chen and Chu (1982) analyzed household expenditure patterns of different age groups while holding income constant. They found that level of income tends not to alter the overall spending patterns, although food is one exception. When income is held constant, the aged spend a smaller proportion of their income on food than do most other age groups (Chen and Chu 1982, 239).

The basic spending patterns reported by Chen and Chu (1982) were similar to those reported in table 15–9. Within each income category, they found that the proportion of income spent on medical care, household utilities, personal care, and contributions increases with age. Even with Medicare and Medicaid, the elderly spend more of their income on medical care than do other age groups. The amount spent on purchasing automobiles and homes decreases with age. Expenditures for clothing, alcohol, and tobacco increase up to middle age and then decrease; the elderly spend a lower percent of their incomes on these items than any other age group. Chen and Chu (1982) observed that recreation expenses decrease with age up to age 65, after which they increase. This reflects the increased leisure activities after retirement.

Summary and Conclusion

The economic well-being of persons over age 65 has increased substantially during the past quarter-century. Between 1959 and 1985, the proportion of the elderly in poverty decreased from 35 percent to 13 percent. The poverty rate among the elderly is now smaller than the poverty rate among the general population. When noncash benefits are taken into account, only 3 percent of the elderly are in poverty, compared with 9 percent of the general population. And fewer of the elderly than nonelderly are dissatisfied with their financial situation.

Among the elderly, economic differences by sex, ethnic group, and marital status are similar to those in the general population. Women are worse off than men, blacks and Hispanics are poorer than whites, and married persons fare better than the unmarried.

Social Security is the major source of income for persons over age 65. Ninety percent of the elderly receive income from Social Security, and it constitutes 40 percent of the total income received by the elderly. Assets and earnings together make up 41 percent of the income of the elderly. High-income elderly persons rely more on assets, earnings, and pensions than do low-income elderly persons.

Compared with persons under age 65, the elderly spend a higher proportion of their incomes on health care, housing, and food and a lower percentage on transportation, clothing, pensions, and taxes. However, when family income is held constant, the elderly spend less on food than most other age groups.

One striking finding is the difference between those who do and those who do not live in families. Only 6 percent of the elderly in family situations are in poverty, compared with 26 percent of those who are not in family situations (U.S. Bureau of the Census 1986, 444). There needs to be more research on why this is the case. One might speculate that the difference is because of the economic plight of women who have lost their husbands. However, there needs to be better documentation of the types of family situations of elderly men and women and how they are related to economic well-being. Much of the research in social gerontology says relatively little about the family (Binstock and Shanas 1985; Riley et al. 1983). Some of the recent work on family relationships in later life says very little about economic well-being (Brubaker 1983, 1985; Treas and Bengtson 1987). These two areas of research need to be joined.

As the number of elderly persons continues to increase, additional research on income levels, sources of income, and expenditures is needed. It would be fruitful to explore how economic characteristics are related to family and social characteristics and to quality of life.

References

Binstock, R. H., and Shanas, E. (eds.). 1985. *Handbook of Aging and the Social Sciences* (2nd. ed.). New York: Van Nostrand Reinhold.

Brubaker, T. H. (ed.). 1983. *Family Relationships in Later Life*. Beverly Hills, CA: Sage Publications.

———. 1985. *Later Life Families*. Beverly Hills, CA: Sage Publications.

Chen, Y.-P. 1983. *Social Security in a Changing Society: An Introduction to Programs, Concepts, and Issues* (2nd ed.). Bryn Mawr, PA: McCahan Foundation.

———. 1985. "Economic status of the aging." In R. H. Binstock and E. Shanas (eds.), *Handbook of Aging and the Social Sciences* (2nd ed.). New York: Van Nostrand Reinhold.

———. 1987. "OASDI bonds could restore confidence in Social Security." *Journal of the American Society of CLU and ChFC* 41:68–73.

Chen, Y.-P., and Chu, K-W. 1982. "Household expenditure patterns: The effect of age of family head." *Journal of Family Issues* 3:233–50.

Leonard, W. M., II. 1982. "Successful aging: An elaboration of social and psychological factors." *International Journal on Aging and Human Development* 14:223–32.

Maxwell, N. L. 1985. "The retirement experience: Psychological and financial linkages to the labor market." *Social Science Quarterly* 65:22–33.

Preston, S. H. 1984. "Children and the elderly: Divergent paths for America's dependents." *Demography* 21:435–57.

Ragan, P. K. 1979. *Aging Parents*. Los Angeles: University of Southern California Press.

Riley, M. W., Hess, B. B., and Bond, K. 1983. *Aging in Society: Selected Reviews of Recent Research*. Hillsdale, NJ: Lawrence Erlbaum Associates.

Seccombe, K., and Lee, G. R. 1986. "Gender differences in retirement satisfaction and its antecedents." *Research on Aging* 8:426–40.

Singh, G. M. P., and Gill, S. 1986. "Problems of widowhood." *The Indian Journal of Social Work* 47:67–71.

Treas, J., and Bengtson, V. L. 1987. "The family in later years." In M. B. Sussman and S. K. Steinmetz (eds.), *Handbook of Marriage and the Family*. New York: Plenum Press.

Upp, M. 1983. "Relative importance of various income sources of the aged, 1980." *Social Security Bulletin* 46:3–10.

U.S. Bureau of the Census. 1986. *Statistical Abstract of the United States: 1987* (107th ed.). Washington, DC: U.S. Government Printing Office.

16
Low Confidence in Social Security Is Not Warranted

Yung-Ping Chen

"When you think of the future, think of Social Security" is a phrase inscribed on a map of the United States exhibited in the Altmeyer Building of the Social Security Administration in Woodlawn, Maryland. That display has been there for several decades. But concern over the program in recent years may be causing some people to amend the phrase to "When you think of Social Security, think of its future."

Erosion in Confidence

The public's confidence in Social Security's future is low today in comparison with a decade or so ago. Between 1975 and 1986, the American Council of Life Insurance commissioned public opinion surveys containing the question,"How confident are you, yourself, in the future of Social Security?" In 1975, about two-thirds (63 percent) felt confident and about one-third (37 percent) expressed no confidence. Ten years later, in 1984, the proportions had nearly reversed themselves: only one-third (32 percent) said they were confident and two-thirds (68 percent) said they were not. In the following several years there was a minor reversal of the downward

For useful data and helpful discussions, the author is indebted to Milton P. Glanz, Stephen C. Goss, Alice Wade (all from the Office of the Actuary, Social Security Administration), Robert J. Myers, Bruce D. Schobel, and George F. Rohrlich. He also appreciates the assistance of Kay Powell, Barbara Price, Holly A. Heline, and Daniel Schulder. None of these individuals or the organizations with which they are associated should be implicated in the opinions expressed, for which he is solely responsible.

This chapter is reprinted with permission from *Journal of Aging and Social Policy*, Volume 1, Fall 1988.

trend in confidence. In 1986, for example, 40 percent of the respondents indicated confidence and 60 percent showed no confidence. The 40 percent confidence rating represented a gain of 8 percentage points since 1984 but was still well below that in 1975 (see table 16–1).

Young people have always had a lower level of confidence than older people. Over the years, however, confidence has been eroding even among the old, as shown in table 16–1. For example, in 1975, 82 percent of those aged 65 or over expressed confidence and 18 percent voiced no confidence. By contrast, in 1982–83 only about 66 percent of this group had confidence. Although in the mid-1980s the attitude has not been as unfavorable as it was earlier, in 1986 the confidence group among those aged 65 or over still stood considerably lower than it was in 1975, by 12 percentage points.

In these statistics answers are classified into two groups: confident and nonconfident. The former includes respondents who were either "very confident" or "somewhat confident," whereas the latter comprises those replying "not too confident" or "not at all confident." A closer analysis of the data in the four-way classification shown in table 16–2 reveals a more troubling trend. From 1975 to 1986 those respondents of all ages who felt "very confident" in the future of Social Security declined from 22 percent to 9 percent; those who were "somewhat confident" declined from 41 percent to 30 percent. On the other hand, the "not too confident" group increased from 27 percent in 1975 to 37 percent in 1986. And the "not at all confident" category rose from 10 percent in 1975 to 21 percent in 1986. The erosion in the level of confidence is all too obvious: The size of the "very confident" group is less than half what it was in 1975, while those "not at all confident" have more than doubled.

It is clear that many people, especially the young but also those of older ages, believe there may not be Social Security in their future because they believe Social Security has no future. What follows is an attempt to show that the pessimistic outlook on Social Security's financing is unwarranted. After identifying two reasons for the low levels of confidence, this chapter analyzes the short-range and long-range financial conditions of the Social Security program, discusses the cost rates in the context of the work environment, and finally calls attention to the meaning of Social Security beyond its role as a retirement income-security measure.

Some Reasons for Low Levels of Confidence

Since Social Security is the cornerstone of the U.S. economic security structure for the elderly, its financial viability is of the utmost importance. Despite the 1983 amendments to the Social Security Act, which were de-

Table 16–1
Confidence in the Future of the Social Security System, by Age, 1975–86 (in percent)

Survey Year	National Conf.	Non-conf.	18–24 Conf.	Non-conf.	25–29 Conf.	Non-conf.	Age 30–34 Conf.	Non-conf.	35–44 Conf.	Non-conf.	45–54 Conf.	Non-conf.	55–64 Conf.	Non-conf.	65+ Conf.	Non-conf.
1975	63	37	45	55	59	41	51	49	62	38	66	34	74	25	82	18
1976	58	43	60	41	46	54	41	60	51	50	55	45	65	35	78	22
1977	50	50	45	55	35	64	37	62	45	54	49	51	64	36	75	25
1978	39	60	32	68	27	73	35	65	24	76	41	60	55	45	62	37
1981	42	57	35	65	24	75	26	75	34	66	40	59	56	43	73	26
1982	32	67	20	80	15	85	15	84	18	82	31	70	57	43	66	34
1983	35	66	28	72	21	79	20	80	25	75	30	69	54	46	67	33
1984	32	68	31	69	19	81	30	70	21	79	26	74	43	57	48	51
1985	37	63	28	72	18	82	29	71	29	71	35	65	53	47	63	37
1986	40	60	30	70	20	80	28	72	31	69	45	55	57	43	70	30

Sources: All these surveys were commissioned by the American Council of Life Insurance: for 1975 through 1984, conducted by Yankelovich, Skelly, and White, published in *Public Opinion* (April/May 1985), 22; for 1985 and 1986, conducted by the Roper Organization, supplied by the American Council of Life Insurance, May 27, 1988.

Note: Confident = "Very confident" + "Somewhat confident"; Nonconfident = "Not too confident" + "Not at all confident." Numbers do not always add up to 100 percent because of rounding.

Table 16–2
Degree of Confidence in the Future of the Social Security System,
1975–86
(in percent)

Survey Year	Very Confident	Somewhat Confident	Not Too Confident	Not At All Confident
1975	22	41	27	10
1976	18	39	32	10
1977	15	35	30	20
1978	8	31	39	21
1981	12	30	39	18
1982	8	24	43	24
1983	9	25	38	26
1984	9	23	43	25
1985	9	26	37	24
1986	9	30	37	21

Source: American Council of Life Insurance, MAP Report, 1986, p. 64.
Note: Numbers do not always add up to 100 percent because of rounding.

signed to assure the financing of the program for the long range and which seem close to doing so according to the intermediate-cost estimate (defined later), many persons are skeptical of the soundness of its funding, and some are even forecasting its doom. The following two reasons may help account for this contrary opinion.

First, there is a definitional problem. Although Social Security is generally understood to mean the old-age, survivors, and disability insurance programs (OASDI), some insist that Social Security must mean not only OASDI but also Medicare. This definitional matter becomes important because the financial status of OASDI is substantially different from that of Medicare. Since the Medicare hospital insurance trust fund is estimated, under the intermediate-cost estimate, to be exhausted in the year 2005, the combined operation of OASDI and Medicare is not viable financially in the long range. However, by design, the 1983 law was enacted to deal with the long-range financial problems of OASDI only, so OASDI financing and Medicare financing should be separately considered.

The second reason concerns the future economic and demographic developments that affect Social Security's income and outgo. The future income and outgo of OASDI depend on many economic and demographic factors, among them the size and composition of the labor force, unemployment, productivity, inflation, fertility, mortality, net immigration, retirement patterns, and disability rates. These factors affect (1) the size of the payroll-tax-paying population and the amount of the payroll taxes they pay, and (2) the size of the OASDI beneficiary population and the magnitude of the benefits they receive. Because precise forecasting of these variables is impossible, estimates by Social Security Administration actuaries are made on the basis of four sets of assumptions, designated as Alternatives I, II-A, II-B, and III. Alternative I presents an optimistic outlook; Alternative III is pessimistic. Alternatives II-A and II-B are based on two sets of assumptions that produce what are generally identified as "intermediate-cost estimates," with II-A being more optimistic than II-B. The Alternative II-B estimates are used by most policymakers as a basis for the best-guess projections. Those who doubt the long-range viability of Social Security, however, think that even Alternative III is too optimistic.

The Current Outlook

What is the current financial outlook for OASDI? During calendar year 1987, the OASDI trust funds increased their assets by $21.9 billion, which represented the excess of income over outgo during the year. The assets in the trust funds at the start of 1988 were $90.5 billion (Board of Trustees 1988, 1, 47).

The financial condition of OASDI may be measured by two indicators: the trust fund ratio (which is a short-range measure) and the actuarial balance (a long-range measure).

The trust fund ratio relates the assets in the trust funds at the beginning of the year to the total payments (benefits and administrative costs) expected to be made in that year. This ratio shows the proportion of the year's outgo that is available at the beginning of the year. For example, the $90.5 billion in the OASDI trust funds on January 1, 1988, represented a ratio of 41 percent, which means that if there were no payroll tax revenue and interest earnings during the year, the system could pay only 41 cents of every dollar of benefits and administrative expenses. Of course, payroll taxes and interest income *are* expected during the year. A ratio of at least 8 to 9 percent is required to pay benefits at the beginning of each month.

On the other hand, as a long-range indicator of the financial status of OASDI, the actuarial balance may be measured by two methods: the average-cost method and the level-financing method. The former is described here, leaving the latter to be explained later. Under the average-cost method, the actuarial balance is measured by the difference between the average income rate and the average cost rate, both expressed as a percentage of taxable payroll. The income rate for each year is the sum of the combined employee and employer taxes collected and the income from income-taxation of benefits, expressed as a percentage of taxable payroll. The revenue from income-taxation of benefits is transferred from the Ceneral Fund of the Treasury to the trust funds. The cost rate for each year, on the other hand, is the annual outgo expressed as a percentage of taxable payroll. For the seventy-five-year valuation period, the actuarial balance calculated on the "average cost" basis is, as stated, the difference between the "average income rate" and the "average cost rate." The average income rate is the sum of the annual income rates during the period divided by 75; the average cost rate is obtained in a like manner. The difference between them is the actuarial balance. If the average income rate exceeds the average cost rate, the system is said, by definition, to have an actuarial surplus. If the average income rate falls short of the average cost rate, an actuarial deficit results. The program is considered to be in "close actuarial balance" for the valuation period if the average income rate is between 95 percent and 105 percent of the average cost rate.

The short-range financial condition is excellent. Very large annual accumulations in the OASDI trust funds are beginning to build up in 1988. As shown in table 16–3, under Alternative II-B, the trust fund ratio will increase from 41 percent in 1988 to 107 percent in 1992, and to 214 percent in 1997. Therefore the short-range outlook (for, say, the next five to ten years) is excellent. The growth in the ratio results from rising payroll tax rates at a time when the cost rates are declining or stabilizing. The tax rate was raised in 1984 and in 1988 and will be raised again in 1990, but the cost rate declined from 11.9 percent in 1982 to 10.7 percent in 1987. It is estimated to remain in the 10 to 11 percent range through 2010, before rising to 13.5 percent in 2020 and 16.8 percent in 2060 (see table 16–4).

Table 16–3
OASDI Trust Fund Ratio, 1988–2048, under Alternative II-B
(in percent)

Calendar Year	Trust Fund Ratio
1988	41
1989	56
1990	71
1991	89
1992	107
1993	127
1994	147
1995	169
1996	191
1997	214
2000	285
2005	404
2010	501
2015	531
2020	497
2025	427
2030	341
2035	251
2040	162
2045	71
2048	exhausted

Source: Compiled from Board of Trustees 1988, 83–84.

Table 16–4
Annual Cost Rates of OASDI, 1980–2060
(as a percentage of taxable payroll)

	Calendar Year	Cost Rate
Actual		
	1980	10.74
	1981	11.36
	1982	11.94
	1983	11.50
	1984	11.24
	1985	11.13
	1986	10.98
	1987	10.69
Projected under Alternative II-B		
	1988	10.73
	1989	10.72
	1990	10.81
	1991	10.80
	1992	10.75
	1993	10.68
	1994	10.61
	1995	10.55
	1996	10.48
	1997	10.43
	2000	10.30
	2005	10.22
	2010	10.67
	2015	11.86
	2020	13.47
	2030	15.88
	2040	16.23
	2050	16.43
	2060	16.80

Source: Compiled from Board of Trustees 1988, 52, 70.
Note: Figures are preliminary for 1983 through 1987.

However, the long-range outlook (for the seventy-five-year valuation period 1988–2062) is not as favorable. Under Alternative II-B, the actuarial deficit is 0.87 percent of taxable payroll. Although 0.87 percent is an improvement over the actuarial deficits shown in trustees' reports during the period 1974 through 1982, it is a higher deficit than estimated in the 1983 to 1987 trustees' reports.

The increase, from the 1987 report to the 1988 report, in the deficit of 0.25 percent of taxable payroll has resulted from several changes in the actuarial estimating procedure and assumptions. One is the reduction in the assumed total fertility rate (the average number of births during the lifetime of a woman) from 2.0 to 1.9. Another is the reduction in the annual rate of growth in real wages, from 1.5 to 1.4 percent. Still another change is the increase in net immigration per year, from 400,000 to 600,000 persons. The final important change is a somewhat smaller improvement (that is, a slower rate of reduction) in future mortality rates. The first two factors increased the actuarial deficit, while the last two reduced the deficit.

There were other changes. First, the change in the valuation period— the seventy-five years covered in the 1988 report begins in 1988 and ends in 2062, whereas for the 1987 report the starting year was 1987 and the ending year was 2061—produced an additional deficit. This is because 2062 is a higher-cost year than the year 1987, which it replaced. In fact, in the future, in each successive year, the actuarial balance will worsen slightly because the relatively low current rate, such as in 1988, is to be replaced by a relatively higher rate for a far-distant future year (like the 2063 rate), thus increasing the cost rate from one valuation period to the next. Second, changes in the actuarial estimating methods have increased the actuarial deficit somewhat. (These changes in the methods used to project the annual income and annual outgo, which have been modified for the 1988 report in order to attain a higher level of consistency between the short-range and long-range projections, are too technical to address in this article.) Third, the assumption on the disability-insured population changed, both as to the size of that population and as to the length of benefit payments, which brought about a slight improvement in the actuarial balance. The net result of all these changes was, as mentioned, that the actuarial balance for the period 1988–2062 was worsened by 0.25 percent of taxable payroll, as indicated.

Is the Estimated Actuarial Deficit Too Low?

Writing for the Americans for Generational Equity, Richard Jackson declared that "if Chief Actuary Harry C. Ballantyne has his way, the 1988 annual report of Social Security's Board of Trustees . . . will reveal that the system's long term balance sheet has plunged into the red" (Jackson 1988). Jackson cited a working memo circulated within the Office of the Actuary in which a number of assumptions relative to actuarial evaluation of OASDI were discussed. According to Jackson, the effect of the proposed revisions would be to double the long-range actuarial deficit for OASDI under Alternative II-B to 1.22 percent of taxable payroll from last year's 0.62 percent, as opposed to the trustees' estimate of a 0.87 percent deficit.

The present author had no access to the quoted internal memo. From Jackson's article, however, it is possible to piece together the assumptions that may account for the difference. The discrepancy between the 0.87 percent deficit (the 1988 trustees' report) and the 1.22 percent deficit (the memo quoted by Jackson) is 0.35 percent of taxable payroll. This difference could have resulted from the memo's assumption of (1) a lower level of net immigration, (2) a larger reduction in the rate of real-wage growth, and (3) a greater impact of AIDS on the OASDI program.

In short, the assumptions that led to a larger actuarial deficit are more pessimistic than ones used by Alternative II-B regarding the demographic and economic conditions in the future. If one were sufficiently pessimistic with unrealistic assumptions, one could believe that apocalypse may be near. But the pessimism about Social Security appears unwarranted, as the remainder of this article attempts to demonstrate.

If the total fertility rate is assumed to be lower than what is now assumed, it seems that the assumption on net immigration should be revised upward (Myers 1988). In a sense, fertility rate and immigration are related measures, and immigration may be regarded as a form of fertility. There is some recognition of this in the 1988 trustees' report. As the total fertility rate was reduced from 2.0 to 1.9, the net immigration was assumed to be 600,000 persons per year instead of 400,000. In the memo, however, when the total fertility rate was assumed to decline from 2.0 to 1.9, the net immigration was estimated to increase from 400,000 persons a year to only 500,000 persons. This explains in part why the actuarial deficit in the memo is higher than in the 1988 trustees' report.

In the 1988 trustees' report, the assumed annual real-wage growth rate was 1.4 percent per year (it was 1.5 percent in the 1987 trustees' report). This is done to reflect the decline in the rate of gain in real earnings over time (real earnings are cash earnings adjusted for inflation). In the memo, the assumed annual rate of growth was even lower, 1.3 percent. When the growth rate in real earnings is lowered for actuarial estimates, it has the effect of raising the actuarial deficit. Since the memo postulated a slower rate of increase than in the 1988 trustees' report, the actuarial deficit shown in the memo is larger.

With the inflation rate assumed to be stable, the decline in the rate of increase in real earnings primarily results from a decline in the rate of gain in productivity and a drop in cash pay as a proportion to total compensation. Although the rate of productivity advancement has slowed in recent years, there is no reason to assume that this downward trend cannot be reversed in the future (The declining fraction of cash pay in the total compensation is taken up in a later section of this chapter).

Another factor responsible for the much larger actuarial deficit is the memo's pessimism about the impact of AIDS on the cost of OASDI. With regard to the disability portion of OASDI, the prediction that AIDS will result in extreme high cost to the program appears exaggerated when one considers (1) the relatively small number of AIDS-related claims, (2) the low average payments to such claimants, (3) the short period of time during which the benefits are paid to them, and (4) the waiting period before eligibility.

Claimants with AIDS represent a minuscule proportion of the total

Social Security disability roll. Currently, some 2.8 million disabled workers receive disability benefits from Social Security. In contrast, AIDS-related beneficiaries number about 6,000. In other words, there are only 21 AIDS claimants for every 10,000 disability beneficiaries under OASDI.

Further, the average benefit level of beneficiaries with AIDS is considerably lower than the average for all disability beneficiaries. Most recipients of Social Security disability benefits are in the 50–64 age group. Nearly 70 percent of AIDS patients are younger than 40, and 90 percent of them younger than 50. Since earning levels are typically lower in younger ages, the average disability benefits are lower for younger beneficiaries. For example, in June 1986, $550 was the average monthly disability benefit for men aged 55 to 64, and half of that—$275—for men under age 25.

Moreover, AIDS claimants receive benefits for a much shorter period of time because of their extremely high mortality rate. About 50 percent of them die within one year. Of the remaining, one-half die in the next twelve months. And of that remainder, one-half of them die in the following twelve months. In other words, nearly 90 percent of them die within three years.

Finally, the Social Security disability program requires a waiting period before benefit payments begin. If an AIDS patient dies within twelve months, the benefit runs for only six months, because of the requirement of five full months of waiting. By comparison, the average Social Security disability beneficiary receives payments for seven and a half years.

Therefore it is unlikely that AIDS victims will add significantly to the cost of the Social Security disability program, unless drugs significantly extend life.

What about the other parts of OASDI? AIDS is likely to be a minor factor as well—and may even reduce costs for OASDI as a whole. Most AIDS patients will not survive long enough to receive the old-age benefits, thus reducing the cost of the old-age program. Since AIDS patients as a group are less likely to have married, and if married to have children, the survivor's benefits attributable to AIDS patients are likely to be minor.

This analysis pertains to benefit payments. On the other hand, AIDS reduces the taxable base that contributes to the support of the program. To the extent that the long-range actuarial projections have underestimated the number of AIDS patients and have assumed that there will be more workers than will actually be the case, the actuarial deficit will be higher than estimated. However, that increase in the actuarial deficit must be offset by the fact that there will be fewer beneficiaries.

Is the Estimated Actuarial Deficit Too High?

Based on the level-financing method, the 1988 trustees' report published another figure for the actuarial deficit: 0.58 percent of taxable payroll. This lower actuarial deficit is a more valid assessment of the actuarial status than the previously cited figure of 0.87 percent of taxable payroll. The lower figure came from a "new" estimating methodology (in effect reverting to elements of the methodology used prior to 1973). The 0.87 percent actuarial deficit is based on the average-cost method, as noted earlier, while the 0.58 percent actuarial deficit is based on the level-financing method explained here. The difference between the two is that the former ignores the current trust fund balance and does not fully take into account the interest earnings on the projected accumulations of trust fund surpluses, whereas the latter does consider the current trust fund balance and fully recognizes future interest income.

As under the average-cost method, the actuarial balance under the level-financing method results from the comparison between the income rate and the cost rate. The concepts of actuarial surplus, actuarial deficit, and "close actuarial balance" are the same under both methods. However, unlike the average-cost method, the level-financing calculations are based on the present value of the income, outgo, and taxable payroll in the future.[1] The income rate over the valuation period is obtained by dividing the present value of the taxable payroll for the period into the present value of the annual incomes for the period. The cost rate over the period is similarly computed: dividing the present value of the taxable payroll for the period into the present value of the annual payments for the period. The actuarial balance is the difference between the income rate (including the current trust fund balance) and the cost rate.

Since the actuarial deficit of 0.58 percent of taxable payroll means that the income rate for the next seventy-five years is within 95 percent of the cost rate, OASDI is in "close actuarial balance," under the definition. This should be reassuring news to the public. Skeptics, however, may question the validity of this alternate methodology. Some may feel that the change is political gimmickry to hide or disguise a real financing problem in OASDI's future.

Is the level-financing method a more valid actuarial procedure than the average-cost method? In assessing the economic position of a person or an organization in a given year, it is not enough to recognize only the *flow* of income and not the *stock* of assets (more accurately, net worth, which is assets minus liabilities). Current money income is, of course, an important measure of a person's or an organization's economic circumstances. But since people with the same current money income may hold widely different amounts of assets and liabilities, the assessment of economic status based on current money income alone is inadequate. A better measure is to recognize both. By the same token, the level-financing method is better than the average-cost method in assessing OASDI's ability to pay benefits because interest earned in the future is a source for paying benefits.

If the level-financing method is superior to the average-cost method, why has it not been used previously? In the early 1970s the estimated actuarial balances were similar under either of the two methods, because the trust fund balances were negligible and were not expected to grow because of the pay-as-you-go or current-cost financing basis then followed. Now, however, sizable trust fund balances are projected to accumulate. It becomes important, therefore, to fully recognize the interest earnings that are projected to accumulate on these balances.

Since the actuarial deficit of 0.87 percent is based on the method that does not reflect the starting assets in the trust funds nor the accumulations of surplus, its usefulness as a measure of the financial condition of the program is limited. By contrast, because the actuarial deficit of 0.58 percent results from the method that fully accounts for both the beginning trust fund balance and the interest income on future surpluses, it is a more accurate portrayal of the OASDI's financial status.

Cost Rates and Taxable Payroll

Thus, according to the more accurate method of actuarial evaluation, OASDI is estimated to be in "close actuarial balance" for the seventy-five-year period 1988–2062. Even though the actuarial balance is the most important single measure of the financial condition of the trust funds, the future of OASDI should not be based solely on the estimated long-range actuarial balance. As the OASDI Board of Trustees has cautioned, the actuarial balance does not fully capture all the information needed for appropriate decision making. The board urges that attention be given to (1) the pattern and ultimate levels of projected annual cost rates and income rates, (2) the size of future fund accumulations, and (3) the year of projected trust fund exhaustion (Board of Trustees 1988, 31–32). The first of these issues will be dealt with here.

The OASDI cost rate and income rate are expressed as percentages of taxable payroll. The payroll taxes for OASDI are levied on the taxable payroll as a percentage. This is a useful convention because cost rates and payroll tax rates may be compared conveniently.

However, only part of total compensation is paid in cash. Over the years the ratio of cash wages to all compensation has declined because employee benefits have grown at a faster rate than wages. The percentage of total compensation paid in cash has continually declined: 83 percent in 1988, compared with 89 percent in 1970 and almost 96 percent in 1940, when Social Security first began paying monthly benefits. As projected for 1988–2062, the proportion of cash pay to total compensation is assumed to decline to approximately 72 percent in the year 2062.

In a given year, the cost of Social Security is customarily expressed as a percentage of the taxable payroll in that year. A given amount of Social

Security expenditures will be represented by a higher percentage on taxable payroll if the taxable payroll declines relatively, as happens when cash pay becomes a smaller part of total compensation. Thus, a significant aspect of the projected increase in the future cost rates (expressed as a percentage of taxable payroll) is the assumption that the ratio of cash pay to total compensation will continue to decline (Chen 1981; Wilkin et al. 1982).

According to this assumption, as employee benefits grow, the taxable payroll shrinks as a proportion of total compensation. Consequently, a given amount of OASDI benefit payments will mean a higher percentage of taxable payroll. For example, suppose that out of $1,000 of employee compensation, $830 is cash pay, and hence, taxable payroll. Suppose $83 is required for paying Social Security benefits. Taking $83 out of $830 means a 10 percent tax on taxable payroll. But suppose that in some future year only $720 of every $1,000 of employee compensation will be in cash (and therefore taxable payroll), and suppose the same amount of Social Security benefit payments, $83, will be required. Taking $83 out of $720 of cash pay means a tax rate of 11.5 percent of taxable payroll. This increase from 10 percent to 11.5 percent does not mean an increase in benefit payments but represents merely the tax rate on cash payroll needed to raise enough revenue to pay the same benefits as before. When the rate rises, it creates an almost indelible but certainly mistaken impression that the cost of Social Security has increased.

The amount of $83 as the future level of Social Security benefits is assumed in the above example to emphasize the point that the same level of payments will imply a higher payroll tax rate when the taxable payroll shrinks, relatively, due to growth in nontaxable employee benefits. In fact, with lowered covered earnings (resulting from cash pay as a smaller percentage of total compensation subject to Social Security taxes), OASDI benefits will also be relatively lower, but not proportionately so.

Another way of analyzing this problem is to compare the OASDI cost as a percentage of Gross National Product and as a percentage of taxable payroll. The estimated cost rate under OASDI as a percentage of GNP differs from the same cost rate when it is related to taxable payroll. For example, related to GNP, the 1988 cost of the OASDI program is 4.7 percent. In 2060 the corresponding cost is estimated at 6.5 percent of GNP. This is an increase of 39 percent over the seventy-two-year period. By contrast, the cost of the OASDI program is estimated at 10.7 percent of taxable payroll for 1988, and 16.8 percent of taxable payroll for 2060. This is an increase of 57 percent over the seventy-two-year period (see Table 16–5). What accounts for the difference in the increase in the two measures of cost?

The answer is the rate of decline in cash pay relative to nontaxable employee benefits as a proportion of total compensation. As mentioned, in

Table 16–5
Estimated Annual Cost Rates of OASDI, 1988–2060, under Alternative
II-B

Calendar Year	Cost Rate	
	As percentage of Taxable Payroll	As Percentage of Gross National Product (GNP)
1988	10.73	4.70
1989	10.72	4.67
1990	10.81	4.69
1991	10.80	4.68
1992	10.75	4.66
1993	10.68	4.63
1994	10.61	4.60
1995	10.55	4.57
1996	10.48	4.55
1997	10.43	4.52
2000	10.30	4.45
2005	10.22	4.39
2010	10.67	4.55
2015	11.86	5.01
2020	13.47	5.64
2030	15.88	6.52
2040	16.23	6.54
2050	16.43	6.49
2060	16.80	6.51
Increase from 1988 to 2060	56.6	38.5

Source: Compiled from Board of Trustees 1988, 70, 136.

1988, cash pay was 83 percent of total compensation. At a 0.2 percent annual compound rate of decline of cash pay, as is assumed in the 1988 trustees' report, only 72 percent of total compensation will be in cash form and hence taxable payroll in 2060. One method of dealing with this development is to adjust the payroll tax rate so as to offset the erosion of the payroll tax base. As the "cash earnings plus taxable employee benefits" portion of total compensation shrinks, the payroll tax rate would increase. This method would result in a payroll tax that taxes total compensation at a constant percentage rate, while preserving payroll tax and income tax exemption for the employee benefits not presently subject to tax (National Commission on Social Security Reform 1982).

OASDI Cost Rates and the Work Environment

Even though the problem posed by the assumed continuing decline in the percentage of total compensation that is cash pay may be solved by a method such as cited above, there is no escaping the fact that in the long range the cost of OASDI will rise substantially. Measured as a percentage of GNP, this cost will increase by 39 percent over the next seven decades, although it is lower than the 57 percent growth based on taxable payroll, indicated earlier. The fundamental reason is population aging—the graying and whitening of America.

Population aging is defined as the growth over time of the proportion of older persons, according to some chronological age, in the total population. The projected magnitude of population aging is generally based on a definition of old age or retirement commencing at age 65. Under the Social Security amendments of 1983, the normal retirement age for full retirement benefits will be gradually raised from 65 to 66 and then to 67 in the first three decades of the next century. If people in general remain in the labor force longer, it will have the effect of at least slightly reducing the cost rates. The recognition of the salubrious cost effect on OASDI must not be interpreted as advocacy for the postponement of retirement age on a mandatory basis. Working longer must be on a flexible and voluntary basis.

The reference to postponing retirement raises objections, or at least reservations, that it runs counter to the early retirement trends evident in recent decades. Even though Americans are now living longer, with some in better health than those in earlier age cohorts, many are deciding to stop working not just at age 65 but even in their early and mid-fifties. A host of factors (physical, psychological, and financial) affect an individual's decision to continue working or to retire and an employer's decision to retain older workers or induce them to leave the workforce.

It is possible that disliking one's job is the primary reason that many people want to stop working. Many workers, perhaps a large majority, feel that society has prescribed a "lock-step approach" for people to follow in their lives—a rigid pattern of going to school, going to work, and then going to retire. Such a pattern is no longer adequate in an aging society, if it ever was adequate in the past. Many people feel trapped in a mismatched job situation—either when they become locked into their trades or professions early in life, or when their interests change after several decades. Therefore, they want to retire as early as possible.

If the concept of lifelong learning is built into our educational and work environments, and into the behavioral expectations of workers and employers, those people who are unhappy with their initial job choices can quit, go back to school, and then start or work toward a new career. If the environment for schooling and work is restructured, then people will be able to go through life with two, three, or more careers—and they will be more satisfied and productive at work through their later years. In recent years, this movement has taken place. But the practice is not as widespread as it should be and as it will become. With each change in career, a person may be moving into a better work environment because of the higher level of interest and ability in the new circumstance. This not only will increase morale for the person but it will also increase efficiency in the workplace with the ultimate beneficiary being the economy as a whole.

It is important for employers to create positive incentives for people to want to stay on the job or to re-enter the labor force. Flexible work schedules and less traditional work arrangements appeal to many older workers. Moreover, businesses will benefit by experimenting and allowing employees various types of phased retirement or sabbaticals. Work alternatives like these represent a low-cost strategy for employers to meet their business demands while promoting employee satisfaction. In addition, a company's positive morale is an important factor not to be overlooked in keeping workers satisfied on the job and productive, and management has much to do with creating that morale.

The preceding discussion has dealt with what the private sector may be able to do. A Social Security system could provide incentives as well. For example, the Social Security systems in Norway and Sweden contain innovative arrangements to offer more choices to older persons (Cinsburg 1985). In the 1970s, both Norway and Sweden introduced partial pension plans into their programs. In Norway, where 67 is the normal age of retirement, flexible and partial pension possibilities are available to people between the ages of 67 and 70. In Sweden, partial retirement is possible beginning at age 60, before the normal retirement age of 65. Sweden's national pension system offers workers aged 60 to 70 a wide range of pension options: (1) a full old-age pension at age 65 without any earnings test; (2) a delayed old-age pension with benefit increases for postponing retirement past age 65 up to age 70; (3) an early old-age pension with permanently reduced benefits, available at age 60; (4) a split pension that allows a worker to collect half the old-age pension before age 65 at a reduced rate, and to collect the other half at age 65 without any benefit reduction; and (5) a partial pension. Serious thought should be given to the possibility of adapting innovative ideas such as these under OASDI so that the environment in which people decide to work or retire may be made more hospitable for continued work. Should future conditions prove conducive to prolonging people's work lives, OASDI cost rates will not rise as rapidly as projected.

The Meaning of OASDI to Families

Although population aging will basically cause OASDI costs to rise some thirty years from now, it is a mistake to think that the term *Social Security* applies only to retired people. More than an income-support program for the elderly, it also provides support for young people, disabled workers and their families, and survivors of deceased workers. There are three basic

Table 16–6
Number of Beneficiaries and Amount of Benefits Under Old-Age,
Survivors, and Disability Insurance (OASDI) Program, by Type of
Program and Category of Beneficiaries, June 1988

Type of Program and Category of Beneficiaries	Number of Beneficiaries (in thousands)	Percent	Amount of Benefits (in millions)	Percent
Old-Age				
Retired workers	23,632	61.5	$12,172	68.5
Wives and husbands	3,082	8.0	819	4.6
Children of retired workers	445	1.2	97	0.5
Survivors				
Widowed mothers and fathers	322	0.8	112	0.6
Children of deceased workers	1,861	4.8	659	3.7
Aged widows and widowers	4,889	12.7	2,302	12.9
Disabled widows and widowers	104	0.3	35	0.2
Disability				
Disabled workers	2,807	7.3	1,428	8.0
Wives and husbands of disabled workers	287	0.7	38	0.2
Children of disabled workers	984	2.6	144	0.8
Total	38,413	100.0	$17,806	100.0

Source: Unpublished Social Security Administration data as of July 14, 1988, courtesy of Rona Blumenthal. These data will be published in a future issue of Social Security Bulletin.

types of cash benefits under Social Security: old-age, survivors, and disability. As shown in Table 16–6, there are ten categories of beneficiaries.

The ten categories of beneficiaries may be summarized into four broad groups: retired workers, disabled workers, spouses or surviving spouses, and children of workers. In June 1988, some 38 million individuals received cash benefits. They were distributed as follows:

	Persons (in millions)	Percentage
Retired workers	23.6	61.5
Disabled workers	2.8	7.3
Spouses (or surviving spouses)	8.7	22.7
Children	3.3	8.6
Total	38.4	100.0

Out of every 100 beneficiaries, 62 were retired workers, 31 were receiving benefits as spouses or children, and 7 were disabled workers.

A somewhat different pattern of distribution is revealed if benefit payments are tabulated by type of beneficiaries. The data for June 1988 show the following distribution:

	Amount (in billions)	Percentage
Retired workers	$12.2	68.5
Disabled workers	1.4	8.0
Spouses (or surviving spouses)	3.3	18.5
Children	0.9	5.0
Total	$17.8	100.0

Although retired workers received more than two-thirds of cash benefit payments, spouses received nearly 19 percent and children 5 percent. The remaining 8 percent was paid to disabled workers. The workers' share of the total benefit dollars was proportionately more than their share of the total number of persons receiving benefits. The reason is that benefits paid spouses and children of workers are auxiliary benefits, which are often based on a fraction of what the workers receive.

As these figures show, Social Security is an income-replacement program not for retired workers alone. Rather, OASDI is a vast program of income support for a wide variety of individuals and families in different covered contingencies. The intergenerational relationship implied in the program should be clearly recognized and acknowledged.

Summary

Between 1975 and 1986, the public's confidence in Social Security has weakened, according to public opinion surveys commissioned by the American Council of Life Insurance. This chapter has attempted to dispel the fear that Social Security is not financially viable in the long range. The major points are summarized here.

1. The expression *Social Security* should refer to OASDI (the federal old-age, survivors, and disability insurance program) but not to Medicare because OASDI financing and Medicare financing are clearly separate, according to the Social Security Act, as amended.

2. The short-range (time horizon of five to ten years) financial outlook is excellent. The trust fund ratio is estimated to rise continuously from 41 percent in 1988 to 214 percent in 1997. A ratio of 214 percent means that at the beginning of 1997 the trust funds will have more than twice as much as needed to pay that year's outgo, not counting revenues from payroll tax and from taxation of benefits.

3. The long-range (seventy-five-year valuation period, 1988–2062) actuarial outlook is estimated under two different actuarial procedures: the average-cost method and the level-financing method. Under the former, the actuarial deficit is 0.87 percent of taxable payroll, whereas under the latter the deficit is 0.58 percent of taxable payroll. Since the level-financing method is a more valid basis for assessing the actuarial status of OASDI, the 0.58 percent deficit, which meets the criterion for being in "close actuarial balance," is the more accurate figure of the two.

4. Despite this reassuring news, some have claimed that the 0.87 percent figure is too low and that the long-range actuarial deficit is 1.22 percent of taxable payroll instead. After analyzing the assumptions used that produced the higher deficit, this chapter concluded that the pessimism is unwarranted.

5. The OASDI cost rates are estimated to remain at the level of 10 to 11 percent of taxable payroll for the next thirty years or so. They are expected to rise to much higher levels starting about 2020. The basic reason is population aging. However, the cumulative effect of the assumed rate of decline in cash pay as a proportion to total compensation is also a factor.

6. It is possible to solve the problem posed by the assumed continual decline in cash pay as a fraction of total compensation by a method that effectively taxes total compensation at a constant percentage rate. It is also possible to reduce the cost rates if educational and work environments could be restructured to accommodate longer work lives of people on a flexible and voluntary basis.

7. Although OASDI cost rates are expected to rise because of population aging, retirement benefits as such are not wholly responsible for the increase in cost. Social Security provides financial support to other types of beneficiaries: disabled workers, spouses, or surviving spouses and children of workers. It is important to acknowledge the meaning of Social Security to families.

In short, the pessimism about Social Security is unwarranted. Its future is what we make of it. Constructive measures will strengthen it, while destructive attitudes may doom it.

Note

1. The concept of present value may be explained in this manner. When a series of future payments, for example, is converted to a single sum payment at the present, the single sum is the "present value" of all payments to be made in the future. The conversion (or discounting) is computed at an assumed rate of interest. The single sum payment is, then, equivalent to all the payments to be made separately in the future. Put another way, the single sum is the amount that could be

invested today, at the assumed interest rate, to produce enough funds to make future payments out of both principal and interest.

References

Board of Trustees. 1988. *Annual report of the federal old-age and survivors insurance and disability insurance trust funds.* House Document 100-192. 100th cong., 2nd sess. Washington, DC: U.S. Government Printing Office, 1988:31–32.

Chen, Y.-P. 1981. "The growth of fringe benefits: Implications for Social Security." *Monthly Labor Review* 104:3–10.

Ginsburg, H. 1985. "Flexible and partial retirement for Norwegian and Swedish workers." *Monthly Labor Review* 108:33–43.

Jackson, R. 1988. "Social Security actuaries raise doubts about the system's solvency." *The Generational Journal* 1:5–6.

Myers, R. J. 1988. "Opinions on the 1988 trustees reports." *Social Security News.* New York: Mercer-Meidinger-Hansen (Summer 1988):7.

National Commission on Social Security Reform. 1982. "Adjusting the payroll tax rate to compensate for the erosion of the tax base due to the growth of fringes." memorandum no. 50 (September 7):5.

Wilkin, J., Gresch, R., and Glanz, M. 1982. "Growth in fringe benefits." Actuarial Note no. 113, Social Security Administration, U.S. Department of Health and Human Services, SSA Pub. no. 11-11500.

Epilogue: Prospects for the Future

Evan T. Peterson
Stephen J. Bahr

Virtually every textbook in social gerontology closes with a chapter dealing with the future of aging—either prospects, issues, or anticipated changes. For example, Cox (1988) discussed the future in terms of the discipline, theories of aging, health, retirement income, family, residential location, postindustrial society, values, work and leisure, power, death, and government services. Atchley (1988) looked primarily at aging and social change and then at the future of social gerontology. This chapter looks at "prospects for the future" in terms of aging and the family, and not in terms of social gerontology.

Demographics

Life Expectancy

In 1900, only 4 percent of the population was 65 years of age or over, but at the close of the 1980s, this figure was close to 12 percent. For the first time in United States history, older people are becoming an important political and economic bloc. It appears that this trend will continue. It is projected that by the year 2000, 13 percent of the U.S. population will be over age 65 (U.S. Bureau of the Census 1987).

The aging of the population has advantages as well as disadvantages. One advantage is that there should be more adequate socialization for old age. Sherman (1986) wrote that the literature on present socialization for roles in the later years ranges from defining the role as a "roleless" one to describing the role in rigidly negative terms. Sherman found that there is now a variety of role models, including parents, grandparents, friends, and the media. As life expectancy increases, there will be more family and friends who will live longer; therefore, more of them will be available for role models. Also, it seems unlikely that the media will continue its largely negative view of the lives of the elderly. As the economic power of the elderly grows, their clout with advertisers should be strong enough to bring about needed changes.

The average American will live for up to twenty-five years after rearing a family; one-fourth of adult life could be spent in retirement (Morris 1987). This has a variety of ramifications. For one, more older couples will spend more of their adult lives together than in previous cohorts. This will require adjustments between wives and husbands, and there might be an increase in divorce rates among older couples. It will mean new kinds of adjustments between elderly parents and their adult children. Strain will increase for women of the "middle generation" because parental care will be added to demands from their own children and employment. Available evidence suggests women who are employed do not spend less time in caregiving than non employed women (Cantor 1983; Horowitz 1985). The same may not be true with sons, but there will be new kinds of adjustments for them also (Stoller 1983).

Especially important are the projections of the elderly 85 years and over. According to Rosenwaike and Dolinsky (1987), the percentage of the population in this group has increased by more than 50 percent in each decade since 1940. They think that this trend is likely to continue. In contrast to earlier periods, the declining mortality rate has been most responsible for the growth in this period. Obviously, the increase in the extremely aged (oldest-old or frail elderly) will have a direct impact on the economy as well as on the family. Hagestad (1987) estimated that close to 70 percent of the elderly have at least one living child, the average age of whom is close to 60 (Torrey 1985). More people who are entering the retirement years will have to think about ways to care for their parents. People in their sixties could well become the new "middle generation." According to Shanas (1980), there has been a growing number of four-or-more-generation families. Therefore, the elderly family of the future could have two or three different cohorts of elderly people in them.

This will also mean that relationships with siblings are long term. For some, eight decades or more of life will be shared. Because there is little research on siblings and other kin, it is difficult to speculate on possible changes that might occur (Troll et al. 1979).

Sex Ratio

Some researchers foresee the sex structure changing as well (Bosco and Porcino 1977). They argue that the family of the twenty-first century will have an elderly population that is mostly female. Among persons over age 65, in 1985 there were 68 men for every 100 women. Among those 75 years or over, there were only 54 men for every 100 women. The elderlys' sex ratio is expected to continue to decrease. By the year 2000, it is projected that there will be only 65 men for every 100 women who are 65 years old or more (U.S. Bureau of the Census 1987, 16).

Some argue that because the women's movement possibly increased stresses for women in the occupational structure, there will be few changes in the sex ratio of the elderly. However, the difference between men and women in life expectancy has been getting wider, not narrower. At current life expectancy rates, the average woman can expect to be a widow for about nine years. Two-thirds of women over age 75 are widowed, compared with only 23 percent of men (U.S. Bureau of the Census 1987, 39). There is no evidence that this will change in the near future.

There will be continued emphasis on women facilitating intergenerational contact (cf. Rosenthal 1985), with special emphasis on the mother-daughter relationship (cf. Kendig and Rowland 1983; Daatland 1983). Women will continue be more involved in caregiving of parents than men (cf. Horowitz 1985).

Caregiving has a great impact on the family as well as on the caregiver, as noted by Brody (1988, 284): "The family is affected by interference with its life-style, privacy, socialization, vacations, future plans, and income, and by the diversion of the caregiver's time from other family members and the negative effects on her health." She suggested that caregiving will be less of a stress if biomedical breakthroughs result in prevention or cure of conditions that cause chronic dependency, such as Alzheimer's disease.

If the scenario of more single elderly women is correct, it is probable that they will be better off financially due to more females in the labor force. According to Coleman (1988, 321), "Future older women are also less likely to view living alone as an undesirable or inappropriate female option." In 1985, more than 40 percent of women over age 65 lived alone, and with improved health and financial well-being, this percentage is likely to increase.

Living Arrangements

More than 80 percent of the elderly live alone or with their spouse. Only 2 percent of elderly women and 3 percent of elderly men live with nonrelatives. Eighteen percent of elderly women and 8 percent of elderly men live with relatives. Forty-one percent of women and 15 percent of men over age 65 live alone (U.S. Bureau of the Census 1986, 46). Although care of the dependent elderly is a concern, the health and financial status of the elderly are likely to enable increasing numbers to be independent, at least during the early years of retirement.

Birthrate

For many years, the birthrate in U.S. society has been going down. The decreasing birthrate suggests that the elderly family of the future will have fewer children and grandchildren. This may not be true in the immediate future due to the baby boom (Cherlin and Furstenberg 1988), but it will probably be true over the long run. In 1985, the total fertility rate in the United States was 1.8 births per woman (National Center for Health Statistics 1987b, 16).

There are several implications for the decreasing birthrate. First, there will be fewer adult children to care for their elderly parents, usually two. Their contribution, even when other agencies are involved, should not be minimized (Giele and Mutschler 1986). Since it seems unlikely that there will be a significant decrease in maternal employment, these adult children will have more responsibilities than others like them have had in previous years. If both of the two adult children are employed, some kind of service agency will have to take care of the parents. Thus, there is likely to be an increase in age-segregated housing and long-term care facilities.

Cherlin and Furstenberg (1988) think that relations between elderly grandparents and grandchildren will be close and intimate for the most part. However, if the economic autonomy of the elderly is weakened (perhaps by a drop in Social Security), they wonder if the "friendly equality" that now exists between the generations might be threatened.

Second, the complex interrelationships within the three- and four-generation families will be somewhat simplified for those families with intact marriages. There will not be as many children, grandchildren, and great-grandchildren with whom to be involved.

Since there are few norms currently operating concerning intergenerational linkages, norms should slowly emerge among such "modified extended families."

Divorce

One factor that will tend to make the family relations of elderly people more complex is the high divorce rate. Although the divorce rate has decreased slightly during the 1980s, it is still very high. Consequently, many aging families will have somewhat complex interrelationships; elderly parents will have new stepchildren as well as stepgrandchildren. The "blended modified extended family" will impact on the elderly couple's relationships with their adult children's children in a direct way. The grandparent-grandchild relationship, already poorly defined, will become even more so due to new members being introduced. How does one relate to his or her stepgrandchild? What happens to the relationship if there is another divorce and the stepchild becomes a former stepchild?

In their study of a sample of white, middle-class families, Johnson and

Barer (1987) observed that the kinship networks of grandparents expanded following divorce. The the mothers and daughters maintained a stronger relationship than did the mothers and sons. They found that it was not unusual for the relationship between the paternal grandmothers and their former daughters-in-law to continue. The grandparents who were more permissive were more likely to have the expanded kinship systems. Furstenberg et al. (1983) argued that marital break-up often intensifies relationships with maternal kin but not with paternal kin. The various in-law relationships expand and consequently make the interrelationships more complex within the "modified extended family."

Divorce will lower the number of golden wedding anniversaries and increase the number of remarriages among the elderly. Although there has been a slight increase in divorce among people over 65, the increase between 1970 and 1985 was very small (National Center for Health Statistics 1987a). The increase was slightly greater for those in the first half of their sixties and still greater for those in their fifties. Of course, for all ages there has been a very pronounced trend in age-specific divorce rates between 1970 and 1980.

Atchley and Miller (1983) presented some evidence that the longer a couple has been married, the higher is their agreement on personal goals. For those marriages that do endure, this could mean greater satisfaction.

Marriages in the later years of life are based on different motivations from those in young adulthood. Older people do not marry because they want to have children, for example, nor because they want to become emancipated from their parental households. They marry for companionship (McKain 1969; Vinick 1979). This focus should cause a change in the leisure activities of the elderly. Those with sufficient financial means and adequate health will want to try different activities with their new spouse.

Single-Parent Families

As a result of the high divorce rate, there will be an increase in the number of single-parent families. This will cause increasing difficulties for grandparent-grandchild interactions. Although some states give visitation rights to grandparents, others do not. There will be increased pressure to obtain legal support for such rights. However, for many of the elderly, relationships with grandchildren who are no longer in the legal custody of their own adult children will undoubtedly become less viable and perhaps completely attenuated.

Morbidity

Along with the increase in life expectancy has come an improvement in physical and perhaps mental health. Elderly couples will be more active.

They will be somewhat more secure financially because the majority will have had two incomes throughout their marriage: both the husband's and the wife's.

Because of improved medical technology and sufficient finances, the elderly should have better health. With better health comes a higher level of activity in both leisure, voluntary activities and in other kinds of things they find interesting.

One of the major difficulties in this somewhat optimistic view of the future is the economy. Halamandaris (1986, 49) predicted that "home care will grow at a meteoritic rate through the end of this century." *Home care* has been defined as in-home diagnosis, treatment, and supportive care as well as rehabilitation involving visiting nurse organizations, community service organizations, commercial home care firms, and others (Nassif 1985). Halamandaris (1986) said that the forces driving this projected growth are "tradition, technology, demographics, and public demand." He foresaw a rationing of health care services, but if that scenario is followed, there will be few changes in the status of the health of the elderly. Home health care, on the other hand, will place some pressures on the family members that will not be blunted by the contributions of the home health care support personnel.

Ethnic Status

In chapter 15, it was noted that elderly blacks and Hispanics are much more economically deprived than whites. There have been improvements in the longevity, health, and financial well-being of minority elderly, and they are starting to live long enough to benefit from Medicare and other programs designed for the elderly. However, there has been an increasing concentration of blacks and Hispanics in poor, urban areas. According to Markides and Levin (1987, 274), "Most poor Hispanics and Blacks are likely to continue to grow old isolated from the economic mainstream of urban America."

Social Security

One of the important social issues for the future is how to finance the Social Security system. The growing elderly population has already put strains on the system, and some maintain that it is not viable in the long run (Chen 1987). "Middle generations may feel increasingly burdened as tax rates to finance Social Security continue to rise along with their burden of care. The resolution of this strain is important for the financial viability of the elderly as well as for the entire government. As noted in chapter 15,

90 percent of the elderly receive Social Security, and it accounts for 40 percent of their income. It is particularly important for poor elderly. The crisis is likely to get worse as the baby boom generation approaches retirement.

One solution to this crisis is to raise the retirement age (Chen 1987). This is likely given the fact that the retirement age has not been raised since 1935 and longevity and health have increased dramatically since then.

Suggestions for Future Research

One obvious conclusion of these projections and speculations is that there will be an increasing need for research in gerontology. Estes (1986, 495) argued that "a firm commitment to aging research and education is essential to the nation's welfare."

Cox (1988, 320) wrote, "Legitimate topics for future research on the family will undoubtedly include adjustment patterns of widows and widowers, second marriages, and alternative family forms during later life." To these could be added the research already suggested in this and previous chapters. For example, there is limited research on relationships among elderly siblings (Gold 1986). Also worth investigating are the dynamics of the changing relationships between people and their kin during the aging process. There may need to be a rigorous theoretical as well as empirical analysis of the relationships between and among relatives in a "modified extended family." What are the relevant dimensions of a relationship in a residential family as compared with the relationships within a kin group whose members may or may not live near other kin? Is the relationship different for those who live long distances apart compared with those who live in the same part of the same community? Should the relationships be studied in terms of psychosocial concepts such as emotions, motivations, and so forth? Or should the relationships be studied in terms of concepts that are easily operationalized, such as distance, frequency of visiting both in person and on the telephone, frequency of letters, frequency of birthday and Christmas cards, and so forth?

We need to know more about the quality of life of women and men in their later years. Women live longer than men, but how do they compare in physical health, functional ability, income adequacy, social contact, psychological distress, and cognitive ability? What characteristics are related to a higher quality of life, particularly family characteristics?

Added to this list should be variables such as socioeconomic status, ethnicity, and the like. One difficulty in studying the elderly family is a sampling problem. It is much easier to study elderly living in some kind of custodial care than it is to study those who are self-sufficient as well as independent. Future research must get more representative samples of elderly people.

Finally, better theoretical constructs that apply to the aging family should be developed. Certainly, the developmental framework would leave the same impression. Just as adults of 21 years of age are different from those of 71 or 81, so do families differ at various stages in the family life cycle. But what are the similarities and differences? Perhaps such family theory should be enmeshed with some of the current theories in social gerontology. Some kind of attempt at integration should be made, without getting involved in the relative strengths and weaknesses of disengagement and activity theories.

References

Atchley, R. C. 1988. *Social Forces and Aging: An Introduction to Social Gerontology.* (4th ed.). Belmont, CA: Wadsworth.

Atchley, R. C., and Miller, S. J. 1983. "Types of elderly couples." In T.H. Brubaker (ed.), *Family Relationships in Later Life.* Beverly Hills, CA: Sage Publications.

Bosco, A., and Porcino, J. 1977. *What Do We Really Know About Aging?* Stony Brook: State University of New York.

Brody, M. E., 1988. "Parent care as a normative family stress." In N. D. Glenn, and M. T. Coleman (eds.), *Family Relations—A Reader.* Chicago: The Dorsey Press.

Cantor, M. H. 1983. "Strain among caregivers: A study of experience in the United States." *The Gerontologist* 23:597–604.

Chen, Y. 1987. "Making assets out of tomorrow's elderly." *The Gerontologist* 27:410–16.

Cherlin, A., and Furstenberg, F. F., Jr. 1988. "The American family in the year 2000." In J.G. Wells (ed.), *Current Issues in Marriage and the Family* (4th ed.). New York: Macmillan.

Coleman, M. T. 1988. "Surviving and doing it well: Options for older women." In N. D. Glenn and M. T. Coleman (eds.), *Family Relations—A Reader.* Chicago: The Dorsey Press.

Cox, H. G. 1988. *Later Life: The Realities of Aging.* (2nd ed.). Englewood Cliffs, NJ: Prentice-Hall.

Daatland, S. O. 1983. "Use of public services for the aged and the role of the family." *The Gerontologist* 23:650–56.

Estes, C. L. 1986. "The challenge to gerontological education in an era of austerity." *Educational Gerontology* 12:495–505.

Furstenberg, F. F., Jr., Peterson, J. L., Nord, C. W., and Zill, N. 1983. "The life course of children of divorce: Marital disruption and parental contact." *American Sociological Review* 48:656–68.

Giel, J. Z., and Mutschler, P. H. 1986. "Frail Elders, formal and informal care." Paper given at the 39th annual meeting of the Gerontological Society of America, Chicago, IL.

Gold, D. T. 1986. "Sibling relationships in old age." Paper presented at the 39th annual meeting of the Gerontological Society of America, Chicago, IL.

Hagestad, G. O. 1987. "Able elderly in the family context: Changes, chances, and challenges." *The Gerontologist* 27:417–22.

Halamandaris, V. 1986. "The future of home health care in America." *Generations* 11:49–51.

Horowitz, A. 1985. "Sons and daughters as caregivers to older parents: Differences in role performance and consequences." *The Gerontologist* 25:612–17.

Johnson, C. L., and Barer, B. M. 1987. "Marital instability and the changing kinship networks of grandparents." *The Gerontologist* 27:330–35.

Kendig, H. L., and Rowland, D. T. 1983. "Family support of the Australian aged: A comparison with the United States." *The Gerontologist* 23:643–49.

Markides, K. S., and Levin, J. S. 1987. "The changing economy and the future of the minority aged." *The Gerontologist* 27:273–74.

McKain, W. C., Jr. 1969. *Retirement Marriage.* Storrs, CT: Agriculture Experiment Station, University of Connecticut.

Nassif, J. Z. 1985. *The Home Health Care Solution.* New York: Harper and Row.

National Center for Health Statistics. 1987a. "Advance report of final divorce statistics, 1985." *Monthly Vital Statistics Report*, vol. 36, no. 8, Supp. DHHS Pub. no. (PHS) 88–1120, Hyattsville, MD: Public Health Service.

———. 1987b. "Advance report of final natality statistics, 1985." *Monthly Vital Statistics Report*, vol. 36, no. 4, Supp. DHHS Pub. no. (PHS) 87-1120, July 17. Hyattsville, MD: Public Health Service.

Morris, R. 1987. "Concluding remarks: Consequences of the demographic revolution." *The Gerontologist* 27:423–24.

Rosenthal, C. J. 1985. "Kinkeeping in the familial division of labor." *Journal of Marriage and the Family* 47:965–74.

Rosenwaike, I., and Dolinsky, A. 1987. "The changing demographic determinants of the growth of the extreme aged." *The Gerontologist* 27:275–80.

Shanas, E. 1980. "Older people and their families: The new pioneers." *Journal of Marriage and the Family* 42:9–15.

Sherman, S. R. 1986. "Socialization for the later years: A qualitative study." Paper presented at the 39th annual meeting of the Gerontological Society of America, Chicago, IL.

Stoller, E. P. 1983. "Parental caregiving by adult children." *Journal of Marriage and the Family* 45:851–58.

Torrey, B. B. 1985. "Sharing increasing costs on declining income: The visible dilemma of the invisible aged." *Milbank Memorial Fund Quarterly/Health and Society* 63:377–94.

Troll, L. E., Miller, S. J., and Atchley, R. C. 1979. *Families in Later Life.* Belmont, CA: Wadsworth.

U.S. Bureau of the Census. 1987. *Statistical Abstract of the United States, 1988* (108th ed.). Washington, DC: U.S. Government Printing Office.

Vinick, B. H. 1979. "Remarriage." In R. H. Jacobs and B. H. Vinick, *Re-Engagement in Later Life.* Stamford, CT: Greylock.

Index

About the Contributors

Clifton E. Barber received his B.A. in sociology from Portland State University, his M.S. in child development and family studies from Brigham Young University, and his Ph.D. in human development and family studies from Pennsylvania State University. He is presently associate professor and coordinator of the Interdisciplinary Studies Program in Gerontology at Colorado State University.

I-Chiao Huang Bowers is currently a doctoral candidate in sociology at Brigham Young University. She received her B.S. in sociology and social work from the National Chung Shing University in Taiwan and her M.S. in sociology from Brigham Young University. Her current interests are social psychology and demography.

Yung-Ping Chen received his undergraduate degree from National Taiwan University in Taipei, Taiwan, and his M.A. and Ph.D. in economics from the University of Washington in Seattle. He presently holds the Frank J. Manning Eminent Scholar's Chair at the University of Massachusetts in Boston. His current interests include Social Security and the economic well-being of elderly persons.

Spencer J. Condie received his B.A. in sociology from Brigham Young University, his M.A. in Social Psychology from the University of Utah, and his Ph.D. in medical sociology from the University of Pittsburgh. He is presently professor of sociology at Brigham Young University. His current interests are family and sociology of aging.

Melanie W. Conlin received her B.S. in sociology from Brigham Young University and is a graduate student in sociology at Brigham Young University. Her research interests include aging and genealogy.

Marie Cornwall received her B.S. in english from the University of Utah, her M.S. in sociology from Brigham Young University, and her Ph.D. in sociology from the University of Minnesota. She is presently assistant professor of sociology at Brigham Young University. Her current interests are religiosity and faith development.

Cardell K. Jacobson received his B.S. in sociology from Brigham Young University and his M.A. and Ph.D. in sociology from the University of North Carolina at Chapel Hill. He is professor of sociology at Brigham Young University. His current interests are race and ethnic relations and social psychology.

Phillip R. Kunz received his B.S. and M.S. in sociology from Brigham Young University and his Ph.D. in sociology from the University of Michigan. He is presently professor of sociology at Brigham Young University. His current interests are complex organizations and family.

Don C. Larson received his B.S. in sociology from Brigham Young University and his M.S. and Ph.D. in sociology from Utah State University. He has completed postgraduate work at Arizona State University and at the East-West Population Center in Honolulu. He is presently a social science researcher for the Church of Jesus Christ of Latter-Day Saints. His current interests include elderly, coping with death, community and intermountain development, and migration.

June Leifson received her B.S. in nursing from Brigham Young University, her M.S. in nursing from Wayne State University, and her Ph.D. in family science from Brigham Young University. She is currently dean and professor of nursing at Brigham Young University. Her current interests include nursing administration, family crisis, and handicapped children.

Millene F. Murphy received her B.S. in nursing from Brigham Young University, her M.S. in psychiatric nursing from the University of Utah, and her Ph.D. in neuropsychology from Brigham Young University. She is presently associate professor of nursing at Brigham Young University. Her current interests include cognitive functioning, infants and elderly, and nursing intervention models.

Brian L. Pitcher received his B.S. and M.S. in sociology from Brigham Young University and his Ph.D. in sociology from the University of Arizona. He is currently associate professor of sociology and head of the Department of Sociology, Social Work, and Anthropology at Utah State University.

Phileon B. Robinson, Jr., received his B.S. in business administration from Brigham Young University, his M.B.A. from Northwestern University, and his Ph.D. in adult education from the University of Nebraska. He is currently associate professor of gerontology and director of the Gerontology Resource Center at Brigham Young University.

Maximiliane Szinovacz received her Ph.D. in sociology from the University of Vienna, Austria. She is presently assistant professor of human development and family ecology at the University of Illinois. Her current research interests include women's retirement, family power, and gender roles.

Melvin White received his B.S. in sociology, his M.S.W. in social work, and his Ph.D. in sociology from the University of Utah. He is presently chief of Social Work Services at the Salt Lake Veterans Administration Medical Center in Salt Lake City, Utah. His current interests are interpersonal relationships, support groups, and gerontology.

About the Editors

Stephen J. Bahr received his B.S. in sociology and M.S. in family relations from Brigham Young University, and his Ph.D. in sociology from Washington State University. He is presently director of the Family and Demographic Research Institute and Professor of Sociology at Brigham Young University. Current research interests include adolescent drug use and the impact of government on families.

Evan T. Peterson received his B.S. and M.S. in sociology from Brigham Young University and his Ph.D. in sociology from the University of Michigan. He is currently professor of sociology at Brigham Young University. His interests are social gerontology and sociology of the family.